Children's Rights Law in the Global Human Rights Landscape: Isolation, Inspiration, Integration?

Children's rights law is often studied and perceived in isolation from the broader field of human rights law. This volume explores the inter-relationship between children's rights law and more general human rights law in order to see whether elements from each could successfully inform the other. Children's rights law has a number of distinctive characteristics, such as the emphasis on the 'best interests of the child', the use of general principles and the inclusion of 'third parties' (e.g. parents and other carers) in treaty provisions. The first part of this book questions whether these features could be a source of inspiration for general human rights law. In Part II, the reverse question is asked: could children's rights law draw inspiration from developments in other branches of human rights law that focus on other specific categories of rights holders, such as women, persons with disabilities, indigenous peoples or older persons? Finally, the interaction between children's rights law and human rights law – and the potential for their isolation, inspiration or integration – may be coloured or determined by the thematic issue under consideration. Therefore, the third part of the book studies the interplay between children's rights law and human rights law in the context of specific topics: intra-family relations, lesbian, gay, bisexual, transgender, queer or questioning (LGBTQI) marginalisation, migration, the media, the environment and transnational human rights obligations.

Eva Brems is professor at the Human Rights Centre of Ghent University, Belgium.

Ellen Desmet is assistant professor of migration law at the Law Faculty of Ghent University, Belgium.

Wouter Vandenhole teaches human rights and holds the UNICEF Chair in Children's Rights – a joint venture of the University of Antwerp and UNICEF Belgium – at the Faculty of Law of the University of Antwerp, Belgium.

Routledge Research in Human Rights Law

Available titles in this series include:

Resolving Conflicts between Human Rights
The Judge's Dilemma
Stijn Smet

Human Rights Education and the Politics of Knowledge
Joanne Coysh

The Istanbul Convention, Domestic Violence and Human Rights
Ronagh J.A. McQuigg

Children's Rights Law in the Global Human Rights Landscape
Isolation, inspiration, integration?
Edited by Eva Brems, Ellen Desmet and Wouter Vandenhole

The Protection of Vulnerable Groups under International Human Rights Law
Ingrid Nifosi-Sutton

Forthcoming titles in this series include:

Freedom of Expression and Religious Hate Speech
You Can't Say That!
Erica Howard

The Right to Food
From Sovereignty to Security
Kirsteen Shields

Business and Human Rights in Africa
History, Politics, Context and Emerging Trends
Uche Ewelukwa Ofodile

Children's Rights Law in the Global Human Rights Landscape

Isolation, Inspiration, Integration?

Edited by
Eva Brems, Ellen Desmet and Wouter Vandenhole

Routledge
Taylor & Francis Group
LONDON AND NEW YORK

First published 2017 by Routledge

2 Park Square, Milton Park, Abingdon, Oxfordshire OX14 4RN
52 Vanderbilt Avenue, New York, NY 10017

Routledge is an imprint of the Taylor & Francis Group, an informa business

First issued in paperback 2018

British Library Cataloguing in Publication Data
A catalogue record for this book is available from the British Library

Library of Congress Cataloging in Publication Data
Library of Congress Cataloging-in-Publication Data
Names: Brems, Eva, editor. | Desmet, Ellen, editor. | Vandehole, Wouter, editor.
Title: Children's rights law in the global human rights landscape : isolation, inspiration, integration? / edited by Eva Brems, Ellen Desmet, and Wouter Vandehole.
Description: Abingdon, Oxon [UK]; New York : Routledge, 2017. | Series: Routledge research in human rights law | Includes bibliographical references and index.
Identifiers: LCCN 2016056483 | ISBN 9781138639010 (hbk) | ISBN 9781315637440 (ebk)
Subjects: LCSH: Children (International law) | Chidlren's rights. | Convention on the Rights of the Child (1989 November 20) | International law and human rights.
Classification: LCC K639. C483 2017 | DDC 341.4/8572—dc23
LC record available at https://lccn.loc.gov/2016056483

ISBN: 978-1-138-63901-0 (hbk)
ISBN: 978-0-367-19658-5 (pbk)

Typeset in Galliard
by Keystroke, Neville Lodge, Tettenhall, Wolverhampton

Contents

Notes on Contributors ix

Children's rights law and human rights law: analysing present and possible future interactions 1
EVA BREMS, ELLEN DESMET AND WOUTER VANDENHOLE

PART I
The broader relevance of features of children's rights law 19

1 **Distinctive characteristics of children's human rights law** 21
WOUTER VANDENHOLE

2 **The broader relevance of features of children's rights law: the 'best interests of the child' principle** 37
HELEN STALFORD

3 **The four general principles of the United Nations Convention on the Rights of the Child: the potential value of the approach in other areas of human rights law** 52
LAURA LUNDY AND BRONAGH BYRNE

4 **The inclusion of 'third parties': the status of parenthood in the Convention on the Rights of the Child** 71
ROBERTA RUGGIERO, DIANA VOLONAKIS AND KARL HANSON

PART II
Inspiration for children's rights from categorical human rights 91

5 **Lessons for children's rights from women's rights? Emancipation rights as a distinct category of human rights** 93
EVA BREMS

6 **Lessons for children's rights from disability rights?** 109
RALPH SANDLAND

7 **Inspiration for children's rights from indigenous peoples' rights** 129
ELLEN DESMET

8 **What young and old can learn from each other: cross-fertilisation between existing human rights law for children and developing human rights law for older persons** 146
ANN-KATRIN HABBIG, ALEXANDER HOEFMANS AND PAUL DE HERT

PART III
The interplay between children's rights law and human rights law in thematic areas 171

9 **Towards an integrated approach to intra-family relations under the CRC and CEDAW: some reflections** 173
TITIA LOENEN

10 **Children's rights and LGBTI persons' rights: some thoughts on their 'integration'** 192
IVANA ISAILOVIC

11 **Undocumented migration: integrating the children's rights concept of nuanced vulnerability in human rights law** 210
JULIE RYNGAERT AND WOUTER VANDENHOLE

12 **Children's rights and media: imperfect but inspirational** 231
EVA LIEVENS

13 Out of isolation: a claim for explicit attention for children in the movement towards recognition of an environmental right 251
DANIELLE VAN KALMTHOUT

14 Children's rights in business and human rights: from the sidelines to the centre field? 273
GAMZE ERDEM TÜRKELLİ

Index 302

Notes on contributors

Eva Brems is senior full professor at the Human Rights Centre of Ghent University. She teaches Advanced Study of Human Rights, Law and Gender (in Dutch) and Islam and the Law (in Dutch). The research of Professor Brems and her team covers numerous topics in domestic, international as well as comparative human rights law. She is particularly interested in issues relating to justiciability of human rights and legal reasoning concerning human rights, as well as in dealing with diversity and gender. Professor Brems is the general coordinator of the Interuniversity Attraction Pole 'The Global Challenge of Human Rights Integration: Towards a Users' Perspective'.

Dr Bronagh Byrne is a lecturer in Social Policy at Queen's University Belfast. She is co-director of the Centre for Children's Rights and co-chair of the University's Disability Research Network. Bronagh has expertise in international human rights law with a particular focus on the application of international human rights standards to local practice in relation to children's rights and disability rights. She has completed a series of projects examining the legal implementation of the United Nations Convention on the Rights of the Child (UNCRC) both nationally and internationally. Her most recent publications have included an examination of the right to inclusive education in international law, the rights of children and young people with disabilities and children's rights in policy and practice.

Paul De Hert is full-time professor at the Vrije Universiteit Brussel (VUB), associate professor at Tilburg University and director of the Fundamental Rights and Constitutionalism Research Group (FRC) at VUB. After having written extensively on defence rights and the right to privacy, De Hert now writes on a broader range of topics including elderly rights, patient rights and global criminal law. Paul De Hert is co-editor in chief of the Supranational Criminal Law Series (Intersentia) and the *New Journal of European Criminal Law* (Intersentia). He is editor in chief of the Flemish human rights journal *Tijdschrift voor Mensenrechten*.

Ellen Desmet is assistant professor of migration law at the Law Faculty of Ghent University. She teaches migration law, coordinates the migration law component of the Human Rights and Migration Law Clinic and co-lectures legal anthropology. Until September 2016, she was the project manager of the Interuniversity Attraction Pole 'The Global Challenge of Human Rights Integration: Towards a Users' Perspective' at Ghent University, and a senior researcher at the Law and Development Research Group of the University of Antwerp. She has a background in human rights law (with a focus on children's rights law and indigenous peoples' rights law) and legal anthropology; her current research concentrates on asylum and migration law and policy.

Gamze Erdem Türkelli is a PhD candidate at the University of Antwerp Law Research School and a member of the Law and Development Research Group. Her doctoral research is on the children's rights obligations of corporate and corporate-like international actors. She received her Bachelor's degree in political science and international relations from Boğaziçi University (Istanbul, Turkey) *summa cum laude* and holds Master's degrees from the University of Paris 1 – Pantheon Sorbonne (France) and from Yale University (US), where she was a Fulbright Fellow. Her research interests include children's rights, transnational human rights obligations and non-state actors in international law.

Ann-Katrin Habbig is a member of the interdisciplinary research group Gerontopole Brussels at the Vrije Universiteit Brussel (VUB), which is conducting research on frailty in the oldest old. Within this project she is focusing on the rights of older persons and on how the capability approach of Amartya Sen and Martha Nussbaum can be applied to older persons. She is also a member of the Research Group Fundamental Rights & Constitutionalism (FRC) at the VUB. Furthermore, she is teaching undergraduate students in European law, international law and human rights.

Karl Hanson is professor in public law and deputy director of the Centre for Children's Rights Studies at the University of Geneva in Switzerland, where he teaches in the *Master interdisciplinaire en droits de l'enfant* (MIDE); he is also the programme director of the *Master of Advanced Studies in Children's Rights* (MCR). His publications and main research interests are in the field of inter-disciplinary children's rights studies and include international children's rights advocacy, child labour and working children, juvenile justice and independent national children's rights institutions. He is an editor of the journal *Childhood* and chairs the Directive Committee of the Children's Rights European Academic Network (CREAN).

Alexander Hoefmans joined the Belgian Ministry of Justice in 2004 as a Human Rights Adviser and, in that capacity, he dealt primarily with the negotiation of international human rights treaties or instruments, their implementation at national level as well as the reporting procedures before the UN and Council of Europe committees. He was national liaison officer to the European Commission against Racism and Intolerance of the Council of Europe as well as to the Fundamental Rights Agency of the European Union. He was also co-agent of the Belgian Government to the European Court of Human Rights and dealt in this capacity with the Belgian case law before the European Court. He also has extensive experience in setting up national independent committees in the field of human rights (children's rights, prevention of torture, national human rights commission). In 2010 he presided over the Working Group on Fundamental Rights of the Council of Ministers during the Belgian EU Presidency preparing, among others, the EU's position in the negotiations on the EU accession to the European Convention on Human Rights. He was also part of the Presidency team that concluded the negotiations on the ratification of the UN CRPD by the EU. From 2012 to 2014 he was seconded first to the Cabinet of the Belgian Minister of Justice as adviser on human rights, trafficking, privacy, hate crime and non-discrimination issues and subsequently to DG JUST of the European Commission as legal and policy officer in the unit responsible for fundamental rights and rights of the child. Currently, he is head of the unit data protection and fundamental rights at the Belgian Ministry of Justice.

Ivana Isailovic is the Emile Noel fellow at New York University (NYU) School of Law. Her research explores the intersections between transnational law and identity and exclusion. Prior to joining NYU she was the Boulton teaching fellow at McGill University Faculty of Law. She received her PhD from Sciences Po Paris and worked as a post-doctoral fellow within 'The Global Challenge of Human Rights Integration' research network coordinated by Professor Eva Brems.

Eva Lievens is Assistant Professor of Law & Technology at the Law Faculty of Ghent University and a member of the Human Rights Centre. From 2003 until 2015, she was a member of the KU Leuven Centre for IT and IP Law (CiTiP) (previously the Interdisciplinary Centre for Law & ICT). Eva obtained her law degree at Ghent University in 2002 and a Master's degree in transnational communications and global media at Goldsmiths, University of London in 2003. A recurrent focus in her research relates to human and children's rights in the ICT and media sector and the use of alternative regulatory instruments, such as self- and co-regulation. Eva is a member of the Chamber for impartiality and the protection of minors of the Flemish Regulator for the Media and the Belgian Film Evaluation Committee. She is the associate editor for the *International Encyclopaedia of Laws: Media Law* (with Prof Peggy Valcke), a member of the editorial committee of *Auteurs & Media* (Larcier) and a contributor for Belgium for the European Audiovisual Observatory's *IRIS newsletter*.

Prof Dr M L P (Titia) Loenen is professor of human rights and diversity at Leiden University. She holds degrees in history and law from the same university. Her research covers human rights and equality issues in an international and comparative perspective. Recent work includes research on the interaction and overlap between European and international human rights protection mechanisms and on (potential) tensions between gender equality and religious freedom. She is also programme director of the advanced LLM European and international human rights law at Leiden Law School.

Professor Laura Lundy is a professor of education law and children's rights and the co-director of the Centre for Children's Rights at Queen's University Belfast, Northern Ireland (www.qub.ac.uk/ccr). Her expertise is in law and children's rights, with a particular focus on children's education rights, the right to participate in decision-making and the implementation of the UNCRC.

Roberta Ruggiero holds an MA in law, an MA in human rights and democratisation, and a PhD in promotion and protection of children's rights. She is a senior research and teaching associate at the University of Geneva's Centre for Children's Rights Studies. She was formerly scientific coordinator of the European Network of National Observatories on Childhood (ChildONEurope), Istituto degli Innocenti (2008–2013), senior lecturer at the University of Padua, Italy, and external professor on children's rights at the University of Molise, Italy. She has also worked as researcher at the IOM Europe Office and at UNICEF–Innocenti Research Office. Her research interests and publications include children's rights in the EU framework of law and policy, independent national human rights institution for children, implementation of children's rights and comparative childhood governmental policies.

Julie Ryngaert is a policy adviser at the Flemish Office of the Children's Rights Commissioner. She studied law at KU Leuven and human rights at the Université Saint-Louis-Bruxelles. In 2015, she obtained her doctoral degree at the Law Faculty of the University of Antwerp. Her PhD studies the interaction between children's rights and human rights, with a particular emphasis on migration.

Ralph Sandland was educated at the University of Kent and Trinity Hall, Cambridge before taking up a lecturing post in the School of Law, University of Nottingham in 1990. He is currently Professor of Law and Difference in the School. Ralph teaches in the areas of family law, children's rights and health care law. His research interests span these areas, as well as jurisprudence, feminist theory and post-modern philosophy. The fourth edition of his leading textbook *Mental Health Law: Policy and Practice* (with Peter Bartlett) was published by OUP in 2013.

Helen Stalford is Professor of Law at the University of Liverpool, England. She is founding director of the European Children's Rights Unit and has written and published extensively on children's rights in a European context. She has a particular interest in developing methods that engage children as research partners, that explore and enhance children's understanding and experiences of the law and that seek to evaluate the impact of legal processes on children's lives.

Danielle Van Kalmthout is a PhD research fellow at the Human Rights Centre at Ghent University. She holds a Master's in international and European law (Leiden University) and a Master's in European studies (University Robert Schuman, Strasbourg). Besides her research, she works at the Policy Research Department of the Flemish League of Families, where she is responsible for sustainable development and environment policies. Her main focus is on environmental and health issues, with a particular focus on vulnerable groups. She also coordinates the interdisciplinary network Childproof. Before, she worked for 12 years for different European networks in the field of environmental affairs and renewable energy policy. Her last position was director at RREUSE vzw (Reuse and Recycling Social Enterprises in the European Union). Her PhD research focuses on 'Environmental rights and the position of children in international environmental law: a children's rights perspective'. In her research, she combines her experience in the domain of law, advocacy work on EU environmental policy and the issue of environment and health focused on children.

Wouter Vandenhole specialises in transnational human rights obligations and economic, social and cultural rights. He holds the chair in human rights and the UNICEF chair in children's rights – a joint venture of the University of Antwerp and UNICEF Belgium – at the faculty of law of the University of Antwerp since 2007. He is the research director of the Law and Development Research Group. Vandenhole serves on the editorial board of several international journals, among which are the *Journal of Human Rights Practice* and *Human Rights and International Legal Discourse*. He has taken up management functions in European research and teaching networks. He is the lead convenor of an international programme on sustainable development and human rights law (SUSTLAW). See www.uantwerp.be/wouter-vandenhole.

Diana Volonakis holds a BA in history from the University of Lausanne, an MA in interdisciplinary children's rights studies from the University Institute Kurt Bösch (Sion) and is currently researching her PhD thesis in the field of educational sciences at the University of Geneva. Her doctoral thesis is a transnational comparative study of youth training and labour in the 19th century watchmaking industry in the USA and Switzerland. Her main research interests include childhood studies, child and youth labour, the history of childhoods and youths, the history of vocational training and school to work transitions.

Children's rights law and human rights law: analysing present and possible future interactions

Eva Brems, Ellen Desmet and Wouter Vandenhole

Introduction

This volume explores whether and how children's human rights law and other branches of international human rights law can inspire and enrich one another. Children's rights law is often perceived and studied in *isolation* from the broader field of human rights law. This book examines to what extent this results in lost opportunities for children's rights law, as well as for general human rights law. Children's rights law has a number of allegedly distinctive characteristics, such as the use of general principles, the emphasis on the 'best interests of the child' and the inclusion of 'third parties' (e.g. parents) in the United Nations Convention on the Rights of the Child (CRC). The question arises whether these features could be a source of *inspiration* for general human rights law or other categorical branches of human rights law.

This is explored in the first part of the volume. The second part reverses the question: could children's rights law draw inspiration from developments in other branches of human rights law that focus on specific categories of rights holders, such as women, persons with disabilities, indigenous peoples or older persons? Finally, the interaction between children's rights law and human rights law – and the potential for isolation, inspiration or integration – may be coloured or determined by the thematic issue under consideration. Therefore, the third part of the book studies the interplay between children's rights law and human rights law in the context of specific topics: intra-family relations, LGBTI marginalisation, undocumented migration, the media, the right to a healthy environment and human rights obligations of business.

For the purposes of this volume, the editors understand the term 'integration' to refer to a deliberate effort from one branch of international human rights law to incorporate concepts, methods or practices that originate from another branch of international human rights law. The term 'inspiration' refers to cases in which direct incorporation of concepts or practices from another branch of international human rights law is not considered appropriate, but where some ideas or dynamics in one branch have nevertheless influenced or could influence ideas or dynamics in another branch. Another way of looking at the difference between 'integration' and 'inspiration' is that it is a matter of degree: 'inspiration' indicates light or indirect forms of influence, whereas 'integration' is used for more far-reaching and/or more direct forms of influence. In this sense, 'integration' may come down in certain cases to an 'uncritical embrace', whereas inspiration may suggest a more critical, deliberated and possibly selective interaction. Finally, the term 'isolation' is used to indicate a (deliberate or not) disregard of what is going on in other branches of international human rights law.

Inspiring other human rights regimes

The first part of the book examines the possible wider relevance of the most salient characteristic features of children's rights law, for both general human rights law and other categorical branches of human rights law. In a first, umbrella chapter, Vandenhole identifies and examines five allegedly distinctive characteristics of the CRC: (i) the indivisibility of civil, political, economic, social and cultural rights; (ii) the inclusion of new substantive norms and elements, particularly as regards non-discrimination, the right to life, the concept of evolving capacities, and the right to education; (iii) the 'best interests of the child' concept; (iv) the use of general principles; and (v) the incorporation of 'third parties' as duty bearers in addition to the domestic state. He shows, among other aspects, that some of these features have either never been (e.g. indivisibility) or are no longer (e.g. general principles) unique to children's rights law.

The following chapters discuss three of these characteristics – arguably those that have been most widely invoked and discussed in children's rights practice and scholarship – in more depth: the best interests of the child (Stalford), the use of general principles (Lundy and Byrne) and the inclusion of third parties in the CRC (Ruggiero, Volonakis and Hanson). The authors analyse the historical and legal basis of these features, their current use in children's rights law and beyond, and their potential future contribution to general human rights law and other specific areas of human rights law. The concept of 'third parties' is approached differently in the two chapters: whereas Ruggiero and others focus their analysis on parents as third parties in the CRC, Vandenhole looks more broadly into non-state actors and extraterritorial obligations.

The overall assessment of the possible added value of these three features for other domains of human rights law runs parallel between the four authors. No calls for a direct integration or transplant of one or more of the features in other areas of human rights law are formulated. The potential for fruitful inspiration is appraised differently for each of the characteristics. Most reluctance is expressed as regards using the best interests principle with respect to adult rights holders. Vandenhole and Stalford caution against 'any naïve transplant' and 'extending the best interests too readily to other decision-making contexts' respectively. The relevance of general principles for other branches of human rights law is more positively assessed, yet also in a qualified way, as contributors point to the weak legal and moral basis of general principles in children's rights law (Vandenhole), and propose a set of criteria that could guide the identification and use of such principles (Lundy and Byrne). Finally, the inclusion of third parties as duty holders is evaluated as holding most promise for influencing other branches of human rights law, a conclusion that is supported both by an analysis of the rights, duties and responsibilities of parents in the CRC (Ruggiero and others) and by an examination of the questions surrounding non-state actors' and extraterritorial human rights obligations (Vandenhole).

Two categorical human rights regimes are explicitly mentioned as possible candidates to be 'inspired' by children's rights law: the rights of persons with disabilities and the emerging regime on the rights of older persons. The Convention on the Rights of Persons with Disabilities (CRPD) has already drawn inspiration from children's rights law, namely by codifying a list of general principles in its Article 3 (as discussed by both Lundy and Byrne, and Vandenhole). In the view of Lundy and Byrne, the principles in the CRPD are too numerous (eight) – 'so all-encompassing that they become dilutionary' – which risks impeding their effective functioning. They prefer the CRC Committee's approach, where the more limited number of principles (four) allows 'for a substantive and focused body of work to develop over time' – an approach that also better fits the reality of limited resources of the UN treaty bodies.

Forward-looking, Ruggiero and others suggest that disability rights law could learn lessons from children's rights law when developing its approach to third parties, limited in the CRPD to a reference to 'families and caregivers' as an additional target group of state measures to prevent exploitation, violence and abuse, next to persons with disabilities themselves (Article 16(2)). In order to conceptualise the legal position of these families and carers, the authors propose that the concept of 'responsibilities' might offer a useful point of departure, influenced by the way 'parental responsibilities' have become understood in children's rights law as 'limited and functional rights aimed at the fulfilment of the rights of the child'.

The older persons' rights regime could, in their view, equally benefit from this concept of 'responsibilities', if third parties are included in its legal framework. The rights of older persons are also mentioned by Vandenhole as an instance where developing a set of general principles could be usefully envisaged.[1] Stalford does not single out particular categorical regimes of human rights as possible destinations of inspiration, and instead discusses the possible application of 'best interests' in relation to adult human rights in general. She does describe, however, how the concept has been used (and abused) 'in a clinical health care context for adults deemed to lack capacity to make decisions for themselves'.

The remainder of this section succinctly reviews the arguments put forward by the authors in favour of and against a broader (adapted) use of best interests, general principles and the inclusion of third parties.

Best interests

Stalford and Vandenhole both note that applying best interests in respect of other so-called vulnerable groups of rights holders seems appealing at first sight. Nevertheless, they warn against too ready an appropriation of this concept in adult human rights contexts, on the basis of various arguments. Both authors refer to the already opaque and indeterminate meaning of the concept in children's rights law, which leads to inconsistent and even opposing outcomes – something which would risk being exacerbated if best interests were broadened towards other human rights domains. In addition, Stalford emphasises the child-specificity of the concept, in three ways: it serves to make children's interests visible in an adult-dominated world; it offers a way to address possible clashes between interests of adults and the interests of the child; and – from a utilitarian perspective – paying attention to the child's best interests enhances general societal welfare. This conceptualisation of best interests makes it difficult, she argues, to extend its application to the realm of adult rights holders. Such an extension could lead, in the words of Parker, to 'an artificial and sterile universalism', dissolving the distinctiveness of the concept. Moreover, Stalford cautions that broadening the use of best interests could undermine the concept's original objective, of protecting children's welfare. Such extension also risks 'entrenching a predominantly paternalistic model of best interests from which, for many years now, activists have been trying to extricate children's rights'.

Finally, Vandenhole and Stalford seem to differ in their view of the weight to be given to the best interests of the child (as prevailing or as (only) carrying greater weight in a balancing exercise). Whereas Vandenhole points to a lack of clarity on this issue, for instance in the jurisprudence of the European Court of Human Rights (ECtHR), for Stalford it is clear that best interests do not imply a trump card for the interests of the child, but that they accommodate the rights of adults. Albeit on the basis of a somewhat different argumentation (unclear weight versus inherent consideration of adult rights), the conclusion of the two authors is similar, namely that this argumentation provides another reason why transposing best interests to other human rights regimes does not seem desirable.

General principles

Tracing the history of the identification of the general principles by the CRC Committee, Lundy and Byrne disclose the difficulty of finding a logical explanation of why precisely Articles 2, 3, 6 and 12 CRC were elevated to the status of general principles. Vandenhole also points to the weak legal and theoretical grounding of the principles, and the fact that the principles of non-discrimination and participation are not child-specific. Notwithstanding their dubious origin, Lundy and Byrne show how the general principles have been predominant in children's rights implementation efforts by state parties and other duty bearers, in advocacy by non-governmental organisations (NGOs) and civil society, and in academic scholarship. Although the general principles thus seem to have contributed to an enhanced understanding and acceptance of the CRC, the authors point out that the key role attached to the general principles may also have led to reduced attention for other substantive treaty provisions.

To assess the added value of the concept of general principles, Lundy and Byrne then proceed to investigate other human rights treaties, adopted prior to and after the CRC. Although they identify provisions in the Convention on the Elimination of All Forms of Discrimination against Women (CEDAW),[2] as well as in the International Convention on the Elimination of All Forms of Racial Discrimination (ICERD) that could serve as general principles, they also wonder 'what if anything has been lost in their absence'. For it can be argued that the lack of general principles has not considerably impacted the implementation of both treaties. On the other hand, as already indicated above, the actual inclusion of general principles in the CRPD does not seem to make a substantial contribution to the convention's implementation either. In their conclusion, Lundy and Byrne formulate some criteria that could guide the identification of convention-specific general principles, including the criterion that the principle has a 'clear basis that enables [it] to apply across the other substantive provisions of the Convention and to do so in a way that enhances implementation', and the criterion that the principle 'addresses a barrier to the realisation and/or a route to fulfilment of the rights of the protected groups and individuals'. Moreover, they submit that the 'sum of the principles must . . . be greater than the parts'. Lundy and Byrne and Vandenhole thus concur that, when carefully selected and well grounded, general principles are an interesting feature of children's rights law that could inspire other human rights fields.

Inclusion of third parties

A final distinctive characteristic of the CRC is that it breaks through the traditional binary relationship in human rights law of individual rights holders versus the state, by introducing 'third parties' – more specifically parents and carers – as holding 'rights, duties and responsibilities'. On the basis of their detailed analysis of the status of parenthood in the CRC, Ruggiero and others identify some advantages and risks of including third parties in other human rights regimes. Two arguments plead against such inclusion. Firstly, bringing in third parties may lead to controversy and polarisation, as the authors illustrate with their account of the dichotomous nature of the relationship between parental rights and children's rights in the United States. Such 'dichotomous vision consistently downplays the contentious nature of the relationship between the family and the State'. Secondly, it has been argued that the triangular relationship in the CRC has led to obscuring the legal obligations of states parties as regards the rights of the child. Critics of the campaign against corporal punishment have argued that this campaign allowed states to hide their direct obligations to combat structural economic inequalities, by shifting the responsibility onto parents. On the other hand, Rugierro and others suggest that other human rights regimes – in particular the rights of persons with disabilities and the rights of older persons – could draw inspiration from the 'conciliatory perspective' as adopted in the CRC, 'which prescribes that a balance needs to be made between the rights of different actors involved by distributing responsibilities, duties and rights among parents/caretakers and the State towards the promotion and realisation of an abstract public good, i.e. the child's well-being'.

Vandenhole draws other, yet complementary conclusions from the inclusion of third parties in the CRC. In his view, the reference to parents in the CRC may contribute to 'opening up the duty-bearer side of human rights law, in order to include other actors than the state'. He pleads for a more consistent use of terminology, however, to indicate the legally binding nature of a certain norm, and warns that the relationship between the obligations and responsibilities of the various actors should be further clarified. Secondly, the multiple references in the CRC to international assistance and cooperation indicate that the CRC goes beyond the domestic state as the only statist duty-holder. As regards the conceptualisation of the responsibilities and obligations of non-state actors as well as of extraterritorial obligations of the domestic state, Vandenhole regrets, however, that the CRC Committee has not yet fully developed this potential. He refers to the work of the Committee on Economic, Social and Cultural Rights (CESCR) as a possible source of inspiration for children's rights law in this respect. The CESCR is not the only human rights treaty body from which children's rights could learn, however, as is explored in the second part.

Learning from other categorical human rights regimes

The chapters in Part II look into other categorical human rights regimes – women's rights, rights of persons with disabilities, indigenous peoples' rights and rights of older persons, in order to examine how these regimes may inspire the human rights of children (and vice versa).

The authors were asked to have their chapters guided by two sets of questions: the first more analytical; the second more normative:

(i) What are distinctive characteristics of the human rights protection of the category of rights holders under consideration? What are best practices? What are pitfalls to be avoided?
(ii) Which general lessons may be drawn from these (sub)disciplines about the protection of the human rights of a specific group? Which aspects may inspire the development of children's rights law specifically?

In the course of this exercise, it became clear that challenges may be common to the categorical regime under scrutiny and children's human rights (that is in particular the case with regard to rights of indigenous peoples), or that children's rights may be a more prominent source of inspiration for other categorical regimes (under construction), as the experience with the rights of older persons seems to suggest.

In what follows, we will look into the most salient distinctive characteristics of each of the three categorical human rights regimes under scrutiny, and draw some inspirational conclusions for children's rights law.

A preliminary caveat is in order, however. The distinctiveness of categorical human rights regimes for women, persons with disabilities, indigenous peoples and older persons must be put into perspective: as Brems points out, all are considered as vulnerable groups and all face the challenge of balancing protection with emancipation or independence. Moreover, intersectionality rather than a particular unique status really seems to matter in practice. So while some of the categorical human rights regimes may have unique characteristics, Brems submits in her chapter on women's rights that they are all emancipation rights that address similar challenges. What unites emancipation rights is that they strongly matter in horizontal relations and require cultural change. The realisation of such a 'cultural' paradigm shift seems most challenging where children are concerned: other categories of so-called vulnerable persons demand that they are not treated like children, hence reinforcing the stereotypes of vulnerability and incapacity that tend to dominate in discourse on children.[3] An interesting avenue for further research on emancipation rights may be the area of work. Whereas the right to work (in dignity) has made quite some leeway with regard to women, persons with disabilities and older persons, developments with regard to children are going in the opposite direction of a ban on all child labour, rather than of the recognition of the right to work in dignity. Indigenous peoples' rights lend support to defining childhood not only in terms of biological age, and in this way possibly also to the recognition of children of a right to work in dignity.

Women's rights together with indigenous peoples' rights seem the most different regimes among these emancipation rights. The commonalities of children's rights, rights of persons with disabilities and rights of older persons indeed stand out in the analysis of these respective regimes: for example, for all three, the debate on capacity rages on, whereas with regard to women's rights and indigenous peoples' rights, the capacity debate seems over. Children's rights, rights of persons with disabilities and rights of older persons face a fluid delineation of the category they are covering. Admittedly, the latter characterises indigenous peoples' rights as well, whereas it is very clear who are considered 'women'.[4] Brems points out: 'The emancipatory challenge of children's rights lies in making people see *not only* children's inherent vulnerability, but *also* their inherent capacity for autonomy, and the gradual development of that capacity. In that sense, children's rights as emancipation rights are both similar to and different from women's rights as emancipation rights' (see Chapter 5; emphasis in original).

Let us now turn to some of the most salient particularities in comparison to children's rights, of each of the categorical regimes under scrutiny.

Women's rights

The women's rights regime may well be the area where the problematic nature of protection dynamics has been most clearly exposed and addressed. As Brems points out, the 'emphasis on vulnerability and protection [is seen] as an expression of paternalism that reinforces gendered stereotypes and that contributes to denying women equal opportunities' (see Chapter 5). In the struggle for realising women's rights as human rights, the emphasis is much more on empowerment and autonomy, and hardly on vulnerability. Protective measures for children have not been delegitimised to the same extent; on the contrary, the very success of children's rights seems to be grounded in the generalised perception of children as vulnerable and the widespread support for maximum protection of children. So, in challenging this myopic emphasis on children's autonomy, children's rights may benefit from women's rights. The need to bring about cultural change to address stereotypes or prejudices means that action has also to be taken in horizontal relations. Brems believes that this is the key learning point for children's rights: cultural perceptions of and practices towards children need to be denormalised, which necessitates the inclusion of a specific provision on the state's obligation to work for cultural change similar to the one in Article 5(a) CEDAW. Such a provision should function as a self-standing obligation, but also as an additional general principle that guides the interpretation of all CRC provisions. A cue could be taken from the work on harmful cultural practices, but efforts should extend far beyond that set of cultural practices.

Rights of persons with disabilities

While acknowledging that in a pessimistic reading any innovative aspect of the CRPD may be repudiated at the general level and in the particular context of the rights of children (with disabilities), Sandland mainly emphasises the major shift in the CRPD's underpinning model or paradigm. The CRPD is premised on a holistic social model of disability. The shift to a *social* model of disability (whereby disability is not seen as an inherent deficiency, but rather as the result of the interaction between persons with impairments and attitudinal and environmental barriers – see the preamble to the CRPD) echoes very much the need for cultural change as argued by Brems. But both authors (and possibly both fields) disagree on the extent to which developments in their own field could or should be paralleled in children's rights. Brems emphasises the persistent difference between women's rights and children's rights. She argues that 'the majority of children have a capacity for autonomy that is significantly lower than that of adults', and that '[t]aking children's capacity for autonomy seriously also means recognising the limits of that capacity'. The optimal balance between protection rights and autonomy rights will therefore differ for women and children. In disability law, the role that the concept of 'capacity', and third-party decision-making in the 'best interests' of persons found to 'lack' capacity used to play, may be argued to have been replaced. Through the notion of supported decision-making, the assumption now prevails that capacity to make one's own decisions is always attainable, if the person with disability is given the necessary assistance.

Sandland submits that the rights of persons with disabilities raise 'questions regarding the continued viability of an essentialist, status-based, non-socialised, construction of children and their rights lack of any comparable "social model of childhood"', and invites to ponder about the effects of a 'social model of childhood'. For one, such a social model of childhood would challenge 'the continued desirability of a role of 'capacity' and 'best interests' as mechanisms for making decisions in relation to children' (see Chapter 6). In other words, the CRPD raises the questions of whether: (i) it is not now time to shift from a status-based to a functionality-based understanding of the limitations that simply being a 'child' as a matter of legal status places on a young person in terms of their abilities to make decisions for themselves and (ii) there should be, if not an abandonment of the best interests principle, then at least the severance of that principle from a substituted judgement framework for those children found to have functional capacity and its attachment instead to a supported decision-making model (see Chapter 6).

The CRPD also adopts a *holistic* approach to rights, which entails the undermining of traditional divisions within orthodox human rights discourse between types of rights (in particular civil and political versus economic, social and cultural rights). The typology impacts the general obligation incumbent on states: the former are to be realised immediately, the latter only progressively subject to the availability of resources. In Sandland's view, the CRPD constructs 'civil and political rights as being interwoven with economic, social and cultural rights', and thereby 'understands the legal subject as being interdependent and relational': 'we *all* need effective economic, social and cultural rights if we are truly to be able to exercise our civil or political rights'. This approach 'undermines the liberal legal subject, seen in political and civil rights terms as being independent, isolated and autonomous' (see Chapter 6; emphasis in the original). Although this comprehensiveness, as it has been called in children's rights literature, has also been identified as characteristic of children's rights, the CRPD seems to push it to a higher level, and children's rights may learn from this.

Finally, Sandland identifies some new rights, and the extension and reconfiguration of existing rights for children (with disabilities): e.g. the evolving capacities of the child and the right to participate effectively in society may have been elevated to general principles; the right to physical and mental integrity is explicitly recognised and the right to life better protected; and the right to physical and mental integrity may provide leverage for access to all spaces open to the public, including private spaces.

Indigenous peoples' rights

Desmet identifies three areas in which children's rights may learn from indigenous peoples' rights: space for flexibility in the definition of the group; the consequences of romanticised constructions; and interpretative guidance for participation and consent.

The field of indigenous peoples' rights uses flexible conceptions of indigenous peoples, with self-identification as a central element. The CRC, on the other hand, employs a static definition of children. However, children grow up in very diverse geographical, cultural and socio-economic contexts. A general upper age limit at 18 is Eurocentric, and may negatively affect certain rights of children, such as a right to work in dignity. Desmet therefore pleads for a multi-dimensional understanding of children, which does not exclusively focus on chronological age but also takes into account self-identification as well as psychological and contextual factors.

Secondly, indigenous peoples and children may be said to have been constructed in a similar way, from historically marginalised to romanticised and idealised today. The romanticised constructions of indigenous peoples and children may have a negative impact on rights protection, and may moreover lead to a lack of critical scientific analysis. Desmet challenges these essentialising tendencies and calls for an increase in efforts 'to unveil assumptions and constructions that essentialise indigenous peoples and children, as well as the impact of these constructions on research, policy and practice' (see Chapter 7).

Thirdly, notions of consultation and consent are legally well developed in the field of indigenous peoples' rights. Indigenous peoples' rights can inspire children's rights law in furthering the theoretical, legal and practical development of the collective dimension of the right of children to be heard (including aspects of representation), and in fleshing out the attributes of the emerging right of children to consent (namely free, prior and informed).

Rights of older persons

The field of rights of older persons is the only one where intersectionality is excluded: children can never belong to this category while being children. Moreover, the codification of the human rights of older persons is still in a rather early stage (no treaty has as yet been adopted), which may explain why the question of inspiration is more prominently in the reverse direction, i.e. which learning points does the CRC contain for the rights of older persons. In Chapter 8, Habbig, Hoefmans and De Hert suggest three points of inspiration. First of all, the paradigm shift that we discussed earlier (from vulnerability to autonomy), although not fully realised in the CRC, is clearly also relevant to address the stereotypes associated with ageing. Moreover, and typical of the CRC, the use of principles in addition to rights is believed to be a good practice. Thirdly, the concept of evolving capacities and the retreating role of parents or other carers may be of relevance to the rights of older persons, although it cannot be simply transplanted: whereas children gradually develop 'towards full capability in decision-making, older persons often see a reverse development'. But the key questions are similar: how to balance and facilitate as much autonomy as possible while dependence increases? And how to define the evolving role, responsibilities and obligations of informal and formal carers?

Children's rights may learn from the older persons' rights regime, as they could from the indigenous peoples' rights regime, how to use a more variable age limit: whether a person is labelled as 'aged', 'old' or 'elderly' depends on the cultural context, economic considerations and the respective life expectancy, and such a more open-ended approach could be beneficial for children's rights too.

Although it is too early to tell, the authors express the hope that if the older persons' rights regime 'strikes the right balance between protection and emancipation, this could be an argument to look more closely at the parallel debate in children's human rights law', in particular with regard to the right to work.

Finally, age-based discrimination has been developed within the older persons' rights regime, but remains by and large a blind spot in children's rights law. The prohibited ground of age is conceptually not yet well developed in children's human rights law, and may benefit from developments within the older persons' rights regime.

In sum, all five regimes are part of a struggle for emancipation. Women's rights and disability rights seem to have been most successful in introducing a paradigm shift, away from protectionism to a better acknowledgement of autonomy. Authors disagree, however, whether children's rights should make a similar shift, towards recognition of full capacity of children, and a supported decision-making model, as one reading of disability rights suggests. Disability rights may also be most inspirational in intertwining civil and political rights, and economic, social and cultural rights, and hence in imposing immediate obligations with regard to economic, social and cultural rights. Indigenous peoples' rights and rights of older persons have adopted a flexible notion of the category concerned, which may inspire children's rights to move beyond a one-size-fits-all approach to the upper limit of 18. Finally, more explicit engagement with age discrimination may sophisticate the children's rights regime.

Situating children's human rights vis-à-vis general human rights in concrete contexts

In the third part of the book, the chapter authors focus on a thematic area to examine the interplay between children's rights law and human rights law. They describe the state of affairs as to the relation between children's rights law and human rights law in the particular thematic area. More specifically, they look for signs that mark this relationship as one of 'isolation', 'inspiration' or 'integration'. In the concrete reality of a specific field, does it seem that children's rights law impacts upon general human rights law or vice versa? In addition to these analytical questions, authors were also asked to ponder some normative questions: what are promising or desirable avenues for further development of the role of children's human rights law vis-à-vis general human rights law in this thematic issue? Should there be isolation, inspiration or integration and, if so, how?

The thematic areas that are examined in this manner are family relations (Chapter 9), LGBTQI marginalisation (Chapter 10), undocumented migration (Chapter 11), media (Chapter 12), environmental protection (Chapter 13) and corporate responsibility for human rights (Chapter 14). From a normative point of view, all the chapters argue in favour of increased inspiration or integration between children's human rights and other fields of human rights law, with some stating that children's human rights should borrow certain elements from other human rights fields, and others claiming that other fields would do well to learn from developments in children's human rights law or to include a focus on children's rights in future normative development.

Enriching children's rights with insights and concerns from other human rights fields

Focusing on the family sphere, Titia Loenen examines (in Chapter 9) how much credit the CEDAW and CRC give to each other in this sphere. Loenen is satisfied that CEDAW provisions pay adequate attention to children's rights through explicit references to the 'best interests of the child principle'. Yet she assesses the limited attention to gender in the CRC, including in the work of the CRC Committee, as insufficient. The CRC Committee is integrating a gender concern by introducing a regular mention of the 'girl child'. However, where parents are concerned, the CRC Committee is generally mute on gender, and prefers the use of gender-neutral language. Loenen draws our attention to the fact that challenging the gender stereotypes and gendered role patterns in the family holds a central position in the CEDAW's theory of change toward gender equality. Indeed, the CEDAW Committee 'links the gendered division of family roles with the overall inferior position of women in society, their economic dependence, poverty and lack of social, economic and political power' (Chapter 9). For Loenen, the fact that the CRC emphasises the shared responsibility of parents for the upbringing of their children is not sufficient.

In addition, she states that the CRC Committee should explicitly address the gendered dimensions of this shared responsibility. By recognising that women are often the primary caretakers of children, the CRC could, according to Loenen, contribute to the empowerment of women. At the same time, she notes that where the CRC and its Committee do pay specific attention to parents' gender, i.e. in the context of motherhood as a biological function, this sometimes results in the instrumentalisation of women, as their interests seem to be subordinated to those of children. Interestingly, Loenen points at a procedural approach that may be best practice in terms of human rights integration: the joint General recommendation/General comment of the CEDAW Committee and the CRC on harmful practices integrates a women's rights approach and a children's rights approach in a manner that Loenen considers optimal.

Women's rights and their focus on relations within the family are a long-standing theme in human rights law, amongst other reasons because the adoption of the CEDAW predates that of the CRC by a decade. Loenen's argument is therefore for the integration within children's rights of the specialised knowledge and experience of a mature specialised system and its expert body. On the other hand, Ivana Isailovic's chapter on children's rights in relation to LGBTI marginalisation (Chapter 10) argues for the integration in children's rights of novel rights protection standards that have only partially gained full recognition in international law as binding standards. Indeed, one can imagine a future LGBTI rights regime comparable to the specialised human rights regimes for women, children, persons with disabilities, etc. However, for now, LGBTI rights as international human rights are found mostly in soft law and in the jurisprudence of supranational monitoring bodies.

Isailovic points out that, on account of their initial focus on sexuality, LGBTI rights have long been conceptualised as adult rights, and the emergence of children in this landscape is a recent development. Until recently, children's rights have been mobilised mostly to counter LGBTI rights. Yet today, the CRC Committee is starting to address LGBTI rights in its General Comments and Concluding Observations. Isailovic's central argument is that the CRC's potential to protect the rights of LGBTI children or children raised by LGBTI parents may or may not be realised, depending on the willingness to embrace new interpretations of CRC provisions. Such new interpretations would have to take into account soft law such as the Yogyakarta Principles, as well as interpretations of other human rights instruments that do justice to the experiences of LGBTI individuals. Isailovic builds this argument through three cases: self-determination rights of intersex children under Article 12 CRC, the interpretation of 'the best interests of the child' (Article 3 CRC) in family life cases, and addressing bullying, intimidation and negative stereotypes in the school context under Article 29 CRC.

Enriching other human rights fields with insights from or a focus on children's rights

The chapters by van Kalmthout on environmental rights (Chapter 13) and by Erdem Türkelli on business and human rights (Chapter 14) likewise discuss dynamic and highly topical fields of human rights law in which normative development is still ongoing. However, unlike Isailovic, they argue not for the integration of general human rights law developments into children's rights, but instead want children's rights to be taken on board in the development of general human rights law.

For Erdem Türkelli, this point of view is based on the finding that, in the area of business and human rights, recent children's rights (soft law) instruments have been developed that have been strongly inspired by general soft law instruments in this field. Indeed, both the Children's Rights and Business Principles and the General Comment 16 of the CRC Committee are heavily inspired by the UN Guiding Principles on Business and Human Rights (UNGP). What is more, the CRC Committee's General Comment goes further in that it corrects or 'improves' the UNGP from a children's rights point of view. In that respect, one might argue that what Isailovic would like to see happen in the field of LGBTI rights, i.e. the reinterpretation of children's rights in line with recent developments in a specific field of general human rights, has in fact happened in the area of business and human rights.

However, Erdem Türkelli deplores the fact that the operationalisation of both frameworks takes place in isolation from one another. The main discussion – in particular on a potential future binding treaty – takes place in the general human rights framework, and 'the momentum on children's rights and business has not yet been translated into a tangible integration of children's rights into the broader human rights discussions on transnational obligations in a meaningful way' (see Chapter 14). This is why she argues that the trend should now be reversed, and that after the integration of business and human rights in the children's rights framework, children's rights should now be integrated in the general human rights frameworks addressing businesses.

In the field of environmental rights, discussed by Danielle van Kalmthout, developments that may lead to the recognition of a binding human right to a healthy environment, have so far not sufficiently included children's specific protection needs. Van Kalmthout therefore argues in favour of integrating children's needs and interests in these debates. However, contrary to Erdem Türkelli, her vision is not one in which children's rights would be incorporated in a general instrument or provision. Instead, for van Kalmthout the integration of children's rights in the debates about a right to a healthy environment should lead to the separate recognition – in the context of the CRC – of a child right to a healthy environment in addition to a general right to the same. In her analysis of the CRC, van Kalmthout identifies numerous provisions that have been interpreted to include some aspects of a child's right to a healthy environment and/or that might be interpreted in a way that would help shape such a right. Yet – and in this her position differs from that of Isailovic – she does not consider reinterpretation a satisfactory solution.

Both Erdem Türkelli and van Kalmthout conceive of the integration of children's rights in general human rights as a way of providing better protection for the human rights of children. Other authors have argued, however, that certain interpretations that have been developed in the context of children's rights may serve as an inspiration to improve general human rights for all, including adults. This line of argument is developed in the chapters on media and undocumented migration.

In Chapter 12, Eva Lievens analyses in detail how the European and UN human rights regimes approach children as consumers, participants and subjects of the media. The combination of hard law, soft law and the interpretations of supranational human rights bodies, results in a very sophisticated regime. Built mainly on three CRC provisions (Articles 12, 13 and 17) it is a three-dimensional approach, including protective measures, in addition to obligations to provide, as well as an emphasis on participation. This is a much richer framework than the general human rights framework that applies to adults in relation to the media, and that includes mainly negative rights. Lievens therefore argues that adult rights holders could benefit from enhanced human rights protection, if the children's rights regime on the media were to inspire the general human rights regime in this field. In addition to positive state obligations, this would entail a right to participate in media governance processes. Moreover, the multi-stakeholder approach of children's rights – conferring responsibilities not only on the state, but also on parents and the media – could prove a useful model to concretise in human rights terms the responsibilities of 'third parties' in the media sector, 'such as journalists, internet service providers, search engines or social network site providers' (see Chapter 12).

The analysis of Julie Ryngaert and Wouter Vandenhole of the use of 'vulnerability' concepts in the context of the rights of undocumented migrants (see Chapter 11) likewise reveals the potential of sophisticated rights reasoning that was developed for children's rights, to have broader application. The concept of vulnerability is mobilised in both children's rights law and general human rights law to single out individuals or groups that need enhanced protection or priority treatment. In general human rights law, children are often considered more vulnerable than adults in this context. The detailed analysis of Ryngaert and Vandenhole shows that the vulnerability concept that is applied (although not always) by the CRC Committee is significantly more sophisticated than that which is used by general supranational human rights bodies, in particular the ECtHR. The sophistication concerns the combination of vulnerability and autonomy, a contextual understanding of vulnerability and attention to diversity within children as a vulnerable group.

Ryngaert and Vandenhole argue, on the basis of empirical studies, that the CRC Committee's nuanced vulnerability approach is more suitable for application to the rights of undocumented migrant children than the ECtHR's approach. This is because each of the nuances introduced by the CRC Committee reflects the reality of undocumented migrant children. However, Ryngaert and Vandenhole do not simply make the argument that the CRC Committee has more expertise on children's rights and experiences than general human rights bodies, and that therefore general bodies 'doing children's rights' should model their approach after that of the CRC Committee. Instead, they argue, again with empirical support, that the CRC Committee's nuanced vulnerability approach is also better suited for addressing the human rights of undocumented migrant adults. They claim that this is a less reductionist approach that better reflects the humanity of undocumented migrants. An additional benefit of this approach, they argue, is that it does away with the dichotomy that pitches undocumented migrant children and their rights against adults (who may even be their parents) in the same situation. In Ryngaert and Vandenhole's interpretation, what may at first sight seem to be a distinctive feature of children's rights protection, is reframed as a state-of-the-art interpretation of general human rights, which happens to be developed in the context of children's rights.

Reasons for pro-integration viewpoints

Across the chapters, the main reasons for normative positions in favour of increased inspiration or integration between children's human rights law and general human rights law or other specific 'branches' of human rights law, are threefold: increasing rights protection, improving rights protection, and doing away with conflicts between the human rights of children and adults.

Increased rights protection for children is the main driver of van Kalmthout's argument: the movement toward formal recognition of a binding right to a healthy environment should, in her opinion, equally lead to the recognition of a parallel children's right. The reason is simple: it has been shown empirically that children suffer more than adults from environmental degradation. Hence, children need enhanced environmental rights protection.

Increased rights protection for both adults and children is what Loenen and Isailovic are seeking. Loenen aims to enlist the CRC's assistance for the realisation of one of the central missions of the CEDAW, which is the elimination of harmful gender stereotypes and role patterns. This approach seems to proceed from an integrated view of human rights that endorses an 'all hands on deck' approach, in which specialised human rights systems should avoid a narrow focus on their area of special interest, but should instead also strive to contribute to optimal human rights protection overall. Isailovic is dealing with a topic that is in the frontline of the dynamic development of international human rights law. Injustice done to LGBTI individuals is finally being recognised and brought under the label of human rights violations. While this process is still not completed, and is also encountering resistance, Isailovic has a vision in which the focused attention for LGBTI rights in specialised instruments goes hand in hand with their mainstreaming in other fields of human rights. Children's rights are particularly salient in this respect for several reasons, which include the vulnerability of LGBTI children, the importance of educating the younger generation if one wants to generate a change of minds, and finally the abuse of children's rights by those who object to LGBTI rights.

Improved rights protection for children or for all as a goal of human rights integration, can refer to the objective of avoiding negative side effects of current – 'unintegrated' – developments in human rights law. In that vein, Ryngaert and Vandenhole propose that general human rights law improves its concept of vulnerability in relation to undocumented migrants so as to avoid reductionism, stigmatisation and disempowerment that may be the by-products of an unnuanced focus on vulnerability. Likewise, Erdem Türkelli proposes integration of children's rights into mainstream debates on business and human rights, to bypass the undesirable effect of the opposite movement, which had resulted in isolating 'children's rights and business' from the momentum on human rights and business. Even without the identification of undesirable side-effects of the current regime, a comparison with children's rights may lead to identifying sophisticated arguments or concepts that can improve general human rights. In the media context, Lievens identified participation rights and the multi-stakeholder approach as promising features of the children's rights approach in this regard.

Finally, several authors conceive of the integration between children's rights and general human rights as a way of appeasing tensions between the rights of children and those of adults. Loenen points out that the CRC Committee instrumentalises biological motherhood at the service of children, disregarding the interests of mothers. In her vision, an integrated approach in which the CRC Committee strengthens its gendered analysis would avoid such statements as a blanket recommendation for mothers to breastfeed their children between six and 24 months without considering the implications for the women concerned. An integrated approach would thus not automatically favour one side in a situation that is characterised by conflicting rights claims, but rather attempt to reconcile both. In other situations, what appears to be a tension between rights of adults and those of children, may disappear as a result of the adoption of an integrated rights approach. Ryngaert and Vandenhole argue that the adoption of a nuanced vulnerability concept for both adult and minor undocumented migrants would deconstruct the dichotomy between the two categories that now leads to different rulings on children and adults in similar situations. In the field of LGBTI rights, Isailovic argues that integration of LGBTI rights thinking in the interpretation of children's rights would dissolve false conflicts between children's rights and LGBTI rights that have often functioned as obstacles to LGBTI rights recognition.

Conclusion: looking beyond

Following the development of different categorical and thematic human rights regimes, human rights scholarship has become increasingly specialised and departmentalised. Academics too rarely look beyond their niche of expertise.

This book shows, however, that much can be learnt by removing our blinkers and widening our gaze. Realising human rights – both in general and with respect to particular groups – may be well served by analysing more in depth the conceptual and practical developments in certain/other subfields of international human rights law. This does not imply that innovative concepts or distinctive approaches should be blindly transposed to other fields. It does mean that carefully analysing the benefits and drawbacks of the particularities of one human rights regime, may contribute to the enhanced effectiveness of human rights law as a whole and also lead to a more integrated experience of human rights.

It is the hope of the editors that this book will not 'remain in isolation', but will inspire other scholars to ask similar questions from points of departure other than children's rights law.

Notes

This research has been funded by the Interuniversity Attraction Poles (IAP) programme initiated by the Belgian Science Policy Office, more specifically the IAP 'The Global Challenge of Human Rights Integration: Towards a Users' Perspective' www.hrintegration.be (last accessed 20 November 2016).

1 See also Habbig, Hoefmans and De Hert (ch 8).
2 For instance CEDAW art 5; see also Brems (ch 5).
3 As Desmet points out, children have also been depicted as noble savages, which seems to show the persistence of stereotypes of indigenous peoples as well. She nonetheless demonstrates that the paradigm shift for indigenous peoples has been more or less successful. It may make sense, therefore, to understand the reasons for that success better, in order to realise a similar paradigm shift for children.
4 With the exception of intersex persons.

Part I

The broader relevance of features of children's rights law

1 Distinctive characteristics of children's human rights law

Wouter Vandenhole

Children's human rights law has a number of distinctive characteristics – presumed and real. This chapter explores and assesses these distinctive characteristics and their potential to enrich the general or other specific (e.g. for women; persons with disabilities etc) human rights regimes.

With children's human rights law (hereafter more succinctly referred to as children's rights law), I refer in the specific context of this publication primarily to the Convention on the Rights of the Child (CRC), to the exclusion of human rights treaties that contain provisions on children's rights (e.g. Articles 6(5), 10(2)(b), 14(1) and (4) and 24 of the International Covenant on Civil and Political Rights (ICCPR); Article 10(3) of the International Covenant on Economic, Social and Cultural Rights (ICESCR); Article 7 of the Convention on the Rights of Persons with Disabilities (CRPD); Article 17 of the Revised European Social Charter (RESC); and Articles 24 and 32 of the EU Charter on Fundamental Rights).[1] I do not limit the analysis to the treaty, but include also the authoritative interpretation given to it by the CRC Committee, as well as scholarly work and sometimes civil society positions.

The following distinctive characteristics will be looked into in particular: the indivisibility of civil, political, economic, social and cultural rights; new substantive norms or elements; the 'best interests of the child' principle; general principles; and the inclusion of 'third parties' (e.g. parents and other carers) as duty-holders beyond the state.

Two hypotheses will inform the chapter. Firstly, many of the alleged distinctive characteristics of children's rights law are in fact not significantly distinctive. Secondly, even the truly distinctive characteristics have a number of weaknesses and limitations. Whereas the second hypothesis does not necessarily preclude integration, nor justifies isolation, it guards against naïve attempts to transplant these distinctive characteristics to the general or specific human rights regimes.

An important element of background information in order to assess the CRC's distinctive characteristics is that there are different readings of the drafting history of the CRC. The CRC is sometimes seen as the historic culmination point of a long struggle for recognition of children as fully-fledged human beings, as subjects of rights.[2] The CRC has therefore been hailed as a 'paradigm shift'[3] from paternalism to the acknowledgement that children are both 'becomings' and 'beings'. This reading has been criticised from at least two perspectives. Some have argued that the CRC has failed to introduce that paradigmatic shift, and keeps focusing on the developing child, i.e. as 'becoming'.[4] Compared to other major struggles for emancipation, it has been argued that children's rights have failed to debunk the ideology of development:

> Jenks argues that while social sciences have critically addressed and debunked dominant ideologies of, for example, capitalism in relation to social class, colonialism in relation to race, and patriarchy in relation to gender, the ideology of development in relationship to childhood had remained relatively intact.[5]

A second alternative reading is offered by an international relations perspective on how the CRC has benefited from changing international relations, such as the change in American presidency and the collapse of the Berlin Wall and the Eastern Bloc in 1989.[6] Poland, which submitted a draft convention to the UN Commission on Human Rights in 1978 and belonged to the group of socialist states, wanted to challenge Western states' leadership in human rights initiatives, in particular that of the then president of the United States, Jimmy Carter.[7] Moreover, it was assumed that a treaty on the rights of the child 'could justifiably be confined to the economic, social and cultural rights to which the Communist countries wanted to accord priority'.[8] When at a later stage the United States gave up its obstruction to a children's rights treaty and sought to add civil and political rights, the US was less motivated by a desire to grant civil and political rights to children, but rather concerned with how it could make the Convention less appealing for Poland and its allies.[9]

Initially, negotiations turned out to be very difficult, for there was little time and quite some ideological obstruction, so that progress on the CRC depended on advancement of work on the Convention against Torture, which was of importance to some Western states.[10] In early 1989, President Reagan was succeeded by President George Bush senior and, by the end of 1989, the former Communist countries were eager to show their commitment to a comprehensive human rights package.[11] These changes made it possible to conclude negotiations without major ideological clashes during the final stages. In the next sections, I examine the five alleged distinctive characteristics that I mentioned above.

1.1 Indivisibility of civil, political, economic, social and cultural rights

The CRC is very comprehensive in scope. It covers the traditional categories of both civil and political rights, as well as economic, social and cultural rights. At first sight, the CRC transcends the long-standing dichotomy between civil and political rights, and between economic, social and cultural rights. It has been hailed as the first (and initially only) instrument to be so comprehensive in scope.[12]

Both claims – first and only – need to be put into perspective. Both the Convention on the Elimination of All Forms of Racial Discrimination (CERD 1965) and the Convention on the Elimination of All Forms of Discrimination against Women (CEDAW 1979) may be said also to cover the two categories of rights, albeit textually through the prism of discrimination (see in particular Article 5 CERD and Articles 7–16 CEDAW). Moreover, since the adoption of the CRC in 1989, other core UN human rights treaties such as the Convention on the Protection of the Human Rights of All Migrant Workers and Members of their Families (CRW 1990) and the Convention on the Rights of Persons with Disabilities (CRPD 2006) include the two categories of rights.

Secondly, whereas the way in which rights are listed in the CRC may emphasise their indivisibility, Article 4 CRC clearly differentiates the general obligation for the realisation of these rights. In the case of economic, social and cultural rights, the general obligation is circumscribed by the reference to 'the maximum extent of their available resources and, where needed, within the framework of international cooperation'.[13] In the CRC Committee's view, the second sentence of Article 4 reflects a realistic acceptance that lack of resources – financial and otherwise – can hamper the full implementation of economic, social and cultural rights in some states; this introduces the concept of 'progressive realization' of such rights.[14]

The CRPD contains a similar general obligation, albeit that it further qualifies the more limited general obligation with regard to economic, social and cultural (ESC) rights by adding that the progressive realisation obligation is 'without prejudice to those obligations contained in the present Convention that are immediately applicable according to international law' (Article 4(2) CRPD). This circumscribed general obligation with regard to the ESC rights of children ensues from a long-lasting debate on the legal nature of ESC rights, which was also central to the negotiations on the CRC, at least in the initial stages. More often than not, they are considered second-class rights in case law and politics. The acceptance that the realisation of economic, social and cultural rights can be achieved only progressively and subject to the availability of resources bears out the recognition of a time dimension and a need for priorities in light of resource constraints.

However, as the Committee on Economic, Social and Cultural Rights (CESCR) has clarified, this recognition does not grant states *carte blanche*: they must begin immediately to take steps in order to realise ESC rights as expeditiously as possible. States also need to adopt a strategy and plan of action to realise these rights. Prioritisation too is subjected to process and substance conditions. The process in which prioritisation is decided needs to be participatory and transparent: all stakeholders must be involved so that all segments of society can express their value judgements regarding priorities. Substantively, core obligations (i.e. obligations pertaining to the minimum essential levels of the rights) should always be complied with or at least be prioritised. Moreover, there is a strong presumption that retrogressive measures are not permissible.[15] Unfortunately, the CRC Committee has mainly paid lip-service to these jurisprudential developments, so that in practice more progress may have been made in general human rights law in considering ESC rights on a par with civil and political rights than in children's rights law.[16]

The lack of conceptual sophistication in interpreting and applying ESC rights in children's rights law may have been worsened, or at least seems to be confirmed, by the popular categorisation of children's rights among children's rights proponents and CRC commentators in the so-called three Ps: rights to protection, provision and participation. Provision rights are typically socio-economic rights.[17] The downside of this categorisation for our current discussion is that the term 'provision rights' tends to confirm the outdated misunderstanding or misrepresentation that economic and social rights are exclusively about provision. It has meanwhile been widely accepted that the obligations relating to economic, social and cultural rights are to be understood as obligations to respect, to protect and to fulfil, and that the latter obligation consists of sub-obligations to facilitate, to promote and to provide. The obligation to fulfil–provide is only incumbent on the state when 'individuals or a group are unable, for reasons beyond their control, to realise that right themselves by the means at their disposal'.[18] Provision, and the concomitant need for the mobilisation of resources, therefore only characterises one tiny fraction of socio-economic rights.

In conclusion, the allegedly distinctive characteristic of children's rights law as reflected in the CRC – in that it fully embraces the indivisibility of civil, cultural, economic, political and social rights – is in fact not significantly distinctive. To the extent that the CRC is indeed premised on the indivisibility of both categories of rights, efforts to transplant this to human rights law must be undertaken cautiously, since the indivisibility is weakened textually in Article 4 CRC, and in the children's rights community by the widespread use of the 3-P typology.

1.2 New substantive norms or elements

Children's rights law, and in particular the CRC, has also been argued to have introduced new substantive norms or new substantive elements, such as additional non-discrimination grounds, a broader notion of the right to life, evolving capacities and additional elements of the right to education. Other innovations that relate rather to children-specific issues or wording (e.g. preamble: the beginning of childhood; Article 7: the right to a name, to acquire a nationality and to know one's parents;[19] Article 8: the right to preservation of identity, including nationality, name and family relations;[20] Article 13: the right to express one's views;[21] Article 14: deference to parents with regard to the freedom of thought, conscience and religion;[22] Article 17: the obligation to ensure the child's access to information and material from a diversity of sources;[23] Article 18: common responsibilities of both parents for upbringing; Article 21: adoption; Article 26: the right to benefit from social security;[24] Article 27: deference to parents with regard to standard of living;[25] Article 30: explicit reference to indigenous children; Article 31: the right of the child to rest and leisure and to participate freely in cultural life and the arts[26]) will in principle not be discussed.

Compared with other non-discrimination clauses, the CRC's non-discrimination provision is broader in that it also offers protection against discrimination on the basis of status, activities, expressed opinions or beliefs of a child's parents, legal guardians or family members. Moreover, it explicitly lists the parent's or legal guardian's race, and the children's ethnic origin and disability as prohibited grounds.[27] At least disability as a prohibited ground of discrimination has meanwhile been mainstreamed in human rights non-discrimination law, *par excellence* in the CRPD. More generally, Article 23 CRC on the rights of disabled children was pioneering at the time,[28] but was matched in human rights law by rights for *all* disabled persons through the adoption of the 2006 CRPD.[29]

The right to life, survival and development is unique in its formulation. Other core human rights treaties protect the right to life only, without mentioning survival and development. The reference to survival was intended to emphasise the positive obligations incumbent on states parties to prolong children's lives. Survival is closely related to a healthy development of children, and thereby introduces obligations of fulfilment.[30] The attention paid to the development of children, to be understood holistically,[31] is closely related to the concept of human development as advocated by the World Health Organization (WHO) and the United Nations Children's Fund (UNICEF) in the 1980s.[32] This concept too emphasises positive obligations. In addition, Article 37(a) CRC contains a prohibition of capital punishment and life imprisonment without the possibility of release.[33]

The CRC is premised on the 'fictitious universal child', which is the 'developing child'.[34] The CRC Committee too tends to see children as becoming rather than as being.[35] This paradigm of the developing child is encapsulated in the notion of the evolving capacities of the child. While being a child-specific notion,[36] it is worthwhile mentioning, since one could imagine an opposite principle with regard to the elderly, i.e. the diminishing capacities. The evolving capacities of the child are mentioned in Articles 5 and 14 CRC, mainly in order to clarify parents' responsibilities. In the words of the CRC Committee:

> the more the child knows, has experienced and understands, the more the parent, legal guardian or other persons legally responsible for him or her have to transform direction and guidance into reminders and advice, and later to an exchange on an equal footing. [footnote omitted] Similarly, as the child matures, his or her views shall have increasing weight in the assessment of his or her best interests.[37]

Article 29 CRC lists extensively the goals of education. CRC specific elements, compared to Article 13 ICESCR, are: respect for one's parents, cultural identity, national values and different civilisations, and respect for the natural environment.[38] The obligation in Article 28 CRC to take measures to ensure that school discipline is administered in a manner consistent with the child's human dignity is innovative,[39] but meanwhile mainstreamed in the CESCR's work.[40]

All in all, the CRC has not been so innovative that it fundamentally challenges human rights norms: it has sophisticated some, and complemented others.

Moreover, some innovations have meanwhile been mainstreamed in human rights law. It is also worth recalling that the CRC was not unequivocally progressive: it also introduced some regressive standard-setting, in particular with regard to the right to education. Whereas the obligation of compulsory and free primary education under the ICESCR is an immediate one, it is watered down to a progressive one in the CRC.[41] Similarly, the ICCPR contains additional safeguards in the context of criminal justice.[42]

1.3 The 'best interests of the child'

Article 3(1) CRC provides that, in all actions concerning children, the best interests of the child shall be a primary consideration. Other CRC provisions too mention the best interests of the child.[43] The CRC Committee has accorded the best interests of the child a threefold status: that of a substantive right, an interpretative legal principle and a rule of procedure.[44] As an interpretative legal principle, the best interests of the child is relatively new in international law; it was introduced to it by the CRC.[45] But it may be very forceful, in that: '[i]f a legal provision is open to more than one interpretation, the interpretation which most effectively serves the child's best interests should be chosen'.[46] Hence, it is a potentially powerful prioritisation of the child's best interests. Sometimes, it goes even beyond prioritisation, so that the child's best interests are the paramount or primary consideration.

The best interests of the child principle is without doubt a distinctive characteristic of children's rights law. One could imagine that a similar prioritisation of the interests of other so-called vulnerable groups is attractive. A transplant of the best interests could therefore be imagined, and the best interests of, for example, persons with disabilities, migrant workers or older persons could be envisaged. So far, with the exception of one almost unnoticed attempt of the CESCR,[47] this has not yet been done. But would it be desirable?[48]

I see two major counter-arguments. Firstly, the meaning of best interests of the child has remained indeterminate and opaque, so that it tends to be invoked from different sides to justify sometimes opposing decisions. In the context of undocumented migration, does the best interests of the child favour a return of the child to its family, or rather the elaboration of a life project in the host country? In the context of neglect or poverty, does it favour alternative care or support for the biological family? The interests of the child can be understood in different ways: as basic interest, developmental interest or autonomy interest,[49] or also in light of children's needs, potential harm to children or their wishes and feelings.[50] The CRC Committee has refrained from defining the best interests of the child. Rather, it has argued that the best interests of the child is 'a dynamic concept that encompasses various issues which are continuously evolving'.[51] 'The concept of the child's best interests is complex and its content must be determined on a case-by-case basis.'[52] Hence, the Committee's general comment on Article 3(1) CRC 'does not attempt to prescribe what is best for the child in any given situation at any point in time'.[53]

It may be too easy and an over-simplification to say that the best interests of the child can be imbued with *any* meaning. For example, in light of the interdependence and interaction between the different rights in the CRC, it has been submitted that the best interests of the child should be understood in light of all other rights and general principles, so that children themselves should have a say in defining what is in their interest.[54] With regard to juvenile justice, the Committee has argued that: 'protecting the child's best interests means that the traditional objectives of criminal justice, such as repression or retribution, must give way to rehabilitation and restorative justice objectives, when dealing with child offenders'[55] and that the 'purpose of assessing and determining the best interests of the child is to ensure the full and effective enjoyment of the rights recognized in the Convention and its Optional Protocols, and the holistic development of the child'.[56]

Secondly, the weight that is to be given to the best interests of the child is unclear: does it imply prioritisation or is it a trump that takes precedence over other rights and interests? Article 3 CRC clearly implies that the best interests of the child shall be (only) '*a* primary consideration', not *the* primary or paramount consideration. The best interests of the child are therefore to be balanced with other interests,[57] although they enjoy 'a larger weight'.[58] In Article 21 CRC, in the context of adoption, the best interests are the decisive factor ('the paramount consideration').

Since its inclusion in the CRC, the best interests principle has also been included in other human rights treaties with regard to children, including for example in Article 7(2) CRPD (on children with disabilities) and in Article 24 EU Charter of Fundamental Rights (on the rights of the child). The best interests principle is also often invoked by the European Court of Human Rights, which seems to oscillate between prevalence and priority in weighing the best interests of the child against other rights and interests.

In sum, the best interests of the child principle is a truly distinctive notion in children's rights law. It has meanwhile been transplanted into human rights law, albeit always with regard to children. Whereas its potential usefulness with regard to other vulnerable groups should not be discarded, the weaknesses and limitations with regard to its substance and weighing caution against any naïve transplant.

1.4 General principles

The CRC is said to be governed by four overarching general principles. These general principles cannot as such be found in the Convention. It was the CRC Committee that identified them as the four general principles of the CRC,[59] drawing on four provisions in the CRC: the right to equality and non-discrimination (Article 2 CRC); the best interests of the child (Article 3 CRC);[60] the right to life, survival and development (Article 6 CRC);[61] and respect for the views of the child/the right to be heard, sometimes also referred to as the right to participation (Article 12 CRC).

The CRC Committee has systematically emphasised their importance in its general comments, and has elaborated a specific general comment on the best interests of the child and on respect for the views of the child.[62] Criticism includes the lack of child-specificity of some of them (i.e. non-discrimination and participation)[63] and their lack of proper theoretical and legal grounding.

The use of general principles in a human rights treaty is no longer unique for the CRC, since the CRPD explicitly lists eight general principles in its Article 3: respect for inherent dignity and individual autonomy; non-discrimination; full and effective participation and inclusion; respect for difference; equality of opportunity; accessibility; equality between men and women; and respect for the evolving capacities of children with disabilities and respect for the right of children with disabilities to preserve their identities. The CRPD Committee has not yet explained its understanding of the general principles very thoroughly.

The *travaux préparatoires* are informative in this regard, and show that inspiration was drawn from the CRC Committee (and environmental law):

> The identification of specific principles to aid in the interpretation and implementation of a treaty is a well-recognized practice in international law. In the context of international human rights law for example, the Committee on the Rights of the Child identified four main principles (non-discrimination, best interests of the child, survival and development, and participation) through its analysis of the text of the Convention on the Rights of the Child. (cf Committee on the Rights of the Child, General Comment No 5, CRC/GC/2003/5), drawing on Articles 2, 3, 6 and 12 respectively.) The approach of the Working Group here is to expressly articulate the principles towards the beginning of the draft treaty text, after the section on objectives/purpose. This is an approach commonly utilized in international environmental treaties which leaves no ambiguity as to the principles to be applied. (cf Convention to Combat Desertification, Article 3; Framework Convention on Climate Change, Article 3).
>
> The principles selected for inclusion in the draft text by the Working Group, are found in numerous existing human rights instruments, including the six core international human rights conventions, the UN Standard Rules on the Equalization of Opportunities for Persons with Disabilities, and the ILO Convention concerning Vocational Rehabilitation and Employment (of Disabled Persons).[64]

The CRPD general principles have also been labelled normative principles or moral compass, since they were in earlier drafts part and parcel of the provision on the purpose of the treaty.[65]

In sum, the inclusion of general principles that clarify the object and purpose of the treaty is no longer unique to the CRC. The CRPD even textually codifies its general principles. The CRC general principles remain weak in legal and theoretical grounding. It is nonetheless an interesting feature explicitly to identify the object and purpose of the treaty, since this may help to assess reservations or to interpret treaty provisions teleologically. General principles are not unique to human rights law, but have also been identified, for example, in sustainable development law. It would therefore make sense to list general principles in a new standard setting, such as on the rights of older persons, as long as they are well grounded.[66]

1.5 Inclusion of 'third parties' as duty-holders beyond the (domestic) state

1.5.1 Beyond the state

Traditionally, human rights law primarily organises the relationship between a state and the individuals within its jurisdiction. Children's rights law, understood as the human rights law of a particular group of individuals, i.e. children, does the same. However, in children's rights law, an *intermediary level* of parents and carers has been included.[67] For example, Article 18 CRC recognises that parents or legal guardians have primary responsibility for the upbringing and development of the child. States are to render appropriate assistance to parents and legal guardians in the performance of their child-rearing responsibilities, as well as to ensure the development of institutions, facilities and services for the care of children.

Article 18 has been criticised for the portrayal of the child as incomplete, hence the need for responsible adults:

> . . . this article secures the hierarchical matrix of the parent over the child, with the state as a backup over the parent. Article 18 talks in terms of responsibility; but 'responsibility for' another person is an enactment of power, and as such is a right held by an adult to exercise power over the child. Responsibility here arguably is about the parent's right to control the child. This responsibility enables the adult to determine and dictate what is or is not in the best interests of the child. Parents' 'responsibility' over the child trumps the child's right to information, thought and religion, [footnote omitted] and even the right to be free from abusive traditional practices . . .[68]

However, I suggest here a different analysis of Article 18 CRC and some other CRC provisions in which the responsibility of parents is mentioned. In my view, it may create space for bringing in other duty-bearers than the state in human rights law. Compare the division of responsibility outlined in Article 27 CRC on the right to an adequate standard of living. That provision goes beyond a traditional understanding of human rights in a vertical relationship between the individual (in this case the child) and the state. For primary responsibility to secure the conditions of living necessary for the child's development lies again with the parents, albeit within their abilities and financial capacities (see Article 27(2) CRC). The corresponding obligation of the state is to ensure that parents fulfil their obligations towards their child (obligation to protect). This attribution of primary responsibility to the parents builds on the Convention's 'conception of the ideal type of setting for the upbringing of the child: a family with the will and the capability to care for the child during its many years, starting with the pregnancy and from birth to full maturity at the age of eighteen'.[69] It goes without saying that parents' capacity to live up to this ideal-type conception is strongly dependent on their resources, material and non-material. If, despite their efforts, parents are unable to ensure proper conditions for the development of the child, the state has an obligation to assist.[70]

Article 27 CRC has been criticised on different grounds. For one, it may be said to portray the child as immature and dependent on adults. Secondly, the subsidiary obligation placed on states in Article 27(3) to assist parents in the implementation of the right, is limited in several different ways. Firstly, it is subject to the means available to the state. Secondly, the state is to intervene only in cases of need, and its intervention appears to be limited to material needs: the state is to provide material assistance and support programmes, particularly with regard to nutrition, clothing and housing (obligation to fulfil).[71] But Article 27 CRC can also be read as opening up the duty-bearer side of human rights law, in order to include other actors than the state.

Unfortunately, unlike the CESCR, the CRC Committee has so far not explicitly drawn attention to the responsibilities of actors other than the state. The CESCR typically includes in its general comments a section dedicated to obligations of actors other than states.[72] On the contrary, the CRC Committee often remains silent on the children' rights responsibilities of other than state actors, even in its general comment on the business sector and children's rights. In the latter, it focused strictly on state obligations, both of individual states and when acting collectively through international organisations.[73] An exception is the 2013 general comment on the right to health, which contains a section on the responsibilities of non-state actors. Non-state actors include parents and other carers on the one hand, and non-state service providers and other non-state actors on the other. The CRC Committee is very affirmative in its language when it comes to the incorporation of the CRC in health service providers' programmes and services ('must'), and with regard to business enterprises' due diligence obligation.[74] Non-state duty-bearers that are singled out in this general comment include in particular pharmaceutical companies, private health insurance companies, mass media organisations and researchers.

Certainly, the conceptual framework governing responsibilities and obligations of non-state actors needs to be clarified. Firstly, as a matter of terminology, 'responsibilities' and 'obligations' may not have the same legal weight. Whereas obligations may be understood as legally binding, responsibilities may be used either to refer to moral responsibilities or to legal duties.[75] A more consistent use of obligations or duties language to indicate legally binding norms, and of responsibility language to refer to moral norms, would be most useful. Moreover, more clarification is needed as to how these obligations and responsibilities of different actors relate to each other. Do they share obligations? Are their obligations parallel obligations, or is there a degree of subsidiarity? Do they share responsibility for violations?[76] Notwithstanding the current conceptual vagueness, the CRC does create space for bringing in other duty-bearers than the state.

1.5.2 Beyond the domestic state

The CRC does not focus exclusively on the territorial state as the sole statist duty-bearer. International assistance and cooperation is mentioned in Articles 4, 7(2), 11(2), 17(b), 21(e), 22(2), 23(4), 24(4), 27(4), 28(3), 34, 35 and 45 CRC. Sometimes there is clearly no intention to refer to cooperation *for development*, sometimes cooperation for development may or may not be encompassed, and in still other instances most likely cooperation for development is at the core of the reference. To the latter category belong the references to international cooperation in the final but one preambular paragraph,[77] Article 4 (general obligation), Article 23(4) (disability), Article 24(4) (health) and Article 28(3) (education).

It is not possible to establish the existence of a general legal obligation under the CRC to cooperate internationally for development, nor of a more specific obligation to provide development assistance for the realisation of economic, social and cultural rights of children in developing countries, commensurate with need. Such obligations would amount to an extraterritorial obligation to fulfil. However, legal obligations to respect and protect economic, social and cultural rights of children in foreign states do apply.[78] The CRC Committee's interpretation states that there is a shared responsibility for development, and that states parties are not only to implement the CRC within their own jurisdiction, but are also to contribute to global implementation, through international cooperation.

Moreover, the CRC Committee has clarified some specific obligations of fulfilment for donor countries, such as, amongst others, the allocation of 0.7 per cent of gross domestic product (GDP) to development assistance, and the adoption of a rights-based approach to development cooperation, in which children's rights are mainstreamed. For example, in its 2013 general comment on the right to health, the CRC Committee argued that: 'States parties to the Convention have obligations not only to implement children's right to health within their own jurisdiction, but also to contribute through international cooperation to global implementation'.[79] It was said that '[i]nternational cooperation should support state-led health systems and national action plans', and that the CRC 'should guide all international activities and programmes of donor . . . States related directly or indirectly to children's health'.[80] States were also reminded of the international 0.7 per cent target for development assistance.[81] Specifically with regard to disaster relief and humanitarian assistance, the individual and joint responsibility to cooperate in providing relief was spelled out, and states were invited to 'consider prioritizing efforts to realise children's right to health . . .'.[82]

It would be good if the CRC Committee moved beyond the focus on the extraterritorial obligation to fulfil, and paid equal or even more attention to extraterritorial obligations to respect and to protect economic, social and cultural rights of children in developing countries. Inspiration for a better understanding of these obligations could be sought in CESCR work.[83] Moreover, questions of subsidiary and shared responsibility for violations arise here as well.

1.6 Conclusion

In order to assess whether and to what extent children's rights law is distinctive from human rights law, the following characteristics in particular have been analysed: the indivisibility of civil, political, economic, social and cultural rights; new substantive norms such as additional non-discrimination grounds, additional aims of education and new wording in a number of provisions; the use of the 'best interests of the child' principle; the use of general principles; and the inclusion of 'third parties' and foreign states as duty-holders beyond the domestic state.

We have argued that many of the alleged distinctive characteristics of children's rights law are in fact not significantly distinctive (anymore). Moreover, the truly distinctive characteristics – to the extent that they are considered to be positive elements that human rights law can copy – have a number of weaknesses and limitations, so that simple transplants are not warranted. 'Best interests of' may work for other vulnerable groups if its substance, meaning and relative weight can be clarified. General principles may be useful in human rights law, provided that their theoretical and legal grounding is strengthened. The inclusion of other duty-bearers than the domestic state needs much more conceptual clarification.

The findings about weaknesses and limitations do not necessarily preclude integration, nor justify isolation, but guard the general and other specific human rights regimes against naïve borrowing from children's rights law.

Notes

1 In principle, I always insist on defining children's rights law much broader than the CRC (see W Vandenhole, 'Children's rights from a legal perspective: children's rights law' in W Vandenhole, E Desmet, D Reynaert and S Lembrechts (eds), *Routledge International Handbook of Children's Rights Studies* (Routledge 2015) 29), but in the context of this exercise, that would create confusion.
2 See e.g. E Verhellen, 'The Convention on the Rights of the Child: reflections from a historical, social policy and educational perspective' in Vandenhole and others (n 1) 44–45.
3 M Freeman, 'The value and values of children's rights' in A Invernizzi, J Williams (eds), *The Human Rights of Children: From Visions to Implementation* (Ashgate 2011) 27; A Invernizzi, J Williams, 'Introduction: human rights of children: from visions to implementation?' in A Invernizzi, J Williams (eds), *Understanding a Human Rights Based Approach to Matters Involving Children: Conceptual Foundations and Strategic Considerations* (Ashgate 2011) 7.
4 See e.g. N Peleg, 'Time to grow up: the UN Committee on the Rights of the Child's jurisprudence of the right to development' in M Freeman (ed), *Law and Childhood Studies* (Current Legal Issues, Oxford University Press 2012) 371–91.
5 A Barnes, 'CRC's performance of the child as developing' in Invernizzi and Williams (n 3) 396–97.
6 P Alston, 'The best interests principle: towards a reconciliation of culture and human rights' (1994) 8 *International Journal of Law and the Family* 1, 6.
7 ibid; A Lopatka, 'Introduction' in Office of the United Nations High Commissioner for Human Rights (OHCHR) (ed), *Legislative History of the Convention on the Rights of the Child* (United Nations 2007) xxxviii.
8 Alston (n 6) 6.
9 ibid.

10 P Cantwell, 'The origins, development and significance of the United Nations Convention on the Rights of the Child' in S Detrick, *The United Nations Convention on the Rights of the Child: A Guide to the 'Travaux Préparatoires'* (Martinus Nijhoff 1992) 23.
11 ibid 7.
12 Verhellen (n 2) 49.
13 Cantwell (n 10) 27. See also Alston (n 6) 7.
14 CRC Committee, 'General Comment No 5: General Measures of Implementation of the Convention on the Rights of the Child' UN Doc CRC/GC/2003/5, para 7.
15 CESCR, 'General Comment No 3: The Nature of States Parties' Obligations (art 2, para 1)' UN Doc E/1991/23; CESCR, 'General Comment No 15: The Right to Water' UN Doc E/C.12/2002/11.
16 J Ryngaert, 'De kruisbestuiving tussen kinderrechten en mensenrechten op het domein van economische, sociale en culturele rechten' [Crossfertilisation between children's rights and human rights in the area of economic, social and cultural rights] (PhD, University of Antwerp 2015); I E Koch, *Human Rights as Indivisible Rights: The Protection of Socio-economic Demands under the European Convention on Human Rights* (Martinus Nijhoff 2009) 101.
17 Verhellen (n 2) 49–50.
18 CESCR, 'General Comment No 14: The Right to the Highest Attainable Standard of Health (Article 12 of the International Covenant on Economic, Social and Cultural Rights)' UN Doc E/C.12/2000/4, para 37. For further details see e.g. W Vandenhole, 'Completing the UN complaint mechanisms for human rights violations step by step: towards a complaints procedure to the International Covenant on Economic, Social and Cultural Rights' (2003) 21 *Netherlands Quarterly of Human Rights* 443–44; E Riedel, G Giacca and C Golay, 'The development of economic, social and cultural rights in international law' in E Riedel, G Giacca and C Golay (eds), *Economic, Social and Cultural Rights in International Law: Contemporary Issues and Challenges* (Oxford University Press 2014) 20.
19 I Ziemele, 'Article 7: the right to birth registration, name and nationality, and the right to know and be cared for by parents' in A Alen, J Vande Lanotte, E Verhellen, F Ang, E Berghmans, M Verheyde and B Abramson (eds), *A Commentary on the United Nations Convention on the Rights of the Child* (Brill Nijhoff 2007).
20 J Doek, 'Article 8: the right to preservation of identity; Article 9: the right not to be separated from his or her parents' in Alen and others (n 19).
21 H Thorgeirsdóttir, 'Article 13: the right to freedom of expression' in Alen and others (n 19).
22 J Tobin, 'Understanding a human rights based approach to matters involving children: conceptual foundations and strategic considerations' in A Invernizzi, J Williams (eds), *The Human Rights of Children. From Visions to Implementation* (Ashgate 2011) 61–98; E Brems, 'Article 14: the right to freedom of thought, conscience and religion' in Alen and others (n 19).
23 S W Sacino, 'Article 17: access to a diversity of mass media sources' in Alen and others (n 19).
24 W Vandenhole, 'Article 26: the right to benefit from social security' in Alen and others (n 19).
25 A Eide, 'Article 27: the right to an adequate standard of living' in Alen and others (n 19).
26 P David, 'Article 31: the right to leisure, play and culture' in A Alen and others (n 19). For a critical discussion from the perspective of the universalist conception of childhood that the CRC Committee employs, see Peleg (n 4) 387–88.

27 W Vandenhole, *Non-discrimination and Equality in the View of the UN Human Rights Treaty Bodies* (Intersentia 2005) 170–72; CRC Committee, 'General Comment No 9: The Rights of Children with Disabilities' UN Doc CRC/C/GC/9.
28 Compare Amnesty International, *Human Rights for Human Dignity. A Primer on Economic, Social and Cultural Rights* (Amnesty International 2014) 113; R Kayess, P French, 'Out of darkness into light? Introducing the Convention on the Rights of Persons with Disabilities' (2008) 8 *Human Rights Law Review* 1, 12–13, who criticise the medical model of disability in that provision.
29 For a general discussion see Kayess and French (n 28). For a specific discussion of children with disabilities in the CRPD see B Byrne, 'Minding the gap? Children with disabilities and the United Nations Convention on the Rights of Persons with Disabilities' in M Freeman (ed), *Law and Childhood Studies* (Current Legal Issues, Oxford University Press 2012) 419–37.
30 M Nowak, 'Article 6: the right to life, survival and development' in Alen and others (n 19) 12–14 and 36–37.
31 CRC Committee, 'General Comment No 5' (n 14) para 12; CRC Committee, 'General Comment No 7: Implementing Child Rights in Early Childhood' UN Doc CRC/C/GC7/2005/Rev1, para 10.
32 Nowak (n 30) 7 and 14. For a criticism of this positive reading see Barnes (n 5) 402–404.
33 W A Schabas, H Sax, 'Article 37: prohibition of torture, death penalty, life imprisonment and deprivation of liberty' in Alen and others (n 19).
34 Barnes (n 5) 392.
35 Peleg (n 4) 371–91.
36 Tobin has argued that this would make a better general principle of the CRC; see Tobin (n 22) 72.
37 CRC Committee, 'General Comment No 14' (n 18) para 44.
38 For a critical discussion from the perspective of the universalist conception of childhood that the CRC Committee employs see Peleg (n 4) 385–87.
39 M Verheyde, 'Article 28: the right to education' in Alen and others (n 19) 9.
40 CESCR, 'General Comment No 13: The Right to Education (Article 13 of the Covenant)' UN Doc E/C.12/1999/10, para 41.
41 The practical impact is in most cases mitigated by art 41 CRC, which provides that: 'Nothing in the present Convention shall affect any provisions which are more conducive to the realization of the rights of the child . . .', whether contained in national or international law applicable to the state concerned. See Verheyde (n 39) 10.
42 G Van Bueren, 'Child criminal justice' in Alen and others (n 19) 8–9.
43 See CRC Committee, 'General Comment No 14' (n 18) para 3.
44 ibid para 6.
45 M Freeman, 'Article 3: the best interests of the child' in Alen and others (n 19) 1.
46 CRC Committee, 'General Comment No 14' (n 18) para 6(a).
47 CESCR, 'General Comment No 13: The Right to Education (Article 13 of the Covenant)' UN Doc E/C.12/1999/10, para 7. The CESCR has argued that when considering the appropriate application of the inter-related and essential features of availability, accessibility, acceptability and adaptability, the best interests of the student shall be a primary consideration.
48 For a rejection of this transplant see Ryngaert (n 16) 143–74.
49 J Eekelaar, 'The importance of thinking that children have rights' (1992) 6 *International Journal of Law and the Family* 230–31.
50 Freeman, 'Article 3' (n 45) 31.
51 CRC Committee, 'General Comment No 14' (n 18) para 11.
52 ibid para 32.

53 ibid para 11.
54 ibid para 43; CRC Committee, 'General Comment No 12: The Right of the Child to Be Heard' UN Doc CRC/C/GC/12, paras 70–74.
55 CRC Committee, 'General Comment No 14' (n 18) para 28.
56 ibid para 82.
57 Freeman, 'Article 3' (n 45) 60.
58 CRC Committee, 'General Comment No 14' (n 18) para 39.
59 They were mentioned for the first time in the CRC Committee's reporting guidelines for initial reports; see CRC Committee, 'General guidelines regarding the form and content of initial reports to be submitted by states Parties under Article 44, Paragraph 1(a) of the Convention' UN Doc CRC/C/5, para 13. For a textual acknowledgement that it was the Committee that identified them as general principles see CRC Committee, 'General Comment No 5: General measures of implementation' UN Doc CRC/GC/2003/5, para 12.
60 See Freeman (n 45).
61 See Nowak (n 30).
62 See e.g. most recently CRC Committee, 'General Comment No 14' (n 18) paras 41–43; CRC Committee, 'General Comment No 13: The Right of the Child to Freedom from All Forms of Violence' (2011) UN Doc CRC/C/GC/11, paras 53–56; CRC Committee, 'General Comment No 12: The Right of the Child to Be Heard' UN Doc CRC/C/GC/12, paras 68–83.
63 See Tobin (n 22) 71.
64 Landmine Survivors Network www.un.org/esa/socdev/enable/rights/wgdca2.htm (last accessed 22 November 2016).
65 Kayess and French (n 28) 27.
66 Contra Ryngaert (n 16) 117–24. See also Habbig, Hoefmans and De Hert (ch 8).
67 As Alston has pointed out, the UN Convention on the Rights of the Child, and by extension, children's rights, do not offer a single answer to the division of responsibility. See P Alston, 'The best interests principle: towards a reconciliation of culture and human rights' (1994) 6 *International Journal of Law and the Family* 2.
68 See Barnes (n 5) 405.
69 See Eide (n 25) 3.
70 ibid 3 and 26.
71 ibid 2.
72 See eg CESCR, 'General Comment No 21: The Right of Everyone to Take Part in Cultural Life (art 15, para 1(a) of the International Covenant on Economic, Social and Cultural Rights)' UN Doc E/C.12/GC/21/Rev1, paras 73–76; CESCR, 'General Comment No 19: The Right to Social Security (art 9)' UN Doc E/C.12/GC/19, paras 82–84; CESCR, 'The right to work. General Comment No 18: Article 6 of the International Covenant on Economic, Social and Cultural Rights' UN Doc E/C.12/GC/18, paras 52–54.
73 CRC Committee, 'General Comment No 16: State Obligations Regarding the Impact of the Business Sector on Children's Rights' (2013) UN Doc CRC/C/GC/16, paras 47–48.
74 CRC Committee, 'General Comment No 15: The Right of the Child to the Enjoyment of the Highest Attainable Standard of Health (Article 24)' (2013) UN Doc CRC/C/GC/15, paras 75–85.
75 Compare the use of responsibility and duties in the Guiding Principles on Business and Human Rights, Principles 1 and 11; see J Ruggie, 'Guiding Principles on Business and Human Rights: Implementing the United Nations "Protect, respect and remedy" framework' UN Doc A/HRC/17/31.

76 For an extensive exploration of these and other questions in human rights law see W Vandenhole, 'Obligations and responsibility in a plural and diverse duty-bearer human rights regime' in W Vandenhole (ed), *Challenging Territoriality in Human Rights Law: Building Blocks for a Plural and Diverse Duty-bearer Regime* (Routledge 2015) 115–135.

77 The final preambular paragraph of the CRC reads: 'Recognizing the importance of international co-operation for improving the living conditions of children in every country, in particular in the developing countries'.

78 For a thorough discussion see W Vandenhole, 'Economic, social and cultural rights in the CRC: is there a legal obligation to cooperate internationally for development?' (2009) 17 *International Journal of Children's Rights* 23–63. See also M Wabwile, 'Re-examining states' external obligations to implement economic and social rights of children' (2009) 22 *Canadian Journal of Law and Jurisprudence* 407–49.

79 CRC Committee, 'General Comment No 15: The Right of the Child to the Enjoyment of the Highest Attainable Standard of Health (Article 24)' UN Doc CRC/C/GC/15, para 86.

80 ibid para 87.

81 ibid para 89.

82 ibid para 88.

83 See inter alia Vandenhole (n 78) 52–55; F Coomans, 'The extraterritorial scope of the international Covenant on Economic, Social and Cultural Rights in the Work of the United Nations Committee on economic, social and cultural rights' (2011) 11 *Human Rights Law Review* 1–35.

2 The broader relevance of features of children's rights law: the 'best interests of the child' principle

Helen Stalford

2.1 Introduction

The best interests principle is the normative axis around which decisions relating to children revolve. While Article 3(1) CRC is the most commonly cited reference for this principle, it finds expression in a number of earlier and subsequent international texts, notably the 1959 Declaration on the Rights of the Child,[1] the 1979 Convention on the Elimination of All Forms of Discrimination against Women[2] and the UN Convention on the Rights of Persons with Disabilities.[3] Despite the fact that best interests is universally regarded as a central tenet of children's rights, its precise definition remains elusive and its application highly inconsistent and contingent upon subjective interpretation. In the words of Mnookin, the enormity of the task associated with determining what is in a child's best interests 'poses a question no less ultimate than the purposes and values of life itself'.[4]

The UN Committee on the Rights of the Child has, somewhat obliquely, characterised the principle as: a substantive right, entailing an intrinsic obligation on all states to ensure that the child's best interests are a primary consideration informing all decisions concerning the child; a fundamental interpretative legal principle requiring that if a legal provision is open to more than one interpretation, the interpretation that most effectively serves the child's best interests should be chosen; and a rule of procedure requiring procedural guarantees to be put in place to enable decisions around what is in the child's best interests actually to occur and be evidenced in practice.[5]

Added to this, it is accepted that the best interests principle does not operate in isolation from other children's rights; on the contrary, it is intimately linked with and instrumental to the exercise and enforcement of other rights set out in the Convention.[6] This, in turn, has generated extensive guidance on how to determine best interests in a range of substantive contexts at international and domestic level. Consider, for example, the best interests determination guidelines of the UN High Commissioner for Refugees,[7] as well as the various welfare checklists[8] and toolkits that have been developed at national level, particularly in a family law and medical law context. Indeed, at the national level, particularly in Western legal systems, the best interests principle has gained considerable traction and even been elevated to a status of 'paramount' importance.[9]

It is not surprising that the best interests principle appeals to other areas of (adult) human rights. The concept offers a neat, rhetorical device that can be shared by the range of professionals and authority figures engaged in decision-making on behalf of vulnerable individuals. It focuses everyone's attention on the common goal of achieving the best possible outcomes for them, and it offers a convenient shorthand for the range of intrinsic and extrinsic factors that are instrumental to protecting individuals' well-being and nurturing their potential in the short, medium and longer term. The principle has been appropriated, in particular, in a clinical health care context for adults deemed to lack capacity to make decisions for themselves. In England and Wales, for example, the Mental Capacity Act 2005 gives statutory force to the best interests test[10] and best interests is a dominant rhetoric informing debates around end-of-life decision-making[11] and forced sterilisation.[12]

Efforts to appropriate the best interests standard are driven by a mixture of pragmatic, philosophical and ethical considerations.[13] But this chapter cautions against extending the best interests too readily to other decision-making contexts, first and foremost because the principle has been developed specifically in a children's rights context to respond to the distinct needs and vulnerabilities of children. It cannot readily be transposed to other human rights contexts without potentially undermining or attenuating the purpose for which it was originally intended. Its explicit focus on children, and particularly its emphasis on paramountcy or primacy, begs the question as to how states and other duty-bearers could meet the obligations inherent in the principle of best interests if it were broadened out to other communities of rights holders, namely adults, on the same terms. This contention will now be considered in more depth.

2.2 Upholding the child-specificity of the best interests principle

It is difficult to imagine the best interests principle, as it is currently conceived, operating effectively in many adult human rights contexts as a general principle, aside from the narrowly defined contexts referred to above involving adults who are mentally and physically vulnerable. Certainly, there is a strong argument in favour of limiting it exclusively to children or, at most, to adults whose cognitive, mental, emotional and physical functions render them comparable to children in terms of their vulnerability and their dependency on adults to make decisions on their behalf. But the best interests principle extends well beyond these paternalistic dynamics. It has evolved with the twin purpose of enabling children to exercise their rights fully by ensuring that obligations towards them are fulfilled and to assist decision-makers in achieving an outcome that will have the most positive (or the least negative) impact on them.[14]

The process of conceptualising and embedding best interests within a rights framework has not been straightforward or uncontested, however. During the drafting of the UN Convention on the Rights of the Child there was considerable debate as to whether a principle grounded in 'interests' and 'needs' should be included at all within a convention that explicitly endorses *rights*.[15] What the drafters arrived at in the end is, in the words of Philip Alston, 'a carefully formulated and balanced statement of values to which [nearly all states] have formally subscribed'.[16]

Since then best interests in the context of children's rights has come to represent a number of ideals and aims. Firstly, it is a mechanism for rendering children's interests visible in decision-making processes that are routinely dominated by adults. As Freeman asserts, 'in a world run by adults, there would otherwise be a danger that children's interests would be completely ignored'.[17] Secondly, it provides an approach to purported clashes between adults' (typically parents') desires and interests and the interests of the child (for instance in the context of disputes around child contact and residence). Such an approach is based on a 'King Solomon-type' philosophy,[18] that a willingness to sacrifice one's own desires for the sake of those of one's child is what being a parent is all about.[19]

It is also generally accepted (in principle at least) that it is right and fair that children's interests should carry more weight in such decisions because their outcome is likely to have much more profound effects on children in the immediate and longer term. Take a family relocation application for instance: the decision to relocate a child, uproot him or her from their school, friends, social commitments, cultural and linguistic environment and, in many cases, from regular contact with the other parent and perhaps even siblings, can have a profound impact on a child's life opportunities, education, sense of identity, health and happiness, arguably to a much greater extent than on that of the parent who has requested the relocation. Such factors have to be weighed up carefully against the likely benefits that such a move might bring, demanding what John Eekelaar refers to as an 'imaginative leap' as to what the child might have chosen for him or herself on reaching maturity.[20] This interpretation links in with the third, more utilitarian function of best interests: that investing in children's interests maximises the welfare of society as a whole; it creates the circumstances in which children can be nurtured to develop into rounded, fulfilled and responsible citizens, contributing to a community that we all want to be part of in the short and longer term.[21]

This cursory overview of how best interests is conceptualised highlights, perhaps, the difficulties of applying such functions to adult-related human rights decision-making. The concern is that this would lead to one of two possible consequences: firstly, it would mark a shift towards what Stephen Parker refers to as 'an artificial and sterile universalism',[22] potentially divesting the principle of any distinctiveness and, ultimately, undermining its effectiveness in protecting children's welfare. Secondly, it risks contriving decision-making processes by seeking to conceptualise them within a (child-focused) framework that is ill-adapted to accommodate the different variables and contexts that shape adults' lives. The following section explores these possible outcomes in more depth.

2.3 Avoiding an artificial and sterile universalism

Any suggestion that best interests be extended to other human rights contexts raises a number of practical and conceptual questions. First and foremost, questions arise as to the ways in which the principle would have to be adapted to respond to the very different variables shaping decision-making around adults. For instance, it is difficult to envisage how the notions of primacy or paramountcy – the cornerstones of the best interests principle – would prevail, particularly in matters concerning both adults and children. What would happen, for instance, if there was a clash between the best interests of the child and the best interests of an adult in a given set of circumstances such as disputes over custody and access, or cases of parental child abduction involving allegations of domestic abuse perpetrated by the father against the mother?

One of the most common arguments in favour of extending the best interests principle to other (adult) parties in such cases is based on notions of fairness and achieving equality of arms. This argument objects to the way in which best interests blindly prioritises children's needs over and above the interests of other parties implicated in proceedings, leading to an artificial, one-sided justice that undermines adult parties' (notably parents') rights, and fails to acknowledge that a more balanced assessment of the different parties' interests might be instrumental to upholding the interests of the child.[23] The way in which child contact is addressed in domestic violence cases provides a good illustration of this tendency. In England and Wales, ongoing contact with the non-resident father is often endorsed in some manner or form, provided it is consistent with the welfare of the child.[24] Many have argued, however, that the interests of the mother are not sufficiently taken into account in such circumstances and that the current legal approach perpetuates circumstances in which the abuser can exert ongoing control and coercion over the mother.[25]

Whilst there are clearly cases in which the welfare of adults in acutely vulnerable circumstances requires specific protection, it should not be to the detriment of enhanced consideration of the interests of children. Children begin at a distinctly disadvantaged position as compared to adults by virtue of the fact that they typically have little control over the living circumstances in which they find themselves. On a day-to-day basis they have very limited autonomy; parents and other adults routinely act as the gatekeepers permitting or refusing their access to and enjoyment of their rights, even for those children who have capacity to make autonomous decisions. They depend on adults to transport them, to support them financially, to feed and clothe them, to guide them in understanding the difference between what is right and wrong, safe or dangerous, healthy or unhealthy. A special mechanism such as best interests enables decision-makers to isolate and distinguish children's needs from those of their parents, particularly in cases where parents are simply unable or unwilling to accept that their children's needs are not coterminous with their own needs or desires.

Of relevance in this regard are developments in new reproductive technologies, which both reflect and endorse growing recognition of individuals' 'right' to parent. Built into most forms of assisted reproduction in the UK now is some obligation to consider the best interests of the child likely to be born as a result of such procedures,[26] but how would such an obligation be affected if the best interests of the adult receiving treatment had to be weighed equally against those of the potential child? Consider the impact that elevation of best interests in favour of adults might have, for instance, on children's right to know their genetic heritage if sperm donors could argue that it is equally in their own best interests to remain anonymous. Consider also how, in a surrogacy arrangement gone wrong, the courts would balance the competing interests of commissioning parents, those of the surrogate mother and the interests of the child if there was an obligation to uphold the best interests of all.[27]

If the best interests of the child is to remain paramount or even primary, that would surely imply an inferior iteration of best interests for adults/parents implicated in the same decision; their interests would have to be a *secondary* or *minor* consideration. Conversely, if the best interests of the child were not to remain paramount but were to be considered in equal measure to the interests of the adults surely this would lead to widespread, routine breaches of the CRC, not to mention the domestic articulation of the principle.

Either way, we end up with a principle that is vulnerable to dilution or corruption if applied too freely to adults. Certainly there is some evidence of this already occurring: in the context of assisted reproduction, for instance, it has been noted that the obligation to consider the welfare of any children born as a result is only superficially adhered to and that, for the most part, adults' reproductive autonomy almost always takes precedence over any speculative child welfare concerns. In a surrogacy context, for instance, there is no requirement to consider the suitability of the commissioning adults to act as parents of a child born of such arrangements.[28] The prevailing (and some would argue, erroneous) presumption is that it is almost always in the child's best interests to be born, save for exceptionally rare instances when he or she would be exposed to a life that is 'not worth living'. Any other approach, it is argued, is tantamount to licensing parenthood in a highly discriminatory way.[29] In the same vein, it is probable that a more explicit obligation to consider the best interests of prospective parents in such contexts would merely reinforce the current, implicit obligation to uphold adults' reproductive autonomy.

There are, of course, numerous situations in which an adult-focused application of the best interests principle is simply inconceivable, particularly where such interests have to be balanced with wider public policy concerns. Take for instance best interests in the context of immigration and asylum law. Immigrants' right to family life is protected under Article 8(1) of the 1950 European Convention on Human Rights. Immigrants' exercise of their right to family life in the host country can be trumped, however, by 'the interests of national security, public safety or the economic well-being of the country, for the prevention of disorder or crime, for the protection of health or morals, or for the protection of the rights and freedoms of others' (Article 8(2)). This provision has spawned an abundant jurisprudence largely endorsing an expansive interpretation of Article 8(2), leading to a situation in which unlawfully resident adult claimants can avoid removal only in the most exceptional of cases, where there are 'insurmountable obstacles'[30] to establishing family life elsewhere.[31]

For the most part, states enjoy a wide margin of appreciation in regulating immigration into their own regions with a view to curbing the injurious economic, political, cultural and social impact of such flows. Effectively, therefore, even if it did have an explicit mediating function, the best interests of immigrants – adults and children alike – will always be relegated to the notional 'best interests' of the broader public, save in the most exceptional of cases. This is not only the case for immigration cases involving adults, however: the fact that states persist (and the UK is a particular culprit) in allowing tens of thousands of unaccompanied children to languish in refugee camps across Europe offers a sobering illustration of how best interests operates as a vacuous mantra rather than as a transparent and coherent call to action.[32] Similarly, the best interests principle in a criminal justice context often pales into insignificance where the focus is on punitive sanctions, avoiding recidivism and obtaining justice for the victim.[33] It is, therefore, highly unlikely that the best interests principle could provide any meaningful, politically palatable framework for determining how to dispose of adult claims in such contexts.

In addition to the more pragmatic difficulties associated with extending the best interests principle is the concern that it would serve to transpose disempowering decision-making opacity commonly associated with children's best interests assessment to adult contexts. This not only risks attenuating adults' right to autonomy and self-determination, but also risks entrenching a predominantly paternalistic model of best interests from which, for many years now, activists have been trying to extricate children's rights.[34]

2.4 Entrenching and reinforcing opaque decision-making

One of the key strengths of the best interests principle (its adaptability to different contexts, depending on how it is interpreted) is also its greatest weakness. Its indeterminacy has been highlighted as rendering it susceptible to manipulation to serve adultist agendas and to sanction '. . . untested assumptions about what is good for children'.[35] Over 40 years ago, Robert Mnookin raised serious concerns about the wisdom of deploying such a speculative, highly subjective and acutely unpredictable framework to inform often life-changing decisions.[36] It has also been questioned whether it is even possible, let alone desirable, to achieve determinacy and predictability in decision-making, particularly when it comes to lives characterised by constant fluctuations in living conditions, family constellations and physical and mental health.[37]

The holy grail of determining what is in the best interests of individuals is all the more elusive when one takes account of what Parker refers to as 'a collapse in consensus over certain kinds of values to do with conformism and individuality, material success and personal contentment, gender differentiation and so on'.[38] In Western democracies, at least, we have increasingly less defined conventions and a less prominent sense of shared values (other than perhaps a shift towards libertarianism) to guide decisions, making it increasingly difficult to ascribe a generalised set of circumstances or ideals to a best interests assessment. Whilst we might still hang onto the artificial assumption that best interests can be determined by reference to shared values or wisdom, in reality best interests assessments are unnervingly instinctive and highly contingent on the subjective assessment and value framework of the decision-maker.

In extending best interests to other human rights arenas, therefore, we risk completely losing grip on what is already a slippery, highly contested concept. This would not only inhibit progress in children's rights, but would risk distorting assessments of adult autonomy and self-determination – quite literally straitjacketing them. One only has to look at the best interests standard in the context of medical decision-making and disability to see how readily it is used to reinforce a highly paternalistic, protectionist agenda and, as a consequence, to divest individuals of their decision-making autonomy. Moral and legal philosophers such as John Stuart Mill have resolutely rejected any attempts to impose constraints on an individual's (adult's) liberty for the purpose of promoting his or her own good. But it is also conceded that there is a class of persons (children, the profoundly disabled or mentally incapacitated) with respect to which paternalistic interventions can be justified because of their inherent vulnerability. And so, there are multiple legal and policy interventions that are paternalistic in nature.

However, the application of this principle to such cases has not been without its problems: legal academics and practitioners alike have grappled with what the components of the best interests formula in such cases might be; what kinds of benefits and burdens can be factored into such decisions; how the interests and well-being of a profoundly disabled, barely communicative person should be assessed and measured; whose perspective/value judgment on quality of life governs; to what extent should the views and wishes of the individual inform determinations of their best interests; and how should those views be elicited and interpreted (whether it is permissible, for instance, to consider the interconnected interests of other persons such as surrounding family and carers). An increasing preoccupation, particularly in times of austerity, is the weight that should be attached to the interests of society more broadly when faced with the financial burden of supporting expensive, specialised and highly individualised treatment.

The lack of coherent guidance on how to interpret best interests in such contexts has led to significant inconsistency and uncertainty in the outcome of decisions. In an adult decision-making context, this has generated ongoing criticism that such decisions are based on the competent decision-maker's assumptions or prejudices about the value and quality of a disabled person's existence, and that decisions are often made more in the interests of protecting public resources than upholding the rights and dignity of the individual.[39]

In England and Wales, for instance, the Mental Capacity Act (MCA) 2005 was heralded as a 'ground-breaking legal framework' to empower and protect those who lack capacity to make decisions for themselves.[40] The best interests principle is a cornerstone of this legislation: 'An act done, or decision made, under this Act for or on behalf of a person who lacks capacity must be done or made, in his best interests'.[41] As a result, the best interests standard forms the basis for all court decisions made and actions carried out on behalf of people who lack capacity to make those decisions for themselves. Section 4 of the MCA provides the relevant checklist of factors that should be taken into account to facilitate this assessment. Yet official reports on its implementation reveal that practitioners are all too quick to assume incapacity in relation to decision-making. Decisions are not always carried out within the best interests framework, and the best interests idiom is too often used as a smokescreen for capricious and stifling paternalism.[42] Practitioners are accused of imposing restrictions on patients 'without any consideration of the person's capacity to consent or the need to maximise decision-making capacity'.[43]

Criticism is also commonly levelled at how vulnerable individuals' views about what is in their best interests in a care or mental health context are only considered *alongside* other factors, such as the view of their carer or health practitioner, thereby diluting the influence of the individual's own views, wishes and feelings. Such were the conclusions of the House of Lords' review in 2014 of the Mental Capacity Act 2005 in England and Wales. Its findings also pointed to a pervasive lack of commitment to the empowerment and enablement promised by the statute and a high degree of inconsistency and confusion as to when best interests should rebut autonomous decision-making.[44] This is made all the more possible by the absence of any reference to paramountcy or primacy within the Act and by the routine absence of any independent assessment.[45] Similar criticisms are advanced by John Coggon, who expresses fears that the best interests test, if not properly monitored and transparently applied with due consideration for the social and cultural values of the patient rather than those of the medical practitioners, cedes too much power to the medical profession.[46]

These concerns resonate with persistent concerns about the dominantly paternalistic approach to best interests in a children's rights context. Despite legal recognition and abundant empirical research that children's best interests can best be determined by hearing directly from the child,[47] the child's right to have a say in determining what is in his or her best interests is routinely ignored or trumped in favour of (often unchallenged) protectionist presumptions. The default position of excluding children from direct participation in public care and private family proceedings is a case in point, as is the ease with which medical practitioners can ignore the views even of the most competent child and administer or withhold treatment, purportedly in the pursuit of his or her best interests.[48]

Even more problematic is the way in which the best interests principle is routinely dispensed with when it comes to securing individuals' access to social and economic rights. Whilst applying best interests to decision-making around children's basic civil rights is challenging, the concept almost completely loses traction when determining how public resources should be allocated in the context of welfare provision, access to education, adequate housing and legal aid, the very scaffolding supporting individual welfare on a day-to-day basis.[49] Similarly, as already noted, in an adult decision-making context, the commitment to best interests is readily calibrated in the light of broader, often highly pragmatic questions about the interests and capacities of the family and carers or around the interests of society in avoiding extraordinary expense or allocating scarce public resources in an equitable fashion.[50] Such concerns point not only to the way in which the best interests principle is interpreted, but also (and perhaps more) to the processes used (or abused/ignored) to determine it and to the (lack of) resources invested in realising it and rendering decision-makers accountable for precisely how they have arrived at their assessment.

Notwithstanding these challenges, a final argument that cautions against extending the principle too readily to adult human rights contexts is that the principle already accommodates the interests of adults as it stands.

2.5 The best interests principle is not antithetic to the interests of adults

It is perhaps useful to be reminded that the best interest principle is not simply a framework for determining whether and how other aspects of children's rights should be fulfilled, or for resolving conflicts between the rights of children and the rights of others. Importantly, it operates to *vindicate* the rights of (adult) others. The text of Article 3(1) is very carefully worded to reflect the fact that the best interests of the child shall be 'a primary consideration', not 'the primary consideration' or 'a/the paramount consideration'. This wording was the product of extensive, heated debate following which the drafters settled on a formula that accommodated situations in which the competing interests of others, justice and society at large should be of equal if not greater importance than the interests of the child. As Stephen Parker notes:

> It is clear that the drafters' preference for the indefinite rather than the definite article in this phrase is intended to indicate that the child's best interests are not to be considered as the single overriding factor . . . The objective implicit in opting for the word 'a' is to ensure that there is sufficient flexibility, at least in certain extreme cases, to enable the interests of those other than the child to prevail . . . Nevertheless, the formulation adopted would seem to impose a burden of proof on those seeking to achieve such a child-centred result to demonstrate that, under the circumstances, other feasible and acceptable alternatives do not exist.[51]

This is certainly the approach of the European Court of Human Rights when interpreting Article 8 ECHR: the best interests of the child prevails only after a detailed consideration of *all* the parties' rights and interests.[52] This is evident, for instance, in the law relating to parental child abduction which discourages, save in the most exceptional of cases, individual assessments of the child's best interests in favour of a policy of immediate, automatic return to their left behind parent and country of habitual residence.[53]

This, it is presumed, is generally in the best interests of all children whilst also protecting the interests of the left behind parent. In more routine domestic proceedings, children's interests are generally balanced against those of adults in a sensitive and successful way. Children's well-being and progress are intimately linked with the well-being and progress of their parents or others with whom they are emotionally and socially connected; an unhappy parent generally implies an unhappy child and vice versa.[54] Relational theorists acknowledge as much in asserting that to polarise children and adults' interests is neither helpful nor realistic.[55] In theory, therefore, best interests should operate to reflect and reinforce healthy interdependency between children and adults rather than subvert it.

A good example of where this has been acknowledged and operated to adults' benefit is in the context of immigration and asylum. The UK Supreme Court, in the seminal case of *ZH Tanzania*, has stated unequivocally that the best interests of children should be placed at the centre of decisions around the deportation of their parents.[56] This represents the culmination of a line of jurisprudence that places significant emphasis on the rights of the child to know and be cared for by their parents in the country with which the former have the most intimate connection, notwithstanding the latter's questionable immigration status. Immigration appeals based on Article 8 of the ECHR, therefore, commonly support a finding that deportation of a family member is disproportionate and unlawful because of its impact on any children residing in the host state.[57] In other words, the best interests of the child are best promoted and exercised by enabling the members of a genuinely supportive family to live in close proximity to one another unless there is a clear justification for ordering otherwise.[58]

The public policy principles associated with upholding immigration control and thwarting applicants' attempts to profit from their unlawful entry and residence can be outweighed by the higher principle of upholding the best interests of the child.[59] Indeed, the narrative of the case law has gone even further in suggesting that foregrounding children's best interests in an immigration context is a public policy device in its own right. In that sense, protecting children's best interests extends beyond an individualised assessment; it is conductive to promoting the interests of the entire family unit and, indeed, the interests of the community at large.[60]

2.6 Conclusion

Exploring arguments to extend the best interests principle to other areas of human rights demands some careful reflection on the value and, indeed, persistent limitations of the concept as it is applied to children. The concept is designed to act as an antidote to processes, cultures of thinking and behaviour which are so often stacked against children. It promises much in terms of protecting and nurturing children's capabilities and positioning them on the best possible trajectory to achieve their potential. One can appreciate its appeal in informing decisions involving adults, particularly those with distinct vulnerabilities akin to those of children.

However, attempts to apply it to such contexts have been less successful than perhaps we might have hoped. There is something inherently problematic about extending a concept that remains fraught with imperfections in terms of its articulation and its application. There is still significant variance in the way that the best interests principle is applied across different contexts by different decision-makers and there is still a lack of understanding or clarity as to how and why children's best interests should be privileged over the interests and rights of other parties, such that in practice it is used to legitimise decisions that may actually be hostile to children's interests. As such, there is still much to be done to create better consistency and certainty in decision-making and to render best interests assessments less vulnerable to misguided or self-interested agendas. Indeed, commentators have explored the value of alternative normative frameworks such as dignity,[61] capability,[62] well-being[63] and the ethic of care[64] to protect and promote individuals' (including children's) essential needs and wishes.

The objectives pursued by children's human rights, and particularly the Convention on the Rights of the Child, of laying down universally applicable standards are necessarily confined to *children* as a discrete community of rights holders. The aim of the Convention was never to create a blueprint of human rights protection for people generally, and it potentially weakens the impact of the best interests principle – and indeed of the Convention more generally – should it be interpreted in such an expansive way. By allowing the principle to be appropriated too readily by decision-makers in an adult human rights context, we risk perpetuating and entrenching what are already undesirable trends or practices, reinforcing exclusively paternalistic approaches that polarise welfare assessments on the one hand and individual autonomy on the other, thereby divesting the principle of any potential it has to act as a persuasive mechanism for promoting children's rights.

Notes

1 Principles 2 and 7.
2 Article 5(b).
3 Articles 7(2), 23(2) and 23(2) and (4).
4 J Mnookin, 'Child custody adjudication: judicial functions in the face of indeterminacy' (1975) 39 *Law and Contemporary Problems* 226, 260, cited in M Freeman, 'Article 3: the best interests of the child' in A Alen, J Vande Lanotte, E Verhellen, F Ang, E Berghmans, M Verheyde and B Abramson (eds), *Commentary on the United Nations Convention on the Rights of the Child* (Brill Nijhoff 2007).
5 CRC Committee, 'General Comment No 14: The Right of the Child to have his or her Best Interests Taken as a Primary Consideration' (2013) UN Doc CRC/C/GC/14, para 6.
6 The best interests principle is explicitly referred to in arts 9(1) and (3), 18(1), 20(1), 21, 37(c) and 40(2)(b)(iii) of the CRC but, as one of the four General Principles, underpins the interpretation of all other rights listed in the Convention. For further discussion of the General Principles see Lundy and Byrne in this volume.
7 UNHCR, 'Field Handbook for the Implementation of UNHCR BID Guidelines' (2011) www.unhcr.org/protection/children/50f6d27f9/field-handbook-implementation-unhcr-bid-guidelines.html (last accessed 22 November 2016).
8 'Welfare' and 'best interests' are commonly used analogously, although the former term implies a rather narrower, paternalistic interpretation whereby decisions are made on behalf of rather than in collaboration with children.

9 See for instance s 1 of the Children Act 1989, which governs public and private family law proceedings involving children in England and Wales and which asserts that the welfare of the child is 'paramount' and contains a checklist of factors that need to be taken into account when determining what is in the welfare of the child.
10 See also S Choudhry, 'Best interests in the MCA 2005: what can healthcare law learn from family law?' (2008) 16 *Health Care Analysis* 240 for an analysis of what decision-makers operating within the scope of the Mental Capacity Act 2005 can learn from family law's practical use of the best interests standard.
11 S Woods, 'Best interests: puzzles and plausible solutions at the end of life' (2008) 16(3) *Health Care Analysis* 279; R Huxtable, 'Autonomy, best interests and the public interest: treatment, non-treatment and the values of medical law' (2014) 22(4) *Medical Law Review* 459.
12 G Cohen, 'Regulating reproduction: the problem with best interests' (2011) 96 *Minnesota Law Review* 423; and G Cohen, 'Beyond best interests' (2012) 96 *Minnesota Law Review* 1187.
13 S McGuinness, 'Best interests and pragmatism' (2008) 16 *Health Care Analysis* 208.
14 Zermatten refers to these functions as the 'control criterion' and the 'solution criterion' respectively. See J Zermatten, 'The best interests of the child principle: literal analysis and function' (2010) 18 *International Journal of Children's Rights* 483–99.
15 For a discussion of the importance of interpreting welfare within a more active, rights-based context see J Fortin, 'Accommodating children's rights in a post Human Rights Act era' (2006) 69(3) *Modern Law Review* 299, 312.
16 P Alston, 'The best interests principle: towards a reconciliation of culture and human rights' (1994) 8 *International Journal of Law and the Family* 1, 19.
17 See Freeman (n 4) 40.
18 For the biblical account of the 'Wisdom of King Solomon' see 1 Kings 3:16–28. For a children's rights critique of this philosophy see J Elster, 'Solomonic judgements: against the best interests of the child' in *Solomonic Judgements: Studies in the Limitations of Rationality* (Cambridge University Press 1989) pt III.
19 See Freeman (n 4).
20 J Eekelaar, 'The emergence of children's rights' (1986) 6 *Oxford Journal of Legal Studies* 161, 170.
21 Although for a critique of this investment model see C Piper, 'Investing in children's future: too risky?' (2010) 22(1) *Child and Family Law Quarterly* 1.
22 S Parker, 'The best interests of the child – principles and problems' (1994) 8 *International Journal of Law and the Family* 26.
23 See for instance C O'Mahony and others, who attempt to shine a spotlight on the oft neglected rights and interests of parents in public law proceedings: 'Representation and participation in child care proceedings: what about the voice of the parents?' (2016) 38(3) *Journal of Social Welfare and Family Law* 302. See also H Reece, 'The paramountcy principle: consensus or construct?' (1996) 49 *Current Legal Problems* 303; J Herring, 'The Human Rights Act and the welfare principle in family law: conflicting or complementary?' (1999) 11(3) *Child and Family Law Quarterly* 223.
24 See *P (Contact: Supervision)* [1996] 2 FLR 314 (applying *Re O (A Minor) (Contact: Imposition of Conditions)* [1995] 2 FLR 124), which affirms that the welfare of the child is of overriding importance; the interests of the parents are only relevant in as much as they have an impact on the child's welfare.
25 See further the evidence of M Coy and others, 'Picking up the pieces: domestic violence and child contact' (Rights of Women and Child and Woman Abuse Studies Unit 2012).

26 Human Fertilisation and Embryology Act 2008 s 13(5).

27 For an example of how this challenging balancing act was achieved with the child's best interests in mind see *Leeds Teaching Hospital NHS Trust v A* [2003] EWHC 259.

28 Surrogacy Arrangements Act 1985. See further B Hale, 'New families and the welfare of children' (2014) 36(1) *Journal of Social Welfare and Family Law* 26; and C Fenton-Glynn, 'Outsourcing ethical dilemmas: regulating international surrogacy arrangements' (2016) 24(1) *Medical Law Review* 59.

29 E Blyth, 'To be or not to be? A critical appraisal of the welfare of children conceived through new reproductive technologies' (2008) 16 *International Journal of Children's Rights* 505.

30 In the UK see *R (Mahmood) v Home Secretary* [2001] 1 WLR 840; *R (Razgar) v Secretary of State for the Home Department* [2004] UKHL 27 [2004] AC 368; and more recently *R (Nagre) v SSHD* [2013] EWHC 720 (Admin).

31 For a comprehensive analysis of how the best interests principle has been interpreted in more than 30 ECtHR cases see C Smyth, 'The best interests of the child in the expulsion and first-entry jurisprudence of the European Court of Human Rights: how principled is the Court's use of the principle?' (2015) 17 *European Journal of Migration and the Law* 70, 79.

32 T Brown, H Johnson, A Adams, K Cronin, R Kohli and B Sandhu, 'Put yourself in our shoes: considering children's best interests in the asylum system' (Law Centres Network 215) www.lawcentres.org.uk/asset/download/464.pdf (last accessed 22 November 2016).

33 K Hollingsworth, 'Bright lines and best interests: children, age and rights in police detention: *R (HC) v Secretary of State for the Home Department*' (2014) 26(1) *Child and Family Law Quarterly* 78.

34 L Kopelman, 'The best interests standard as threshold, ideal and standard of reasonableness' (1979) 22 *Journal of Medicine and Philosophy* 271; C Piper, 'Assumptions about children's best interests' (2000) 22(3) *Journal of Social Welfare and Family Law* 261.

35 J Eekelaar, 'Beyond the welfare principle' (2002) 14(3) *Child and Family Law Quarterly* 237.

36 See Mnookin (n 4) 226.

37 J Eekelaar, 'The interests of the child and the child's wishes: the role of dynamic self-determinism' (1994) 8 *International Journal of Law, Policy and the Family* 42, 43; S Holm and A Edgar, 'Best interest – a philosophical critique' (2008) 16(3) *Health Care Analysis* 197.

38 See Parker (n 22) 36.

39 I Wise and M Spurrier, 'A gilded cage is still a cage' (May 2014) *New Law Journal* 7.

40 T Spencer-Lane, 'Lost in translation' (June 2013) *New Law Journal* 8.

41 UNCHR, 'Guidelines on determining the best interest of the child' (2008) s 1(5) *www.unhcr.org/4566b16b2.pdf (last accessed 22 November 2016).*

42 See Spencer-Lane (n 40).

43 See Care Quality Commission, 'Monitoring the use of the MCA deprivation of liberty safeguards in 2011–12' (2003), cited in Spencer-Lane (n 40).

44 Select Committee on the Mental Capacity Act 2005, Mental Capacity Act 2005: Post-Legislative Scrutiny, HL Paper 139 (March 2014). For further discussion see E Cave, 'Determining capacity to make medical treatment decisions problems implementing the Mental Capacity Act 2005' (2015) 36(1) *Statute Law Review* 86–106. Similarly, the UK Supreme Court has responded to an established trend in holding people with disabilities in care placements that are tantamount to forced imprisonment, concluding that even arrangements purported to be made in disabled people's best interests may still violate their fundamental rights

and require stringent justification. See further *Cheshire West* [2014] UKSC 19, discussed in Wise and Spurrier (n 39).

45 See Choudhry (n 10).

46 J Coggon, 'Mental capacity law, autonomy, and best interests: an argument for conceptual and practical clarity in the Court of Protection' (2016) *Medical Law Review*, forthcoming.

47 See for example D Archard, M Skivenes, 'Balancing a child's best interests and a child's views' (2009) 17 *International Journal of Children's Rights* 1; Kay Tisdall, Fiona Morrison, 'Children's participation in court proceedings when parents divorce or separate: legal constructions and lived experiences' (2012) 14 *Law and Childhood Studies: Current Legal Issues* 156.

48 M Freeman, 'Rethinking *Gillick*' (2005) 13 *International Journal of Children's Rights* 201; E Cave, 'Goodbye *Gillick*? Identifying and resolving problems with the concept of child competence' (2014) 34(1) *Legal Studies* 103.

49 B Kelly, 'Best interests, mental capacity legislation and the UN Convention on the Rights of Persons with Disabilities' (2015) 21(3) *British Journal of Psychiatric Advances* 188.

50 See the ECtHR decision in *McDonald v UK*, Application no 4241/12, judgment of 20 May 2014, for an illustration of how states can defer to their margin of appreciation and public policy arguments to justify the constriction of social care for the disabled, even if it is acknowledged as contrary to their well-being. N L Cantor, 'The bane of surrogate decision-making: defining the best interests of never-competent persons' (2005) 26 *Journal of Legal Medicine* 155, 156.

51 See Parker (n 22) 12–13.

52 See Choudhry (n 10).

53 Convention of 25 October 1980 on the Civil Aspects of International Child Abduction; Council Regulation (EC) No 2201/2003 of 27 November 2003 concerning jurisdiction and the recognition and enforcement of judgments in matrimonial matters and the matters of parental responsibility, OJ L 338/6, art 1.

54 For a very recent empirical insight into the complexities of disentangling children's interests from those of their parents see R George, A Gallwey and K Bader, 'How do parents experience relocation disputes in the family courts?' (2016) 38(4) *Journal of Social Welfare and Family Law* 1.

55 G Mannion, 'Going spatial, going relational: why "listening to children" and children's participation needs reframing' (2007) 28(3) *Discourse: Studies in the Cultural Politics of Education* 405.

56 *ZH v (Tanzania) (FC) v Secretary of State for the Home Department* [2011] UKSC 4. See also s 55 of the Borders, Citizenship and Immigration Act 2009, which imposes a statutory duty on the Secretary of State and those acting on his behalf to ensure that all decisions relating to entry and residence of immigrants safeguard and promote the welfare of any children concerned.

57 See for example *Nunez v Norway*, Application no 55597/09, ECtHR judgment of 28 June 2011.

58 See further H Wray, 'Greater than the sum of their parts: UK Supreme Court decisions on family migration' in M Sunkin (ed), *Public Law* (Sweet & Maxwell 2016) 839.

59 H Stalford, S Woodhouse, 'Rights realised or rights defeated? Responses to family migration in the UK' in J Eekelaar *Family Law in Britain and America in the New Century: Essays in Honor of Sanford N. Katz* (Brill Nijhoff 2016) 265. Subsequent cases reinforce this point. See *H (H) v Deputy Prosecutor of the Italian Republic, Genoa* [2012] UKSC 25 para 98 (Lord Kerr); *JO and Others (section 55 duty) Nigeria* [2014] UKUT 517 (IAC); *MK (section 55 – Tribunal options)* [2015] UKUT 223 (IAC); and *EV (Philippines) & Ors v Secretary of State for the Home Department* [2014] EWCA Civ 874.

60 See Lord Kerr in *H (H)* (n 59): 'although the child has a right to her family life and to all that goes with it, there is also a strong public interest in ensuring that children are properly brought up' (para 33).
61 M Freeman, 'Why it remains important to take children's rights seriously' (2007) 15 *International Journal of Children's Rights* 5.
62 R Dixon, M Nussbaum, 'Children's rights and a capabilities approach: the question of special priority' (2012) 97 *Cornell Law Review* 550.
63 K Tisdall, 'Children's rights and children's wellbeing: equivalent policy concepts?' (2015) 44(4) *Journal of Social Policy* 807.
64 J Herring, *Caring and the Law* (Hart Publishing 2013).

3 The four general principles of the United Nations Convention on the Rights of the Child: the potential value of the approach in other areas of human rights law

Laura Lundy and Bronagh Byrne

3.1 Introduction

One of the best known and most-cited features of the UN Convention on the Rights of the Child (CRC) is a concept that is, in fact, entirely extra-Conventional. This is the proposition that four of its articles are not just rights in themselves but enjoy a special cross-cutting status in the implementation of the whole CRC. These four articles (Articles 3, 4, 6 and 12) were identified by the UN Committee on the Rights of the Child at a very early stage in the Convention's life as 'general principles'. While the concept of 'general principles' has a long history in human rights discourse,[1] the notion that a particular Treaty could have its own bespoke principles was at the time they were adopted entirely novel. How these four principles fared in the wake of their identification by the Committee is thus worthy of analysis, of interest not just to those concerned with the implementation of the rights of the child but also to those engaged in other spheres of human rights.

This chapter begins with a review of the four principles, how and why they were identified and their intended use and value. This is followed by a discussion of the ways in which they have since been adopted and embraced by states parties and others working in the area of child rights. The objective is to assess their contribution to child rights discourse and practice, drawing some lessons on the value of this approach for other areas of international human rights law. With a view to this, we reflect on the potential and actual value of the CRC's approach in the context of other UN treaties: first, the Convention on the Elimination of Discrimination against Women (CEDAW) and the Convention on the Elimination of Racial Discrimination (CERD), both adopted prior to the CRC and operating since then without general principles;[2] and then the Convention on the Rights of Persons with Disabilities (CRPD), emerging after the CRC and including an extensive list of general principles in its core text. The chapter concludes with some reflections on the considerations that might be taken into account by those deciding whether the general principles approach, pioneered by the Committee on the Rights of the Child and now with 25 years of experience under its belt, might be useful for the furtherance of other human rights.

3.2 The general principles

In 1991, the newly appointed UN Committee on the Rights of the Child met and agreed its first set of working guidelines for states parties on the implementation of the CRC.[3] Tucked into these, at paragraphs 13 and 14, were the following statements (CRC/C/5) under the title 'General Principles':

> 13. Relevant information, including the principal legislative, judicial, administrative or other measures in force or foreseen, factors and difficulties encountered and progress achieved in implementing the provision of the Convention, and implementation priorities and specific goals for the future should be provided in respect of:
>
> (a) Non-discrimination (art 2)
> (b) Best interests of the child (art 3)
> (c) The right to life, survival and development (art 6)
> (d) Respect for the views of the child (art 12).
>
> 14. In addition, States parties are encouraged to provide relevant information on the application of the principles in the implementation of articles listed elsewhere in these guidelines.

There is no published minute of the discussion that led to the decision to collate and elevate these four individual articles. However, Abramson has tracked the progress of the general principles in the Committee's records, demonstrating that Articles 2, 3 and 12 were first collated under the heading of 'The Child and the Law'; Article 6 was added and the heading became 'Basic Principles'; and finally the heading was changed to 'General Principles'.[4] Research with the key actors involved (the first 10 member Committee) would undoubtedly shed some light on the accompanying discussion that took place and the reasons they were chosen. What is known is that, with the unprecedented uptake of the treaty, the first Committee had an urgent need to write and publish guidance for the 80-odd states parties who were to submit their initial reports for review imminently.[5] Like previous treaty bodies, the Committee was tasked with giving direction about the information needed for the reporting process. It is unlikely that there was a great deal of time to debate or reflect on the conceptual basis for general principles or indeed to discuss in any depth which of the agreed articles should feature in them. Like many processes of this nature, the publication of the first committee is most likely to have been the product of a relatively tight for time exercise in negotiation and compromise between its inaugural members.

To list all of the requirements for reporting under each of the 42 substantive articles would have been cumbersome and repetitive, so some sort of grouping of the articles in themes was a pragmatic necessity, although it has also been suggested that the key motivation underpinning the clustering was a desire to demonstrate the inter-relationship of the many rights and the fact they need to be considered holistically.[6] Many of the themes that emerged are relatively self-evident (e.g. basic health and welfare, civil rights and freedoms).[7]

The decision to pool Articles 2, 3, 6 and 12 is less apparent, particularly as each of them had the potential to be incorporated elsewhere and some of them had a natural fit under the other chosen themes. Article 12, for example, has an obvious alliance with the other participation rights, Articles 13, 14, 16 and 17. We can speculate that someone may have suggested that one or more of the articles (perhaps Articles 3 or 12?) had a particular cross-cutting dimension or role in the implementation of the Convention as a whole and other members will have responded by suggesting other articles which they perceived to have similar qualities. What is not clear is what the qualities were that justified the decision that they should fall under the same umbrella and merit the use of the term 'general principles'.

In the absence of an official explanation of the rationale underlying the decision to have a set of general principles, the intent has to be inferred from the text of the 1991 guidelines. The first thing that is apparent is that they were intended to enjoy an additional status over and above the other substantive rights. The title 'general principles' is, of course, open to interpretation but, on the face of it, suggests first that the articles have a 'general' application, applying across all aspects of the Convention and thus children's rights and lives. Paragraph 14 reinforces the notion that these provisions are not just rights in themselves but should be considered across the implementation of other CRC articles since states are asked to 'provide relevant information on the application of the principles in the implementation of articles listed elsewhere in these guidelines'.[8] This expectation of usage in relation to other substantive provisions attributes the four articles a cross-cutting role. Secondly, the provisions are attributed the status of 'principles' as well as substantive rights. While the term 'principles', open to interpretation, is left undefined, it has been suggested that they are 'underlying and fundamental values that are relevant to the realization of all children's rights'.[9]

It has also been suggested that describing them as principles is inaccurate as they are rules.[10] While attributing them an additional role as principles should not detract from their standing and remit in law as individual articles of the Convention, there is an argument to be made that the Committee in choosing to do this was overstepping its mark, effectively adding something to the content of the CRC that was not intended (nor possibly foreseen by the drafters or those who adopted it). If the drafters had intended for there to be a set of principles, they might well have positioned these four alongside each other in the text; as it stands, Article 12 sits apart from the other three in what could be seen as its natural positioning alongside the other participation/autonomy rights. Articles 4 and 5, which also have a 'general' quality, are excluded from the list, even though they break the consecutive flow from Articles 3 to 6. On the other hand, the Committee, like the other UN Treaty bodies, has the power to give authoritative guidance on the interpretation of the Convention[11] and what they did with these four articles was not questioned then or since by the subsequent committee members[12] nor the states parties who ratified the original text and report on their progress in implementing it according to the guidance published.[13]

Also open to question is why the Committee chose the four that they did. To consider this fully, it is necessary to examine the actual text of the articles, rather than the phrases the Committee employs to summarise them in paragraph 13 of the guidelines above. The core elements of each of the selected four articles are set out in full below:

> Article 2.1: States Parties shall respect and ensure the rights set forth in the present Convention to each child within their jurisdiction without discrimination of any kind, irrespective of the child's or his or her parent's or legal guardian's race, colour, sex, language, religion, political or other opinion, national, ethnic or social origin, property, disability, birth or other status.
>
> Article 3.1: In all actions concerning children, whether undertaken by public or private social welfare institutions, courts of law, administrative authorities or legislative bodies, the best interests of the child shall be a primary consideration.
>
> Article 6.1: States Parties recognize that every child has the inherent right to life. . . . States Parties shall ensure to the maximum extent possible the survival and development of the child.
>
> Article 12.1: States Parties shall assure to the child who is capable of forming his or her own views the right to express those views freely in all matters affecting the child, the views of the child being given due weight in accordance with the age and maturity of the child.

The choices are not justified by the Committee in the 1991 guidelines. However, since the intention was to identify articles of the Convention that had a more general quality (and one that should be reported upon in the information provided on the implementation of other articles), the choices need to be justified from the Committee's original rationale. This means that the principles should be capable of being applied in the implementation of the other articles of the CRC. Article 2 clearly has that quality, since it is not a stand-alone right and refers explicitly to the need to ensure 'the rights set forth in the present Convention'.[14] Articles 3 and 12 have similar statements, which convey a more general application. Article 3 refers to 'in all actions concerning children' and Article 12 defines the scope of the provision to be 'all matters affecting the child'. While the terms 'actions' and 'matters' are not synonymous with rights of children, they are arguably wider than that, encompassing all of the issues addressed in the Convention, and thus have a potential application in relation to the other articles of the CRC.

It is less obvious perhaps how Article 6 has 'general' application. Not all challenges to children's rights are matters of life and survival. Development could arguably be impacted by a denial of many of the rights that are included in the CRC but it is difficult to see how states could report on it specifically across the Convention, as opposed to reporting on progress in relation to the many articles that deal with children's development directly (e.g. Article 24 on health and Article 29 on the aims of education) and indirectly (e.g. Article 13 on freedom of expression or Article 39 on recovery and reintegration).[15] It might be speculated that Article 6 may have made it to the shortlist because it addresses issues which are profoundly fundamental rather than of general application. That said, the Committee has reasserted its significance as a general principle, suggesting that it should be understood as a 'holistic concept, embracing the child's physical, mental, spiritual, moral, psychological and social development'.[16] Even then, in practice the Committee has a tendency to define the violation of other children's human rights as a violation of the right to development or define development as the protection of other human rights.[17]

What is also unclear is why some of the other CRC provisions were left out of the list. Article 4, for example, has general application, although its focus is squarely on implementation and the article has no substantive content. More perplexing is the omission of Article 5, which provides as follows:

> States Parties shall respect the responsibilities, rights and duties of parents or, where applicable, the members of the extended family or community as provided for by local custom, legal guardians or other persons legally responsible for the child, to provide, in a manner consistent with the evolving capacities of the child, appropriate direction and guidance in the exercise by the child of the rights recognized in the present Convention.

The provision is undoubtedly of general application across all other rights. It specifically refers to 'the exercise by the child of the rights recognized in the present Convention'; one of its core terms, 'the evolving capacities of the child', is often used and cited in discussions of the CRC, albeit that sometimes that involves an erroneous assumption that it is integral to Article 12; and it addresses a fundamental tenet of the Convention and defence to many of its critics, by positioning parents and guardians at the centre of the implementation of children's rights. For reasons unknown, it did not make it into the group of general principles along with the other four.

Treaty bodies are known to interpret conventions in ways that do not always lend themselves to standards of rationality and predictability.[18] Whatever the logic, or lack of it, underpinning the selections and omissions, having settled on the chosen four in 1991, the Committee has been remarkably consistent in referring to and drawing on these. In 2003, the Committee published guidance on the implementation of the Convention, which states that: 'The development of a children's rights perspective throughout Government, parliament and the judiciary is required for effective implementation of the whole Convention and, in particular, in the light of the following articles in the Convention identified by the Committee as general principles . . .'.[19] Moreover, each of the general comments which appeared in the wake of the adoption of the general principles refers to them, often drawing out their implications for particular issues or affected groups. A typical example of this is the General Comment on rights of children in the early years, which expands on what is needed for the full implementation of the rights for younger children, suggesting for example in relation to Article 2 that 'young children are especially at risk of discrimination because they are relatively powerless and depend on others for the realisation of their rights'.[20]

The guidelines in which the general principles debuted were revised and replaced in 2010 and 2015 in the wake of the Committee's experience of monitoring and reporting. The current guidelines once again highlight the same four articles under the same heading of 'general principles'.[21] There are, however, some little noted yet significant changes in the descriptions of what is expected of states parties in relation to the chosen four. Article 2 is discussed individually and further detail given about the need for information for certain categories of discrimination (gender, disability, children belonging to minorities and indigenous children). Articles 3 and 12 are grouped together, with the guidelines saying that 'states parties should provide updated information on legislative, judicial, administrative or other measures in force, particularly on how the principles of the best interests of the child (art. 3) and respect for the views of the child (art. 12) are addressed and implemented in legislative, administrative and judicial decisions'.[22]

Article 6 is also discussed in a dedicated section, but this time the Committee requests specific information on capital punishment for offences committed under 18, deaths and extrajudicial killings of children and measures to prevent suicide and eradicate infanticide.[23] It is telling that the focus is on Article 6 as a substantive right and not a cross-cutting principle, a revised position that supports the argument above that it is different in character to the other three.

The guidelines do not repeat the statement in their predecessor that 'states are encouraged to provide relevant information on the application of the principles in the implementation of articles listed elsewhere in these guidelines'. That is a potentially significant omission, given the import attributed to the previous statement in the 1991 guidelines. However, the intention can be inferred in two subsequent general comments dedicated to Articles 12 and 3 respectively. In its General Comment 12 on the Right to be Heard, the Committee highlights the fact that this article establishes not 'only a right in itself, but should also be considered in the interpretation and implementation of all other rights'.[24] This is a clear reassertion of the original vision for the general principles at their inception. In contrast, the General Comment on Article 3 does not repeat this statement. Instead the comment states that Article 3 fulfils three roles: an intrinsic obligation for states; a fundamental, interpretative legal principle; and a rule of procedure.[25] This distinguishes this provision from the other three and arguably expands its cross-cutting role in implementation.

In summary, the Committee's intention for the four general principles, while not crystal clear at the outset, has become muddier over time. There is a lack of consistency in the 'general' application that they have both individually and collectively. Had the drafters envisaged the need for general principles during the decade of discussion on the text of the CRC, they might have given it some thought and this would then have been reflected in both the choices and text. That said, this discussion is now by-the-by. The fact remains that the first Committee envisaged a role for them in the effective implementation of the CRC and its successors have not deviated greatly from this original choice since. In order to assess whether they can play a role in other areas of human rights, the important question then is not why they exist but how they are operating and what, if anything, they have achieved.

3.3 The contribution of the general principles to the advancement of children's rights

The four principles individually and collectively have received an enormous amount of attention since they appeared in the 1991 guidelines. The following sections trace their development and reception from the perspective of some key stakeholders: the states parties and other duty bearers who are charged with implementation; the NGOs and civil society who advocate for change; and the academics whose scholarship critiques and reflects on them and their impact in the furtherance of children's rights. Missing from this list, regrettably, are children who are the rights holders under the Convention. Children's views were not taken into account during the drafting of the CRC and the Committee did not seek or consider their views when they drafted and reviewed the reporting guidelines.[26] There is an interesting piece of research yet to be conducted that would ask children what cross-cutting principles should be considered in relation to the implementation of their rights.

3.3.1 States parties and other duty bearers

Engagement with the general principles by governments has been widespread, albeit largely due to the periodic reporting requirements; states are asked to report under the headings in the guidelines and have, for the most part, complied. States party reports are problematic for a number of reasons. Reports are often tardy[27] and their content can be partial and superficial.[28] Some of these limitations may be exacerbated when it comes to the general principles given the sheer scope of their application. A review of the content of states party reports specific to the general principles across a representative sample of countries would be necessary to draw general conclusions. However, taking the example of a country that has reported recently in the interim, it is obvious that reporting about each of the four principles across all of the other substantive rights was not considered necessary nor possible. For example, the UK State Party report, submitted in 2014, refers to a very narrow range of issues across the four articles; the entire content of the information sent to the Committee by the UK in relation to Article 3 is as follows:

> 2. The principle of the best interests of the child is enshrined in legislation, policy and practice across the UK. In England Section 1 of the Children Act 1989 (CA 1989) provides that, in any proceedings relating to the upbringing of a child or the administration of the child's property or application of any income arising from it, the child's welfare is the paramount consideration. This applies to both private family law proceedings under Part 2 of the CA

1989 and public law proceedings – emergency protection orders, care orders and supervision orders.

3. New measures introduced through the Children and Families Act 2014 to strengthen arrangements for adoption, promote family life and reform support for children with special educational needs, are all predicated on the assumption that decisions affecting children should be in their best interests and take account of their views, wishes and feelings.[29]

Leaving aside the inexplicable lack of any reference to developments in the three other jurisdictions of the UK (Wales, Northern Ireland and Scotland), the reporting is limited to legislation in very specific areas of children's lives with no mention of other areas of the CRC where the best interests principle may also be important (e.g. immigration and juvenile justice). Space is, of course, limited (just over 20,000 words in total) and the practical realities require a huge degree of selectivity in terms of what is reported under the heading of the general principles. However, it is possible that the dedicated section for reporting affords states an excuse to ignore some of these matters when reporting under substantive content. In practice, this narrows rather than expands the application of the general principles across the Convention.

The general principles have had a discernible impact on domestic law. Articles 3 and 12 are the provisions of the CRC that are most likely to be incorporated into domestic legislation.[30] They have also been included in post-CRC constitutions, with Ireland as one of the most recent examples.[31] The reasons why these provisions are chosen are undoubtedly complex but linked to the Committee's insistence that they are translated into law. However, while their incorporation in domestic law is a goal of implementation, there is a danger that the ready embrace of Articles 3 and 12 has been at the expense of the other substantive articles. On the other hand, it is equally open to question whether there would have been anything adopted and included in domestic law at all had these two articles not been rendered accessible as part of the four general principles. In effect, Articles 3 and 12 offer a 'quick fix' for incorporation which, while it falls short of full incorporation, nonetheless represents a potent first step on that journey.

Professionals working with children such as social workers, health professionals and teachers have also embraced the general principles to some degree in their professional training and/or competency frameworks. There are recurring examples of the four being used to reflect and critique on existing professional expertise such as paediatric ethics, social work, education and child care.[32] While most of the literature on children's rights and professional practice is critical of the extent to which the CRC is known and applied,[33] where there is evidence of understanding and engagement, it is often clustered around or built upon the general principles, individually and/or as a set. A readily accessible four-point package is more easily understood and disseminated than a lengthy treaty with over 40 detailed articles, some of which may not seem to have direct relevance to those who are at the front line of delivering children's rights. A downside is that this 'capsule' of articles may undermine the obligation to make all of the provisions of the CRC widely known to adults and children alike under Article 42.

3.3.2 Non-governmental organisations and civil society

Non-governmental organisations (NGOs) and other civil society organisations embrace the four general principles with enthusiasm. Key publications by all of the major children's rights NGOs often open by setting them out in full, with a variety of explanations as to their value for programming and advocacy.[34] The influential Children's Rights Information Network (CRIN), for example, describes their value as follows: 'Addressing these four rights can help explain the reasons behind rights violations and serve as a guide to preventing them'.[35] Part of their appeal to NGOs may also lie in their simplicity, both in terms of building staff capacity to use the CRC but also in terms of their interactions and advocacy with duty-bearers. More targeted approaches are those which link the principles squarely to substantive child rights issues such as health, juvenile justice and the abolition of physical punishment. Here too, issues of non-discrimination, best interests and participation are most commonly drawn upon rather than Article 6, other than instances when Article 6 is itself at risk and the child's survival or development is under threat.

While the four principles provide a neat package on which to design programmes and build advocacy, it would be simplistic to suggest that this is their only attraction to civil society. What is of most value is their capacity to capture the essence of a rights-respecting approach to children, one that recognises their equality and capacity for autonomy as well as their need to have decisions taken for them in their best interests and to secure their development. Save the Children, for example, in its much used guide to child rights programming, states: 'If the duty-bearer–rights-holder relationship is to work effectively for children, it requires a 'rights climate' in which the four general principles of the UNCRC are fulfilled'.[36] This notion of a 'rights climate' generated through a focus on these four principles is interesting. Individually and collectively, the four Articles are perceived to provide a powerful insight into some of the fundamental underpinning concepts of human rights for children which, if understood fully and operationalised effectively, would go some way to ensuring that children's rights were respected in every sphere of their lives. While they are not all of the child rights agenda, they seem to provide an accessible beginning and a substantial tool on which to base advocacy.

3.3.3 Academic scholarship

The general principles have provided rich fodder for academic scholarship. The vast majority of this, however, focuses on them individually rather than as a collective. As discussed earlier, Article 3 in particular has received a good deal of attention, some of it critical of its lack of clarity[37] but others defending its value.[38] Article 12 has probably received the most attention, its visibility enhanced by the significant academic attention given in childhood studies to child participation.[39] Article 2 is rarely discussed on its own[40] but features strongly in analysis of other substantive rights such as the right to education.[41] Article 6 received relatively little attention by itself until recently.[42] The consideration that they have enjoyed as individual articles may be linked in some way to their elevation into general principles. It could also explain why Article 5 has received comparatively little analysis.

While many books and journal articles on children's rights will acknowledge their existence or use the principles as a frame for analysis, there has been sparse attention given to them as a concept or a set. An important exception is John Tobin, who acknowledges that the four are often described as foundational to a child rights based approach with little scrutiny as to the basis of that claim.[43] He identifies a different set of 'specific express principles' for children's rights (in contrast to 'general express principles' such as accountability and 'implied principles' such as dignity) to include: the best interests principle, the right to survival and development, the principle of due deference and the principle of evolving capacities. More often the principles appear in academic scholarship as a kind of set piece at the beginning of any general explanation of the CRC. In this way, academics have to a large degree bought into the approach of the Committee on the Rights of the Child and, along with NGO advocates, have employed the concept of general principles willingly as a device for analysis and critique.

In summary, it is clear that the decision by the Committee on the Rights of the Child in 1991 to collate four of the articles of the CRC under the banner of 'general principles' has had far-reaching and ongoing consequences for children's rights implementation, advocacy and scholarship. The principles have a significant degree of visibility and buy-in from stakeholders. This appears to have increased understanding and acceptance of the CRC generally, albeit that this focus may have diverted attention from some of the other substantive provisions in the CRC. One lesson from the experience to date is that, if general principles are to be adopted, it is worthwhile taking the time to ensure that they are chosen carefully.

3.4 What can the 'general principles' approach contribute to other areas of human rights law?

The notion of 'general principles' is not new to human rights. Underpinning values such as equality, dignity and respect are also referred to frequently as human rights 'principles'.[44] What is distinct about the approach adopted for the CRC is that it singles out specific provisions of the text and affords them the status of being cross-cutting values to guide implementation. This is something that had not occurred with any of the UN treaties adopted prior to the CRC, although it became an explicit and in-text feature of the major treaty adopted subsequently – the UN Convention on the Rights of Persons with Disabilities. The implications for these other areas of human rights are explored below, acknowledging this distinction.

3.4.1 Human rights treaties adopted prior to the CRC

The UN treaties that preceded the CRC did so by quite some years. While they often (CRC included) tend to follow a common structure (definitions, civil and political rights, social and economic rights, monitoring and enforcement), the CRC reads differently not least because it is significantly longer and its provisions more detailed than its antecedents. The length and detail may be attributable to the differences in the drafting process, in particular the extensive involvement of NGOs and other parts of civil society.[45] The text which followed undoubtedly owes much to their insights on the challenges that are faced by children in terms of the realisation of their rights and can, at least in part, explain the presence of innovative provisions such as Article 3 and Article 12.

At the outset, it is important to acknowledge that all of the main UN treaties address non-discrimination. In fact, it is the focus of CEDAW and CERD. Moreover, non-discrimination has been officially identified as a cross-cutting principle for almost all of the treaties which precede the CRC. The guidelines for the Common Core document reference discrimination as a principle, stating that the report should '. . . contain general information on whether the principle of non-discrimination is included as a general binding principle in a basic law, the constitution, a bill of rights or in any other domestic legislation and the definition of and legal grounds for prohibiting discrimination (if not already provided in para. 42(a)). Information should also be provided on whether the legal system allows for or mandates special measures to guarantee full and equal enjoyment of human rights'.[46]

Non-discrimination aside, it is worth considering whether there is anything in the text of the other treaties that lends itself to adoption as a cross-cutting principle, merits consideration in the application of other rights and addresses some core barrier to the realisation of rights common to the protected group. Taking CEDAW as an example, the article that could, possibly, provide the basis for a general principle is Article 5, which provides:

> States Parties shall take all appropriate measures:
>
> (a) To modify the social and cultural patterns of conduct of men and women, with a view to achieving the elimination of prejudices and customary and all other practices which are based on the idea of the inferiority or the superiority of either of the sexes or on stereotyped roles for men and women;
>
> (b) To ensure that family education includes a proper understanding of maternity as a social function and the recognition of the common responsibility of men and women in the upbringing and development of their children, it being understood that the interest of the children is the primordial consideration in all cases.

The first paragraph (Article 5(a)) could clearly have cross-cutting status, addressing as it does many of the underlying challenges to the realisation of women's rights in the various contexts addressed in the rest of CEDAW (education, health). So too could the emphasis on maternity and equality in child upbringing in Article 5(b), albeit that the ambit of this provision is narrowed *ab initio* with its stated focus on 'family education'.

The CERD does not have a set of general principles either. Like the CEDAW, the whole Convention is about eliminating discrimination, which makes that 'principle' unnecessary. There are, however, several articles that might lend themselves to general principles.[47] For example, Article 2(e) tackles a cross-cutting issue of racial integration as follows:

> Each state party undertakes to encourage, where appropriate, integrationist multiracial organisations and movements and other means of eliminating barriers between races, and to discourage anything which tends to strengthen racial discrimination.

Article 4 might also be a contender:

> States Parties condemn all propaganda and all organizations which are based on ideas or theories of superiority of one race or group of persons of one colour or ethnic origin, or which attempt to justify or promote racial hatred and discrimination in any form, and undertake to adopt immediate and positive measures designed to eradicate all incitement to, or acts of, such discrimination and, to this end, with due regard to the principles embodied in the Universal Declaration of Human Rights and the rights expressly set forth in article 5 of this Convention, inter alia:
>
>> Segregation and policies promoting the inferiority of a racial group will inevitably strike at the ability to deliver equality and it is thus possible to imagine a justification for these being used as guiding principles in the interpretation of other rights. The Committee on the Elimination of Racial Discrimination has not identified these as 'general principles' but it has underlined their significance through dedicated recommendations.[48]

Thus, while it is possible to identify aspects of these two UN treaties pre-existing the CRC that could lend themselves to use as general principles, it is also worth asking what if anything has been lost in their absence. There is an argument that the lack of a set of general principles has made little difference to implementation here. Not only is non-discrimination recognised as a general principle irrespective, other fundamental challenges have been articulated by the treaty bodies in their publications and monitoring processes, all of which consistently urge states parties to tackle the barriers to the realisation of rights for women and racial minorities. On the other hand, what is not known is whether upfront early identification of some cross-cutting articles may have increased their visibility, facilitated a cultural shift in understanding the distinctive challenges faced by the groups they are designed to protect and thus contributed in some way to furthering the realisation of rights.

3.4.2 Treaties adopted after the CRC: the CRPD

The CRPD was adopted in December 2006. Unlike the CRC, the general principles of the CRPD are explicitly set out in the treaty text, a development that was undoubtedly influenced by the high profile of the CRC's general principles. This in itself could be viewed as innovative and progressive, moving beyond the CRC by including the general principles in the text from the outset. Much has been made of the transformative potential of the CRPD[49] with Kanter[50] arguing that the process of drafting the Convention was the result 'of unprecedented collective and collaborative action', and the Ad Hoc committee meetings the most inclusive in the UN's history. It is within this context that the explicit identification of the general principles at this stage can be understood. Analysis of the *travaux préparatoires* indicates that substantive discussion of what the general principles might look like took place during the Working Group sessions in 2004. At this stage, the principles of autonomy, participation, equality and respect for difference were commonly agreed as having particular significance and general applicability for disabled people's lives. These were extended in the final draft to encompass eight general principles under Article 3 in total, as follows:

> The principles of the present Convention shall be:
>
> (a) Respect for inherent dignity, individual autonomy including the freedom to make one's own choices, and independence of persons;
> (b) Non-discrimination;
> (c) Full and effective participation and inclusion in society;
> (d) Respect for difference and acceptance of persons with disabilities as part of human diversity and humanity;
> (e) Equality of opportunity;
> (f) Accessibility;
> (g) Equality between men and women;
> (h) Respect for the evolving capacities of children with disabilities and respect for the right of children with disabilities to preserve their identities.

Each of these principles can be viewed as having general applicability across disabled people's lives in varying ways. There is concern, for example, that disabled people are often excluded from making decisions about their lives while accessibility barriers whether physical, communicational or attitudinal, can impact on the effective realisation of a range of rights. Notwithstanding, the sheer number of principles contained in Article 3 runs the risk of becoming cumbersome when it comes to their implementation and monitoring; so all-encompassing that they become dilutionary, favouring breadth rather than depth. In this vein, the CRC's four distinctive, rather than eight, general principles allow for a substantive and focused body of work to develop over time; a task which perhaps lends itself more appropriately to the practical realities of the limited Committee resources.

The attempt to be radical and ground-breaking in advancing the rights of disabled people could be perceived as falling short if we examine the substantive content of the principles more closely. In contradistinction to the CRC, where each general principle is a stand-alone article, not all of the principles enumerated above are explicitly stipulated or expanded upon in the remainder of the CRPD. The general principle of accessibility, for example, is the subject of Article 9, while non-discrimination and equality is the subject of Article 5. On the other hand, there is no direct comparator to the principle of 'respect for difference', and 'respect for the evolving capacities of children with disabilities and for the right of children with disabilities to preserve their identities' do not directly appear in Article 7 on children with disabilities.[51]

Indeed, it is not apparent why the latter principles are set out in Article 3 as opposed to in Article 7, particularly when we consider that Article 7 contains two of the CRC's general principles: best interests and the right of the child to express their views. This creates something of a disconnect whereby some general principles appear to be indirectly elevated over others. Of particular note is the principle of equality, which appears in three different forms in Article 3: non-discrimination, equality of opportunity and equality between men and women. The latter is interesting as it does not specify 'disabled' men or women. The limitations of equality of opportunity in general and specifically in relation to disability are well documented.[52] In fact the CRPD has been lauded for introducing the concept of reasonable accommodation for the first time in a treaty text in a nod to the importance of substantive equality.[53] It is also odd that these principles are not grouped together or simply referred to as 'equality and non-discrimination'.

The weaknesses of the CRPD's general principles can be seen more clearly if we look at the observations and commentary of the Committee on the Rights of Persons with Disabilities. In its reporting guidelines, the Committee requires states parties to report on Articles 1 to 4 together, and that this should include information on:

> In what manner the general principles and obligations established under articles 3 and 4 of the Convention have been implemented, and how it intends to ensure their effective realization, in particular the principle of promotion of the full realization of the rights under the Convention without discrimination based on disability as provided under article 4 and provide examples (2009 CRPD/C/2/3 para 4).

However, states parties are also required to report on each of the other articles separately, including Article 5 on equality and non-discrimination, Article 9 on accessibility and Article 19 on living independently and being included in the community. This format is repeated in the structure of the Committee's concluding observations. It is noteworthy that the second general comment produced by the Committee has focused on accessibility, clarifying that this is a vital precondition for the effective and equal enjoyment of civil, political, economic, social and cultural rights of disabled people.[54]

An examination of the 27 sets of concluding observations published to date indicates that the Committee has not explicitly referred to any of the general principles in its analyses of Articles 1–4, preferring to focus on general obligations and measures of implementation.[55] Instead, each of the general principles is commented on in their stand-alone form elsewhere. For example, in its response to Sweden in 2014, the Committee recommended under Article 5 of its observations that the state party 'take all appropriate steps to ensure that reasonable accommodation is provided in all spheres of society . . . based on the principle of *equal opportunities* for all'.[56] Outside of this minor reference – an exception rather than the norm – it is difficult to see how the so-called general principles are treated differently from the remaining articles of the CRPD and how they can be said to add value to the overall implementation of the CRPD in practice. Whilst acknowledging the relatively early days of the CRPD Committee, it is not clear how states parties to the CRPD can utilise the general principles in an effective manner if these are not acknowledged and treated as such by the Committee.

3.5 Conclusion

The CRC marked a qualitative departure in human rights treaty drafting, the effects of the conversation between states and civil society imprinted in its lengthy text. That same text leaves considerable scope for interpretation in its application and the Committee on the Rights of the Child, perhaps emboldened by its scope and ready endorsements, used its newly appointed remit to introduce a creative and hitherto untried approach to the implementation of human rights standards. What happened subsequently was unforeseen and unforeseeable. The four articles identified as general principles, individually and as a set, have acquired significant attention over and beyond what they may have enjoyed had they been integrated within other substantive clusters of rights. The four general principles have shaped implementation of, advocacy for and the scholarship on the Convention. They enjoy a visibility and a traction that would not have existed but for the decision to classify them as general principles.

A review of the uses of the general principles in the wake of their adoption would suggest that they have on the whole been a beneficial device that aids understanding and boosts implementation. Yet it is not clear that the CEDAW and CERD Conventions adopted prior to the CRC have been diminished in the absence of something similar nor that the CRPD has been enhanced by formal adoption of the general principles approach in its core text. What is apparent, however, is that for Convention-specific general principles to be most effective in this context, the principles must have a clear basis that enables them to apply across the other substantive provisions of the Convention and to do so in a way that enhances implementation. Non-discrimination is a straightforward case in point and it is understandable that its role as a cross-cutting provision is widely recognised in other treaty texts and in implementation guidance.

In other cases, there is a need to ask what added value the 'principle' might play across the treaty. It is submitted that a potential test would be (a) that the provision addresses a barrier to the realisation and/or a route to fulfilment of the rights of the protected groups and individuals and (b) that integrating consideration of it will facilitate implementation of other rights. Article 12 of the CRC is a good example of a provision that achieves this in relation to the CRC. Moreover, it is submitted that the sum of the principles must also be greater than the parts; the combination should be capable of creating the optimal conditions for the kind of 'rights climate' envisaged by Save the Children.[57] Each treaty will be different; while human rights are universal, the factors that challenge their realisation vary with the groups and individuals they are designed to protect. A thoughtful, considered approach to these and their potential to be translated into principles, while not a human rights 'must-have', is nonetheless an endeavour worthy of consideration.

Notes

1 See M Lafferty, M O Boyle, 'General principles and constitutions as sources of human rights law' in D Shelton (ed), *The Oxford Handbook of International Human Rights Law* (Oxford University Press 2013).
2 Space does not permit a review of all of the preceding treaties. These two have been chosen as the two best known Conventions addressing the rights of specified groups.
3 CRC Committee, 'General Guidelines Regarding the Form and Content of Initial Reports to be submitted by States Parties under Article 44, Paragraph 1(a) of the Convention' UN Doc CRC/C/5.
4 B Abramson, 'Article 2: The right of non-discrimination' in A Alen, J Vande Lanotte, E Verhellen, F Ang, E Berghmans, M Verheyde and B Abramson (eds), *A Commentary on the United Nations Convention on the Rights of the Child* (Brill Nijhoff 2008).
5 D McGoldrick, 'The United Nations Convention on the Rights of the Child' (1991) 5(2) *International Journal of Law, Policy and the Family* 132.
6 G Lansdown, 'The reporting process under the Convention on the Rights of the Child' in P Alston, J Crawford (eds), *The Future of UN Human Rights Treaty Monitoring* (Cambridge University Press 2000).
7 CRC Committee (n 3).
8 ibid.
9 M Santos Pais, *A Human Rights Conceptual Framework for UNICEF* (Unicef Innocenti 1999).
10 See Abramson (n 4).
11 D B Hollis, *The Oxford Guide to Treaties* (Oxford University Press 2012).
12 Abramson (n 4) at 65 reports that when Committee members were asked why they kept to them: 'Their replies boil down to "We speak of the four general principles because we have always spoken of the four general principles"'.
13 States parties' reports are consistently structured according to the guidelines with the 'General Principles' as a routine heading.
14 But see Abramson (n 4) above for an argument that Article 2 cannot be a general principle.
15 For an argument that development should be interpreted more broadly to include participation in political, social and cultural development, see M Novak, 'Article 6: The Right to Life Survival and Development' in A Alen and others (n 4).
16 CRC Committee, 'General Comment No 5: General Measures of Implementation' UN Doc CRC/GC/2003/5, para 7.

17 N Peleg, 'Time to grow up: the UN Committee on the Rights of the Child's jurisprudence of the right to development' in M Freeman (ed), *Law and Childhood Studies* (Oxford University Press 2012).
18 K Mechlem, 'Treaty bodies and the interpretation of human rights' (2009) 42 *Vanderbilt Journal of Transnational Law* 905.
19 CRC Committee, 'General Comment No 5', para 12.
20 CRC Committee, 'General Comment No 7: on Implementing Child Rights Early Childhood' UN Doc CRC/GC/2005/7, para 11.
21 CRC Committee, 'Treaty-specific Guidelines Regarding the Form and Content of Periodic Reports to be Submitted by States Parties under Article 44, Paragraph 1 (b), of the Convention on the Rights of the Child' CRC/C/2015/58.
22 ibid para 25.
23 ibid para 26.
24 CRC Committee, 'General Comment No 12: on the Right of the Child to be Heard' UN Doc CRC/GC/2009/12, para 2.
25 CRC Committee, 'General Comment No 14: on the Right of the Child to have his or her Best Interests taken as a Primary Consideration' UN Doc CRC/GC/2013/12. The approach appears to have been based on the work of one of the Committee members, Professor Jean Zermatten, outlined prior to the Comment in the following article: J Zermatten, 'The best interests of the child principle: literal analysis and function' (2010) 18(4) *International Journal of Children's Rights* 483.
26 M Freeman, 'The future of children's rights' (2000) 14(4) *Children and Society* 277; L Lundy, E Welty, B Blue Swadener, N Blanchet Cohen, K Smith and D Devine, 'What if children had been involved in drafting the United Nations Convention on the Rights of the Child?' in A Diduck, N Peleg and H Reece (eds), *Law in Society: Reflections on Children, Family, Culture and Philosophy* (Brill 2015) 223.
27 N Pillay, 'Strengthening the United Nations human rights treaty body system: a report by the United Nations High Commissioner for Human Rights' (2012) United Nations Human Rights: Office of the High Commissioner, 100.
28 L Lundy, 'Children's rights and educational policy in Europe: the implementation of the United Nations Convention on the Rights of the Child' (2012) 38(4) *Oxford Review of Education* 393–411.
29 CRC Committee, 'Consideration of reports submitted by States parties under article 44 of the Convention: Fifth periodic reports of States parties due in 2014: United Kingdom' (2014) CRC/C/GBR/5, paras 2, 3.
30 L Lundy, U Kilkelly and B Byrne, 'Incorporation of the United Nations Convention on the Rights of the Child in law: a comparative review' (2013) 21(3) *International Journal of Children's Rights* 442.
31 The Thirty-first Amendment of the Constitution (Children) Act 2012 includes the following: 'Provision shall be made by law for the adoption of any child where the parents have failed for such a period of time as may be prescribed by law in their duty towards the child and where the best interests of the child so require'; and 'Provision shall be made by law for securing, as far as practicable, that in all proceedings referred to in subsection 1° of this section in respect of any child who is capable of forming his or her own views, the views of the child shall be ascertained and given due weight having regard to the age and maturity of the child'.
32 R Reading, S Bissell, J Goldhagen, J Harwin, J Masson, S Moynihan and E Webb, 'Promotion of children's rights and prevention of child maltreatment' (2009) 373 *The Lancet* 332; K Winter, 'The UNCRC and social workers' relationships with young children' (2011) 20(6) *Child Abuse Review* 395; J Elwood, L Lundy, 'Revisioning assessment through a children's rights approach: implications for policy, process and practice' (2010) 25(3) *Research Papers in Education* 335.

33 L Jerome, L Emerson, L Lundy and K Orr, *Children's Rights Education: A Study of Implementation in 26 Countries* (UNICEF 2014).
34 See, for example, the International Child and Youth Care Network: 'These four principles contribute to a general attitude towards children and their rights' www.cyc-net.org/today2001/today011120.html (last accessed 5 October 2015).
35 CRIN, 'General principles' www.crin.org/en/home/rights/themes/general-principles (last accessed 5 October 2015).
36 K O'Neill (ed) *Getting it Right for Children: A Practitioners' Guide to Child Rights Programming* (International Save the Children Alliance 2007) 10.
37 J Elster, 'Solomonic judgments: against the best interest of the child' (1987) *University of Chicago Law Review* 54, 1.
38 P Alston, 'The best interest's principle: towards a reconciliation of culture and human rights' (1984) 8(1) *International Journal of Law, Policy and the Family* 1.
39 R A Hart, *Children's Participation: From Tokenism to Citizenship* (UNICEF Innocent Research Centre 1992); L Lundy, '"Voice" is not enough: conceptualising Article 12 of the United Nations Convention on the Rights of the Child' (2007) 33 *British Educational Research Journal* 927.
40 But see Abramson (n 4).
41 M Roth, F Moisa, 'The right to education of Roma children in Romania: European policies and Romanian practices' (2011) 19(3) *International Journal of Children's Rights* 501; B Byrne, 'Hidden contradictions and conditionality: conceptualisations of inclusive education in international human rights law' (2013) 28(2) *Disability & Society* 232.
42 But see Peleg (n 17).
43 J Tobin, 'Understanding a human rights based approach to matters involving children: conceptual foundations and strategic considerations' in A Invernizzi, J Williams (eds), *The Human Rights of Children: From Visions to Implementation* (Ashgate Publishing 2013) 61–98.
44 Lafferty and others (n 1).
45 C P Cohen, 'The role of non-governmental organizations in the drafting of the Convention on the Rights of the Child' (1990) *Human Rights Quarterly* 137–47.
46 Compilation of Guidelines on the form and content of reports to be submitted by States Parties to the International Human Rights Treaties (2009) UN Doc HRI/GEN/2/Rev 6, para 52.
47 Another contender for a place in the general principles could be Article 7 which provides as follows: 'States Parties undertake to adopt immediate and effective measures, particularly in the fields of teaching, education, culture and information, with a view to combating prejudices which lead to racial discrimination and to promoting understanding, tolerance and friendship among nations and racial or ethnical groups, as well as to propagating the purposes and principles of the Charter of the United Nations, the Universal Declaration of Human Rights, the United Nations Declaration on the Elimination of All Forms of Racial Discrimination, and this Convention'.
48 UN Office of the High Commission on Human Rights, 'General Recommendation No 1: States Parties' Obligations (Art 4)' UN Doc Gen/Rec/No 1 (General Comments) (1972).
49 R Kayess, P French, 'Out of darkness into light? Introducing the Convention on the Rights of Persons with Disabilities (2008) 8(1) *Human Rights Law Review* 1.
50 A Kanter, 'The challenge and promises of the UN Convention on the Rights of Persons with Disabilities' (2007) 34 *Syracuse Journal of International Law and Commerce* 287, 294.
51 It is noteworthy that the principle of evolving capacities has been given primacy in the CRPD as a standalone general principle rather than integrated into Article 7 alongside other CRC general principles.

52 See for example I M Young, 'Equality of whom? Social groups and judgments of injustice' (2001) 9(1) *Journal of Political Philosophy* 1; A Silvers "'Defective" agents: equality, difference and the tyranny of the normal' (1994) *Journal of Social Philosophy* 25th anniversary issue, reprinted in R Manning, R Trujillo (eds), *Social Justice in a Diverse Society* (Mayfield Publishing Company 1996); B Byrne, 'Reconciling sameness and difference in disability rights ideology: the case of student identity' in G Quinn, C O'Mahony (eds), *The United Nations Convention on the Rights of Persons with Disabilities* (Intersentia forthcoming).

53 See Kayess and French (n 49); O M Arnardottir, 'A future of multidimensional disadvantage equality?' in O M Arnardottir, G Quinn (eds), *The UN Convention on the Rights of Persons with Disabilities: European and Scandinavian Perspectives* (Martinus Nijhoff 2003) 41.

54 Committee on the Rights of Persons with Disabilities, 'General Comment No 2: Article 9 Accessibility' (2014) UN Doc CRPD/C/GC/2, para 4.

55 For example, Concluding Observations: Denmark (2014) CRPD/C/DNK/CO/1, Concluding Observations: Azerbaijan (2014) CRPD/C/AZE/CO/1 and Concluding Observations: Germany (2015) CRPD/C/DEU/CO/1.

56 Concluding Observations: Sweden (2014) CRPD/C/SWE/CO/1, emphasis added.

57 See O'Neill (n 36).

4 The inclusion of 'third parties': the status of parenthood in the Convention on the Rights of the Child

Roberta Ruggiero, Diana Volonakis and Karl Hanson

4.1 Introduction

This chapter analyses the inclusion of parents as 'third parties' in the Convention on the Rights of the Child (CRC) as a particular feature of the CRC compared with general human rights law instruments. While the child is the central figure of the CRC, the Convention also makes repeated reference to 'third parties', namely parents, whose identities and roles are commented upon throughout scattered provisions. The CRC does not include a comprehensive definition of parents and parenthood. In order to fill this conceptual void, the present contribution borrows from David Archard's work *Children: Rights and Childhood*, where 'biological parenthood' is defined as the 'existence of a physical causal tie between begetter and offspring', and moral parenthood is defined as 'the giving to a child of continuous care, concern and affection with the purpose of helping to secure for her the best possible upbringing'.[1]

Following this distinction, the present contribution holds parents to be individuals biologically and/or emotionally linked to the child through the provision of care, concern and affection guided by the best interest of the child. In the framework of this chapter, the figure of the 'legal guardian' (Article 18 CRC) does not fall within the definition of parent, considering the absence of biological and or affective ties of this figure to the child. In addition, 'members of the extended family' (Article 5 CRC) are equally excluded from the present analysis, given that distant family relatedness also falls outside the scope of parenthood.

In order the better to understand the roles, duties and responsibilities of parents as developed in the CRC, the contribution will begin with a general legal analysis of the key provisions in relation to parents: Articles 3(2) and (3), 5 and 18 of the CRC. This section is followed by a more detailed analysis of the parental role in relation to the child's right to freedom of religion contained in Article 14 CRC. This provides an interesting case study of the current relevance, benefits and drawbacks of the inclusion of parents as holders of rights, duties and responsibilities in the CRC.

The legal analysis leads to two contrasting perspectives on the relation between children's rights and the rights, duties and responsibilities of parents. A first perspective explores the dichotomisation of children's rights and parental rights. We will address this dichotomy by reflecting on the emergence of the parental rights movement in the USA, which has sparked intense discussions, particularly among North American legal circles, on the problems linked to the parental rights/children's rights binary.[2] A second perspective is of a conciliatory nature, and points at the possibility of heightened cooperation between family and public sphere stakeholders towards the realisation of children's rights. This perspective will be addressed by questioning the philosophical, legal and social implications, which arise from the designation of parents as 'rights holders', 'duty bearers' and holders of 'parental responsibilities'. In addition, we will identify the tensions which the multiple facets integral to the status of parenthood pose, and its impact on distributions of power between the child, the parent, and the state.

To summarise the debates, we will briefly address arguments against – and in favour of – the potential inclusion of parents as well as possible other third parties in global human rights law for other groups. We believe that other branches of international human rights law can find inspiration from the conciliatory perspective within children's rights law in order to address the rights, duties and responsibilities of third parties.

4.2 Parents in the CRC: legal analysis of Articles 3(2) and (3), 5 and 18 CRC

Of the 16 articles that mention parents in the CRC, three provisions have been selected on the basis of their centrality to understanding the role of parents as third parties in the CRC: Articles 3(2 and 3), 5, and 18.[3] The following paragraphs will submit each of the said articles to legal analyses.

Article 3(2) CRC states:

> States Parties undertake to ensure the child such protection and care as is necessary for his or her well-being, taking into account the rights and duties of his or her parents, legal guardians, or other individuals legally responsible for him or her, and, to this end, shall take all appropriate legislative and administrative measures.

The provision bestows upon parents the primary responsibility to ensure the protection and care of the child, both elements thought to be integral to the notion of 'well-being'. It further asserts that the realisation of the child's well-being is dependent upon the rights and duties of parents, and state obligations. Article 3(2) CRC acts as a 'backstop provision'[4] bestowing on states parties an overarching obligation to support parents' primary responsibilities. The state's empowering role is further highlighted in other CRC provisions, which require state party intervention in cases of absent, fragile or abusive parents' inability to perform. This is for example the case in Articles 5 and 18 CRC, which concern parent–child relations in general, as well as in Article 27 concerning adequate standards of living, in Article 20(2) on alternative care and in Article 21 on intercountry-adoption.

Elements contained in Article 3(2), such as 'protection', 'care', 'necessity', 'child well-being' and the 'rights and duties of parents' are not defined in the CRC.[5] Therefore, state-by-state interpretation of such central concepts are carried out on the basis of domestic legal systems, which most frequently refer to 'parental responsibility' rather than 'parental rights'.[6] The term 'responsibility' is thought to be preferred since it is deemed more conciliatory, allowing the concept of the family as a network of reciprocal, non-authoritarian relationships, thus guaranteeing due regard for the child's equal status as rights holder.[7]

Parental responsibilities include providing guidance in a manner consistent with the child's evolving capacities. This is further addressed in Article 5 of the CRC, which reads as follows:

> States Parties shall respect the responsibilities, rights and duties of parents or, where applicable, the members of the extended family or community as provided for by local custom, legal guardians or other persons legally responsible for the child, to provide, in a manner consistent with the evolving capacities of the child, appropriate direction and guidance in the exercise by the child of the rights recognized in the present Convention.

Article 5 CRC serves to emphasise that parental prerogatives and obligations grow increasingly limited by the child's increase in personal autonomy, understanding and decision-making power. This implicit time-limitation imposed on parental prerogatives and obligations constitutes the uniqueness of the provision in relation to other international and regional legal standards. Article 5 states that parents are endowed with the right to provide 'appropriate direction and guidance in the exercise by the child of the rights recognised in the present Convention'. Parents' prerogatives are therefore *limited* and *functional*, i.e. parents provide oversight over the child's exercise of his or her rights, and factors such as young age or disability may affect parents' degree of involvement in the assistance provided to the child.

External factors may equally influence the scope of parental involvement in the child's exercise of his or her rights: if the wrong done to a child requires a legal remedy, procedural complexity well beyond the child's comprehension may require a heightened degree of parental commitment. Thus it is the child who is the beneficiary of the rights, *stricto sensu*, contained in the Convention. The parents' right to oversee the child's exercise of his or her rights is *limited* and *functional*, and can be interpreted as a supplementary protective framework to ensure that the child's best interest is safeguarded.

It becomes apparent that nowhere does the Convention explicitly endorse parents' abilities to exercise a right in the stead of a child. Nevertheless, concrete cases in which such situations may unfold are all too common. One may only consider the vast array of parental decisions taken in regard to the daily life of a child, who – owing to his or her young age or disability – is excluded from the decision-making process. Such decisions may concern living arrangements, schooling, health, religion, recreation etc. However, this does not mean, per se, that parents are exercising the right in place of the child. Rather, based on the CRC provisions, parents act as representatives of the child, with the child's best interests in mind.

The final provision of the CRC, which makes general reference to the status of parents, is Article 18 on parental responsibilities for the upbringing and development of the child, which reads as follows:

1. States Parties shall use their best efforts to ensure recognition of the principle that both parents have common responsibilities for the upbringing and development of the child. Parents or, as the case may be, legal guardians have the primary responsibility for the upbringing and development of the child. The best interests of the child will be their basic concern.
2. For the purpose of guaranteeing and promoting the rights set forth in the present Convention, States Parties shall render appropriate assistance to parents and legal guardians in the performance of their child-rearing responsibilities and shall ensure the development of institutions, facilities and services for the care of children.
3. States Parties shall take all appropriate measures to ensure that children of working parents have the right to benefit from childcare services and facilities for which they are eligible.

Article 18 supplements Articles 3(2) and 5 CRC, directly bestowing on parents the primary responsibility for the rearing and development of the child, further underlining that parental decisions should always be taken with due consideration of the best interests of the child (Article 18(1)). Furthermore, it is complementary to Article 27(2), which charges parents with the responsibility to secure 'the conditions of living necessary for the child's development'. It also reiterates states parties' obligation to provide appropriate assistance to parents in the performance of their child-rearing responsibility (Article 18(2)). The combined reading of Article 18(2) and Article 3(2) and (3)[8] bestow on states parties the responsibility to render appropriate assistance to parents in the performance of their child-rearing responsibility, namely through the creation of 'institutions, facilities and services for the care of the child' and monitoring of the latter's compliance with quality standards.[9] Both provisions are therefore closely intertwined, even though Article 3(3) does not exclusively refer to institutions dedicated to child-rearing, but also to those dedicated to child protection more generally.[10]

Following the analysis of Articles 3(2), 5 and 18 CRC, it has been established that parents are endowed with a spectrum of rights, duties and/or responsibilities for the fulfilment of two aims: first, to secure the child's well-being through the purveyance of protection and care (Articles 3(2) and 18) and, secondly, to provide evolving and age-appropriate guidance to the child in the child's exercise of his or her rights (Article 5).

Moreover, the CRC imposes upon states parties the *obligation to respect* parents' roles, by refraining from arbitrary interference in the exercise of parental responsibility and the *obligation to fulfil*, by taking all appropriate legislative and administrative measures to nurture parental resources – both in terms of personal skills and availability of support facilities. As a consequence, the CRC provides a framework for a *social contract* between parents and the state, where protection from undue state interference coexists with the right to receive state support.[11] In this framework, parents enjoy a degree of discretion as holders of what has been defined as *limited*[12] and *functional* rights.[13] Each of these concepts will be addressed in turn in the following sections. The limitations are of a twofold nature. Firstly, parental rights are limited by the evolving capacity of the child: as the child becomes more mature, parents' rights will be automatically restricted or reshaped as to their content and scope. Secondly, parents' rights should be exercised in full respect of the best interests of the child and his or her enjoyment of the full range of rights included in the CRC.

In order to highlight the multiple problems that the concept of limited rights entails, the following section will provide a case study of the tensions emerging between parental rights and children's rights related to freedom of religion.

4.3 Parental rights, duties and responsibilities in relation to the child's right to freedom of religion

In the CRC, the child's right to religious freedom is contained in Article 14, which reads as follows:

> 1. States Parties shall respect the right of the child to freedom of thought, conscience and religion.
> 2. States Parties shall respect the rights and duties of the parents and, when applicable, legal guardians, to provide direction to the child in the exercise of his or her right in a manner consistent with the evolving capacities of the child.
> 3. Freedom to manifest one's religion or beliefs may be subject only to such limitations as are prescribed by law and are necessary to protect public safety, order, health or morals, or the fundamental rights and freedoms of others.

Article 14(1) CRC confirms the child as a rights holder whose right to freedom of thought, conscience and religion must be protected. This right is also protected by Article 9(1) of the European Convention on Human Rights (ECHR), which states that 'everyone' has the right to freedom of thought, conscience and religion. The European Court of Human Rights (ECtHR) has explicitly recognised the freedom of thought, conscience and religion as an individual right of the child. It has done so by analysing, in its case law on religious freedom in the context of the right to education and the state school system, if the right to freedom of religion of the child was respected in practice.[14]

The right to freedom of thought, conscience and religion encompasses three closely related dimensions. A first dimension concerns the *internal freedom of religion* and has an absolute character, implying that no restrictions can be imposed on this internal dimension of the freedom.[15] The existence of a right to freedom of religion also comprises a negative aspect, namely the right of individuals not to be required to reveal their faith or religious beliefs and not to be compelled to assume a stance from which it may be inferred whether or not they have such beliefs.[16] A second dimension is the child's *freedom to change his or her religion or belief*.[17] The third and most visible dimension is the *freedom to manifest one's religion or belief*. This includes worship, teaching of a religion or belief, and the practice and observance of religious prescripts.

The right of the child to freedom of thought, conscience and religion is a classic freedom right, in the sense that the state has the obligation to protect everyone against unlawful interference with the exercise of this freedom. According to the escape clause in Article 14(3) CRC, the limitations on the right to freedom of religion are only applicable on the freedom to *manifest* one's religion or belief. The internal freedom of religion, as well as the freedom to change one's religion or belief that does not involve any public manifestation, cannot be restricted. The aim of this approach is to reconcile the interests of various groups in democratic societies and to ensure that everyone's beliefs are respected.[18] In case the right protected in Article 14(1) CRC is at stake, an assessment needs to be made if the limitation on the exercise of this right complies with the criteria provided in Article 14(3). The question whether there has been an interference in children's autonomous freedom to manifest their religion or belief has been discussed in several European countries, for example in the context of the debate on the place of the Islamic headscarf in state education.[19]

As stated above, the CRC does not contain a corresponding right of parents to ensure the religious education of their children in conformity with their own convictions. It does, however, require states parties to respect the rights and duties of the parents to provide direction to the child in the exercise of his or her right in a manner consistent with the evolving capacities of the child (Article 14(2) CRC). The formulation that parents have rights and duties in the exercise of the child's freedom of religion or belief is in line with the general conception of parental responsibilities in the CRC discussed above as limited and functional rights, which need to be exercised in a manner consistent with the evolving capacities of the child (Article 5 CRC), with the best interests of the child as their basic concern (Article 18(1) CRC).

An important difference between the provision of Article 14(2) CRC about the right of parents to provide direction to the child in the exercise of his or her right to freedom of thought, conscience and religion, and the rights of parents to ensure the religious education of their children in conformity with their own convictions is that the former concerns the exercise of the child's freedom, whereas the latter is concerned with the convictions of the parents.

General human rights instruments include, however, further rights of parents in this respect. As such, Article 2 of Protocol No 1 to the ECHR provides that the state shall respect the right of parents to ensure the education and teaching of their children in conformity with their own religious and philosophical convictions. This provision is binding upon the contracting states in the exercise of each and every function that they undertake in the sphere of education and teaching. According to the ECtHR, that duty is broad in its extent as it applies not only to the content and implementation of school curricula but also to the performance of all the functions assumed by the state.[20] It includes the organisation and financing of public education, the setting and planning of the curriculum, the conveying of information or knowledge included in the curriculum in an objective, critical and pluralistic manner (hence forbidding the state to pursue an aim of indoctrination that might be considered as not respecting parents' religious and philosophical convictions), as well as the organisation of the school environment, including the presence of crucifixes in state-school classrooms.[21]

A similar provision is contained in Article 18(4) of the International Covenant on Civil and Political Rights (ICCPR), according to which states parties undertake to have respect for the liberty of parents and, when applicable, legal guardians to ensure the religious and moral education of their children in conformity with their own convictions.

In the exercise of his or her right to freedom of religion and beliefs, a very young child is entirely restricted by the decisions made by his or her parents, who act according to their responsibilities, rights and duties towards their children. In a case before the European Commission of Human Rights, an applicant complained that he had been baptised a few weeks after his birth, and requested that this imposed commitment might be annulled. However, the Commission declared that this case did not breach Article 9 of the ECHR[22] because, when the child is older, parents need to take into account his or her evolving capacities. In the absence of a fixed legal age from which children and young people can exercise their own right to religious freedom, a case-by-case approach will be necessary to assess how far the evolving capacities of the child allow him or her to make (gradually more) autonomous decisions about the exercise of his or her right to freedom of thought, conscience and religion.

When conceptualising the exercise of children's freedom of religion, traditionally pre-eminence was given to the rights of parents to determine the religious and moral upbringing of their children rather than to the child's right to religious freedom. In such a view, children were excluded from the autonomous exercise of the right to religious freedom; at most they had a right to practise the religion of their parents.[23] The wording of Article 26(3) of the Universal Declaration of Human Rights (UDHR) that '[p]arents have a prior right to choose the kind of education that shall be given to their children' was a deliberate choice of the drafters. Through this formulation, they wanted to restrict the power of the state to determine religious education and instead favoured parents' freedom of choice.[24]

In case of a conflict, only two elements needed to be balanced against each other, namely the prerogative of parents to determine the religious upbringing of their children and the monitoring role of the state to tackle potential abuses of this right. Until today, this view is upheld in many states, which is illustrated by the relatively high number of reservations and interpretative declarations made regarding the right of the child to freedom of thought, conscience and religion contained in Article 14 of the CRC.[25] Upon ratification of the CRC, Jordan for example explicitly stated that it does not consider itself bound by Article 14 of the CRC because it considers the child's right to freedom of choice of religion incompatible with the precepts of the tolerant Islamic Shariah.

The explicit recognition of the child's own right to freedom of thought, conscience and religion, in conjunction with the provision that parents have the rights and duties to provide direction to the child in the exercise of his or her right in a manner consistent with the evolving capacities of the child, have considerably altered the existent relation between the different fundamental freedoms. In case of conflict over the religious freedom of children, not only the respective roles of parents and the state need to be balanced against each other, but also the right of the child itself to religious freedom needs to be taken into account. For Eva Brems, Article 14(2) of the CRC signals a paradigm shift, because 'the parental right is an accessory to the child's right, rather than an autonomous right on an equal footing'.[26] This provision hence illustrates the findings which were reported above that it is the child who is the main beneficiary of the rights contained in the CRC, and that parents, as 'third parties', have only limited, instrumental rights.

The analysis of the provisions in the CRC that deal with the rights, duties and responsibilities of parents in the field of children's religious freedoms leads to two contrasting perspectives on the relation between children's rights and the rights, duties and responsibilities of parents with which we will deal in the following sections. The first perspective is characterised by dichotomy; the second by conciliation.

4.4 The children's rights/parental rights dichotomy in the US campaign to ratify the CRC

In their critical review of the academic literature produced on the topic of the CRC between 1989 and 2009, Reynaert and others identify the children's rights/parental rights dichotomy as one of the three predominant themes explored in the social sciences and humanities literature.[27] The authors stress that the CRC precipitated a considerable shift in the nature of parental rights, from negative rights (non-involvement of the state within the family sphere) to positive rights (enlarged state involvement through the purveyance of institutional support concerning areas of child care and protection). The authors further state that: '[t]his shift in parenting has been an important concern for scholars in children's rights. Frequently, this changing relationship is described as a dichotomy whereby children's rights are placed in tension with the rights of parents'.[28] The rights-based approach is said to create potentially contentious situations within the family, when the child's and parents' divergent interests require different and mutually unacceptable outcomes. As discussed above, such a contentious situation for instance arises when children's own religious convictions clash with the rights of their parents to determine the religious upbringing of their children.

In order to illustrate further the dichotomy between children's rights and parental rights, we will now turn to the American context, where the trichotomous structure of child/parents/state relations constitutes the core of ongoing debate within and outside the academic sphere. Over the past two decades, a wealth of literature has been produced in the United States by academics and civil society actors engaged in the analysis, promotion or defence of children's rights. Unsurprisingly, in discussing broader children's rights issues, the authors ultimately take a stance in favour of the future ratification of the CRC by the US government. In response, a social movement identified as the American parental rights movement has consistently voiced opposition to the treaty, by mobilising the children's rights/parents' rights dichotomy to further their agenda.[29]

A review of the literature produced between 1989 and 2016 on the topic of the US ratification of the CRC has highlighted publications which critically address the concept of parental rights in the American context.[30] The literature indicates that, in this national setting, the debate can be said to tackle both micro and macro power struggles. On the one hand, debate is centred on the effects of the shift in power relations within the family, stemming from the recognition of children as rights holders. Parental capacity to shape the moral character of children is inhibited by child empowerment, which further serves to undermine patriarchal authority and create intergenerational conflict. On this point, Rutkow and Lozman stress that CRC provisions conferring participatory rights to children are most highly problematised by those who oppose US–CRC ratification, which charge the Convention with enabling children to resist parental authority.[31]

On the other hand, a parallel debate concerns the nature and scope of governmental action the state is entitled to wield in the name of the child's best interests. The tension arising from state intervention in the private family sphere, and its potentially damaging effects on parents' decision-making authority in the performance of child-rearing duties, is a point of contention consistently mobilised by American actors as an argument against CRC ratification.

Parental rights are a concept of which the origin is difficult to pinpoint: McCarthy situates the recognition of parental rights in the early 20th century, when the United States Supreme Court progressively addressed tensions involving state interference in the parent–child relationship.[32] The author further states that the concept is defined by its supporters as the 'precept declaring that parental interests in the custody, care, and control of their children are constitutionally protected from unwarranted State interference'.[33] In the American context, therefore, parental rights are a concept deeply rooted in the negative–positive rights tradition. McCarthy deftly deconstructs this definition, highlighting what he claims to be an inextricable paradox: while activities pertaining to the areas of 'custody' and 'care' of children are said to merit heightened protection from state intervention by virtue of an inalienable quality characteristic of the parent–child bond, the author notes that the same areas are precisely those subject to frequent state intervention, e.g. federal and state legislation pertaining to vaccination, compulsory schooling, child labour or child abuse.[34] The argument that parents and carers should enjoy unrestricted liberty in their exercise of care and upbringing of children appears then to lack sound legal grounding.

Furthermore, the argument that it is an individual's right to 'control' one's offspring is equally disputed by Dwyert, in claiming that: 'the American legal system does not recognise an individual's rights tocontrol the lives of other people. There is an in-principle limitation on legal rights that confines them to protection of a rights holder's personal integrity and self-determining activities'.[35] In this perspective, the authority to exercise child-rearing activities is conceptualised as a privilege granted to parents by the state, but which may be revoked if deemed in the best interests of the child.[36] McCarthy and Dwyert's stances converge around the idea that legal disputes involving parents, children and the state are thought to be best resolved through a children's rights approach. In a conciliatory effort, McCarthy suggests the potency of reconceptualising parental rights as 'family integrity or autonomy rights',[37] considered more consensual by the author, although he admits that 'the use of a family rights method of analysis gets one no further ahead in attempting to isolate a theory of parental rights, and in the end may generate more problems'.[38]

Considering the lack of a coherent and persuasive legal definition of parental rights in the US, it is unsurprising that American courts have treated these rights with marked ambivalence. According to McCarthy, 'the Supreme Court has given conflicting signals about these rights, [and] it should be no surprise that lower courts have had great difficulty with cases that raise questions concerning the protection of parental rights in circumstances beyond those that are clearly covered by direct precedent'.[39] While the Supreme Court would appear to accept the principle of parental rights as fundamental rights, the Court does not follow through with this stance once application is warranted, thereby creating great confusion among legal experts and the general public as to the legal value of parental rights in the US. Lane echoes Kilbourne and Dwyert in lamenting the fact that 'in all of the rhetoric of parental rights, there is little or no mention of the rights of children. Certainly their rights to a safe, non-abusive, and enjoyable childhood environment should be a factor in the parent/child calculus'.[40]

Gunn breaks with previous research by advancing that the CRC's symbolic character is the true motive fuelling the opposition's attacks.[41] The author contends that the symbolic struggle is in fact 'divorced from the actual language or effect of the CRC'.[42] In this view, anti-CRC rhetoric is based on an idealised account of the family, which 'leads them [the opposition] to completely ignore the plight of children who do not fit within the traditional family'.[43] The opposition's concern with safeguarding an idealised view of middle-class, bi-parental family life is said not to take into account the needs of children and families outside this model, e.g. homoparental families, children living in poverty, unparented children, and abused and/or neglected children.

In the context of the United States, political organisations have seized upon the children's rights/parental rights dichotomy towards the construction of anti-CRC rhetoric. Those actors who subscribe to the views expressed by the US parental rights social movement appear to take more serious issue with state intervention within the family sphere than with an eventual power struggle within the family. The American case is of particular relevance, since it allows an understanding that parental rights are political and cultural constructions, understood and problematised within specific contexts. Conceptually speaking, on the international stage, parental rights can be said to have received less attention from governments and civil society, as compared to the international support enjoyed by children's rights both as an idea and as a movement. In order to mediate the tension created by the emergence of two seemingly irreconcilable stances, the subsequent section will focus more closely on an alternative, more conciliatory view on the inclusion in the CRC of rights, duties and responsibilities linked to the parental status.

4.5 Conciliation between children's rights and parental rights, duties and responsibilities

A second perspective on the relationship between children's rights and parental rights is of a conciliatory nature, and points at heightened cooperation between family and public sphere stakeholders in the realisation of children's rights. This perspective will be addressed by questioning the philosophical, legal and social implications which arise from the designation of parents as 'rights holders', 'duty bearers' and holders of 'parental responsibilities' in the CRC. In addition, we will identify the tensions that the multiple facets integral to the status of parenthood pose, and their impact on distributions of power between the child, parents and the state.

Reynaert and others venture to mend the rift posed by the dichotomy between children's and parents' rights, by conceptualising parental rights as '*functional* rights'.[44] The authors further stress that the scope of parental functional rights is inversely proportional to the child's age, experience and capacity for autonomous thinking and acting. The successful exercise of these functional rights is grounded on a set of implicit premises: that fuelled by benevolence and altruism, parents aim for a fair determination and effective fulfilment of the child's best interests and evolving capacity (*limited rights*).

As stated by Van Bueren, by introducing a rights-based approach to the family sphere, international law shifted attitudes, from initially safeguarding the privacy of the family, with no intention of monitoring the quality of the relationship between family members, to a more intrusive state role.[45] This new approach defines the family as an increasingly public institution, allowing state interference within the family sphere in order to protect the rights of those composing the family unit.

Without denying the primordial nature of family, which remains based on personal relationships, the CRC endorses this shift by introducing talk on 'children's rights'. Consequently, rights-based rhetoric introduces an understanding of the parent–child relationship as 'quasi-contractual' ties, which are 'limited, and directed to the promotion of an abstract public good',[46] i.e. the child's well-being. This allows state intervention in order to protect the human rights of all members of the family. By introducing the talk on 'children's rights', as we have seen in the case of the child's right to freedom of religion, the CRC therefore moves children into the public realm, thereby preventing them from being at the sole mercy of their parents.[47] In parallel, the CRC recognises family autonomy, requiring states to respect the autonomy of parents while also monitoring the quality of parental care. The state's intervention in case of a violation of children's rights is therefore a consequence of parental shortcomings.

Based on this analysis, 'effective parenthood' becomes a matter of public interest. Hence, the use of concepts such as 'guidance' and 'direction' recasts the role of parents as enablers of the child's well-being and full enjoyment of the rights enshrined in the CRC. As Kamchedzera has underlined, the parent is a 'key participant in – and not the determinant of – the child's life'.[48] As a consequence, fostering a rights approach recognises the child as a holder and exerciser of rights, acting as a dynamic participant in both relational processes of 'guidance' and 'rearing'.

The CRC defines this key parental role by referring to the combination of parental 'responsibilities', 'rights' and 'duties' (Articles 5 and 18 CRC). The three terms appear together in Article 5, whereas Article 18 refers exclusively to parental 'responsibility' pertaining to tasks related to child-rearing. Based on Kamchedzera, it would appear that Article 5, by encompassing 'all the three words . . . indicates its spirit to be as encompassing as possible in ensuring that those who have parental roles provide appropriate guidance to the child'.[49] Kamchedzera further underlines that previous commentaries on Article 5 CRC have been reluctant to address 'the jurisprudential differences between "responsibilities", "rights" and "duties" in relation to the general correlative duty on the part of key caregivers'.[50] This specific aspect is briefly discussed in the following paragraphs.

4.5.1 Duties

The duty is a 'legal requirement to carry out or refrain from carrying out any act'.[51] In other words, it is 'a legally-defined responsibility to perform certain acts or meet certain standards of performance'.[52] Duties can be mandated by law or may be the result of a voluntary decision, such as those assumed under a contract. Parental duties are the result of both these dynamics. They are the result of the parent's willingness to take on the duties devolved to them by national and international legal provisions, and of an autonomous decision to assume this role. To cite Archard: 'parents who do undertake the task of rearing their own child should also honour the duty' in providing adequate care for their children.[53]

The CRC does not provide any definition of 'duties', but makes reference to the term in Article 5 with the intention of identifying the parental obligations pertaining to the 'appropriate direction and guidance in the exercise by the child of the rights recognised' in the CRC. The 'duties' mentioned in Article 5 are correlative to the child's right to receive appropriate direction and guidance, in general and in response to specific, contextualised needs. In performing these duties as 'duty bearer', parents become accountable for their actions and decisions performed in the private sphere of the family. By doing so, the CRC attributes to states the obligations to support the parent and to monitor parental performance in order to fulfil the correlative rights of the child. Therefore, parental duties, such as the duty to educate and financially support the child, are legally enforceable.

4.5.2 Rights

Rights are commonly understood as 'any other interest or privilege recognized and protected by law'[54] and may imply the 'freedom to exercise any power conferred by law'.[55] Based on Archard's position, parents are entitled to the protection and recognition of their interests in rearing their child, a position reflected in the CRC which recognises the same entitlement within the limits of parents' overarching responsibility in guiding and rearing the child. Hence, we agree with Kamchedzera's statement that the 'right' attributed to parents in Article 5 'pertains to claims that parents and other key carers should have in providing appropriate direction and guidance. Included are rights that are instrumental for the provision of parental guidance, such as the right to reside with the child'.[56]

In other words, Article 5 generally recognises legal or moral entitlements in the framework of decisions and actions for people *in loco parentis* against other actors: the state and children (to name a few). It does not provide a list of these rights nor a definition, but generally refers to them. Therefore, it is arguable that any right to provide guidance recognised to parents as a consequence of their parental responsibility, derives from and is limited by the duty to ensure that the child is adequately guided.

4.5.3 Responsibilities

Law and Martin define parental responsibility as the cohort comprised of all 'the rights, duties, powers, and responsibilities that by law a parent of a child has in relation to the child and his or her property'.[57] This 'responsibility' is paired, at the same time, with all the duties and rights parents enjoy in order to take autonomous decisions in the performance of the parental role and to achieve the final public interest: the child's well-being.[58]

By defining responsibility in this manner, it is arguable that responsibility, at least as far as the parental role is concerned, is the most encompassing term. It includes in itself all the range of statuses pertaining to the parental position. 'Responsibility' refers at once to parental duties towards the child and the state, to the parents' right to perform their role free from arbitrary state interventions, and the right to benefit from different forms of state support (care services, educational and economic support etc).

The CRC does not provide a definition of 'responsibility', but it nonetheless makes reference to the term in several provisions referring to parents' key position. For example, in Article 18(1), the CRC bestows upon parents the primary responsibility for the upbringing and development of the child, and Article 27(2) confers on parents the primary responsibility to secure 'the condition of living necessary for the child's development in the limits of their abilities and financial capacities'. Based on these provisions, it would therefore appear that, in the CRC, the use of the term 'responsibility' is intended to refer to the broad spectrum of parental duties and rights.

In short, from a legal point of view, 'responsibility' implies, on the one hand, parental rights over under-aged children (including, for example, the rights to provide physical care and oversight, to monitor their education, including religious education, to consent by proxy to medical treatment, to administer their property and to represent them in legal proceedings) and, on the other hand, parental duties, such as, for example, the duty to educate and economically support the child. All duties pertaining to child rearing (Article 18), akin to those identified in Article 5, can be legally enforced in cases of omission or inconsistency with CRC principles. Therefore, the concept of 'parental responsibility' is indicative of both the duties relative to immediate child-rearing (upbringing), to long-term physical and cognitive progression into adulthood (development) and to the means parents may employ to ensure that the child's exercise of his or her rights is fully realised, without being unduly limited owing to the child's personal characteristics (age, maturity, disability) and/or procedural inadequacy/complexity. Furthermore, primary parental responsibility not only encompasses duties, but also the rights related to enabling the child's exercise of his or her rights, and to 'the upbringing and development of the child'. The duties can be legally enforced by state intervention when parental performance is unsuited to the fulfilment of the child's complementary right to adequate guidance and rearing.

4.6 Inclusion of third parties in other human rights law instruments

From our analysis of the status of parenthood in the CRC, we can provide some thoughts on potential pitfalls and benefits of including 'third parties' in other human rights law instruments as well.

Some arguments can be given against the idea of granting rights, duties or responsibilities to third parties in international human rights instruments that deal with specific groups. A major risk is that with third party rights more controversy slips into human rights instruments, as has been the case with the binary view of children's rights versus parents' rights, as discussed above, which appears to confine potential tensions to power struggles occurring within the family sphere. The dichotomous vision consistently downplays the contentious nature of the relationship between the family and the state, asserting that state intervention is limited to the purveyance of support in habitual cases, and to the removal of the child from the family in extreme cases of neglect or abuse.

Furthermore, the inclusion of parents as 'third parties' in the CRC has repeatedly been used to conceal the legal obligations of state parties as duty bearers towards children as rights holders, as is the case in the agenda to combat all forms of violence against children. For instance, the campaign to protect children from corporal punishment in their homes, which is led by a large coalition of international non-governmental child rights organisations with strong support from the Committee on the Rights of the Child and the 2006 UN Secretary-

General's study on violence against children has, according to this campaign's critics, allowed states to hide their own direct duties to tackle economic inequality and other forms of structural violence.[59] According to the anti-violence campaign, children are victims of violence perpetrated by their parents or carers, rather than of structural violence.

Other arguments can be formulated that plead in favour of transposing third parties in other human rights instruments directed at particular groups. Inspiration can therefore be found in the conciliatory perspective, which prescribes that a balance needs to be made between the rights of the different actors involved by distributing responsibilities, duties and rights among parents/carers and the state towards the promotion and realisation of an abstract public good, i.e. the child's well-being. We think that this perspective can be particularly relevant for international human rights law pertaining to people with disabilities, where some reference to third parties already exists but could be further developed.

The Convention on the Rights of Persons with Disabilities (CRPD), adopted in December 2006, emphasises third party responsibility and rights which are instrumental to the fulfilment of the rights of individuals with disabilities, but to a far lesser extent compared to the CRC. In the CRPD, the state is the exclusive responsibility holder. The involvement of third parties is foreseen in Article 16 CRPD; however, without the intention of bestowing on them a direct responsibility, duty or right. The provision requires states parties to take measures to protect persons with disabilities from exploitation, violence and abuse within and outside the home. In particular, Article 16(2) asks states parties to take preventive measures by ensuring appropriate assistance and support not only for persons with disabilities themselves but also for 'their families and caregivers'. The provision hence bestows on states parties the obligation to support families and carers in order to avoid, identify and report cases of exploitation, violence and abuse; however, without recognizing any specific form of responsibility, duty or rights to family members or carers.

Therefore, the CRPD is perceived as falling short for three reasons. Firstly, the recognition of the carer's rights, duties and responsibilities is completely absent from the Convention. Secondly, conversely to what characterises the CRC, in the CRPD the 'well-being' of persons with disabilities is mentioned exclusively in the preamble as a programmatic principle. Thirdly, it would appear that the drafting procedure of the CRPD aimed to confirm the state's primary responsibility towards people with disabilities (in terms of obligations to respect, fulfil and protect), without considering the personal and moral ties characterising the relationship between a person with disabilities and his or her carer and/or legal representative. This is mirrored in the wording of the different Articles, which are formulated, with few exceptions,[60] from a *negative perspective*. In other words, CRPD Articles are not addressed directly to the subjects concerned by identifying them as holders of rights (*positive perspective*), but instead identify state obligations meant to overcome physical and social obstacles characterising the daily life of this specific group of people.

Therefore, the CRPD could be further strengthened by adopting a rights-based approach such as the one adopted by the CRC. In this perspective, it is possible to enforce a system based on both individual autonomy and mutual accountability between the person with disabilities, carers (*sensu lato*) and the state.

The concept of 'responsibilities', which includes functional rights aimed at the fulfilment of the rights of the individual with disabilities, might provide a starting point for new thinking on this topic.

4.7 Conclusion

While parental rights have acceded to the forefront of public debate, as illustrated by contemporary debates in the USA on CRC ratification, the concept remains highly elusive. The prerogatives and duties inherent in parental status can be said to be context specific, and vary greatly depending on cultural representations of 'adequate' parenting and parents' access to resources and state support. As such, it is impossible to attempt to construct a comprehensive enumeration of the tasks and obligations that parenthood entails; nor is it possible to impose strict definitions on three resolutely vague categories of parental rights, duties and responsibilities.

Conservative interest groups have claimed that children's rights would be fundamentally incompatible with parental rights. In reaction to this stance, we have argued that such a binary model does not give due space to the state and its role in organising, monitoring and supporting the family. Moreover, such a dichotomous view on parental rights versus children's rights is contrary to the nuanced positions contained in the CRC, which conceptualises parents as aiding the child's exercise of his or her rights until the latter is able to act autonomously. By advancing a family framework which is based at the same time on the child's individual autonomy and on mutual accountability, the CRC calls for consideration of a dynamic relationship between the child, parents and the state towards achieving outcomes which are mutually acceptable to all the parties involved. We think that other human rights instruments can take inspiration from the ways in which CRC provisions and scholarly literature have developed 'parental responsibilities' as including limited and functional rights aimed at the fulfilment of the rights of the child. In this regard, the current elaboration of an international framework for the promotion and protection of the rights of older people may open new avenues for reconsidering the relevance of including third parties in human rights treaties.

Notes

1 D Archard, *Children: Rights and Childhood* (2nd edn, Routledge 2004) 152.

2 D Volonakis, 'Advocating for human rights treaties in the USA. A comparison between CRC and CRPD advocacy' (2016) 11(6) *Discourse, Journal of Childhood and Adolescence Research* 193.

3 See G Kamchedzera, 'Article 5: the child's right to appropriate direction and guidance' in A Alen, J Vande Lanotte, E Verhellen, F Ang, E Berghmans, M

Verheyde and B Abramson (eds), *A Commentary on the United Nations Convention on the Rights of the Child* (Brill Nijhoff 2012) 1–5.

4 M Freeman, 'Article 3: the best interests of the child' in A Alen, J Vande Lanotte, E Verhellen, F Ang, E Berghmans, M Verheyde (eds), *A Commentary on the United Nations Convention on the Rights of the Child* (Brill Nijhoff 2012) 66–67.

5 ibid 67–69.

6 ibid 69.

7 ibid 69–71.

8 Article 3(3) reads as follows: '3. States Parties shall ensure that the institutions, services and facilities responsible for the care or protection of children shall conform with the standards established by competent authorities, particularly in the areas of safety, health, in the number and suitability of their staff, as well as competent supervision'.

9 See Freeman (n 4) 71–72; S Detrick, *A Commentary on the United Nations Convention on the Rights of the Child* (Martinus Nijhoff Publishers 1999) 295.

10 See Freeman (n 4) 72.

11 S Brennan, R Noggle, 'The moral status of children: children's rights, parents' rights, and family justice' (1997) 23 *Social Theory and Practice* 14.

12 See Archard, (n1)149. For further discussion, even if leading to different conclusions, see H Brighouse, S Swift, 'Parents' rights and the value of the family' (2006) 117(1) *Ethics* 82.

13 D Reynaert, M Bouverne-de-Bie and S Vandevelde, 'The review of children's rights literature since the adoption of the Unites Nations Convention on the Rights of the Child' (2009) 16 *Childhood* 525.

14 See for instance *Valsamis v Greece* Application no 21787/93 (ECtHR, 18 December 1996) and *Efstratiou v Greece* Application no 24095/94 (ECtHR, 18 December 1996).

15 *Darby v Sweden* Application no 11581/85 (ECtHR, 23 October 1990).

16 *Alexandridis v Greece* Application no 19516/06 (ECtHR, 21 February 2008); *Grzelak v Poland* Application no 7710/02 (ECtHR, 15 June 2010).

17 J Duffar, 'La liberté religieuse dans les textes internationaux' (1994) *Revue de Droit Public* 939.

18 *Kokkinakis v Greece* Application no 14307 (ECtHR, 25 May 1993).

19 See *Leyla Şahin v Turkey*, Application no 44774/98 (ECtHR, 10 November 2005); *Dogru v France* Application no 27058/05 (ECtHR, 4 December 2008); *Kervanci v France* Application no 31645/04 (ECtHR, 4 December 2008). See in the literature E Brems, 'Above children's heads: the headscarf controversy in European schools from the perspective of children's rights' (2006) 14(2) *International Journal of Children's Rights* 119; K Hanson, 'A la découverte des droits de l'enfant dans le débat sur des symboles religieux ostentatoires' (2000) 6(1) *Bulletin suisse des droits de l'enfant* 12.

20 See the relevant case law of the ECtHR: *Kjeldsen, Busk Madsen and Pedersen v Denmark* Application nos 5095/71, 5920/72 and 5926/72 (ECtHR, 7 December 1976); *Valsalmis v Greece* Application no 21787/93 (ECtHR, 18 December 1996); *Folgerø and Others v Norway* Application no 15472/02 (ECtHR, 29 June 2007); *Hasan and Eylem Zengin v Turkey* Application no 1448/04 (ECtHR, 9 October 2007); *Lautsi and Others v Italy* Application no 30814/06 (ECtHR, 18 March 2011).

21 *Lautsi and Others v Italy* Application no 30814/06 (ECtHR, 18 March 2011).

22 *X v Iceland* Application no 2525/67 (ECtHR, 6 February 1967) ; R Goy, 'La garantie européenne de la liberté de religion: l'article 9 de la Convention de Rome' (1991) *Revue de droit public* 31.

23 A Scolnicov, 'The child's right to religious freedom and formation of identity' (2007) 15 *International Journal of Children's Rights* 251, 257.
24 ibid 262.
25 E Brems, 'Article 14: the right to freedom of thought, conscience and religion' in A Alen, J Vande Lanotte, E Verhellen, F Ang, E Berghmans, M Verheyde (eds) *A Commentary on the United Nations Convention on the Rights of the Child* (Brill Nijhoff 2006) 7.
26 ibid 25.
27 See Reynaert, Bouverne-de-Bie and Vandevelde (n 13) 518.
28 ibid 524.
29 S Kilbourne, 'US failure to ratify the U.N. Convention on the Rights of the Child: playing politics with children's rights' (2006) 6 *Transnational & Contemporary Problems* 437; D Smolin, 'Overcoming religious objections to the Convention on the Rights of the Child' (2006) 20 *Emory International Law Review* 81.
30 The parental rights movement, a social movement which came into existence in the 1990s, continues to advocate in favour of the legal recognition of parental rights. According to Kilbourne (n 29) and Smolin (n 29), multiple identities are present among those who support the movement, and are most often either politically conservative and/or religiously conservative (the one not necessarily entailing the other).
31 L Rutkow, J T Lozman, 'Suffer the children? A call for the United States ratification of the United Nations Convention on the Rights of the Child' (2006) 19 *Harvard Human Rights Journal* 159.
32 F B McCarthy, 'Confused constitutional status and meaning of parental rights' (1988) 22 *Georgia Law Review* 975.
33 ibid 962.
34 ibid 977.
35 J G Dwyert, 'Parents' religion and children's welfare: debunking the doctrine of parents' rights' (1994) 82(6) *California Law Review* 1371, 1450.
36 ibid 1372.
37 McCarthy (n 32) 979.
38 ibid 975.
39 ibid.
40 L L Lane, 'The parental rights movement' (2008) 69 *University of Colorado Law Review* 825, 849.
41 T J Gunn, 'The religious right and the opposition to U.S. ratification of the Convention on the Rights of the Child' (2006) 20(1) *Emory International Law Review* 111.
42 ibid 122.
43 ibid 128.
44 See Reynaert, Bouverne-de-Bie and Vandevelde (n 13) 525.
45 G Van Bueren, *The International Law on the Rights of the Child* (Brill Nijhoff 1998) 68–72.
46 F Schoeman, 'Rights of children, rights of parents, and the moral basis of the family' (1980) 91 *Ethics* 6, 11, cited in Brennan, Noggle, 'The moral status of children' (n 11) 1, 14.
47 See Brennan and Noggle (n 11).
48 See Kamchedzera (n 3) 14.
49 ibid 24.
50 ibid.
51 Jonathan Law, Elizabeth A Martin *A Dictionary of Law* (7th edn, Oxford University Press 2014).
52 ibid.
53 See Archard (n 1) 149.

54 See Law and Martin (n 51).
55 ibid.
56 See Kamchedzera (n 3) 30.
57 See Law and Martin (n 51).
58 See Archard (n 1) 149.
59 United Nations General Assembly (UNGA), 'Right of the Child: Report of the Independent Expert [P S Pinheiro] for the United Nations Study on Violence Against Children' (2006) UN Doc A/61/299.
60 Article 5 – Equality and non-discrimination, Article 10 – Right to life, Article 12 – Equal recognition before the law, Article 17 – Protecting the integrity of the person, Article 22 – Respect for privacy, Article 23 – Respect for home and the family; Article 24 – Education, Article 25 – Health, Article 27 – Work and employment and Article 28 – Adequate standard of living and social protection.

Part II

Inspiration for children's rights from categorical human rights

5 Lessons for children's rights from women's rights?

Emancipation rights as a distinct category of human rights

Eva Brems

5.1 Women and children in international human rights law

Women and children are two categories of rights holders that are regularly discussed together or in relation to each other. This occurs in different configurations. One example is the concept of 'vulnerable groups' that merit priority or to which states should pay special attention in acting upon their human rights obligations. In that context, women and children often find themselves included in the same list, together with other groups such as minorities and indigenous peoples. For example, in its General Comment on the right to water, the United Nations Committee on Economic, Social and Cultural Rights (CESCR) states:

> Whereas the right to water applies to everyone, States parties should give special attention to those individuals and groups who have traditionally faced difficulties in exercising this right, including women, children, minority groups, indigenous peoples, refugees, asylum seekers, internally displaced persons, migrant workers, prisoners and detainees.[1]

In addition, the effort of mainstreaming women's rights as well as increasing attention to the implications of intersectionality, have put forward 'the girl child' as a special focus of attention, both from a women's rights perspective and from a children's rights perspective. This shared interest of women's rights defenders and children's rights defenders has led amongst others to the unique initiative of a joint General Recommendation of the Committee on the Elimination of Discrimination against Women (CEDAW Committee) and the Committee on the Rights of the Child (CRC Committee) on the topic of harmful cultural practices.[2]

Finally, it should be noted that in the context of children's rights, women play a role as mothers. This role (and that of fathers) is recognised in international human rights law, as the Convention on the Rights of the Child (CRC) includes both rights and obligations of parents and other carers of children.[3] In this context, the rights of mothers and children can concur, yet they can also be in conflict. The latter situation can occur in particular when a state has a duty under international human rights law to protect a child against her or his parent(s).[4]

However, none of the configurations sketched above is the focus of this chapter. In line with this volume's overall purpose, the chapter will explore what lessons might be drawn from the experience with the international protection mechanisms for women's human rights (especially CEDAW, which dates from 1979) that might benefit the international protection of children's rights, knowing that the latter has a decade less experience. In this context, the term 'women' in this chapter refers to adult women, unless mentioned otherwise. Moreover, this chapter is not specifically interested in women's parental role. The chapter will address the qualification of women and children as 'vulnerable' mostly as a background against which to focus on the degree to which this qualification is *not* applicable and on the extent to which it might hamper the protection of the human rights of women or children.

The focus will be on some of the characteristics of women's rights as human rights and some of the experiences with women's rights as human rights that may be relevant for children's human rights. These shared characteristics will be discussed as functions of women's rights and children's rights belonging to the same distinct category of human rights, which will be described as 'emancipation rights'. The following sections will first make the case for emancipation rights as a distinct category of human rights, of which women's rights are the most senior member, and to which children's rights also belong. It will highlight some of the characteristic challenges of realising emancipation rights. Next, and in order to deliver on the intent of identifying legal features of women's human rights protection that may be of interest for children's human rights protection, the focus will be on Article 5 CEDAW, a provision that is designed to tackle some of these challenges.

5.2 Emancipation rights: a distinct category of human rights

In human rights discourse, it is common to distinguish categories of human rights that share distinct characteristics, in particular the category of 'civil and political rights' and that of 'economic, social and cultural rights'. Recent scholarship has focused mostly on challenging or nuancing this categorisation, on the ground that it has contributed to unjustified constructions of unsurmountable differences between both categories.[5] Against this dominant tendency of scepticism vis-à-vis categorisation in human rights law, it is submitted that it would nevertheless be useful to distinguish a separate category of 'emancipation rights'. In line with the overall purpose of the present volume, which breathes a dynamic of human rights integration,[6] this categorisation is intended to emphasise similarities and common challenges among the members of the group, rather than emphasising difference as compared to some other group. The category of emancipation rights is not part of any binary set.

It is proposed to use the analytical category of emancipation rights to indicate those rights that are intended to correct a legacy of structural discrimination of specific groups and to provide to members of such groups equal opportunities and equal enjoyment of their human rights. This is the case for most instances in which international human rights law has developed special texts or mechanisms for the protection of the human rights of a specific target group. But the category need not be limited to these instances, as the identification and recognition of groups that merit such treatment tends to proceed through different steps and may not necessarily always result in separate treaties.[7]

Women's rights are the standard bearer of the category of emancipation rights. But children's rights are also emancipation rights, and so are the rights of ethnic and cultural minorities, the rights of indigenous peoples, the rights of persons with disabilities, the rights of the elderly and LGBTI rights. One crucial feature that these and other emancipation rights have in common is that the sustainable realisation of these rights does not only (or even predominantly) take place in the vertical relations between individuals and the state, but that they present some of their main challenges in the horizontal relations among individuals in society. This implies that the realisation of emancipation rights requires cultural change, which is focused in particular on the way in which societies perceive members of that group and the way in which societies frame issues affecting them. For example, the realisation of LGBTI rights mandates new definitions of central social concepts such as 'family', 'couple' and 'marriage'. The realisation of transgender rights requires a dynamic conception of sex/gender.[8]

The Convention on the Rights of Persons with Disabilities (CRPD) proposes a new perception of a disability as something that is not a characteristic of a person, but that instead 'results from the interaction between persons with impairments and attitudinal and environmental barriers'.[9] Realising emancipation rights thus requires individuals to change not only their actions and expressions, but even their way of thinking. It is submitted that the nature and magnitude of this challenge justifies separate analysis and discussion of this category. The present chapter will examine how this challenge is being addressed in the CEDAW context, and will explore what this might mean for children's human rights. In its comparison of women's rights and children's rights *qua* emancipation rights, this chapter makes two claims.

Firstly, it is claimed that, to a certain extent, the challenges of 'seeing differently' an identified category of individuals, are similar for the categories of women and children. For both categories, a central part of this endeavour is a critical unpacking of protection dynamics. The emancipatory drive in emancipation rights requires that, for children's rights as well as for women's rights, the problematic nature of some protection dynamics is recognised, and that it is in part replaced by an emphasis on autonomy.

Secondly, it is claimed that, within the context of this similarity, women's rights and children's rights are nevertheless different, and that an important distinction lies in what can be considered to be the optimal balance between protection rights and autonomy rights, which is not the same for both groups.

5.3 Women's rights and children's rights as emancipation rights

The coupling of 'women and children' in a context that emphasises an increased need for protection as compared to adult men was of course not invented by human rights law. Rather, international law in this respect reflects widespread perceptions that associate both women and children with vulnerability and weakness. This can occasionally be extensive, such as in the UN Declaration on the Protection of Women and Children in Emergency and Armed Conflict (1974),[10] which generally depicts both women and children as passive victims of armed conflict, naming them 'defenceless' (Article 2) and 'the most vulnerable members of the population' (Article 1).

Yet neither in its intent nor in its results should this emphasis on the vulnerability of women and children be considered as negative per se. It is beyond question that protection against human rights violations is a good thing, and that more protection is generally better than less protection. Yet, in human rights as in the broader societal context, the movement for women's emancipation has come to see an emphasis on vulnerability and protection as an expression of paternalism that reinforces gendered stereotypes and that contributes to denying women equal opportunities. One might say that part of women's struggle for emancipation has been about resisting being treated 'like children'. The equation of women and children, based on vulnerability as their perceived dominant trait, could historically be seen in all sorts of societal contexts. In international law, prominent examples can be found in international labour law. The regulation of night work is a case in point.

In 1919, the International Labour Organization (ILO) concluded two conventions on night work. Convention No 4[11] (based on a pre-ILO Convention of 1906) forbids employing women for night work. Convention No 6[12] forbids employing young persons under the age of 18 for night work, making however some exceptions for young people from the age of 16. Hence, at that time, protective bans for women were stronger than those for 16 and 17-year-old children. The revised night work conventions No 41 of 1934[13] and No 89 of 1948[14] were still about banning women from night work.[15] From the 1970s onwards, the ban on night work for women became the focus of feminist action resisting this paternalist protection and seeing the ban as an unjustified limit on women's autonomy and on women's opportunities. In Europe in the early 1990s, the European Commission and the European Court of Justice[16] stated that the ban violated European norms of gender equality, which prevailed over ILO Treaties.[17] Henceforth, the dominant legal and political position is that women are free to choose night work, just like men. The move has thus been away from a paradigm of protection that went so far as to force protection upon women by banning them from certain choices, and toward autonomy. The only remaining pocket of gender-specific protection in the context of night work concerns maternity protection.[18]

Where children are concerned, the movement has been in the opposite direction, extending from bans on specific types of work, such as night work, to a general ban on child labour (albeit with some exceptions), in the ILO Minimum Age Convention No 138 (1973).[19]

In more general terms, it can be said that protective measures specifically targeting women have been delegitimised in many contexts, including measures that do not go as far as banning women from certain choices.[20] In human rights law in particular, the struggle for realising women's rights as human rights hardly relies on discourses of vulnerability. The emphasis is much more on empowerment, autonomy, fairness and equal treatment. This is prominent even in contexts in which an empirical case for special vulnerability can be made, such as the human rights approach to gender-based violence. A clear illustration is the CEDAW Committee's General Recommendation No 19 on Violence against Women (1992),[21] which frames violence as an infringement on women's autonomy and equality, starting with its first paragraph: 'Gender-based violence is a form of discrimination that seriously inhibits women's ability to enjoy rights and freedoms on a basis of equality with men'.

Protective measures for children have not been similarly delegitimised, and the success of children's rights instruments and institutions is largely explained by the generalised perception of children as vulnerable and the widespread support for maximum protection of children. Yet arguably the single most distinctive characteristic of children's rights as human rights is their emphasis on children's capacity for autonomy and on participation rights that build on this capacity. Verhellen argues that the CRC countered the long-standing paternalistic perception of children as incomplete and dependent human beings; yet, rather than making it disappear entirely, proclaimed 'the simultaneous importance of both dependency and autonomy for children'.[22] In that perspective, 'the CRC demonstrates that there has been a growing consensus about the fact that children should not only be considered as passive objects of protection, but should also be regarded as active bearers of rights'.[23]

While protectionism prevails in the CRC, its most innovative feature – the feature that justifies its qualification as an instrument of emancipation rights – lies in its provisions on children's (gradual) autonomy. The emancipatory challenge of children's rights lies in making people see *not only* children's inherent vulnerability, but *also* their inherent capacity for autonomy, and the gradual development of that capacity. In that sense, children's rights as emancipation rights are both similar to and different from women's rights as emancipation rights.

The shared challenge lies in steering the gaze of the international community away from an exclusive focus on the group's protection needs, and making visible its autonomy needs. It is about the realisation that the recognition of specific protection needs should not go at the expense of autonomy needs. It has come to be recognised that women are best protected against human rights violations not by denying them choices, but by empowering them to make well-informed choices for themselves.[24] The women's movement has been extremely successful in changing ways of thinking about women. Adopting a human rights perspective to children similarly implies focusing not only on the child's capacities that are not yet there (and which make the child vulnerable), but also on those capacities that are already there, and to do justice to the child's capacities. In that perspective, the CRC provides for duties on parents as well as on the state to facilitate and support children's exercise of their autonomy rights. This is a very different paradigm from one in which parents and public authorities make decisions about children without involving them. In the CRC, protection goes hand in hand with autonomy. In the words of Van Bueren, 'children are protected not only by giving the state, i.e. adults, greater powers of intervention, but also by giving children power to consent to and challenge decisions which affect their lives'.[25]

Similar challenges apply to other groups that claim emancipation rights. For example, much of the focus of the CRPD is on facilitating the participation of persons with disabilities in all spheres of life. Yet arguably the realisation of a paradigm shift is particularly difficult where children are concerned. An indicator in that sense might be the fact that other groups looking for emancipation will commonly use children as a reference point in the negative sense: 'don't treat us like children' say persons with disabilities, elderly people and indigenous peoples,[26] amongst others.

At the same time, there is a limit to the parallel between women's rights and children's rights as emancipation rights. Children aged 0 to 17 cannot all handle the same degrees of autonomy. As a result, arguably the majority of children have a capacity for autonomy that is significantly lower than that of adults. Taking children's capacity for autonomy seriously also means recognising the limits of that capacity. Too much autonomy can be harmful for children. A state can even be found to violate children's rights for granting children too much autonomy, and hence not offering sufficient support for and control over children's exercise of their human rights.[27]

The same cannot be said about women and women's rights. Both in the current state of international human rights law and in the views of most activists for women's rights and/or children's rights, the optimal balance between protection and autonomy in the realisation of the human rights of women shows a rather different picture than for the human rights of children. In the area of women's rights, protective needs remain very real, but, with the notable exception of pregnancy and maternity protection, have been reframed in such a way that they are strongly intertwined with discourses of autonomy and non-discrimination/equality, which dominate the field of women's rights. Conversely, the field of children's rights remains dominated by a discourse of vulnerability and protection. Within this context, concerns of autonomy and participation are, however, very prominently promoted. A specific feature of children's rights is the principle of progressive autonomy as a function of the 'evolving capacities of the child' (Article 5 CRC): as the child grows older, the balance between protection needs and autonomy needs shifts, with the former decreasing and the latter increasing.

What does this mean for the purpose of the chapter, i.e. finding out how children's rights can draw on the experience of women's rights to realise the cultural change that emancipation rights require? Both for women's rights and for children's rights, the historical starting point is a model based on protection, and the emancipation challenge is to claim space for an autonomy paradigm that is in part complementary to, and in part in competition with, the protective paradigm. The reason that the special focus of emancipation rights is on children's autonomy rights, and not on their protection rights, is not that the former are somehow considered more important than the latter. They are not. Nor is it that the protection rights are generally well protected, while autonomy rights are not. This is not the case, as huge challenges remain for children's protection as well. The reason is that the need for protective measures for children is generally recognised, whereas the need to recognise and facilitate children's autonomy is not. Hence, in the sphere of protection rights, the obstacles for rights realisation are situated in the gap between theory and practice. For autonomy rights, these obstacles exist as well, yet in addition there is a preliminary obstacle, namely the need to make room in people's minds for a perception of children as (partially) autonomous actors. That is exactly what women's rights activists were historically confronted with. Women's rights discourse has been so successful in eliminating this preliminary obstacle that, at least in Western societies, views of women as somehow less capable of autonomously exercising rights have largely disappeared from collective memory. The next section will focus on the specific provision of CEDAW that addresses this challenge of cultural change to make room for autonomy, i.e. Article 5 CEDAW.

5.4 A crucial emancipation tool: Article 5 CEDAW

Article 5(a) CEDAW explicitly recognises the fact that emancipation requires seeing women differently and changing long-held cultural perceptions and expectations. It reads:

> States Parties shall take all appropriate measures:
>
> (a) To modify the social and cultural patterns of conduct of men and women, with a view to achieving the elimination of prejudices and customary and all other practices which are based on the idea of the inferiority or the superiority of either of the sexes or on stereotyped roles for men and women; . . .

In addition, Article 5(b) addresses 'the most universal traditionalist cultural norm that disadvantages women, which is the stereotypical assignment of sole or major responsibility for child care to women'.[28] It requires states parties to take all appropriate measures to ensure that family education includes a proper understanding of maternity as a social function and the recognition of the common responsibility of men and women in the upbringing and development of their children.

The state's obligation to bring about cultural change for gender equality is further strengthened by Article 2(f) CEDAW, imposing an obligation to 'modify or abolish . . . customs and practices' that discriminate against women.

A number of crucial insights can be drawn from CEDAW's approach to anti-emancipatory practices, behaviour and perceptions.

At the basis, there is the fundamental insight that the emancipatory dimension of women's rights requires changes in the horizontal relations among individuals and in society at large. Emancipation rights cannot be realised solely in the vertical relationship between an individual and the state.

The logical, but radical consequence drawn from that is that the state has to intervene to realise cultural change. The fact that emancipation rights are a matter of horizontal relations does not allow state authorities to consider them to be outside their realm. Human rights law mandates the inclusion of emancipatory change within the state's realm. State authorities cannot use cultural perceptions or cultural patterns of behaviour as an excuse for slow progress on emancipation rights. Instead, they should take on the responsibility of addressing these cultural factors.

Commentators have argued that Article 5(a) CEDAW can be viewed both as a separate norm, and as a general principle or guideline that can be applied in interpreting other CEDAW provisions.[29] For some rights, this is supported by the text of the Convention[30] or by a General Recommendation of the CEDAW Committee.[31] Cook and Cusack argue that for CEDAW provisions for which this is not the case, 'the State Party is still obligated to examine how wrongful gender stereotypes inhibit the exercise of that right'.[32]

Moreover, this provision can be made concrete and enforceable along the same lines as other CEDAW provisions. This implies that state responsibility under Article 5(a) CEDAW can be analysed in terms of the classical tripartite model that distinguishes duties to respect, protect and fulfil human rights.[33] The duty to respect is the duty of public authorities to refrain from expressing or acting upon gender stereotypes or prejudice. The duty to protect is the duty to take necessary and appropriate measures to address prejudicial or stereotyping behaviour and perceptions by non-state actors. The duty to fulfil is the duty to adopt positive measures to clear away obstacles to the enjoyment of women's rights that result from cultural practices, prejudice or bias.

Likewise, the means through which states are required to realise their obligations under Article 5 CEDAW are similar to those under other CEDAW provisions. That is to say, they require changes within the law, as well as legal and societal structures and institutions that can tackle the persistence of gender stereotypes at a structural level.[34] In addition, states are expected to tackle gender bias through their role in education, and through awareness-raising campaigns.[35]

Through its practice, the CEDAW Committee has shown that it can monitor states' obligations under Article 5 CEDAW in the same manner as obligations under other CEDAW provisions, both through concluding observations on state reports, and through decisions in the individual communications procedure. In the latter context, the CEDAW Committee has most notably found violations of Article 5(a) and Article 2(f) on account of judicial rulings upholding wrongful gender stereotypes in cases of rape,[36] domestic violence[37] and dismissal,[38] and on account of decisions of medical authorities in the sphere of reproductive health,[39] as well as the behaviour of male prison staff against female detainees.[40] This shows that 'the duty to eliminate gender stereotypes corresponds with an individual right not to be subjected to gender stereotypes'.[41] It offers perspectives for enforcing this right also at the domestic level.

Another important insight from Article 5 CEDAW is that women's rights are to some extent group rights. This is so in the sense that the need to change cultural practices and ideas about women is not so much related to individual women as to women as a group, or at least a subcategory of that group (e.g. working women or mothers). To the extent that the emancipatory challenge concerns (perceptions of) group characteristics and practices vis-à-vis individuals on account of their group belonging, emancipation rights are group rights. That does not mean that these rights are exercised by groups rather than individuals but rather that, in such cases, the human rights violation affects an entire category of persons.

An additional lesson to take away is that women's emancipation requires changes in the gendered perceptions and in the patterns of conduct of both women and men. It is vital for efforts in education and awareness raising to target men as well as women, even though the objective of sensibilisation is different for each group: for men this is about giving up some privileges and learning to share dominance; for women it is about empowerment, about exercising autonomy and claiming one's share.

A final point that needs to be made concerns the pervasiveness of cultural perceptions and practices that are the target of Article 5 CEDAW. Cultural practices that stand in the way of women's emancipation are not only the so-called 'harmful cultural practices', such as female genital cutting, forced marriage or polygyny. Gendered practices that stand in the way of women's equal rights reach much further and are much more widespread than that. They include 'benevolent' gender stereotypes such as those that consider that women naturally excel at caring. They also include role patterns and opinions on maleness and femaleness that are widely shared within societies, by women as well as men.[42]

In fact, their widespread character and general interiorisation are among the chief reasons why emancipation proves to be so difficult, and hence why the obligations under Article 5 CEDAW are needed. This point has two implications. Firstly, when discussing cultural challenges for emancipation, there is a need to resist the tendency to downplay outstanding emancipation challenges among the majority population at home, and to focus preponderantly on 'other women': women in other parts of the world, or minority women in the Global North. This should not be misunderstood as minimising the problems that those 'other women' experience, nor the need to address them. However, vigilance is required to avoid the trap of letting a focus on types of practices that are not found among the majority population at home increase the invisibility of the problematic practices that do exist there.

Secondly, one of the objectives of the realisation of emancipation rights is to make visible types of harm that people did not previously see. Emancipation involves de-normalising practices that were generally accepted by men as well as by women who had internalised cultural norms. The women's rights movement has a long track record in this field. One can think for example of the denormalisation of such practices as sexual harassment in the workplace or on the street[43] and the use of sexist stereotypes in advertisements and in the media,[44] as well as the challenging of glass ceilings and horizontal segregation at work.[45]

5.5 Lessons for children's rights

It is submitted that most of the arguments presented above are applicable *mutatis mutandis* to emancipation rights generally. This final section will examine the extent to which they can be applied to children's rights.

It has been argued above that the realisation of children's autonomy rights requires a change of mindset about the category of 'children'. In that respect, children's emancipation rights are also group rights. Again in parallel with women's emancipation rights, children's emancipation rights aim at changing the attitudes of children as well as adults: they want to empower children to claim and use their autonomy, as well as to change behaviour in adults, to make them create room for children's exercise of autonomy.

The fundamental insight that emancipation rights have realised to an important degree in private relations is self-evident in the context of children's rights, as far as they concern the family setting. Indeed, the CRC includes parents and other carers among the rights holders and duty bearers of children's rights.[46] In the CRC context, this is by no means limited to children's autonomy rights. Nevertheless, the CRC Committee does not as a rule name the specific challenge of changing cultural perceptions of children and cultural practices that do not provide sufficient room for children's autonomy. As a result, neither does it discuss how to prepare the ground for such cultural change.

This reflects broader tendencies in the discourse about children and their rights. For example, it is not common to use the language of stereotyping in this context. The CRC Committee has discussed in detail the obligations of states parties to the CRC to realise children's participation rights under Article 12 CRC without discussing this as a cultural challenge, except for the final paragraphs, where it states that '(a)chieving meaningful opportunities for the implementation of Article 12 will necessitate dismantling the legal, political, economic, social and *cultural* barriers that currently impede children's opportunity to be heard and their access to participation in all matters affecting them,'[47] before emphasising the need to build 'a culture of respect for children and their views'.[48]

In practice however, and as aptly illustrated in the same context, the CRC Committee's tacit requirement of cultural change entails a combination of governmental obligations that is comparable to the CEDAW Committee's explicit requirement of cultural change. For example, for the realisation of children's participation rights within the family, the CRC Committee states that authorities should adopt legislation and policy to encourage parents to listen to children and give due weight to their views in matters that concern them.[49] In addition, states should 'support the development of parenting styles respecting the child's right to be heard', and 'promote parent education programmes, which build on existing positive behaviours and attitudes and disseminate information on the rights of children and parents enshrined in the Convention'.[50] The Committee concludes by stating that: '(t)he media should play a strong role in communicating to parents that their children's participation is of high value for the children themselves, their families and society'.[51]

The CRC Committee hence appears to recognise that the participation rights in the CRC require a different way of looking at children compared to what is common in most societies. Nevertheless, the CRC does not include a provision that is intended to outline the state's role in facilitating this change. The only exception is Article 24(3), which states that: 'States Parties shall take all effective and appropriate measures with a view to abolishing traditional practices prejudicial to the health of children'.

This provision does, however, present several limitations. First, it targets only cultural practices, excluding cultural perceptions. Moreover, it is limited to practices that are harmful from a health perspective. Finally, the provision envisages only the top-down solution of state abolition. Hence, this provision is not concerned with the recognition of children's autonomy, but rather with physical harm. What is more, this provision has typically been interpreted as dealing with 'harmful cultural practices' in the Global South.[52] It is not usually mobilised with respect to widespread cultural practices in the Global North that are harmful to children's health, such as for example smoking in the presence of children. With reference to the argument that was made above about women's rights, it seems that the CRC risks encouraging a bias in the cultural dimension of children's rights, which should be avoided.

As has been argued with respect to women's rights, the cultural challenge of the realisation of children's rights includes harmful cultural practices, but extends much beyond those to encompass also widespread and normalised behaviour in the Global North, such as taking decisions about children's lives without consulting them. As is the case with women's rights, children's rights aim to denormalise such practices. To some extent, this applies also to protection rights. One can think in particular of the example of corporal punishment of children at school and in the family.

The strong similarities between children's rights and women's rights that relate to their shared characteristics as emancipation rights plead in favour of the integration in the CRC or in its interpretation of a rule resembling Article 5(a) CEDAW. This conclusion is strengthened by the finding that recent human rights texts in fields that include a strong emancipation load have also opted for the inclusion of a specific provision on the state's obligation to work for cultural change. In the field of women's rights this is the case for the Council of Europe Convention on preventing and combating violence against women and domestic violence (Istanbul Convention 2011), which echoes Article 5(a) CEDAW in its Article 12(1):

> Parties shall take the necessary measures to promote changes in the social and cultural patterns of behaviour of women and men with a view to

> eradicating prejudices, customs, traditions and all other practices which are based on the idea of the inferiority of women or on stereotyped roles for women and men.

In addition, the UN Convention on the Rights of Persons with Disabilities has embedded similar language in a provision that additionally outlines the measures states parties are required to take to facilitate cultural change for emancipation rights: public awareness campaigns, education policy, media policy and training programmes.[53]

It was noted above that Article 5(a) CEDAW acts simultaneously as an autonomous right and as an interpretative principle for the entire Convention. That is a concept that is very familiar in the CRC context, where the CRC Committee has given a similar double role to several provisions that have been elevated to the level of guiding principles underlying the interpretation of the entire CRC.[54] It is submitted that a state obligation to modify cultural patterns in society that stand in the way of children's exercise of their rights could act both as a self-standing obligation and as a general principle guiding the interpretation of other CRC provisions, whenever appropriate. It is submitted, moreover, that the CRC Committee might elect to interpret the first paragraph of Article 4 CRC[55] in such a manner as to include this obligation.

5.6 Conclusion

Looking for best practice under CEDAW that might usefully be repeated under the CRC, this chapter thus proposes the interpretative integration in the CRC of state obligations to promote cultural change where this is needed to enable children to exercise their human rights fully. The argument is based on the similarity of some of the challenges for the realisation of women's human rights and children's human rights respectively, more specifically the challenges of defying paternalistic conceptions that look at women/children through a single lens of protectionism and of making room for another perspective that is based on autonomy. The broader argument made in this chapter is that it is relevant to distinguish within international human rights law a category of 'emancipation rights' to which both women's rights and children's rights belong.

Notes

This research has been funded by the Interuniversity Attraction Poles Programme initiated by the Belgian Science Policy Office, more specifically the IAP 'The global challenge of human rights integration: towards a users' perspective' www.hrintegration.be (last accessed 8 December 2016).

1 Committee on Economic, Social and Cultural Rights, 'General Comment No 15: The Right to Water' E/C.12/2002/11, para 16. The paragraph continues with an enumeration of the specific challenges for each of these groups concerning the realisation of the human right to water.

2 CEDAW and CRC, 'Joint general recommendation No 31 of the Committee on the Elimination of Discrimination against Women/general comment No 18 of

the Committee on the Rights of the Child on harmful practices' (2014) UN Doc CEDAW/C/GC/31 – CRC/C/GC/18.

3 See CRC arts 3, 5, 7, 9, 10, 14, 18, 24, 27.

4 Cf CRC arts 9 and 19 on protection of the child against violence, abuse and neglect.

5 See amongst others F Coomans, 'The International Covenant on Economic, Social and Cultural Rights: from stepchild to full member of the human rights family' in F Gomez Isa, K de Feyter (eds), *International Human Rights Law in a Global Context* (Humanitarian Net 2009) 293 ff.

6 See E Brems, 'Should pluriform human rights become one? Exploring the benefits of human rights integration' (2014) 4 *European Journal of Human Rights* 447–70.

7 LGBTI rights are an example of this; there is one soft law instrument for this category (the 2006 Yogyakarta Principles on the Application of International Human Rights Law in relation to Sexual Orientation and Gender Identity), yet there is currently no perspective of a separate treaty or monitoring mechanism.

8 See ch 10 by Ivana Isailovic in this volume.

9 UN Convention on the Rights of Persons with Disabilities (2006) preamble (e).

10 UN OHRCR, 'Declaration on the Protection of Women and Children in Emergency and Armed Conflict' GA Res 3318 (XXIX), 29 UN GAOR Supp (No 31) 146, UN Doc A/9631 (1974).

11 ILO, 'Convention concerning Employment of Women during the Night, known as Night Work (Women) Convention' (1919) (No 4).

12 ILO, 'Convention concerning the Night Work of Young Persons Employed in Industry, known as Night Work of Young Persons (Industry) Convention' (1919) (No 6).

13 ILO, 'Convention concerning Employment of Women during the Night (Revised), known as Night Work (Women) Convention (Revised)' (1934) (No 41).

14 ILO, 'Convention concerning Night Work of Women Employed in Industry, known as Night Work (Women) Convention (Revised)' (1948) (No 89).

15 In the same year, Convention No 45 bans women from underground work in mines: ILO, 'Convention concerning the Employment of Women on Underground Work in Mines of all Kinds, known as Underground Work (Women) Convention' (1935) (No 45).

16 Case *C-158/91 Levy* [1993] ECR I-4287 (ECJ). See P Humblet, 'De invoering en de afschaffing van het verbod op nachtarbeid door vrouwen. Vragen bij een (de)mobilisatie' in E Brems, L Stevens (eds), *Recht en Gender in België* (Die Keure 2011) 57 ff.

17 In 1990, the ILO adopted a Protocol to Convention No 89, providing for the possibility of sectoral exemptions from the night work ban, as well as Convention No 171 on night work in general, which treats women as a separate category only in the context of pregnancy and maternity protection: ILO, 'Night Work Convention' (1990) (No 171) art 7.

18 The revised European Social Charter of 1996 (art 8(4)) provides that states parties have to ensure the effective exercise of the right of maternity protection amongst others by regulating the employment in night work of pregnant women, women who have recently given birth and women nursing their infants.

19 Concerning night work for young persons, intermediate steps were the Night Work of Young Persons (Non-industrial Occupations) Convention 1946 (No 79) and the Night Work of Young Persons (Industry) Convention (Revised) 1948 (No 90).

20 For example, the above-cited UN Declaration on the Protection of Women and Children in Emergency and Armed Conflict (n 10).

21 Contained in document A/47/38.

22 E Verhellen, 'The Convention on the Rights of the Child: reflections from a historical, social policy and educational perspective' in W Vandenhole, E Desmet,

D Reynaert and S Lembrechts (eds), *Routledge International Handbook of Children's Rights Studies* (Routledge 2015) 50.

23 ibid.

24 It should be noted, however, that paternalism lingers in some contexts. One may think in particular of the treatment of minority women in Europe, who still find themselves confronted with prohibitions that are claimed to be in their best interest (e.g. bans on Islamic headscarves and face veils).

25 G Van Bueren, *The International Law on the Rights of the Child* (Martinus Nijhoff 1995) 21.

26 See ch 7 by E Desmet in this volume.

27 A (hypothetical) example of such a situation could be a euthanasia law that puts the decision entirely in the child's own hands.

28 F Raday, 'Culture, religion and CEDAW's article 5(a)' in H B Schöpp-Schilling, C Flinterman (eds), *The Circle of Empowerment* (The Feminist Press 2007) 74.

29 R Holtmaat, 'Article 5' in M A Freeman, C Chinkin and B Rudolf (eds), *The UN Convention on the Elimination of All Forms of Discrimination against Women: A Commentary* (Oxford University Press 2012) 143.

30 See art 10(c) on the obligation to eliminate 'any stereotyped concept of the roles of men and women at all levels and in all forms of education by encouraging coeducation and other types of education which will help to achieve this aim and, in particular, by the revision of textbooks and school programmes and the adaptation of teaching methods'.

31 See General Recommendation No 19 on Violence Against Women (n 21), paras 11 and 12: '11. Traditional attitudes by which women are regarded as subordinate to men or as having stereotyped roles perpetuate widespread practices involving violence or coercion, such as family violence and abuse, forced marriage, dowry deaths, acid attacks and female circumcision. Such prejudices and practices may justify gender-based violence as a form of protection or control of women. The effect of such violence on the physical and mental integrity of women is to deprive them the equal enjoyment, exercise and knowledge of human rights and fundamental freedoms. While this comment addresses mainly actual or threatened violence the underlying consequences of these forms of gender-based violence help to maintain women in subordinate roles and contribute to the low level of political participation and to their lower level of education, skills and work opportunities.

12. These attitudes also contribute to the propagation of pornography and the depiction and other commercial exploitation of women as sexual objects, rather than as individuals. This in turn contributes to gender-based violence.'

32 R J Cook, S Cusack, *Gender Stereotyping: Transnational Legal Perspectives* (University of Pennsylvania Press 2009) 75.

33 ibid 76–84.

34 CmEDAW, General recommendation No 25 on art 4 para 1 of the Convention on the Elimination of All Forms of Discrimination against Women, on temporary special measures, para 7.

35 For a detailed analysis of the state obligations that the CmEDAW has derived from art 5 (in particular in its concluding observations on state reports) see Holtmaat (n 29) 161 ff.

36 CmEDAW, *Karen Tayag Vertido v The Philippines*, Communication No 7/2008, CEDAW/C/46/D/18/2008 (2010).

37 CmEDAW, *VK v Bulgaria*, Communication No 20/2008, CEDAW/C/49/D/20/2008 (2011); CmEDAW, *Isatou Jallow v Bulgaria*, Communication No 32/2011, CEDAW/C/52/D/32/2011 (2012).

38 CmEDAW, *RKB v Turkey*, Communication No 28/2010, CEDAW/C/51/D/28/2010 (2012).

39 CmEDAW, *TPF v Peru*, Communication No 22/2009, CEDAW/C/50/D/22/2009 (2011).
40 CmEDAW, *Inga Abramova v Belarus*, Communication No 23/2009, CEDAW/C/49/D/23/2009 (2011).
41 A Śledzińska-Simon, 'Making progress in elimination of gender stereotypes in the context of gender-based violence: the role of the CEDAW Committee' (2013) 16(1) *Tijdschrift voor Genderstudies* 41, 45.
42 Examples include the opinion that women are better than men at childrearing, and at caring in general, and the opinion that men are more ambitious than women and more eager to exercise power. For an elaborate development of this argument see R Holtmaat, J Naber, *Women's Human Rights and Culture: From Deadlock to Dialogue* (Intersentia Publishers 2011).
43 See e.g. A Bernstein, 'Law, culture and harassment' (1994) *University of Pennsylvania Law Review* 1227 ff.
44 See for example the Gender Ads Project www.genderads.com (last accessed 7 March 2016).
45 See e.g, Feminist Majority Foundation, 'The glass ceiling: how women are blocked from getting to the top' www.feminist.org/research/business/ewb_glass.html (last accessed 7 March 2016).
46 See CRC arts 3(2), 5, 7(1), 10, 14(2), 18, 19(2), 24(2)(d) and (f), 27.
47 CmRC, General Comment No 12 (2009) 'The right of children to be heard' CRC/C/GC/12, para 135. Emphasis added.
48 ibid para 136.
49 ibid para 92.
50 ibid para 93.
51 ibid para 96.
52 The *travaux préparatoires* of the CRC reveal that the delegates of Canada, the United Kingdom and the United States had proposed a text that included explicit reference to female genital cutting (FGC). This was later omitted upon the insistence of especially the Senegalese delegate. See D Johnson, 'Cultural and regional pluralism in the drafting of the UN Convention on the Rights of the Child' in M Freeman, P E Veerman (eds), *The Ideologies of Children's Rights* (Brill 1992) 109–10. While the wording now avoids targeting Africa alone, it remains clear that practices such as FGC are the main target of this provision.
53 CRPD art 8 (entitled 'Awareness raising') reads:

1. States Parties undertake to adopt immediate, effective and appropriate measures:
    a. To raise awareness throughout society, including at the family level, regarding persons with disabilities, and to foster respect for the rights and dignity of persons with disabilities;
    b. To combat stereotypes, prejudices and harmful practices relating to persons with disabilities, including those based on sex and age, in all areas of life;
    c. To promote awareness of the capabilities and contributions of persons with disabilities.

Measures to this end include:

a. Initiating and maintaining effective public awareness campaigns designed:
    i. To nurture receptiveness to the rights of persons with disabilities;
    ii. To promote positive perceptions and greater social awareness towards persons with disabilities;
    iii. To promote recognition of the skills, merits and abilities of persons with disabilities, and of their contributions to the workplace and the labour market;

b. Fostering at all levels of the education system, including in all children from an early age, an attitude of respect for the rights of persons with disabilities;
c. Encouraging all organs of the media to portray persons with disabilities in a manner consistent with the purpose of the present Convention;
d. Promoting awareness-training programmes regarding persons with disabilities and the rights of persons with disabilities.

54 See Lundy and Byrne, ch 2 in this volume.
55 CRC art 4 reads: 'States Parties shall undertake all appropriate legislative, administrative, and other measures for the implementation of the rights recognized in the present Convention'.

6 Lessons for children's rights from disability rights?

Ralph Sandland

6.1 Introduction: is there anything new for children in the CRPD?

6.1.1 A pessimistic reading

This chapter asks whether international child law (ICL) can learn any lessons from recent developments in international disability law (IDL). At first glance, this might perhaps seem to be an odd question. After all, the main instrument of ICL, the United Nations Convention on the Rights of the Child (CRC), is now more than 25 years old whereas the IDL equivalent, the United Nations Convention on the Rights of Persons with Disabilities (CRPD), is a much younger document. It was adopted by the United Nations General Assembly on 13 December 2006, opened for signing in March 2007 and came into force, following its 20th ratification, on 3 May 2008.[1]

In a sense, the CRC is the adult and the CRPD is the child, and it might appear more likely that the CRPD could take lessons from the CRC than vice versa. One reason for holding this view is that ICL has in the 21st century moved decisively from questions relating to the articulation of rights in abstract textual form to their realisation in practice. A decade or so ago, Kofi Annan called, in the context of child soldiers, for an 'era of application',[2] and this is an apt description of the current state of international children's rights more generally. Children's rights were closely interwoven into the pursuit of the Millennium Development Goals (MDGs) set in 2000, and we have in recent times seen time-bound campaigns aimed at the abolition of the worst forms of child labour by 2016; education for all by 2015; the eradication of female genital mutilation (FGM) 'within a generation'; the eradication of child soldiers; and a whole host of sub-goals. All of these developments, grounded in ICL, were well underway whilst those interested in disability rights were still trying to agree the substantive content and scope of IDL and the text of the CRPD. As a consequence, for example, the MDGs do not make any mention of disability.

Moreover, when the finished text of the CRPD did emerge, it was presented, in UN discourse at least, as not particularly innovative. The CRPD was conceptualised as an 'implementation convention',[3] designed not to create new rights but, rather, to implement existing human rights law[4] in the field of disability: all prior existing international human rights treaties (bar the CRC: see below) having been silent on the particular difficulties faced by people with disabilities. According to the *United Nations Disabilities Handbook for Parliamentarians*, 'The Convention is a complement to existing international human rights treaties. It does not recognize any new human rights of persons with disabilities, but rather clarifies the obligations and legal duties of States to respect and ensure the equal enjoyment of all human rights by all persons with disabilities'.[5] This is reflected in Article 1, the first of two interpretative articles, which states that the purpose of the CRPD is to:

> Promote, protect and ensure the full and equal enjoyment of all human rights and fundamental freedoms by all persons with disability, and to promote respect for their dignity.

Article 1 is buttressed by the statement of the general obligations of state parties in Article 4, which is to bring about 'the full realisation of all human rights and fundamental freedoms for all persons with disabilities'. The CRPD was, in essence, presented at the time of its emergence as a corrective rather than an innovative measure, as far as the broader human rights landscape was concerned.

A quick perusal of the text of the CRPD appears to confirm a conservative view of its wider import. It contains what looks like a fairly standard list of political/civil and social, economic and cultural rights. Political and civil rights in the CRPD include:

- Article 10: Right to life
- Article 13: Access to justice
- Article 14: Liberty and security of the person
- Article 15: Freedom from torture or cruel, inhuman or degrading treatment or punishment
- Article 16: Freedom from exploitation, violence and abuse
- Article 18: Liberty and nationality
- Article 21: Freedom of expression
- Article 22: Privacy
- Article 23: Home and family
- Article 29: Participation in political and public life.

Social, economic and cultural rights in the CRPD include:

- Article 24: Education
- Article 25: Health
- Article 27: Work and employment
- Article 28: Standard of living and social protection
- Article 30: Participation in cultural life, recreation and sport.

Moreover, the CRPD apparently stays on traditional ground as far as the realisation of human rights is concerned. Article 4(2) uses the familiar form of words which provides that, although political and civil rights are 'immediately applicable according to international law', a state party must work towards the full realisation of economic, social and cultural rights 'to the maximum of its available resources'. There is little scope here, or so it would seem, for the CRPD to provide some 'added value' to the CRC.

The repudiation of any innovative aspect to the CRPD at the general level is repeated in the particular context of the rights of children. Although containing a number of specific provisions relating to children with disabilities, the CRPD has been presented as being concerned primarily with the rights of adults, and it has not attracted much attention from those in the academic community interested in the rights of children.[6] This may be because of an understanding that the approach taken in the CRPD is to channel the rights of children with disabilities back into the rights regime that applies to other children under the CRC. Paragraph (r) of the preamble to the CRPD recognises that children with disabilities 'should have full enjoyment of all human rights and fundamental freedoms on an equal basis with other children', and recalls 'obligations to that end undertaken by State Parties to the Convention on the Rights of the Child'. Article 7 of the CRPD, which is headed 'Children with disabilities', is as follows:

> 1. States Parties shall take all necessary measures to ensure the full enjoyment by children with disabilities of all human rights and fundamental freedoms on an equal basis with other children.
> 2. In all actions concerning children with disabilities, the best interests of the child shall be a primary consideration.
> 3. States Parties shall ensure that children with disabilities have the right to express their views freely on all matters affecting them, their views being given due weight in accordance with their age and maturity, on an equal basis with other children, and to be provided with disability and age-appropriate assistance to realize that right.

Articles 7(2) and 7(3) are of course familiar to international child lawyers as reworked versions of Articles 3(1) and 12 of the CRC. Read together with the reference to 'other children' in Article 7(1) and in the preamble, it seems clear that the intention behind the CRPD in relation to children is as it is more generally, to offer the same level of human rights protection to the target group as is enjoyed by other citizens, to remove discrimination and equalise the position of children with disabilities, but not to enhance the rights protection of children generally.

As preamble para (r) makes clear, the CRPD was drafted with the existing provision in respect of children with disabilities in the CRC in mind. Article 2 CRC prohibits discrimination against a child for a number of reasons, including disability. Article 23 provides a rare pre-2006 example of a stand-alone provision regarding disability rights and commits state parties to ensure the provision of 'special care' for children with disabilities in a wide variety of fields on account of their 'special needs':

> 1. States Parties recognize that a mentally or physically disabled child should enjoy a full and decent life, in conditions which ensure dignity, promote self-reliance and facilitate the child's active participation in the community.
> 2. States Parties recognize the right of the disabled child to special care and shall encourage and ensure the extension, subject to available resources, to the eligible child and those responsible for his or her care, of assistance for which application is made and which is appropriate to the child's condition and to the circumstances of the parents or others caring for the child.
> 3. Recognizing the special needs of a disabled child, assistance extended in accordance with paragraph 2 of the present article shall be provided free of charge, whenever possible, taking into account the financial resources of the parents or others caring for the child, and shall be designed to ensure that the disabled child has effective access to and receives education, training, health care services, rehabilitation services, preparation for employment and recreation opportunities in a manner conducive to the child's achieving the fullest possible social integration and individual development, including his or her cultural and spiritual development.
> 4. States Parties shall promote, in the spirit of international cooperation, the exchange of appropriate information in the field of preventive health care and of medical, psychological and functional treatment of disabled children, including dissemination of and access to information concerning methods of rehabilitation, education and vocational services, with the aim of enabling States Parties to improve their capabilities and skills and to widen their experience in these areas. In this regard, particular account shall be taken of the needs of developing countries.

Given the prior existence of Article 23 CRC, many delegates were of the opinion during the drafting of the CRPD that there should be no reference to children in the new convention,[7] and specific mention was ultimately made of children with disabilities in the CRPD only on the basis that to do so would not conflict with Article 23 CRC.[8] All of this seems to indicate that we should not expect too much in terms of innovation for children's rights from this quarter, particularly as Article 23(2) identifies the right of the disabled child to special care as a social right, and the extent of its realisation therefore subject to the availability of resources.

6.1.2 An optimistic reading

The above sketch of the CRPD bears scant resemblance to the way in which the convention has been analysed in some of the academic literature. For Amita

Dhanda, for example, the CRPD can be seen in terms of nothing less than 'constructing a new human rights lexicon'.[9] For Frédéric Mégret, in a similar vein:

> . . . the Disabilities Convention has an approach to the issue of rights which rather cavalierly (but very beneficially) ignores or reinvents some perennial dichotomies of the 'mainstream' of human rights. This is, I contend, because disability forces human rights lawyers to reexamine some core assumptions about what the needs of human beings are, and how these relate to society and the state. There is a lesson in this for human rights itself, of course, which can gain tremendously from the resulting, more holistic, concept of rights that emerges.[10]

Mégret argues that disability forces this re-examination because of the radical developments in its underpinning model which have occurred over the past few decades. It is not contentious to state that the field of disability has been transformed over that period at the level of its conceptual base. From a starting position that viewed disability in welfarist, charitable and medicalised terms, with state policy the collective expression of pity for the inherent disability of the sufferer, disability is now seen instead in terms of human rights and equality 'premised on a holistic "social model"'[11] of disability, which understands, as it is put at paragraph (e) of the preamble to the CRPD, that 'disability results from the interaction between persons with impairments and attitudinal and environmental barriers that hinder their full and effective participation in society on an equal basis with others'.

The CRPD itself is the best and most concrete expression of this change of thinking. The point is put more concisely by Thomas Hammarberg, at the time Council of Europe Commissioner for Human Rights, writing the keynote introduction to a special edition of the *European Human Rights Law Review* on the CRPD published in 2011: 'we have come to see the source of the problem: the society's attitude towards persons with disabilities'.[12] This may be putting the point too strongly. As Judith Butler for one has pointed out,[13] as embodied beings there is a material reality to our existence which is beyond social or psychic construction, just as the child exists beyond any social or cultural construction of childhood. Social attitudes are not the sole cause of individual disability. But social attitudes, norms and practices are certainly major and variable vectors of disability-related discrimination. They may not constitute the entirety of 'the problem', of what is problematic about disability, but they do constitute a very significant part of it, and it is the part which can, in theory at least, be most readily attended to and even prevented from arising by state action underpinned by a discourse of rights and equality.

How this links to the way in which rights are understood is that a 'holistic' approach entails the undermining of traditional divisions within orthodox human rights discourse. For example, the right to vote is for a person with a perambulatory disability of little use unless the polling station is accessible to persons with his or her particular disability. Hence, the exercise of a political right – the right to vote – depends intimately for its realisation in practice on the reality of a social right – the right of access. To generalise the point, it is that the realisation of political and civil rights is dependent on the prior or simultaneous realisation of social, economic and cultural rights. Work in this area chimes with the development of theories of vulnerability by writers such as Fineman,[14] who argues that it is the vulnerability that constitutes us all in our humanity which should underpin human rights, because to realise that we are all vulnerable to illness, disability or other misfortune is, again, to recognise the social underpinning of the civil and political rights of the individual.

It is on this basis that Mégret proceeds to argue that the CRPD reconfigures four major distinctions in international law, between types of rights (political and social, negative and positive, and so on); between actors (state as principal actor and other actors); in terms of the 'intensity' of rights (immediate realisation and progressive realisation); and modes of implementation (law and policy). Indeed, returning to Article 7(3) of the CRPD, it can be seen that the modification of that article by comparison to Article 12 CRC, which is achieved by adding its final stanza, requires that a child with disabilities is afforded not merely the right to free expression of his or her views and for those views to be given due weight, but also the right 'to be provided with disability and age-appropriate assistance to realize that right'. The assistance, as well as the substantive right to be heard, must be 'ensured' by the state (the whole of Article 7(3) being governed by the state's obligation to 'ensure' that its aims be achieved). The right to assistance – a social right – has been tagged on to the right to be heard – a civil right – and, seemingly, made subject to the same obligation to immediate realisation. This indivisibility of rights gives expression to a prior understanding of the indivisibility of needs and, ultimately, the indivisibility of the self.

In addition, Article 4(2) – although repeating the orthodox distinction between, on the one hand, civil and political rights, which are 'immediately applicable according to international law' and, on the other, economic, social and cultural rights, which are subject to progressive realisation as resources permit – is worded differently from other versions of the distinction, such as that found in Article 4 CRC. The distinction in the CRPD must be read according to Article 4(2) 'without prejudice to those obligations contained in the present Convention that are immediately applicable according to international law'. It might be that 'those obligations' refers only to civil and political rights, but if that was the case, civil and political rights could have been explicitly mentioned in Article 4(2) and contrasted with economic, social and cultural rights – which Article 4(2) *does* specifically refer to – and so arguably the best interpretation of its final stanza is that it countenances that some CRPD rights conventionally seen as economic, social or cultural could nonetheless be subject to immediate realisation; which lends support, for example, to the above reading of the significance of Article 7(3). At the very least, the final stanza of Article 4(2) introduces some ambiguity into interpretations of its potential scope and effect.

Other elements of the CRPD are equally intriguing and thought-provoking for international children's rights strategists. For instance, the CRPD exhibits an attitude towards a role for a test of capacity which lies somewhere between sceptical and downright hostile. It has been argued by some, including the UN High Commissioner for Human Rights,[15] that capacity as a mechanism for the removal of rights has been jettisoned altogether by the CRPD, which if correct means that only ICL retains faith in the concept of capacity as an acceptable mechanism to regulate the exercise of rights by the right holder, and suggests that it is at least worthwhile to investigate whether the same arguments that have been so influential in IDL should also be considered in ICL. It is important to understand that there is controversy and, as of yet, a lack of clarity about exactly what the CRPD represents in terms of innovation. Some academic voices are circumspect about the extent to which the CRPD can be seen as a radical departure from existing norms of both international human rights law and practice and disability law and practice,[16] but there is a broad consensus that, even if the CRPD does not as it stands exemplify the claims made for it by Mégret, then it certainly has the *potential* to do so.

There are further factors which suggest that the possible impact of the CRPD on ICL may be worth pondering. The CRPD follows earlier conventions such as the CRC by establishing a committee of experts, the Committee on the Rights of Persons with Disabilities (in Article 34), to which state parties must report, initially within two years of the convention coming into force in the jurisdiction in question, and thereafter every four years (Article 35) on progress in meeting the requirements of the convention. And as with the CRC, there is an Optional Protocol (OP) to the CRPD,[17] under the terms of which the Committee on the CRPD can hear complaints made by or on behalf of individuals. But unlike the CRC, the OP to the CRPD was opened for signature alongside the main convention in March 2007, whereas the OP to the CRC was only added recently, more than two decades after the parent convention.[18] That the CRC existed for many years without such an OP perhaps demonstrates that it is in some sense 'old-fashioned', the product of the thinking of an earlier, more cautious generation of human rights advocates. Certainly, in the years after 1989, public international law has at a general level begun to encompass the claims of individuals, rather than regulating only the relationship between states. Perhaps, then, the CRPD does contain what Dhanda has termed 'the wisdom of a straggler'.[19]

The final reason for optimism is that the arguments against specific mention of children in the CRPD, although forcefully made, were, as seen, ultimately unsuccessful. The day was won by the opposing view: that it was necessary to include specific provision for children with disabilities in the new convention because such children must often deal with issues that are not faced by other children or by adults with disabilities: issues such as the failure to register the birth of a disabled child or the particular discrimination and threats including violence that are faced by children with disabilities. So, although allegedly not conflicting with Article 23 CRC, the CRPD *is* intended to extend and increase the protection given to the rights of children with disabilities, over and above that provided by the CRC, to the extent necessary to equalise the position of all children. In fact, as will be discussed shortly, not only does the CRPD make specific provision for children with disabilities in Article 7, it also weaves the rights of children with disabilities right across the text of the convention.

The remainder of this chapter will pursue this optimistic reading of the potential for the improvement of the rights of children offered by the CRPD. I will first discuss the new rights for children with disabilities to be found in the CRPD, and then consider the extent to which the convention provides new rights for all, before moving on to discuss the ways in which it also extends and reconfigures existing rights. Finally, I shall give some space to the implications for the continued desirability of a role for 'capacity' and 'best interests' as mechanisms for making decisions in relation to children, in the light of the significant departures in this respect contained in the CRPD.

6.2 New rights for children with disabilities

The CRPD aims to implement a sophisticated strategy in pursuit of the goal of equal rights for children with disabilities. It adopts a different approach from that taken in the CRC. In the CRC, as seen above, one article is allocated specifically to the rights of children with disabilities, leaving those interpreting the convention to read those rights into its other articles for themselves, albeit with rather belated assistance from the Committee on the Rights of the Child.[20] The CRPD, by contrast, both highlights the specific situation of children with disabilities (in Article 7, discussed above) and weaves the particular rights and entitlements of children with disabilities by way of numerous further references into the final text of the CRPD more generally. This strategy is perhaps something that any revised version of the CRC could usefully adopt.[21] In terms of the second strand of this strategy, which can be called 'mainstreaming':

- one of the general principles of the CRPD, Article 3(h), requires 'Respect for the evolving capacities of children with disabilities and respect for the right of children with disabilities to preserve their identities'
- there is an obligation placed on state parties to consult persons with disabilities in developing national law and policy in conformity with the CRPD, which extends to children with disabilities, albeit through their representative organisations (Article 4(3))
- there is an obligation placed on state parties to foster at all levels of the education system, including in all children from an early age, an attitude of respect for the rights of persons with disabilities (Article 8(2)(b))
- there is an obligation placed on state parties to put in place effective legislation and policies, including child-focused legislation and policies, to ensure that instances of exploitation, violence and abuse against persons with disabilities are identified, investigated and, where appropriate, prosecuted (Article 16(5))
- there is an obligation imposed on state parties to take effective and appropriate steps to ensure, inter alia, that all persons with disabilities, including children, retain their fertility on an equal basis with others (Article 23(1)(c))

- there is an obligation placed on state parties to ensure that children with disabilities have equal rights with respect to family life. With a view to realising these rights, and to prevent concealment, abandonment, neglect and segregation of children with disabilities, state parties shall undertake to provide early and comprehensive information, services and support to children with disabilities and their families (Article 23(3))
- children with disabilities have a right not to be separated from their parents against their parents' will except by legal process which acts only in the best interests of the child, and 'In no case shall a child be separated from parents on the basis of a disability of either the child or one or both of the parents' (Article 23(4))
- there is an obligation placed on state parties, where the immediate family is unable to care for a child with disabilities, to undertake every effort to provide alternative care within the wider family, and failing that, within the community in a family setting (Article 23(5))
- children with disabilities have a right not to be excluded from the general education system and from free primary and secondary education on the basis of disability (Article 24(2)(a))
- there is an obligation placed on state parties to provide those health services needed by persons with disabilities specifically because of their disabilities, including early identification and intervention as appropriate, and services designed to minimise and prevent further disabilities, including among children and older persons (Article 25(b))
- there is an obligation placed on state parties to ensure that children with disabilities have equal access to play, recreation and sporting facilities (Article 30(5)(d)).

There is also specific mention of the rights of blind, deaf and deafblind children,[22] and of the rights of girl children with disabilities.[23]

There are two issues here. The first is the technical question of whether the concept of mainstreaming is better supported, as it is in ICL, by one dedicated article in the text of the convention supported by an explanatory General Comment, or by specific and systematic sequence of references on the face of the convention itself. It seems clear that the latter course, the one adopted with the CRPD, is preferable. The second issue concerns substance. The language relating to children in the main body of the CRPD, as with that used in Article 7, the dedicated article, is sometimes borrowed wholesale from the CRC. For example, Article 23(4) CRPD contains the right of the child 'not be separated from his or her parents against their will, except when competent authorities subject to judicial review determine, in accordance with applicable law and procedures, that such separation is necessary for the best interests of the child' found in Article 9 CRC. But there are clearly new rights for children with disabilities included in the above list.

Some of these are addressed as wrongs that have historically been suffered by children and families living with disability. One important example is the obligation placed on states to ensure that 'all persons with disabilities, including children, retain their fertility on an equal basis with others', found in Article 23(1)(c), which prohibits eugenic or quasi-eugenic practices incompatible with the right to procreate of persons with disabilities. Further examples include Article 23(4)'s stipulation, that 'in no case shall a child be separated from parents on the basis of a disability of either the child or one or both of the parents', and Article 23(5)'s requirement that states '[u]ndertake every effort to provide alternative care within the wider family, and failing that, within the community in a family setting' when it is necessary in the best interests of a child to remove him or her from the parental home.

It might be argued that Article 23(4), which seems to place an absolute embargo on factoring disability into best interests-based decision-making, actually goes considerably further than was needed to address the discriminatory practice of removing children with disabilities from their families and raising them instead in state institutions. There will, inevitably, be situations in which a contextualised, reasonable and sometimes morally imperative judgment will be made that, because of the presence of some physical or mental impairment of either parent and/or child, it is in the best interests of the child to be separated from his or her family, whether permanently or temporarily (and Article 23(4) contains no temporal reference). Such situations are by definition extreme in their facts and should be rare, but they will and do arise.

Here the CRPD seems to exhibit dogma which does not countenance (what will sometimes be) the realities of the situation. But concerns that this provision has been drafted too widely or too clumsily in no way detract from its importance or, indeed, necessity, as a mechanism to condemn and, ultimately, facilitate the eradication of state policies and practices which prefer or allow the routine institutionalisation of children with disabilities. Shifting care wholly out of institutions and into the family or, failing that, the wider community, as required by Articles 23(4) and 23(5), naturally entails the reallocation and, most probably, the provision of further resources, and provides leverage for non-governmental organisations (NGOs) and the international community at large to bring pressure to bear on recalcitrant governments. These provisions, then, do enhance the protection of children with disabilities over and above that offered by Articles 2 and 23 CRC. They are also a long way, in philosophical terms, from accepting the propriety of the 'placement in suitable institutions for the care of children' of children removed from their families, licensed by Article 20(3) CRC.

Some rights found in the CRC, namely the right, in Article 5, to have evolving capacities recognised, or that in Article 8, to have one's identity preserved, have been elevated to the status of a general principle in the CRPD. Others – such as the obligation placed by Article 16(5) CRPD on states in respect of exploitation, violence and abuse suffered by children with disabilities – which is reminiscent of Article 19 CRC, provide added value because, unlike that article, Article 16(5) CRPD contains specific reference to the obligation to prosecute where appropriate.

Other rights still are genuinely novel. The right of disabled children to be consulted by states when bringing national law into conformity with the CRPD, found in Article 4(3) CRPD, goes beyond anything guaranteed by the CRC. The obligation on the state to ensure that disabled children have equal rights with respect to family life in Article 23(3) CRPD is couched in much more positive terms than the negative formulation of Article 16 CRC, which merely forbids 'arbitrary or unlawful interference with his or her privacy, family, home or correspondence'. Moreover, Article 23(3) provides further that: 'With a view to realizing these rights, and to prevent concealment, abandonment, neglect and segregation of children with disabilities, States Parties shall undertake to provide early and comprehensive information, services and support to children with disabilities and their families'. Again, there is no comparable obligation to be found in the CRC.

As can be seen, at least some of these rights entail positive obligations being placed on state parties, and even if the scope of these obligations is (albeit to an uncertain extent) limited by Article 4(2) in respect of economic, social and cultural rights, these are positive developments for children with disabilities. For example, the right of children with disabilities, not to be excluded from the general education system and from free primary and secondary education on the basis of disability in Article 24(2)(a) should trigger reinterpretation of the way in which 'special care' and 'special needs' in Article 23(2) and 23(3) CRC have often been interpreted, which is that children with disabilities should be educated outside of mainstream or general education. This is buttressed by the requirements, in Article 30(5)(d) CRPD, that children with disabilities are afforded equal access to play, recreation and sporting facilities 'including those activities in the school system', and in Article 8(2)(b), to foster an attitude of respect for children with disabilities 'at all levels of the education system, including in all children from an early age'.

Finally, in terms of new rights, the obligation placed on states by Article 25(b) to provide bespoke health services, including preventative services, for children with disabilities is a potentially very valuable addition to the rights of children with disabilities, and compares favourably with the requirement of Article 23(3) CRC, which provides only that children with disabilities be afforded 'effective access' to health and other services. In summary, the CRPD can be seen as providing disability rights advocates, and those advocating the rights of children with disabilities, with a truly dynamic set of rhetorical and political tools to encourage change, which is as much a matter of adopting new ways of thinking about children with disabilities as it is to do with the dedication of additional resources.

6.3 New rights for all?

Don Mackay, the chair of the Ad Hoc Committee on a Comprehensive and Integral Convention to Promote and Protect the Rights and Dignity of Persons with Disabilities, did not actually say that the CRPD was not intended to create new rights. Rather, he said that the CRPD does not 'for the most part'[24] create new rights, which is not the same thing at all, and the CRPD does indeed contain some rights that may have the potential to benefit all children.

A key example is Article 17, which provides that 'Every person with disabilities has a right to respect for his or her physical and mental integrity on an equal basis with others'. There is no equivalent stand-alone right to respect for integrity in any other UN human rights convention. This article reflects, albeit obliquely, concern for the particular vulnerability of persons with intellectual disabilities or mental health difficulties to compulsory medical treatment and detention, but in its final form is of more general, and unspecified, scope and application.

It is an open question whether the presence of Article 17 in the CRPD indicates that earlier conventions, including the CRC, should be modified in some way so as to also include this right. The right to physical and mental integrity is inherent in many of the CRC's articles, such as the Article 19 right to freedom from all forms of physical or mental violence, injury or abuse, neglect or negligent treatment, maltreatment or exploitation, including sexual abuse; or the Article 39 right to physical and psychological recovery and social reintegration of a child victim of any form of neglect, exploitation, or abuse, torture or any other form of cruel, inhuman or degrading treatment or punishment, or armed conflicts. But these articles have so far proven blind to such problematic issues as, for example, the circumcision of boy children,[25] whereas a right to physical and mental integrity might have more purchase in this regard.

Additionally, Articles 3(f) and 9 place an obligation on state parties to ensure access to the physical and virtual environment and to transportation for disabled persons, and to develop and promulgate minimum standards and guidelines for access to all spaces open to the public, including private spaces. Space precludes fuller discussion here, but there may be scope to adapt Article 9 to the situation of children/the CRC. Indeed, it may be that compliance with Article 9 as it stands will be of benefit to all persons, including children, not just those with disabilities, if it entails the improvement of the local environment or the provision of facilities such as play areas, for example.

6.4 Extending and reconfiguring existing rights

The significance of the CRPD lies as much in how existing rights are presented and refashioned as it does in providing new rights. For example, although the right to life in Article 10 CRPD merely 'reaffirms' that right and seeks to ensure its effective enjoyment by persons with disabilities on an equal basis with others, Article 11 extends that protection explicitly to 'situations of risk, including situations of armed conflict, humanitarian emergencies and the occurrence of natural disasters'. One might question whether this extension will make much practical difference in such situations, but it is welcome if for no other reason than it strengthens the hand of children's rights advocates, and this is at least one idea that could usefully be borrowed by the CRC. Indeed, it seems odd that the right to life of a disabled child is better protected in this sense than the right to life of other children. This is not the only example of existing rights being extended in novel ways: another is the elevation of the right to participate effectively in society to a general principle (Articles 3(c) and 29), which goes beyond the narrow scope of Article 12 CRC and which could usefully be followed in other areas including ICL.[26]

With regards to reconfiguring, the CRPD gives old rights a new twist. At several points, the convention blurs the distinction between civil/political rights and economic, social and cultural rights. For instance, the right to liberty of movement, in Article 18, is followed, in Article 19, by the right to live independently in the community, involving the positive obligation of state parties to provide a range of permanent residential accommodation (for those who desire it) and provide those services to persons with disabilities in their own homes and at locations within communities which are necessary to facilitate 'full enjoyment' of that right. Article 20 similarly requires state parties to facilitate the personal mobility of persons with disabilities 'and at an affordable cost'. It is clear from the way that these articles unfold that the view embedded in the convention is that civil and political rights depend for their realisation on the parallel realisation of economic, social or cultural rights.[27]

Elsewhere, political/civil rights are conflated with economic, social and cultural rights within the same article, which is an even more radical restructuring of the relationship between them. For example, the right of equality before the law is interwoven by Article 13(1) with an obligation placed on state parties to provide 'procedural and age-appropriate accommodations, in order to facilitate their effective role as direct and indirect participants, including as witnesses, in all legal proceedings, including investigative and other preliminary stages', coupled with training for criminal justice personnel (Article 13(2)). It seems, as access to justice is a political right, that lack of resources is not a good reason to fail to implement Article 13.

The same pattern is found in Article 21, which opens with a fairly standard version of the right to freedom of expression and opinion and requires state parties to ensure equal exercise of that right to persons with disabilities. It then goes considerably further, imposing positive obligations on state parties to provide information intended for the general public in a form suitable for persons with disabilities at no cost (Article 21(a)), to facilitating the use of sign language, Braille and 'all other accessible means, modes and formats of communication' at the choice of the person with disabilities (Article 21(b)), as well as 'urging' private entities and the mass media to do the same (Article 21(c) and (d)). This has been described by Kayess and French as 'intriguing'.[28] This is because in their view Article 21 seemingly implements a civil right (freedom of expression and opinion): and yet, on a natural reading, it seems that the economic, social and cultural aspects of Article 21 are subsumed by its overarching quality as a civil/political right.

This reading is supported by the structure of Article 21, which renders the civil/political right, in Article 21(1), as the main focus of the article, with the positive obligations then placed on state parties to realise that right as Article 21(1)(a), 21(1)(b) and 21(1)(c), which suggest that they are sub-components of that right; there is no Article 21(2). If this analysis is correct, then the CRPD demonstrates how it is possible, in effect, to convert an aspiration into a positive obligation to be realised immediately. This might be a lesson of value to children's rights strategists – although it seems to require change at the level of the wording of the text of the CRC to import this into children's rights. If the CRPD proves to set some sort of blueprint for the future articulation of rights – this novel conflation of the civil and the political with the economic, social and cultural – then the CRC will appear increasingly out of date.

It remains to be seen, however, whether the reading offered by Kayess and French will be shared by state parties and the CRPD Committee. It might be a neat textual conjuring trick to convert the aspirational into the enforceable in the way done by Article 21 and other articles within the CRPD, but that does not sit comfortably with the retention of the orthodox division between the two types of rights which is expressly made by Article 4(2) (although as suggested at 6.1.2 above, the scope of Article 4(2) is open to debate). Moreover, changing texts does not in and of itself change realities. The financial limitations on states will continue to constrain the extent to which the subcomponents of Article 21 can be realised. If Article 21 was expressly designed to challenge orthodoxies of international law obligations that entail significant financial implications, then it is a risky strategy. On the one hand, it risks the right to freedom of expression itself being seen as subject to progressive realisation; on the other, it risks undermining goodwill towards and compliance with the convention if developing states are required to invest resources beyond their means in order to secure the immediate realisation of all elements of Article 21.[29] And even then, such immediate realisation simply will not be possible for all, perhaps many, state parties.

But at a deep philosophical and jurisprudential level something fundamental has irrevocably shifted here, as Mégret suggests. The blurring of political/civil rights with economic, social and cultural rights undermines the liberal legal subject, seen in political and civil rights terms as being independent, isolated and autonomous. This is because, in constructing civil and political rights as being interwoven with economic, social and cultural rights, the CRPD understands the legal subject as being interdependent and relational:[30] we *all* need effective economic, social and cultural rights if we are truly to be able to exercise our civil or political rights. In this sense, the CRPD may be the vanguard of very fundamental change, the scope and impact of which we cannot really yet determine.

6.5 Revisiting capacity: status, functionality, best interests and supported decision-making

The single most radical element of the CRPD is that it marks an attempt, which cannot yet be judged to have been successful or unsuccessful, to shift the paradigm with respect to the role that the concept of 'capacity' and third-party decision-making in the 'best interests' of persons found to 'lack' capacity has in disability law and practice. The CRPD states boldly, in Article 12, which is headed 'equality before the law', that:

1. States Parties reaffirm that persons with disabilities have the right to recognition everywhere as persons before the law.

2. States Parties shall recognize that persons with disabilities enjoy legal capacity on an equal basis with others in all aspects of life.
3. States Parties shall take appropriate measures to provide access by persons with disabilities to the support they may require in exercising their legal capacity.

For some, perhaps most, of those involved in the drafting of the CRPD this article was intended to prohibit national law from utilising 'capacity' as a mechanism to regulate both whether a person with disabilities is accorded legal rights and whether he or she is permitted independently to exercise those rights. This was based, first, on the conviction that even what is generally seen as the most morally defensible model of capacity – a 'functional' model which asks if the person in question can understand, retain and process information relevant to a decision, and communicate that decision to relevant others[31] – has proven inadequate at prohibiting the values and preferences of third parties from percolating into the assessment of capacity, such that in truth often a covert 'status-based' test[32] is deployed. In addition, the consequences of a finding of incapacity – most often a form of substituted judgment by a third party, ostensibly designed to make decisions in the best interests of the person found to lack capacity – was seen as licensing decision-making that alienated the person lacking capacity from their own life choices, and by implication often led to best interests judgments that did not in fact meet or even focus on the needs of the person with disability.

Article 12(3) demonstrates the clear preference of the drafters of the CRPD for an alternative approach – supported decision-making – in preference to substituted judgment. The key difference is that supported decision-making is posited on the assumption that capacity to make one's own decisions is always (or virtually always) in fact attainable, if the person of limited capacity is given the necessary assistance. For those in favour of supported decision-making, an approach which determines the extent to which a person has or may act on their rights by reference to a test of capacity breaches the prohibition on discrimination which is recognised as both a fundamental principle[33] and a general obligation of state parties;[34] and, to underline its importance, is also accorded its own article[35] in the CRPD.

If this is correct, then it might be seen as unfortunate that the approach taken in the CRPD was to separate children with disabilities from adults with disabilities, and render children subject to the substituted judgment/best interests approach which dominates the CRC. If the CRPD had not made such provision, then children with disabilities would have had the same entitlement as adults with disabilities, to a supported decision-making rather than a substituted judgment approach. This would have in turn raised questions as to why children with disabilities had a greater entitlement to autonomous decision-making than other children, and exerted pressure to consider fundamental reform of the text of the CRC along the same lines. To me, it seems that one challenge – in terms of research needed – is to be able to articulate mechanisms which would bring supported decision-making for children into reality as the norm. This might involve, for example, the use of advocates or other support workers who take instruction from or act together with one or more children (depending on the situation), and of course training of professionals in a wide range of fields to provide such persons with the skills necessary to provide children with such support. No doubt other mechanisms could and should also be deployed.[36]

Beyond this, there is an even greater potential significance to the adoption of a supported decision-making framework, which is deftly identified by Amita Dhanda:

> By setting up the paradigm of supported decision making, the CRPD unequivocally declares that it is possible to obtain support without being lessened or diminished. This paradigm of interdependence should be empowering and emancipatory for all of humanity and not just persons with disabilities.[37]

All this may be jumping the gun. As I have said, it remains to be seen whether this understanding of Article 12 becomes established internationally.[38] Article 12(4) is in tension with Articles 12(1)–3. Article 12(4) provides:

> 4. States Parties shall ensure that all measures that relate to the exercise of legal capacity provide for appropriate and effective safeguards to prevent abuse in accordance with international human rights law. Such safeguards shall ensure that measures relating to the exercise of legal capacity respect the rights, will and preferences of the person, are free of conflict of interest and undue influence, are proportional and tailored to the person's circumstances, apply for the shortest time possible and are subject to regular review by a competent, independent and impartial authority or judicial body. The safeguards shall be proportional to the degree to which such measures affect the person's rights and interests.

This provides for the possibility that a person will not in fact, even if Article 12(3) has been complied with to the fullest extent possible, have the capacity to make the decision in question. It therefore goes against the grain of the philosophy of the earlier elements of Article 12. And the drafting of Article 12 was a see-saw affair between the two camps, of substituted judgment and supported decision-making respectively.[39] So it may be that the abandonment of capacity in this context is not yet upon us.[40]

Nonetheless, it seems odd that the CRPD, which is so clearly intended to remove discrimination on any grounds against persons with disabilities, including discrimination based on that person's age[41] nonetheless supports and enhances, but does not challenge, the age-based discrimination which is inherent in the very idea that, by reason of age alone, children should be afforded less and lesser legal rights than adults, to be compensated merely with an obligation placed on an adult decision-maker to give due weight to their views when making a substituted best interests judgment on their behalf. In other words, the paradigm-shifting question is why do the same arguments against status-based and functionality-based models of capacity which apply to adults with disabilities not also apply to the application of those models to people below the age of 18 years? The answer seems to be that those arguments are blocked and stymied by an essentialist understanding of children as a legal–political class which permeates and indeed animates the CRC: childhood in other words, as a matter of law, is constituted as a status-based limitation which is seen to affect, and delimit the capacity of, all children, regardless of actual ability. In the CRC, the essence of childhood is constructed in terms of a lack of capacity.

It does seem innocuous that – whereas for adults the key issue of the moment is whether there will be a wholesale abandonment of capacity as a mechanism to determine who can make decisions for themselves and its replacement by a supported-decision-making model, with virtually no support left amongst the international community for a status-based approach – for children the shift from status to functionality has barely begun. Possible switch points – and as an English lawyer my point of reference is the decision in the case of *Gillick v West Norfolk and Wisbech AHA* [1986] AC 112, in which it was held that a child, on being able to demonstrate sufficient competence to pass a functional capacity test, should be entitled in law to make his or her own decisions – have been neutralised subsequently by being made subject to overriding best interests principles grounded in the status of that person as a child.[42]

At the very least, it can be suggested that the coming into being of the CRPD raises the questions of whether: (i) it is not now time to shift from a status-based to a functionality-based understanding of the limitations that simply being a 'child' as a matter of legal status places on a young person in terms of their abilities to make decisions for themselves, and (ii) there should be, if not an abandonment of the best interests principle, then at least the severance of that principle from a substituted judgment framework for those children found to have functional capacity and its attachment instead to a supported decision-making model. The main difference is that the former is 'objective' (decision made by an adult), whereas the latter is 'subjective' (decision made by the child) in orientation. In short, a child with capacity would have the legal right to decide his or her own best interests.

The more radical question, of whether: (iii) it is possible to shift the default position from childhood denoting presumptive lack of capacity, to childhood not being of itself sufficient to displace the presumption of capacity which applies to adults, is also raised (and with it a host of related questions such as whether the balance between protection and autonomy is currently appropriately figured). To put this differently, if there is widespread consensus that human rights are best protected by a 'social' model of disability, which locates the essence of the problem in the way in which society at large fails to make adequate accommodation for people with impairments, rendering such persons at risk of discrimination, how do we explain the lack of any comparable 'social model of childhood', which similarly views childhood as a time of vulnerability by reason of the same 'attitudinal and environmental barriers that hinder their full and effective participation in society on an equal basis with others'? What would the CRC and ICL in general look like if a 'social model of childhood' were to be adopted, whereby different treatment is prima facie discrimination and disempowerment? And if this is not the right question to ask, why not? And what is the right question?

6.6 Concluding comments

In this chapter I have considered the implications of the arrival of the CRPD for ICL and the CRC in particular. I have suggested that not only does the CRPD contain important new rights and entitlements for children with disabilities, but that some of its provisions have the potential to improve the situation for children more generally, and, taken in its totality, the 2006 convention does justify the paradigm-shifting claims that have been made for it. At the least, the CRPD demonstrates how various rights in the CRC could be made more robust, and it points the way to greater involvement of individuals, communities and other actors such as NGOs in the formulation of law and policy. Beyond this, the way the CRPD restructures orthodox understandings of rights and their limits, rejects tests of capacity as disempowering and discriminatory, and does so on the philosophical basis of a 'social model' of disability, raises far-reaching and awkward questions regarding the continued viability of an essentialist, status-based and non-socialised construction of children and their rights.

Notes

1 As of 26 May 2016, the Convention had been signed by 160 and ratified by 164 state parties. Its Optional Protocol had attracted 92 signatures and 89 ratifications by the same date www.un.org/disabilities/ (last accessed 26 May 2016).

2 United Nations General Assembly (UNGA), 'Children and Armed Conflict Report of the Secretary General', UN Doc A/58/546–S/2003/1053, para 104.

3 UN Press Releases, 'Chairman says draft convention sets out "detailed" code of implementation and spells out how individual rights should be put into practice' (15 August 2005) SOC/4680 www.un.org/News/Press/docs/2005/soc4680.doc.htm (last accessed 11 December 2016).

4 Namely the Universal Declaration of Human Rights 1948, the International Covenant on Civil and Political Rights 1966 (ICCPR) and the International Covenant on Economic, Social and Cultural Rights 1966 (ICESCR). Both the CRC and the CRPD are included in the nine core UN treaties: see 'The core International human rights instruments and their monitoring bodies' www.ohchr.org/EN/ProfessionalInterest/Pages/CoreInstruments.aspx (last accessed 11 December 2016).

5 UN Secretariat for the Convention on the Rights of Persons with Disabilities, Secretariat for the Convention on the Rights of Persons with Disabilities, Office of the United Nations High Commissioner for Human Rights (OHCHR), *United Nations Handbook for Parliamentarians, From Exclusion to Equality, Realizing the Rights of Persons with Disabilities* (Inter-Parliamentary Union No 14, United Nations 2007) 5.

6 For a rare example see G Mulheir, 'Deinstitutionalisation: a human rights priority for children with disabilities' (2012) 9 *Equal Rights Review* 117.

7 M Schulz, *Understanding the UN Convention on the Rights of Persons with Disabilities* (3rd edn, Handicap International 2009) 69.

8 ibid.

9 A Dhanda, 'Constructing a new human rights lexicon: Convention on the Rights of Persons with Disabilities' (2008) 8 *International Journal of Human Rights* 43.
10 F Mégret, 'The Disabilities Convention: towards a holistic concept of rights' (2008) 12(2) *International Journal of Human Rights* 261, 262.
11 G de Búrca, 'The European Union in the negotiation of the UN Disability Convention' (2010) *European Law Review* 174, 175.
12 T Hammarberg, 'Disability rights: from charity to equality' (2011) 6 *European Human Rights Law Review* 638, 639.
13 J Butler, *Bodies that Matter: On the Discursive Limits of 'Sex'* (Routledge 1993).
14 M A Fineman, 'The vulnerable subject: anchoring equality in the human condition' (2008) 20 *Yale Journal of Law and Feminism* 1.
15 UN High Commissioner for Human Rights (UN HCHR), *Annual Report* A/HRC/10/48 (26 January 2009) paras 45, 47.
16 P Fennell, U Khaliq, 'Conflicting or complementary obligations? The UN Disability Rights Convention, the European Convention on human rights and English law' (2011) 6 *European Human Rights Law Review* 662, 669; P Bartlett, 'The United Nations Convention on the Rights of Persons with Disabilities and mental health law' (2012) 75(5) *Modern Law Review* 752.
17 UNGA, 'Optional Protocol to the Convention on the Rights of Persons with Disabilities (2007) UN Doc A/RES/61/106.
18 UNGA, 'Optional Protocol to the Convention on the Rights of the Child on a communications procedure' (2012) UN Doc A/RES/66/138.
19 See Dhanda (n 9) 48.
20 The CRC published a General Comment on the rights of children with disabilities in early 2007 (prompted, it seems, by activity around the CRPD), advising state parties that the rights of children with disabilities must be implemented 'in a comprehensive manner which covers all provisions of the [CRC]'. See CRC Committee, 'General Comment No 9: the rights of children with disabilities' UN Doc CRC/C/CG9 (27 February 2007) para 6.
21 The CRC Committee implicitly acknowledges this lacuna in the protection offered to children with disabilities by the CRC by elaborating a mainstreaming programme in its General Comment No 9.
22 CRPD art 24(3)(c).
23 ibid preamble para (q); art 6(1) and art 28(2)(b).
24 UN (n 3).
25 There is a huge literature on this topic. Examples include: J S Svoboda, 'Circumcision of male infants as a human rights violation' (2013) 39 *Journal of Medical Ethics* 469; J Mazor, 'The child's interests and the case for the permissibility of male infant circumcision' (2013) 39 *Journal of Medical Ethics* 421; P W Adler, 'Is circumcision legal?' (2013) 16(3) *Richmond Journal of Law and the Public Interest* 439.
26 The Committee on the Rights of the Child has recognised art 12 CRC as having the status of a general principle of the CRC (CRC Committee, 'General Comment No 12: on the Right of the Child to be Heard' (2009) UN Doc CRC/C/GC/12 (1 July 2009) para 2), but the way in which art 12 has been interpreted to date has often led to participation which is less than 'effective': see for example L Lundy, 'Voice is not enough: conceptualising Article 12 of the United Nations Convention on the Rights of the Child' (2007) 33(6) *British Educational Research Journal* 927; A Nolan, 'The child as "democratic citizen": challenging the "participation gap"' (2010) 4 *Public Law* 767.
27 Although I do not agree with Kayess and French that the rights in arts 19 and 20 are, as they claim, 'despite their appearance, civil and political rights'. See R Kayess, P French, 'Out of darkness into light? Introducing the Convention on the Rights of Persons with Disabilities' (2008) 8(1) *Human Rights Law Review* 1, 29.
28 ibid.

29 As Bartlett (n 16) 757 notes, discussing the point, 'Neither choice seems particularly appealing'.

30 For discussion of these concepts see for example M A Fineman, 'Equality, autonomy and the vulnerable subject in law and politics' in M A Fineman, A Grear (eds), *Vulnerability: Reflections on a New Ethical Foundation for Law and Politics* (Ashgate 2013).

31 This model of capacity is seen as morally defensible because it does not judge the outcome of decision-making, leaving those with reduced but sufficient capacity to make their own decisions even when, from an objective point of view, the decision in question is unwise. Instead, this test asks only if the functional ability to process the relevant information is present. The English Mental Capacity Act 2005 is a fairly typical national law example of such an approach, and fairly typically the 2005 Act is headed by general principles of minimum interventionism: an assumption that capacity is present, with the onus on those disputing that to displace that assumption; an obligation to take 'all practicable steps' to help a person achieve capacity; as well as an embargo on judging capacity by reference to the substance of the decision made.

32 By contrast to a functional test, a status-based test simply assumes that membership of a class of persons – such as persons with learning disabilities, or children – necessarily entails lack of capacity. In the field of mental disability, status-based tests are these days almost universally condemned as discriminatory and unfit for purpose.

33 CRPD art 3(b).

34 ibid art 4(1).

35 ibid art 5.

36 See *mutatis mutandis* P Weller, 'The Convention on the Rights of Persons with Disabilities and the social model of health: new perspectives' (2011) *Journal of Mental Health Law* 74, 77.

37 See Dhanda (n 9) 50.

38 Some state parties entered reservations in respect of art 12 for fear that it would render their own substituted judgment mechanisms for dealing with persons found to lack mental capacity unlawful, and others signed up to art 12 but made an interpretative declaration upon ratification, to the effect that art 12 would be interpreted in such a way as to permit substituted decision-making. On the other hand, the Committee on the Rights of Persons with Disabilities, in its recent 'Concluding Observations on the initial report of New Zealand' CRPD/C/NZL/CO/1 (31 October 2014) para 22, advised the state, which utilises substituted judgment, that it must 'take immediate steps to revise the relevant laws and replace substituted decision-making with supported decision-making'. See also Committee on the Rights of Persons with Disabilities, 'General Comment No 1 Article 12: equal recognition before the law' (2014) CRPD/C/GC/1, para 3, wherein the Committee notes that there has been 'general failure to understand that the human rights-based model of disability implies a shift from the substitute decision-making paradigm to one that is based on supported decision-making'.

39 A Dhanda, 'Legal capacity in the disability rights convention: stranglehold of the past or lodestar for the future?' (2006–2007) 34 *Syracuse Journal of International Law and Commerce* 429.

40 See Fennell and Khaliq (n 16) and Bartlett (n 16).

41 See CRPD preamble, para (P) art 8(1)(b).

42 This situation has been theorised, for example, by Eekelaar's concept of 'autonomy interest', which subsumes autonomy and rights within a 'best interests' framework. See J Eekelaar, 'The emergence of children's rights' (1986) 6 *Oxford Journal of Legal Studies* 161.

7 Inspiration for children's human rights from indigenous peoples' rights

Ellen Desmet

7.1 Introduction

Although there are many and obvious differences between children and indigenous peoples, there are also a number of similarities, especially in how international human rights law and academic research have addressed the claims of these groups. This chapter focuses on three domains in which children's rights and indigenous peoples' rights share certain challenges, in order to explore whether and how both branches of human rights law could inspire each other: (i) the demarcation of the personal scope of rights, and the divisions and dichotomies generated by the establishment of categorical human rights; (ii) the way in which indigenous peoples and children have been constructed, especially from a Western perspective, and the consequences thereof; and (iii) participation and consent. I will argue that children's rights law could draw inspiration from indigenous peoples' rights law in defining its rights holders, in developing the collective dimension of the right to be heard and in conceptualising the right of children to give consent. On the other hand, an area in which research and practice on both indigenous peoples' rights and children's rights should increase efforts concerns addressing the adverse consequences of idealised constructions.

This chapter has developed in an organic way, following the flow of my professional life. In my PhD research, I analysed the rights of indigenous peoples and local communities in the context of nature conservation initiatives, with ethnographic fieldwork in the Peruvian Amazon.[1] After that, I delved into children's rights through my work at the Flemish Children's Rights Knowledge Centre.[2] Working on both indigenous peoples' rights and children's rights, I have at times been struck by parallels in how these two groups have been approached in law and research. The notes and reflections on those parallels gathered over the years form the backbone of this chapter.

7.2 The personal scope of indigenous peoples' and children's rights law

7.2.1 The definitional tangle

A first challenge that is common to indigenous peoples' rights law and children's rights law concerns the demarcation of their personal scope. Who can invoke the protection of these categorical forms of rights protection? And who has the power to decide this?

Definitions of 'indigenous peoples' in international law have evolved over time and differ in the elements they emphasise. The most influential definitions are those of Conventions No 107 and – especially – No 169 of the International Labour Organization (ILO), as well as the one provided by Martínez Cobo in his 'Study on the problem of discrimination against indigenous populations'.[3] No definition of indigenous peoples has been universally endorsed, however. Interestingly, the lack of a universally accepted definition has not prevented the global rise of the indigenous movement and the development of an extensive body of legislation, case law and doctrine concerning the rights of indigenous peoples.

Indigenous peoples themselves emphasise that a definition of 'indigenous peoples' is 'not necessary or desirable' and stress the right of self-identification.[4] Such a right of self-identification has two components: the right of an individual to identify him- or herself as indigenous, and the right of a group to define its membership. Of these two components, the former, the right of an individual to choose to belong to a particular people or 'to opt out', takes precedence over the latter.[5] Any other approach would unduly encroach upon individual liberty – a cornerstone of human rights law. Various reasons underpin the importance attached by indigenous peoples to self-identification. Firstly, given the enormous diversity in the historical and current situation of indigenous peoples throughout the globe, any definition risks being under-inclusive in certain contexts or over-inclusive in others. Moreover, attributing definitional power to an external actor, such as a state or international organisation, would imply that the latter would also have the possibility *not* to recognise indigenous peoples.[6] History is a powerful witness of the adverse consequences entailed by such a denial of the existence of indigenous peoples and their rights.

The Working Group on Indigenous Populations, which was established in 1982, followed this position of indigenous peoples, as it decided not to adopt a formal definition.[7] This absence of a definition did not prevent the Working Group from acting efficiently and successfully. On the contrary, the Working Group has been praised for its openness and flexibility.[8] The Committee on the Elimination of Racial Discrimination (CERD) has also stated that the identification as members of a particular racial or ethnic group shall be based upon self-identification, 'if no justification exists to the contrary'.[9] The UN Declaration on the Rights of Indigenous Peoples (UNDRIP) does not contain a definition of indigenous peoples either. Pursuant to Article 33(1) UNDRIP, '[i]ndigenous peoples have the right to determine their own identity or membership in accordance with their customs and traditions'.[10]

To resolve questions of indigenousness in concrete settings, various authors have proposed a flexible approach. Erica Daes, the former Chairperson-Rapporteur of the UN Sub-Commission on Prevention of Discrimination and Protection of Minorities, has identified various 'factors considered relevant to the concept of indigenous', namely priority in time, the voluntary perpetuation of cultural distinctiveness, self-identification and recognition by other groups, and an experience of marginalisation.[11] She has stressed, however, that these factors 'do not, and cannot, constitute an inclusive or comprehensive definition. Rather, they represent factors which may be present, to a greater or lesser degree, in different regions and in different national and local contexts'.[12]

Similarly, in his 'constructivist approach', Kingsbury suggests combining different criteria in a nuanced and flexible way.[13] As such, he identifies four uncontested and indispensable characteristics of the concept of indigenous peoples: (i) self-identification as an ethnic group; (ii) historical experience of, or contingent vulnerability to, severe disruption, dislocation, or exploitation; (iii) long connection with the region; and (iv) the wish to retain a distinct identity. Three further criteria, namely (i) non-dominance in the state or region, (ii) close cultural affinity with a particular territory or land, and (iii) continuity based on historical priority, must be interpreted with some flexibility. Moreover, these latter criteria do not necessarily have to be present all three simultaneously, so as not unjustly to exclude certain groups from the qualification as indigenous peoples. Other additional indicators such as language and race are not essential, but may support the case in favour of qualification as an indigenous people. Sieder and Witchell have also pleaded for 'flexible and dynamic conceptions' of indigenous peoples.[14]

Finally, in response to the particular challenges relating to indigenousness on the African continent, the African Commission's Working Group on Indigenous Populations/Communities has advanced a 'modern analytic understanding' of the term indigenous, with three fundamental characteristics: (i) self-definition; (ii) cultural difference, most prominently expressed in the distinctive relationship of indigenous peoples to their ancestral territory and natural resources; and (iii) an experience of marginalisation and dispossession.[15] The criterion of priority in time would, in the eyes of the Working Group, not allow an adequate analysis of the continuing structural inequalities within African independent states.[16]

Such flexible conceptions of indigenous peoples, with self-identification as a central element, take into account the specific characteristics of indigenous peoples, while leaving enough space for regional and local particularities. This approach seems more appropriate than establishing a 'one-size-fits-all' definition at the international level, which would fit uneasily with various local contexts.

In contrast with this rather open approach towards defining indigenous peoples, we understand who 'children' are – or at least we think we do. Article 1 of the quasi-universally ratified Convention on the Rights of the Child (CRC) reads: '*For the purposes of the present Convention*, a child means every human being below the age of 18 years unless under the law applicable to the child, majority is attained earlier'.[17] Even though Article 1 explicitly confines its scope to the CRC, this definition has been widely adopted in national, regional and international legal frameworks and policies on children.[18] The consensus to apply children's rights to persons below 18 years of age is thus very broad, especially when compared to the heated debates on the definition of indigenous peoples. Such a univocal definition of children obviously has its advantages, among which would be simplicity, clarity, a global common understanding of children and the facilitation of cooperation between different jurisdictions.

This wide endorsement of the CRC definition does not mean that there is no debate regarding the starting point of children's rights, namely its application to the unborn child,[19] or the upper age limit of the definition of children. With respect to the latter, findings in neuroscience that the brain continues to develop until the age of 25 have generated calls to extend the scope of children's rights up to that age.[20] As discussed in the next subsection, a more flexible approach towards the boundary between 'children' and 'youth' may be warranted. Moreover, children are not a homogeneous group, but grow up in very diverse geographical, cultural and socio-economic contexts. Establishing a general cut-off age at 18 years of age to define children appears to be something of a Eurocentric approach. In non-Western contexts, other factors besides chronological age also play a role in establishing the boundary between childhood and adulthood. Examples include the concept of maturity in Muslim legal tradition,[21] 'possessing understanding' in Bangladesh[22] and having productive and reproductive capacities in southern and eastern Africa.[23] Children in Africa are often more autonomous and independent at an earlier age than those growing up in a nuclear Western family, but they are also more accountable to their communities.[24] Denying children certain rights, such as a right to work in dignity,[25] because of their formal status of children may then go against their best interests.

Does the indigenous rights regime provide inspiration to address these challenges concerning the demarcation of the personal scope of children's rights law? In line with the complex and flexible approaches towards defining indigenous peoples, this chapter suggests moving towards a multi-dimensional understanding of children, which does not exclusively focus on chronological age.[26] When thinking about children's rights and to whom to apply them, importance should also be attached to elements other than the number of years one has been walking around on this globe. Firstly, in line with the right of self-identification of indigenous peoples, more attention should be paid to how children perceive themselves. Not giving children a say in determining who can invoke children's rights seems to be a continuation of the paternalistic and protectionist approach that predominated in the early children's rights movement, and goes against children's right to express their views in matters affecting them and to have these views given due weight (Article 12 CRC).

Secondly, factors other than chronological age may be relevant in determining the scope of children's rights law, such as socio-psychological development, the role taken up in one's family, community and society, as well as the cultural, socio-economic, historical and geographical context. The relevance of psychological development in the application of children's rights law is already reflected in the concepts of 'maturity', as co-determining the impact of children's expressed views (Article 12 CRC), and 'evolving capacities', as delineating the scope of the duty of parents and legal guardians to provide guidance to the child (Articles 5 and 14 CRC). The identification of the particular characteristics to be taken into account in defining the personal scope of children's rights law in a certain context should then occur at the appropriate international, regional, national or local level.

The proposal of a multi-dimensional approach towards defining children, i.e. going beyond chronological age to take into account self-identification as well as psychological and contextual factors, should not be understood as implying or suggesting lowering the standard of children's rights law. On the contrary, a more flexible and contextualised approach towards defining children may lead to a more tailored and thus more adequate realisation of human and children's rights. The experience of indigenous peoples has shown that a definitional approach combining various criteria in a flexible and nuanced way, may not be as problematic as one may think at first sight. For instance, one could think of a situation where a teenager does not consider herself as a child anymore (self-identification), has the corresponding socio-psychological capabilities and is taking up adult duties within her family and community. In these circumstances, the rights of this teenager may be better protected by not considering her as a child, but by ensuring the realisation of her (general) human rights.

7.2.2 Creating dichotomies . . . and building some bridges?

During the last decades, categorical rights have been created within human rights law to rectify historical situations of substantive inequality, discrimination and marginalisation of certain groups (e.g. women, children, indigenous peoples, migrant workers and persons with disabilities).[27] It was considered that the general human rights instruments did not adequately recognise and protect the specific needs and rights of these groups. Nevertheless, such categorical rights inevitably generate divisions between those who belong to a certain category and those who do not. Groups marginally over the edge, who cannot invoke the protection of a particular categorical rights regime, may then be among the first ones to fall through the cracks of the human rights system.

As indigenous peoples are concerned, this may be particularly the case for low-earning communities.[28] Historically as well as today, indigenous peoples have suffered from disdain, discrimination and human rights violations. Nowadays, however, a stronger international legal framework has turned indigenousness into a potentially 'positive' factor, as the indigenous identity comes with greater land and resource rights, as well as more autonomy. Indigenous peoples may also more easily attract funding from international donors, as they are more 'exotic' and thus appealing than the 'grey' low-paid communities next door. So whereas before 'nobody wanted to be indigenous anymore',[29] today the pendulum seems to a certain extent to have swung the other way, and this to the detriment of the recognition of and respect for the rights of local non-indigenous communities. As a consequence, national minorities are increasingly redefining themselves as indigenous peoples, to gain access to this broader catalogue of rights to autonomy, land and legal pluralism.[30]

The recognition of broader territorial, land and resource rights as well as greater participation rights of indigenous peoples may be particularly problematic for communities that share many characteristics that are usually associated with indigenous peoples – such as a close connection with the land – but that do not qualify as 'indigenous peoples'.[31] In Latin America, this is for instance the case for Afro-descendant maroon communities, whose ancestors escaped from slavery to establish their own communities: 'These Afrodescendant groups developed separate racial/cultural collective identities distinct from those of the dominant *mestizo* majority, and forged a relationship to land or territory in the colonial period before the establishment of state sovereignty of the areas they occupied'.[32] In recent years, the boundaries between the rights of indigenous peoples and these Afro-descendant maroon communities have become blurred. For instance, the Inter-American Court of Human Rights has extended its jurisprudence on collective property rights of indigenous peoples to the Afro-descendant maroon communities in two cases against Suriname.[33]

Similarly, the establishment of children's rights divides the human population into children on the one hand, and adults – such as parents and teachers – on the other. Children's rights also separate children from 'young adults'. Because of the cut-off age of 18, these young adults lose the protection of children's rights law, even though the life of a 19-year-old may not be so different from that of a 17-year-old, and some 19-year-olds may find themselves in a more vulnerable situation than some 17-year-olds. Just as the Inter-American human rights jurisprudence has recognised the communal land rights of Afro-descendant maroon communities to the image of the land rights of indigenous peoples, it seems relevant to build more bridges between the rights of children and those of young adults. This is already being done in various situations. For example, the UN Guidelines for the Alternative Care of Children are not only applicable to children, but also, as appropriate, to 'young persons already in alternative care and who need continuing care or support for a transitional period after reaching the age of majority under applicable law'.[34] This provision prevents a rupture in care during the – often complex – transition to adulthood. In Flanders, a child and youth impact report (JoKER) must be elaborated for draft decrees that have a direct impact on the interests of persons under the age of 25.[35] Both minors and young adults are thus included in its personal field of application, although another cut-off age (namely 25 years) is established.

It is concluded that within both indigenous peoples' rights law and children's rights law, steps are being taken to mitigate some of the potentially undesirable consequences of categorical rights systems, by extending part of their protection to those who just fall outside their personal scope. From a general human rights perspective, this evolution is to be applauded and should continue where appropriate, so as to avoid that categorical protection creates new vulnerabilities.

7.3 Western constructions

A second domain characterised by some remarkable parallels concerns the way in which children and indigenous peoples have been represented and constructed in Western society, not only in popular discourse but also in scholarship. A multiplicity of child images and constructions of indigenousness can be identified and situated on a continuum ranging from (overly) 'negative' to (overly) 'positive' appreciations. Different and even opposite images are often simultaneously present in a certain context, their strength depending on the particular intersection of time, place and actors involved. Within the confines of this chapter, it is not possible to do justice to the richness of analysis in historiographies on the constructions of childhood and indigenousness.[36] Nevertheless, from an analytical perspective, some parallels between constructions of indigenous peoples and constructions of children may be identified, especially at both extremities of the continuum.

Historically, particularly during colonial times, indigenous peoples were often considered 'primitive' and 'backward': they needed to be civilised and proselytised. Such constructions underpinned the doctrines of *terra nullius* and guardianship.[37] Similarly, in Western society, children were long seen as the private property of their fathers, or as 'not-yet' human beings.[38] Both groups were marginalised in society: they were not considered fully; nor was their specificity acknowledged.

Since then, an enormous shift in the perception of and approach towards indigenous peoples and children is noticeable, to the extent that today, both groups are often romanticised and idealised. Indigenous peoples have been represented as the guardians and stewards of Mother Earth, living in harmony with nature. The romantic image of Indians as noble savages, expressed in the writings of Locke and Rousseau, was taken up again in the 20th century to refer to the supposedly balanced relationship of indigenous peoples with their natural environment. The 'ecologically noble savage' was born; indigenous peoples were seen as 'natural conservationists'.[39] Similarly, the attitudes towards children changed tremendously. Zelizer, for instance, has argued that from the late 19th century onwards, childhood underwent a process of 'sacralisation' in America: children were not only invested with emotional significance, but they were also separated from their economic value – rendering them 'priceless'.[40]

At the other far end of the continuum, less benign images of indigenous peoples and children can be discerned. Some Western conservationists, for instance, argue that nature conservation requires strict preservation, which is not reconcilable with human presence or resource use.[41] They claim that sustainable resource use cannot sufficiently protect biodiversity, and point to instances of environmental destruction by indigenous peoples. This perception of fundamental incompatibility between humankind and nature is rooted in and still influenced by the American idea of wilderness preservation as it developed in the 19th century.[42] Comparably, children that do not conform to the image of innocent angels tend to be sent away as dangerous. A shift is being observed from welfare-oriented approaches for children 'at risk' towards perceiving children 'as risk', leading to the image of the 'problem child'. The behaviour of children and young people is today increasingly problematised – and often criminalised – especially in the public space.[43]

Particularly interesting for the purposes of this chapter is that the image of both children and indigenous peoples has been used to characterise and essentialise the 'other' category. As such, '[o]ne of the most common observations in literature about colonial relations has been that indigenous populations are invariably cast as childlike in their nature'.[44] Such infantalisation of native populations was used by the colonisers to legitimate paternalistic policies and the exploitation of native economies.[45] Similarly, children have been constructed as either 'primitives' or 'noble savages'. For instance, Gagen has argued that: 'US colonial policy did not simply construct the natives of the Philippines, Puerto Rico or Guam as primitive, but Western child development theories themselves constructed the American child as inherently primitive'.[46] From such an evolutionary perspective, children were situated in a prehistorical phase of development and needed to evolve towards modernity, as in America's 'underdeveloped' colonies. Jenks has referred to this image of the child as being primitive and wild as the Dionysian child.[47] By contrast, when considering children as intrinsically good, they have been portrayed as 'noble savages', Jenks invoking here the mythological image of the Apollonian child.[48]

Many of the constructions of indigenous peoples and children referred to above are linked to the presumed 'natural' character of these groups, which may be assessed positively ('noble savage') or negatively ('wild and primitive'). These images stand in opposition to the 'civilised' Western world in general or adults in particular. The new sociology of childhood has tried to break through this binary construct of natural children versus civilised adults.[49] Also in indigenous rights studies, the environmental harmony image has been deconstructed.[50]

What are consequences of these constructions of indigenousness and childhood? In general, such constructions seem problematic, because they violate the competence of the group members and 'their right to be valued on their own terms'.[51] Although 'negative' images have not disappeared, it seems that today idealised constructions of indigenous peoples and children predominate in Western society, often coupled with sentimentalism. Both groups arouse strong emotions in the 'other' (Western society or adults), who feel a need to 'preserve' or 'protect' them respectively. Therefore, I will now discuss two shared consequences of romanticised constructions of indigenous peoples and children, namely an adverse impact on rights protection and a lack of critical scientific analysis.

First, if romantic images of indigenous peoples as guardians of Mother Earth and of children as inherently good turn out not to be supported by reality, this may have detrimental consequences for the recognition of and respect for the rights of these groups. For instance, the assumption of a harmonious relationship of indigenous peoples with nature has had the contradictory consequence that higher expectations have been attached to the attitudes and actions of these peoples towards the environment. The ecological footprint of an average conservationist residing in an industrial country is usually much larger than the one of an indigenous person.[52]

Nevertheless, when practices of the latter are unfriendly to the environment, conservationists are very indignant. As Cronon has formulated it: 'Why in the debates about pristine natural areas are "primitive" peoples idealized, even sentimentalized, until the moment they do something unprimitive, modern, and unnatural, and thereby fall from environmental grace?'[53] These unrealistic standards regarding the conservationist behaviour of indigenous peoples have had a negative impact on the potential to realise indigenous peoples' rights. In the words of Niezen: '[t]he high – or one may say impossible – expectations of environmental stewardship applied to indigenous peoples have a tendency to intrude upon their rights and thus their ability to prosper'.[54] However, the rights of indigenous peoples do not depend on their conservationist behaviour. Similarly, children who do not behave as responsible citizens but become 'a problem' may be deprived of the specific protection of the children's rights regime. For example, Belgian minors who are 16 or older when they commit a criminal office can be referred to the criminal law system if the youth judge is of the opinion, on the basis of a societal and medical-psychological examination, that the minor is not 'suitable' for youth protection measures.[55] The only criterion that can be taken into account is the subjective one of the personality of the minor. Similar systems in Europe exist in the Netherlands (also from the age of 16) and England and Wales (from the age of 10). However, in England and Wales, the judge can only decide to refer to the criminal law system on the basis of objective elements, such as the characteristics and seriousness of the criminal offence, or having an accomplice of age. In the Netherlands, a referral can be based on either subjective elements (related to the personality of the offender) or objective elements (related to the criminal offence).[56] Notwithstanding the particularities of each system, they have in common that children who commit an offence may be referred from the juvenile justice system to the adult criminal law system.

Secondly, idealised constructions may limit the possibility of adopting a critical perspective in research, a dynamic that seems to be at play in research on both indigenous peoples' rights and children's rights. For instance, according to Smith – a well-known anthropologist in Peru – one of the reasons explaining the absence of much critical research on the process of political organisation in the Amazon region is the attitude prevailing in the small academic and non-governmental organisation world accompanying the indigenous movement: 'an attitude that combines romanticism with a feeling of guilt towards the indigenous, which hampers a critical and objective examination of indigenous political actions'.[57] By the same token, the image of children as being vulnerable, innocent and intrinsically good may contribute to an understanding of children's rights as being 'intrinsically good' for children as well. Combined with the observation that much work remains to be done as regards the implementation of children's rights, it is then often considered 'not done' to examine children's rights from a critical perspective – be it with the aim of contributing to a more effective realisation of children's rights.[58]

By way of conclusion, is there then something to be 'learnt' in this domain of constructions and representations from (research on) indigenous peoples' rights for (research on) children's rights? In my opinion, both fields should increase efforts to unveil assumptions and constructions that essentialise indigenous peoples and children, as well as the impact of these constructions on research, policy and practice. Such essentialising tendencies do not account for the multiple and complex layers of identity within every person and each group, and may have a negative impact on rights protection.

7.4 Participation and consent

Parallels between indigenous peoples' rights and children's rights may also be drawn in the domain of participation. In an effort to move away from assimilationist policies (towards indigenous peoples) and protectionist approaches (towards children), participation rights have taken on particular importance for both groups. Moreover, these rights have been conceptually developed in ways tailored to the specificities of indigenous peoples and children. Next to a general right to participation of indigenous peoples to at least the same extent as other sectors of the population,[59] this has implied the establishment of a specific right of indigenous peoples to free, prior and informed consultation 'whenever consideration is given to legislative or administrative measures which may affect them directly' (Article 6(1)(a) ILO Convention No 169).[60] Moreover, the right to free, prior and informed *consent* of indigenous peoples is being increasingly recognised, as elaborated below. Children, on the other hand, have the right to express their views freely on all matters affecting them, and to these views being given due weight in accordance with their age and maturity (Article 12 CRC), which has been briefly referred to as 'the right to be heard'.[61]

In the area of participation, consultation and consent, I suggest that indigenous peoples' rights law could inspire children's rights law as regards two aspects: the further theoretical, legal and practical development of the collective dimension of the right of children to be heard, and the fleshing out of the attributes of the emerging right of children to consent (namely free, prior and informed). This section starts with a brief comparison between the two key provisions on participation in both fields of law, and closes with the identification of some common challenges in the realisation of the participation rights of indigenous peoples and children.

Comparing Article 6 of ILO Convention No 169 and Article 12 of the CRC leads to the following observations. As far as the material scope is concerned, governments should consult indigenous peoples 'on legislative or administrative measures', whereas the right of children to be heard broadly applies to 'all matters'. The link between the matter and the right holder triggering the right is also formulated widely in the CRC (matters 'affecting the child'). ILO Convention No 169 requires a direct impact of the envisaged measure on indigenous peoples,[62] but explicitly accounts for the uncertain nature of such impact (measures 'which *may* affect them directly').[63] The possible influence on the eventual decision is similar: neither the right to consultation nor the right to be heard imply a veto power. Consultation of indigenous peoples should be carried out 'with the objective of achieving agreement or consent to the proposed measures', but an absence of agreement does not invalidate the consultation.[64]

The views of children 'are to be given due weight in accordance with the age and maturity of the child', providing the decision-maker some leeway. Whereas the CRC does not offer further guidance on the modalities or quality criteria that should characterise the participation process, consultation of indigenous peoples should take place 'through appropriate procedures and in particular through their representative institutions' (Article 6(1)(a) ILO Convention

No 169). Moreover, consultation must be undertaken 'in good faith and in a form appropriate to the circumstances' (Article 6(2) ILO Convention No 169). A final difference is that the right to consultation is a collective right of indigenous peoples (as evident from the 'representative institutions' requirement), whereas the right of the child to be heard is both an individual and a collective right.

In General Comment No 12, the Committee on the Rights of the Child explicitly makes a distinction between 'the right to be heard of an individual child and the right to be heard as applied to a group of children (e.g. a class of schoolchildren, the children in a neighbourhood, the children of a country, children with disabilities, or girls)'.[65] It argues that this is a relevant distinction, because 'the task of assessing a child's age and maturity . . . is made more difficult when children express themselves collectively'.[66] The Committee continues to emphasise that '[e]ven when confronting difficulties in assessing age and maturity, States parties should consider children as a group to be heard, and the Committee strongly recommends that States parties exert all efforts to listen to or seek the views of those children speaking collectively'.[67] The Committee then announces that:

> [i]n section A (Legal analysis) of the general comment, the Committee deals with the right to be heard of the *individual child*. In section C (The implementation of the right to be heard in different settings and situations), the Committee considers the right to be heard of both the *individual child* and *children as a group*.[68]

The Committee does not provide any explanation or justification for this different approach of the right to be heard of the individual child and of children as a group. The absence of a legal analysis of the right to be heard of children as a group seems a missed opportunity. Moreover, in the implementation section, the Committee does not clearly distinguish between the individual and group right to be heard. To develop the collective dimension of children's right to be heard further, some lessons may be learnt from the experience built up regarding the consultation of indigenous peoples, for instance with regard to representativity. The functioning of indigenous organisations at the local, national, regional and international level has shown the challenges in ensuring that indigenous leaders at a higher level are still voicing the concerns of those they claim to represent. Maintaining open channels of communication and guaranteeing accountability are two ways in which these challenges can be mitigated.

A related area of possible inspiration concerns the right to give consent. Indigenous peoples have the right to free, prior and informed consent in case of relocation (Article 16(2) ILO Convention No 169; Article 10 UNDRIP) and the storage or disposal of hazardous materials in indigenous lands or territories (Article 29(2) UNDRIP).[69] According to the Inter-American human rights jurisprudence, free, prior and informed consent is also required when 'large-scale development or investment projects . . . would have a major impact' on the territory of the people concerned.[70] The Committee on the Elimination of Racial Discrimination has broadly stated that member states should ensure that 'no decisions directly relating to the rights and interests [of indigenous peoples] are taken without their informed consent'.[71] Other UN human rights treaty bodies have also referred to the norm of free, prior and informed consent in relation to indigenous peoples, mostly in the context of resource-extraction activities.[72] Indigenous peoples themselves insist on the recognition of a wide right 'to veto any developments proposed on our lands without our consent'.[73]

The CRC does not give children a right to consent. In General Comment No 12, however, the right of a child to give consent is mentioned a few times. First, child offenders must give their 'free and voluntary consent' in case of diversion, and 'must be given the opportunity to obtain legal and other advice and assistance in determining the appropriateness and desirability of the diversion proposed', the latter requirement thus ensuring an informed consent.[74] In health care, '[t]he Committee welcomes the introduction in some countries of a fixed age at which the right to consent transfers to the child, and encourages States parties to give consideration to the introduction of such legislation'.[75] Moreover, the 'informed consent' of children must be obtained concerning their participation in paediatric research and clinical trials.[76]

The elements of 'free' and 'prior' are not mentioned here. In line with the recognition of children as legal subjects and agentic actors, it seems relevant to rethink more broadly under which circumstances children should not only have a right to be heard, but a right to give consent as well. In the conceptualisation of this right to consent and its attributes, inspiration could be drawn from how the elements of 'free', 'prior' and 'informed' have been developed in the legal framework, jurisprudence and literature on indigenous peoples' rights to consultation and consent.[77] More specifically, clear and accurate information must be provided in a language and format comprehensible for the target group (for instance, in indigenous peoples' mother tongue and in child-friendly terms respectively). The information must be available sufficiently beforehand so that there is time to process and discuss the information, before engaging in the actual consultation process ('informed'). This consultation must be held before the decision is taken ('prior') and without unduly exercising pressure ('free').

Finally, indigenous peoples and children face some common challenges regarding participation. To start, unequal power relationships usually exist in the outward relationship: between indigenous peoples, an individual child or a group of children, on the one hand, and those who seek their opinion or listen to them, normally state representatives, on the other. When a *group* of indigenous peoples or children is consulted or being heard, power dynamics may also play internally. Subaltern or weaker voices risk receiving less attention. People who unite various markers of identity that are more prone to give rise to discrimination (such as gender, disability, ethnic origin, sexual orientation etc), often experience more difficulty in having their voices heard. However, these challenges in relation to power dynamics are shared by other groups as well.

Other participatory challenges seem more particular for indigenous peoples and children. Because their ways of thinking and behaving tend to differ from those of Western society and adults respectively, indigenous peoples and children are usually perceived as difficult-to-reach target groups. As a consequence, participation is often reduced to a mere presence at meetings, without sufficient efforts being made to really listen and try to understand their views.[78] Moreover, indigenous peoples and children share the challenge of avoiding tokenism.[79] Both groups have been put on the stage of international events, for instance at the United Nations, but – especially in earlier decades – unfortunately often more as an exotic 'bonus' than as real stakeholders to be reckoned with. Summing up, for both indigenous peoples and children, the right to have their views being considered has developed in particular ways, as the 'right to consultation' and 'the right to be heard' respectively. When expanding the collective dimension of the right to be heard of children as a group, some of the lessons learnt in indigenous peoples' rights law could be drawn upon. Also, the more advanced conceptual development of the right to free, prior and informed consent in indigenous peoples' rights law could inspire children's rights law.

7.5 Conclusion

This chapter has reflected on whether and how indigenous peoples' rights law could inspire children's rights law. A careful infusion of the flexible and contextual approach used to define indigenous peoples was suggested, in this way going beyond the criterion of chronological age when thinking about the personal scope of children's rights law. Moreover, children's rights law could benefit from the conceptual advances within indigenous peoples' rights law to strengthen the collective right of children to be heard as a group, and to develop the right to free, prior and informed consent of children. A domain in which both (research on) children's rights law and indigenous peoples' rights law should increase efforts concerns addressing the adverse consequences of idealised constructions.

Notes

This research has been funded by the Interuniversity Attraction Poles Programme initiated by the Belgian Science Policy Office, more specifically the IAP 'The global challenge of human rights integration: towards a users' perspective' www.hrintegration.be (last accessed 11 December 2016).

1 See E Desmet, *Indigenous Rights Entwined with Nature Conservation* (Intersentia 2011).
2 Children's Rights Knowledge Centre www.keki.be (last accessed 11 December 2016).
3 UN Human Rights Sub-Commission on Prevention of Discrimination and Protection of Minorities, 'Study of the problem of discrimination against indigenous populations [J R Martínez Cobo, Special Rapporteur]' UN Doc E/CN.4/Sub.2/1986/7/Add.4 paras 379–81.
4 UN Commission on Human Rights, 'Working Paper by the Chairperson-Rapporteur, Mrs Erica-Irene A Daes, on the concept of "indigenous people"' UN Doc E/CN.4/Sub.2/AC.4/1996/2 para 35.
5 See N Rouland, S Pierré-Caps and J Poumarède, *Droit des minorités et des peuples autochtones* (Presses Universitaires de France 1996) 442–43.

6 See F Mackay, *Los Derechos de Los Pueblos Indígenas En El Sistema Internacional* (Asociación Pro Derechos Humanos and Federación Internacional de Derechos Humanos 1999) 74–75.
7 UN Sub-Commission on Prevention of Discrimination and Protection of Minorities, 'Report of the Working Group on Indigenous Populations on its Second Session' UN Doc E/CN.4/sub.2/1983/22, 22–23. See also Russel Lawrence Barsh, 'Indigenous peoples: an emerging object of international law' (1986) 80 *American Journal of International Law* 369, 373–76.
8 See UN Sub-Commission on Prevention of Discrimination and Protection of Minorities, 'Note by the Chairperson-Rapporteur of the Working Group on Indigenous Populations, Ms. Erica-Irene Daes, on criteria which might be applied when considering the concept of indigenous peoples' UN Doc E/CN.4/Sub.2/AC.4/1995/3, 3. See also H Hannum, *Autonomy, Sovereignty, and Self-Determination: The Accommodation of Conflicting Rights* (University of Pennsylvania Press 1992) 91.
9 UN Committee on the Elimination of Racial Discrimination, 'General recommendation No 8: Interpretation and application of article 1(1) and (4) (identification with a particular racial or ethnic group)' UN Doc A/45/18 (1990), preamble.
10 UN General Assembly, 'Resolution adopted by the General Assembly 61/295. United Nations Declaration on the Rights of Indigenous Peoples' UN Doc A/RES/61/295 (2007), Annex.
11 UN Sub-Commission on Prevention of Discrimination and Protection of Minorities, 'Working Paper by the Chairperson-Rapporteur, Mrs Erica-Irene A Daes, on the concept of "indigenous people"' UN Doc E/CN.4/SUB.2/AC.4/1996/2, para 69.
12 ibid para 70.
13 B Kingsbury, '"Indigenous peoples" in international law: a constructivist approach to the Asian controversy' (1998) 92 *American Journal of International Law* 414, 453–55.
14 R Sieder, J Witchell, 'Advancing indigenous claims through the law: reflections on the Guatemalan peace process' in J K Cowan, M-B Dembour and R A Wilson (eds), *Culture and Rights: Anthropological Perspectives* (Cambridge University Press 2001).
15 African Commission on Human and Peoples' Rights, *Report of the African Commission's Working Group of Experts on Indigenous Populations/Communities* (ACHPR and IWGIA 2005) 92–93.
16 ibid 92.
17 Emphasis added.
18 At the regional level, Article 2 of the African Charter on the Rights and Welfare of the Child states: 'A child means every human being below the age of 18 years'. The children's rights policies of the European Union, the Council of Europe and the United Nations also adopt the CRC definition. See E Desmet, 'Implementing the Convention on the Rights of the Child for "youth": who and how?' (2012) 20 *International Journal of Children's Rights* 3, 10.
19 See e.g. M Cornock, H Montgomery, 'Children's rights in and out of the womb' (2011) 19 *International Journal of Children's Rights* 3; R Joseph, *Human Rights and the Unborn Child* (Martinus Nijhoff 2009).
20 See e.g. P E Veerman, 'The ageing of the UN Convention on the Rights of the Child' (2010) 18 *International Journal of Children's Rights* 585.
21 See K Hashemi, 'Religious legal traditions, Muslim states and the Convention on the Rights of the Child: an essay on the relevant UN documentation' (2007) 29 *Human Rights Quarterly* 194, 199.
22 See C Banks, 'The discourse of children's rights in Bangladesh: international norms and local definitions' (2007) 15 *International Journal of Children's*

Rights 391; S C White, 'Children's rights and the imagination of community in Bangladesh' (2007) 14 *Childhood* 505.

23 See A Armstrong and others, 'Towards a cultural understanding of the interplay between children's and women's rights: an Eastern and Southern African perspective' (1995) 3 *International Journal of Children's Rights* 333.

24 See J Whiting, B Whiting, *Children of Six Cultures: A Psycho-Cultural Analysis* (Harvard University Press 1975), referred to in K Cheney, 'Killing them softly? Using children's rights to empower Africa's orphans and vulnerable children' (2012) 56 *International Social Work* 92, 98.

25 See K Hanson, D Volonakis and M Al-Rozzi, 'Child labour, working children and children's rights' in W Vandenhole and others (eds), *Routledge International Handbook of Children's Rights Studies* (Routledge 2015).

26 A parallel could be drawn with the evolution in anti-poverty policies from a purely economic approach to poverty (as lack of income) towards a multidimensional understanding of poverty.

27 In addition, 'thematic' conventions have been adopted to protect *everyone* (not just a particular category of persons) against – at the United Nations level – racial discrimination, torture and enforced disappearances.

28 See F von Benda-Beckmann, 'Citizens, strangers and indigenous peoples: conceptual politics and legal pluralism' in R Kuppe, R Potz (eds), *Law & Anthropology: International Yearbook for Legal Anthropology*, vol 9 (Martinus Nijhoff Publishers 1997).

29 As a man of indigenous origin told me during my fieldwork in the Peruvian Amazon (*Nadie quiere ser indígena ya*).

30 See W Kymlicka, 'The internationalization of minority rights' (2008) 6 *International Journal of Constitutional Law* 1.

31 See further E Desmet, 'Identifying rights-holders in natural resource regimes: a critical assessment of the Peruvian protected areas legislation' (2016) 8 *The Hague Journal on the Rule of Law* 135.

32 See J Hooker, 'Afro-descendant struggles for collective rights in Latin America: between race and culture' (2008) 10 *Souls: A Critical Journal of Black Politics, Culture and Society* 279, 285. Hooker distinguishes between four types of Latin American Afro-descendants: (i) *Afro-mestizos*, descendants of slaves who did not develop a separate racial/cultural group identity; (ii) descendants of slaves who developed a strong racial group identity, such as the *movimento negro* in Brazil; (iii) descendants of 'maroon' communities, such as the Quilombos in Brazil, Creoles in Nicaragua and Garifuna in Honduras, Nicaragua and Guatemala; and, in Central America, (iv) descendants of West Indian immigrant labourers.

33 See IACtHR, *Moiwana v Suriname*, Ser C, no 124 (15 June 2005) and IACtHR, *Saramaka People v Suriname*, Ser C, no 172 (28 November 2007).

34 UN General Assembly, 'Guidelines for the alternative care of children' UN Doc A/RES/64/142 (2009), para 28.

35 See E Desmet, H Op de Beeck and W Vandenhole, 'Walking a tightrope: evaluating the child and youth impact report in Flanders' (2015) 23 *International Journal of Children's Rights* 78.

36 See e.g. H Cunningham, *Children and Childhood in Western Society Since 1500* (2nd edn, Pearson Education Limited 2005); J Dahl, *The Indigenous Space and Marginalized Peoples in the United Nations* (Palgrave Macmillan 2012).

37 See P Thornberry, *Indigenous Peoples and Human Rights* (Manchester University Press 2002) 74.

38 See E Verhellen, 'The Convention on the Rights of the Child: reflections from a historical, social policy and educational perspective' in W Vandenhole and others (n 24) 44.

39 See K H Redford, 'The ecologically noble savage' (1991) 15(1) *Cultural Survival Quarterly* 46.
40 V A Zelizer, *Pricing the Priceless Child: The Changing Social Value of Children* (Princeton University Press 1994).
41 See e.g. R Kramer, C van Schaik and J Johnson, *Last Stand: Protected Areas and the Defense of Tropical Biodiversity* (Oxford University Press 1997); J Terborgh, *Requiem for Nature* (1st edn, Island Press 2004).
42 See e.g. R Nash, *Wilderness and the American Mind* (4th edn, Yale University Press 2001).
43 See S Pleysier, 'Kind als gevaar. De nieuwe preventie en criminalisering van gedrag' (2012) *Tijdschrift voor Jeugd en Kinderrechten* 278.
44 See E A Gagen, 'Reflections of primitivism: development, progress and civilization in imperial America, 1898–1914' (2007) 5 *Children's Geographies* 15, 18.
45 ibid.
46 ibid.
47 C Jenks, *Childhood* (Routledge 2005) 62.
48 ibid 64.
49 See e.g. A James, A Prout, *Constructing and Reconstructing Childhood: Contemporary Issues in the Sociological Study of Childhood* (Psychology Press 1997).
50 See e.g. K von Benda-Beckmann, 'The environmental protection and human rights of indigenous peoples: a tricky alliance' (1997) 9 *Law and Anthropology* 302; E Alden Smith, M Wishnie, 'Conservation and subsistence in small-scale societies' (2000) 29 *Annual Review of Anthropology* 493.
51 See Gagen (n 43) 17, drawing on S C Aitken *Geographies of Young People: The Morally Contested Spaces of Identity* (Routledge 2001), in relation to children.
52 See J W Clay, 'Cultural survival and conservation: lessons from the past twenty years' in M L Oldfield, J B Alcorn (eds), *Biodiversity: Culture, Conservation, and Ecodevelopment* (Westview Press 1991) 248.
53 W Cronon, 'The trouble with wilderness; or; getting back to the wrong nature' in W Cronon (ed), *Uncommon Ground: Rethinking the Human Place in Nature* (W W Norton & Company 1996) 85.
54 R Niezen, *The Origins of Indigenism: Human Rights and the Politics of Identity* (University of California Press 2003) 182.
55 See A Nuytiens, J Christiaens and C Eliaerts, *Ernstige jeugddelinquenten gestraft? Praktijk van de uithandengeving* (Academia Press 2005).
56 ibid 50. Moreover, in the Netherlands, a young person is still tried before the youth court, be it on the basis of the adult criminal code. ibid 49.
57 The other reasons he identified were: (i) the reluctance of indigenous organisations to being critically evaluated, which complicates access by outsiders like researchers or journalists; (ii) the fragile trust between the indigenous movement and non-indigenous persons, as a consequence of which few persons dare to endanger their relationship with the movement by publishing critical analyses; and (iii) the fact that the indigenous political movement was long not considered an appropriate topic of academic research, so few resources were available to do so. R Chase Smith, 'Los indígenas Amazónicos suben al escenario internacional: reflexiones sobre el accidentado camino recorrido' in F Morin, R Santana (eds), *Lo Transnacional: Instrumento y Desafío para los Pueblos Indígenas* (Abya-Yala 2002) 207.
58 But see e.g. Vandenhole and others (n 24), adopting an approach of critique in the study of children's rights.
59 See ILO Convention No 169 art 6(1)(b) and UNDRIP art 18.
60 See J S Anaya, *Indigenous Peoples in International Law* (2nd edn, Oxford University Press 2004) 154.

61 See e.g. CRC Committee, 'General Comment No 12: The Right of the Child to Be Heard' (2009) UN Doc CRC/C/GC/12.
62 But see UNDRIP art 19, where 'directly' has disappeared from the formulation.
63 Emphasis added.
64 See R L Barsh, 'An advocate's guide to the Convention on Indigenous and Tribal Peoples' (1990) 15 *Oklahoma City University Law Review* 209, 219.
65 CRC Committee, 'General Comment No 12' (n 60), para 9.
66 Such assessment may be facilitated when the group in question 'is a component of an enduring structure, such as a family, a class of schoolchildren or the residents of a particular neighbourhood'. ibid para 10.
67 ibid.
68 Emphases added. ibid para 14. These 'settings and situations' are: in the family; in alternative care; in health care; in education and school; in play, recreation, sports and cultural activities; in the workplace; in situations of violence; in the development of prevention strategies; in immigration and asylum proceedings; in emergency situations; and in national and international settings.
69 Moreover, when the lands, territories and resources of indigenous peoples have been 'confiscated, taken, occupied or damaged without their free, prior and informed consent', indigenous peoples are entitled to restitution or other appropriate redress (UNDRIP art 28).
70 IACtHR, *Saramaka People v Suriname* (n 32) para 134.
71 CERD, 'General Recommendation No 23: Indigenous Peoples' (1997) UN Doc CERD/C/51/misc13/rev4, para 4(d).
72 See e.g. CCPR, 'Concluding observations: Nicaragua' (2008) UN Doc CCPR/C/NIC/CO/3, para 21; CESCR, 'Concluding observations: Ecuador' (2004) UN Doc E/C.12/1/Add.100, para 12.
73 International Alliance of the Indigenous and Tribal Peoples of the Tropical Forests, 'Charter of the indigenous and tribal peoples of the tropical forests' art 21.
74 CRC Committee, 'General Comment No 12' (n 60), para 59.
75 ibid para 102.
76 ibid para 103.
77 See e.g. IACtHR, *Saramaka People v Suriname* (n 69); IACtHR, *Kichwa Indigenous People of Sarayaku v Ecuador*, Ser C, no 245 (27 June 2012); UN General Assembly, 'Report of the Special Rapporteur on the rights of indigenous peoples' (2011), UN Doc. A/66/288, paras 77–91, (on the duty to consult); Desmet (n 1) 314–317.
78 See e.g. S Bessell, T Gal, 'Forming partnerships: the human rights of children in need of care and protection' (2009) 17 *International Journal of Children's Rights* 283, 290; Desmet (n 1) 600–607.
79 See e.g. R A Hart, *Children's Participation: From Tokenism to Citizenship* (UNICEF International Child Development Centre 1992).

8 What young and old can learn from each other: cross-fertilisation between existing human rights law for children and developing human rights law for older persons

Ann-Katrin Habbig, Alexander Hoefmans and Paul De Hert

Quels conseils les 'anciens' pourraient donner aux 'nouveaux' afin d'éviter des erreurs de débutant(e) et vice versa

8.1 Introduction

The most recent UN World Population Prospects forecast a population growth that shatters previous predictions. By 2100 the world population is expected to increase to 11.2 billion people,[1] with the base of young people shrinking and the proportion of older persons growing.[2] This demographic transition has a tremendous influence on the economy by means of public expenditures for inter alia pensions, healthcare and long-term care. Whilst general healthcare costs are only estimated to increase moderately, a stronger effect is expected from the use of new technologies in healthcare (for which older persons are an important target group) and growth in long-term care.[3] Many states formerly known as 'welfare states' are in the current times of financial difficulties cutting back expenditure for social benefits and healthcare.[4]

These changes and their expected socio-economic impacts, combined with an increase in fundamental rights discourse, illustrate why more and more people focus on (the elaboration of) rights of older persons. Whilst children and the protection of their rights have been a major concern during the last decades, the rights of older persons have not received the same attention and recognition.[5] For some, this is no longer justified, since in their view current human rights instruments do not sufficiently articulate the needs and requirements of older persons. It is therefore argued that because the societal constraints imposed by the 'burden' of demographic change become ever more pressing, there is a need for more empowerment of older people by ensuring the protection of their rights becomes visible. This challenge can be informed by the field of other person-based human rights conventions. In particular, the success story of the

Convention on the Rights of the Child (CRC)[6] serves as an encouraging model to elaborate on the development of further person-based treaties. After decades of struggling for the recognition of children's rights, the CRC has been a major achievement in promoting and strengthening the rights of a nevertheless still vulnerable group.

The heterogeneity of the group of older persons might be used to argue against the creation of specific rights. Although the group is indeed diverse, this should not hinder the creation of specific rights. Many other groups which can be considered as heterogeneous – such as children or women – are covered by international conventions and do receive special protection. Following these examples, the creation of specific rights for older persons is a possibility, despite the heterogeneity of the group.

Even though there is a clear lack of binding instruments, there is an ongoing discussion on an international level. In the first section, this contribution discusses the lengthy history of the struggle for human rights for older persons (section 1). In the next section we elaborate on the movement of human rights law towards a possible convention on the rights of older persons (section 2). Then we discuss the added value of human rights monitoring (section 3) and the necessity of adding principles (section 4) to the rights listed in section 5. The CRC can clearly serve as an inspiration when it comes to the use of principles rather than creating a merely rights-based convention. In the last section the involvement of third parties in the CRC is considered as an interesting option for enriching the discussion on the rights of older persons (section 6). Finally, we conclude that the CRC is a thought-provoking example of the development towards the personification of human rights which can serve us as a fruitful source of new ideas to revive and advance the process of creating a convention on the rights of older persons. We will push the analysis in the other direction and highlight some of features of this older persons' human rights law to come, which could inspire further amendments and improvements in children's human rights law. In doing this we also look at some of the improvements contained in the 2006 Convention on the Rights of Persons with Disabilities (CRPD).

8.2 Movement towards a convention for older persons

Already at the time that the Universal Declaration of Human Rights (UDHR) was signed, there were discussions about the necessity of specific human rights for older persons.[7] Since then there have been many attempts by the UN to create specific human rights for older persons, although none has been successful. Therefore, the following inventory is indicative of a history of failure conerning enshrining specific rights of older persons in human rights instruments.

In 1948, Argentina introduced a Draft Resolution on the Declaration of Old Age Rights.[8] This draft is considered as one of the first attempts to draw attention to the rights of older persons. The point of time is very remarkable as the UDHR had just been adopted and no other UN human rights documents existed at that time. Argentina states in the draft 'that old age rights, having the same origin and purpose as other universal social safeguards, are essential for the improvement of the living conditions of the worker and for his welfare when his physical strength is at an end and he is exposed to poverty and neglect'.[9] The draft is focusing on the following rights: the right to assistance, the right to accommodation, the right to food, the right to clothing, the right to the care of physical health, the right to the care of moral health, the right to recreation, the right to work, the right to stability and the right to respect. These rights cover the areas of adequate standard of living (including housing), the right to health, the right to dignity and the right to work; topics which are still considered very relevant for older persons. The original draft resolution has never been adopted. Instead, the UN General Assembly in 1948 published a short resolution referring to the draft declaration by the Argentinian delegation.[10]

The 1982 Vienna International Plan of Action on Ageing, drafted by the first World Assembly of Ageing, is considered to be the first international document on ageing and an important step towards the realisation of specific rights for older persons. It represents a concentrated response to the challenges that were and are expected from an ageing society by including the needs and the potential of older persons. The focus is developmental and its recommendations for action span from research and health to employment.[11] The plan is part of a broader framework of strategies which had been developed in the years before.[12] It acknowledges a gender dimension of ageing by taking into account the longevity of women, who are expected to form the majority of the older population.[13]

The 1991 UN Principles for Older Persons are built on the affirmation of faith in general human rights and were adopted by UN General Assembly Resolution A46/91 (1991). The principles cover five areas: independence, participation, care, self-fulfilment and dignity.[14] The area of independence includes the provision of income and support in order to guarantee access to food, water and healthcare. Older persons should have access to education and be able to work and determine themselves when to withdraw from the workforce. Secondly, they should be able to live at home independently for as long as they want. Participation in society, associations and movements is another focus point. Thirdly, older persons should benefit from (health) care, social and legal services. Then, through access to educational and spiritual services older persons should be able to develop their full potential. Finally, the dignity of older persons needs to be safeguarded by protecting them from abuse and guaranteeing non-discrimination.[15]

Following the 10th anniversary of the Vienna Plan in 1992, the UN General Assembly adopted a Proclamation on Ageing, asking to promote the 1982 Vienna Plan as well as the 1991 Principles.[16] A (second) World Assembly on Ageing took place in 2002. It adopted the Madrid International Plan of Action on Ageing that focuses on three priority themes: development; health and well-being; and enabling environments.[17] The idea was to further advance the philosophies developed in Vienna 20 years earlier,[18] and to focus on the protection of human rights of older persons and the elimination of age-based discrimination. The adopted document also included a political *declaration* emphasising equal rights for everyone.[19]

The 2002 Declaration and the 2002 Action Plan were endorsed by the UN General Assembly in the 2003 Resolution 57/167. However, despite the creation of regional action plans, the awareness about these initiatives remained low and there was a lack of effective implementation.[20]

In 2010, a Working Group on Ageing was established by the UN General Assembly with the intention to improve the protection of human rights of older persons.[21] An important follow-up step was the establishment in 2013 of an independent expert (Resolution 24/20) on the enjoyment of all human rights by older persons.[22] The independent expert was expected to assess the implementation of existing international instruments and to identify current gaps, to consult stakeholders and consider regional and national human rights mechanisms, to inform older persons about their rights, to pay particular attention to vulnerable groups (such as women and disabled persons) and to cooperate with states to strengthen the implementation of rights for older persons.[23]

These international developments were complemented by several regional initiatives. Significant for Europe, for example, is the Council of Europe 2014 Recommendation on the rights of older persons.[24] This recommendation promotes the fight against discrimination, autonomy and participation, the protection from violation and abuse, social protection and employment, care (consent, homecare, institutional and palliative care) and the administration of justice. A particular feature of this recommendation is that it gives good practices from all over the world to illustrate the possible use and implementation of the respective rights.

8.3 A new treaty would create a double opportunity if the scope is controlled

In past contributions, we have pointed to the advantages of reflecting on the need to adopt new legal instruments going beyond the core UN covenants.[25] This is contrary to others that are sceptical about the pursuit for a convention of rights for older persons.[26] There are in existing human rights law relevant provisions for the protection of older persons, but there is no comprehensive instrument ensuring a general application of the rights of older persons. The existing international documents on the rights of older persons are not binding and do not address the government's positive obligations towards older persons. The lack of internationally binding treaties on human rights for older persons leads to major problems: missing attention of states, as well as the absence of human rights bodies and monitoring bodies on the rights of older persons. Consequently, specific rights for older persons should not only be brought forward in non-binding documents but should be protected with the creation of specific human rights.

This process, undoubtedly leading to proliferation of human rights treaties (see below), creates two opportunities. First, it can help calling things by their name, and allowing for the injection of new ideas, new or adapted legal standards as well as improved methods to address the implementation gap existing treaties encounter. In a next section we will discuss improved methods of monitoring human rights policies as an example of a novel idea. Ultimately, it can lead to treaties focusing on either a phenomenon or a treatment one can be subjected to (such as forced disappearances, torture or racial discrimination) or a group of persons in society facing particular difficulties to achieve full enjoyment of their human rights (such as women, children, migrants and persons with a disability).

This latter category of treaties – the outcome of a process of personification of human rights[27] – focuses on the needs and challenges of specific vulnerable groups. This focus should make possible a more interpretative, contextual and functional rights-based approach allowing a degree of dynamism other treaties may lack. The developments to strengthen the rights of older persons, in particular through a new UN treaty (see above), therefore constitute an opportunity to take this reflection further, not only to take stock of existing mechanisms but also to search for avenues of cross-fertilisation[28] and to bring together rights and ideas that are now separated in traditional human rights documents but are in fact interdependent.[29]

Secondly, several of the challenges that specific groups of persons, such as older persons, have to deal with are nurtured by archaic notions and perceptions deeply rooted in our societies. They lay at foundations that perpetuate inherent limitations to the exercise of human rights. These notions and perceptions can be reversed through the introduction of substantial and structural paradigm shifts.[30] Previous treaties have increasingly addressed the existing barriers groups of persons experience in enjoying their human rights. A treaty on the rights of older persons would be well served with such paradigm shifts addressing stereotypes associated with ageing.[31]

Creating new rights and instruments produces the risk of proliferation of human rights and feeds a concern that this would dilute the authority of the existing rights, treaties and their monitoring mechanisms. The problem, however, lies not so much with the adoption of new instruments but rather with the lack of consensus to apply new methods to negotiating human rights treaties. Indeed, rather than the copy and paste exercise which parts of such negotiations often entail we plead for a thorough discussion based on the adaptation of core rights to the context of older persons on the one hand and a dynamic approach to monitoring and enforcement on the other hand.[32] Only by taking into account the constraints of other treaties and treaty bodies can a new legal instrument bring added value and, in turn, other treaties and treaty bodies can benefit from the dynamics of negotiating innovative approaches and new legal standards.

In this respect a discussion on the scope of rights of a future UN treaty for older persons is fundamental. Should a future treaty address all human rights of older persons or rather focus on specific rights? In the latter case, on what basis should we select the rights to be withheld and developed according to an interpretative, contextual and functional rights-based approach? In our view a selective approach would not only help muster the necessary political support to move the UN towards a new legal instrument, it would ultimately also benefit the authority of the legal standards adopted and an effective implementation of the treaty.[33]

Firstly, a future treaty could be limited to clusters of rights addressing the most significant challenges older persons face in society. In his first report to the General

Assembly on the rights of older persons, Secretary General Ban Ki-moon stressed the following four key human rights issues: poverty, violence and abuse, discrimination, lack of specific measures and services.[34] We will highlight in section 5 some of the rights requiring particular attention. Secondly, a new treaty should hold a substantive general provision stipulating that relevant standards adopted and developed by other UN human rights treaties are to be considered as an integral part of the treaty on the rights of older persons. Currently, any bridges between the treaties are only taken up in the section elaborating the monitoring of the treaty and the means of cooperation between UN bodies or through savings clauses such as in Article 41 CRC.[35] We see added value in also providing for an interconnection between treaties as to their substantive provisions.[36]

8.4 Monitoring of human rights: making it smarter

The call for a more comprehensive and substantively binding instrument addressing the rights of older persons cannot be dissociated from a system of monitoring and enforcement of internationally agreed standards. In the same vein, reinforcing existing instruments or moving towards a new mechanism of monitoring specifically for the rights of older persons should be connected to the broader discussion of the efficiency of the current models.[37] The Committee on the Rights of the Child can be considered as a benchmark amongst existing UN committees but it suffers from constraints that are inherent to the overall set-up of UN human rights treaties monitoring. Negotiating a UN treaty on the rights of older persons would present an opportunity to inject new methods of monitoring into the UN system that could ultimately inspire other committees. It could also consolidate or build on innovative practices that have already been developed. A step forward would be to make it impossible for states to express reservations with regard to the provisions regarding monitoring.[38]

The 2009 General Guidelines on periodic reports[39] seek to harmonise practices, ensure consistency and create synergies by encouraging state parties not to repeat all of the information set out in previous reports but rather describe developments, in terms of legislation and domestic practice, update the data previously supplied and inform the committee on the follow-up to the concluding observations. The common core document details the overarching human rights framework which defines the implementation of all treaties. The committees also increasingly cross-reference their recommendations in concluding observations. This enhances coherence but often merely amounts to a reiteration of previous concerns. While these are laudable efforts, the extent to which they render the UN monitoring system swifter and more thorough is questionable.

Coming back to our reflection on the scope of the future treaty (see section 2), a treaty on the rights of older persons confined to a selective or cluster approach would redirect a committee's energy and resources to areas where it would be most beneficial. At the same time, it would imply a more meaningful dialogue with state parties and civil society. The guidelines on reporting currently underscore the need for all periodic reports to indicate 'factors and difficulties' encountered by the state in the implementation of the treaties and to specify 'implementation priorities' and 'specific goals for the future'. Combining the obligation for periodic reports to reflect the rationale of state policies and priorities with the requirement to deliver concise but informative reports which cover the entire scale of rights and principles of a treaty is a daunting task. Given the timeframe of each cycle – here particularly problematic in the case of the CRC – and both the retrospective and forward-looking exercise, periodic reporting as a means to control and navigate state parties can be considered an under-achieving tool, rather than providing the 'positive monitoring climate' as was initially intended.[40]

In the absence of a general overhaul of the UN monitoring system and to avoid burdening already strained existing committees, we still favour the creation of a separate committee on the rights of older persons. However, thought should clearly be given to setting up a more focused committee rather than the copy and paste exercise that took place in the more recent Committee on the Rights of Persons with Disabilities.

8.5 Adding principles to the listed rights

Now let us turn to the more substantive issues when shaping a treaty on older persons' rights. We have already insisted on the need to be selective when choosing rights and to look for synergies with existing treaties. A first question to be addressed is whether we need to be thinking rights *only*, or rights ***and*** principles. Children's human rights law seems to suggest a positive answer to the latter: there are four general principles enshrined in this area of law based on the CRC: non-discrimination; the best interests of the child; the right to life, survival and development; and respect for the views of the child. These are guiding principles meant to help interpret the Convention as a whole. Furthermore, they are considered to establish the core rights of the CRC.

The four general principles were not, however, explicitly portrayed as general principles from the outset but have rather been recognised as such through interpretation by the Committee on the Rights of the Child. A good example is the right of children to be heard, provided for in Article 12 CRC. The Committee has identified Article 12 as one of the four general principles of the Convention, thus highlighting the fact that this article establishes not only a right in itself, but should also be considered in the interpretation and implementation of all other rights.[41] Principles such as 'the best interest' are fluid and flexible. Children's human rights law teaches us that principles will not be used as an alibi for individual arbitrariness.[42]

Whereas we do not dispute the usefulness of incorporating principles in the treaties, the activist approach of the Committee on the Rights of the Child to lift several principles to a more prominent level in the CRC has resulted – albeit in a limited way – in a fragmentation of rights and principles. Firstly, the principles are scattered throughout the substantive provisions of the CRC. Secondly, some rights have also been categorised as principles, whereas some principles are clearly not rights (such as the best interests of the child). Thirdly, the best interests of the child principle is distinguished as the superlative principle to which all rights and principles in the CRC should be held and therefore seems to constitute a category on its own.[43] This asymmetry has to some extent been rectified through the CRC treaty specific reporting guidelines[44] but only by regrouping them for purposes of monitoring implementation.

A different approach has been taken in the 2006 Convention on the Rights of Persons with Disabilities (CRPD), where state parties are presented in Article 3 with a coherent, self-standing and equal set of principles.[45] We would favour a similar provision for a future treaty on the rights of older persons. Even when following the selective approach to the scope of rights to be incorporated in a future treaty, we still see an added value in having a separate article with general principles. The addition of principles in a treaty does not necessarily limit their effect to only interpreting the rights withheld in the substantive provisions. Given that principles have a different status and purpose than rights, they could bridge the gap to all human rights of older persons and to other treaties and treaty bodies as partially self-standing provisions equally requiring implementation. A general provision could be included stipulating the obligation of state parties to facilitate the realisation of the rights and principles of the treaty, rather than only the rights.[46] This would confirm their complementary nature.

Regardless of the scope of the rights included, a future treaty on older persons would also need to take into account the traditional division between immediately applicable rights and those rights that allow for progressive realisation. Considering where many of the challenges lie for older persons, a margin of implementation of socio-economic rights will be required, much in line with Article 4(1) CRC, which obliges states to 'undertake all appropriate legislative, administrative, and other measures' for the implementation of the rights recognised in the Convention, but clarifies in Article 4(2) that 'with regard to economic, social and cultural rights, state parties shall undertake such measures to the maximum extent of their available resources'. This approach, that gives states leeway in the implementation of economic, social and cultural rights, is to our taste, incomplete in view of the current insufficient protection of economic and social rights and their interdependence with other rights. General principles can also be considered as additional leverage to move states to adopt measures with the aim of implementing socio-economic rights.[47]

A radical, alternative approach is to move away from the resources perspective and to turn to the capability approach as developed by Sen and Nussbaum. This approach has been employed in welfare economics to foster certain human rights for quite some time now.[48] The capabilities approach – contrary to many other approaches on development – does not focus on economic growth but wants to foster people's opportunities – the so-called capabilities.[49] During the last decades the capability approach has been applied to several (vulnerable) groups such as children and women.[50] One group that received little attention in this context is the growing group of older persons. According to Nussbaum's version of the capabilities approach, everyone can be recognised as the rights bearer of certain basic fundamental entitlements (the so-called central capabilities).[51] Nussbaum identifies the following list of 10 entitlements: life; bodily health; bodily integrity; senses, imagination, and thought; emotions; practical reasoning; affiliation; other species; play; and control over one's environment.[52]

Thinking in terms of capabilities shifts the focus away from the resources issue. Rather than fostering the image of older people as consumers or recipients of goods, it (also) provides them with agency concerning their rights and identifies what is needed for them to act and lead their lives. Sen's aim is to prioritise equality of capabilities over equality of income and to make contextualisation possible.[53] Respect for basic capabilities as a principle could be one way of overcoming the divide between groups of rights (as is done in Article 4 CRC) that are as a matter of fact interdependent.

8.6 Highlighting specific principles and rights

8.6.1 General: useful approaches taken from the CRC

We saw in the foregoing that the CRC can serve as an inspiration when it comes to the use of principles, rather than creating a merely rights-based convention. Undeniably, an adaptation of several principles to the specific situation of older people is indispensable.[54]

There is more to learn from children's rights law. The CRC approaches the rights of children in different ways. There are on the one hand articles that foresee concrete rights and state obligations[55] and on the other hand articles which only provide a general framework or very generally formulated rights.[56] Both approaches are worth considering for the rights of older persons.[57] Whilst specific targeted rights provide clear standards, a more general set-up leaves space for a certain degree of interpretation.

In the following we identify, using the CRC and the CRPD as reference points, several rights and principles that, to our mind, seem to be of particular importance for older persons. Particular attention will be paid to provisions on participation and the right to be protected against age-based discrimination (both of which can also be considered as principles), the right to work and education, the right to health, the right to social security, the right to housing and the right to freedom from violence and abuse.

8.6.2 Participation as a principle and right

The introduction of the right for children to have their views heard in matters that concern them (Article 12 CRC) has been a cornerstone of the CRC and has set a benchmark for subsequent treaties. We saw above that the Committee on the Rights of the Child, recognising the importance of this right, transformed it into one of the four general principles of the CRC thereby stressing its transversal applicability. The right to be heard, while remaining a self-standing provision, thus evolved into the broader concept of participation which state parties are required to implement throughout the CRC.[58] Interestingly, the CRPD has included full and effective participation as an explicit general principle in its Article 3 but does not provide for a substantive provision on the right of persons with disabilities to be heard in matters concerning them. Rather, the CRPD stresses the procedural element of participation by requiring state parties to consult and actively involve persons with disabilities through their representative organisations.

Our take is to propose both: participation as a principle and as a set of rights (for instance the right to participation in cultural life).[59] There is much to be said about participation and a self-standing provision along the lines of the CRC or Article 25 of the EU Charter on Fundamental Rights could allow this to be accommodated. Particularly relevant for a future treaty on the rights of older persons is the notion of evolving capacities that the CRC introduced in relation to participation.[60] Article 12 CRC refers to age and maturity as criteria to determine the weight to be given to a child's opinion. Using these criteria to establish the capacity of a child, the CRC does not only acknowledge a child as an active rights holder, but also recognises the development that a child undergoes and the impact this has on the way a child can enjoy his or her rights on the one hand and the way state parties should implement the provisions of the CRC on the other. Interestingly again, the notion of evolving capacities has only been marginally recognised in the CRPD in one of its recitals[61] and in relation to children with disabilities.

A future treaty on the rights of older persons should combine the different approaches developed through the CRC and the CRPD. Participation is a principle that works in both directions. On the one hand, it can be a tool that empowers older persons to plead their cause and set progress in motion by their own doing. On the other hand, participation ensures that state parties involve those who are affected by their decisions and develop policies that take into account different capacities of rights holders.[62]

8.6.3 The right to be protected against age-based discrimination

Age-based discrimination is one of the principal struggles and even human rights violations of older persons. Interestingly, the CRC does prohibit discrimination but does not refer to age at all. This might be due to the fact that the CRC gives a clear definition of its target group in Article 1.[63] This definition is not as clear-cut when describing older persons. Whether a person is labelled as 'aged', 'old' or 'elderly' depends on the cultural context and the respective life expectancy. When looking at the statistics of the EU, the cut-off for inclusion within the group 'older persons' is 65 years and above.[64] Economic planning and in particular social schemes are based on specific understandings of the age group of older persons. Economic terminology such as the aforementioned 'age dependency rate' suggests that all people older than 65 years are no longer economically productive. This cut-off, however, does not reflect empirical reality, obfuscating the fact that many stop working before reaching this age whilst others remain within the workforce for far longer. As mentioned above, the idea of an 'old' person also depends heavily on the cultural context, and in countries with an average life expectancy below 60 years (which is still the reality in several sub-Saharan countries) a cut-off of 65 years seems not only unrealistic but even cynical. The UN therefore designates a person as older if he or she is aged 60 or more.[65]

The principle of non-discrimination is normally phrased as a 'catch-all' expression that does not pay attention to age.[66] The Universal Declaration of Human Rights (UDHR) entails a provision that has been a model for many other human rights treaties and contains a list of forbidden distinctions.[67] Even though it is said that this list is non-exhaustive it is still noticeable that age is not mentioned.[68] The UDHR and the other general treaties do forbid distinctions based on 'other status', but it is disputed whether this open term includes older persons.[69] Interestingly, the (more recent) European treaties entail provisions that include age amongst the prohibited grounds for discrimination.[70] Article 21.1 (on non-discrimination) of the EU Charter forcefully states that '*any* discrimination based on any ground such as sex, race, disability, *age* or sexual orientation shall be prohibited'.[71]

It would in our option not be recommended to stop there. In line with children's human rights law, the prohibition of age discrimination should be a matter of 'principle' *and* 'right', giving the right's immediate effect in all matters, including the field of economic, social and cultural rights, and should therefore be modelled along the lines of the relatively broad CRC provision on non-discrimination.[72] Also, the relevant provisions should pay explicit attention to very urgent problems such as discrimination against older women and should be complemented and clarified, where necessary, in provisions that relate to other specific rights .[73]

Barbara Mikolajczyk makes a strong case for specific provisions on protection against discrimination on the basis of old age, especially in the European context, since the Member States could rectify specific well-known flaws in the European Convention on Human Rights (ECHR): Article 14 ECHR having a limited scope and being silent on discrimination on the basis of old age; Protocol No 2 to the ECHR (prohibiting discrimination in all spheres of life) only ratified by relatively few countries. European Member States do not seem willing to endorse new general anti-discrimination provisions, Mikolajczyk writes, but they might be more willing to accept laws exclusively limited to the prohibition on discrimination on the grounds of age (older age) in various spheres of human life.[74] If this observation is correct, it might be an option to explore an equal treatment approach, rather than a non-discrimination approach,[75] a road not taken in children's rights law.

8.6.4 The right to health

The idea of weak and frail older persons is still persisting in our minds, although older persons are often robust, independent and physically and socially active. This is reflected in the appreciation of the development of future healthcare costs; the same are not expected to rise radically owing to the demographic transition.[76] Nonetheless, the right to health plays an important role for older persons, particularly if seen in the context of access to healthcare and the provision of long-term care. Successful ageing – thus the upkeep of a high physical and mental function – and the demographic transition also illustrate the success of modern medicine and the more widespread access to it. In order to foster successful ageing the right to health therefore needs to be realised by providing easy access to healthcare – specifically prevention programmes. Despite numerous active older citizens, the need for care at a high age should not be neglected. The right to health therefore also needs to ensure the realisation of long-term care.

The question if there is a right to health still provokes an ongoing academic debate. Many human rights documents, international and regional, include this right. However, this is not incorporated in all human rights treaties and also not accepted by all states.[77] We observe in passing that the EU Charter of Fundamental Rights does not formulate a right to health, although it does address the more specific right to healthcare.[78] The right to health is explicitly recognised in the International Covenant on Economic, Social and Cultural Rights (ICESCR), which states in Article 12 that there is a 'right of everyone to the enjoyment of the highest attainable standard of physical and mental health'.[79] Article 12 mentions very specific steps that should be taken by state parties to achieve a full realisation of the right to health. State parties should furthermore take the requirement of 'the creation of conditions which would assure to all medical service' in Article 12.2(c) into consideration.[80]

More preferable as a source of inspiration is, again, the CRC, which acknowledges the right 'to the enjoyment of the highest attainable standard of health and to the facilities for the treatment of illness and rehabilitation of health'.[81] With this statement the CRC goes further than the ICESCR, and undeniably further than many other human rights treaties that only recognise a relatively 'abstract' idea of health rather than a specific right of access to healthcare. Furthermore, the CRC provides a list of 'targets' for children's health that poses clear positive obligations on all state parties. Although the needs of children will be different from those of older persons, the list can serve as an inspiration for the latter in order to emphasise the importance of the responsibility of the state in facilitating the right to health for older persons in general and access to healthcare and the promotion of healthy and active ageing in particular.

One of the 'targets' of the CRC is the information and education of parents and children about health.[82] The right to health is often focused on the right to receive healthcare and the aspect of receiving information and proper education is often neglected. These aspects are also of high importance for older people. Still, the CRC seems cautious here in recognising the right of children to take their own decisions regarding their health. This right is closely related to dignity and self-determination (the right to take one's own decisions regarding healthcare). This includes consent to medical treatment – meaning that treatment can also be refused. For both groups, the young and the old, the question of the ability to consent is an important one. Mental health issues can impact the decision-making capacities of older persons and entail a loss of autonomy with regards to this right,[83] whilst children might not be considered mature enough to take their own decisions.

8.6.5 The right to work

An area where older persons often suffer discrimination is 'work'. Mandatory retirement ages often limit the opportunities of older persons and force them into retirement against their own will. Naturally, the right to work requires a different approach when it comes to children. Contrary to employing a maximum age, the CRC focuses on the protection of children from economic exploitation, thus requiring a minimum age and the regulation of working hours and other employment conditions.[84]

The real challenge will consist in finding a balance between protection and emancipation or independence. The right to work can fulfil an important function when working towards the recognition of older persons as an important part of society. The recognition of the valuable experience and knowledge this group might have is an important step towards re-evaluating the value older people can have as a part of the workforce. Mandatory retirement age can be justified in certain cases.[85] It is, however, important to realise that this mandatory regime – which is handled in some countries or with regard to certain professions – can strongly impact an older person's life and force him or her to withdraw from economic activities that might be essential for maintaining a reasonable standard of life, or lead to social isolation and have a psychological impact.[86] We are aware of the debate with regard to a right to work for children and some advocating in favour of such a right. If older persons' human rights law strikes the right balance between protection and emancipation, this could be an argument to look more closely at the parallel debate in children's human rights law.

8.6.6 The right to education

Whereas it is obvious to consider education when examining the rights of children,[87] the right to education of older persons has only recently received more attention. Concepts such as life-long learning are currently high on policy agendas and aim to encourage people of all ages to continue educating themselves throughout their lives.

The right to education is recognised – amongst others – in Article 13 of the ICECSR.[88] According to the General Comment No 6, two dimensions of this right have to be taken into account: the benefit of education programmes and the transfer of knowledge to younger generations.[89] Similar to the right to work, the right to education can be a measure for empowerment. In a world of constant technological change, tailored education programmes can ensure that older persons can keep up with the developments and actively participate in discussions surrounding these issues.

8.6.7 The right to social security and an adequate standard of living

Articles 22 and 25 of the UDHR promote the right to social security and to an adequate standard of living.[90] Article 22 states: 'Everyone, as a member of society, has the right to social security and is entitled to realization, through national effort and international co-operation. . .'.[91] We have already touched upon the right to social security and the need to include a non-discrimination dimension within. As is the case for children, it is useful to discuss separately the contours of a right to social security for older persons.[92] Similar to children, older persons may not be economically active. This is not only attributable to their possible inability (physically or mentally) to work but is often the result of a mandatory retirement age. Additionally, many people will have saved money during their economic life in order to retire at a certain age and enjoy some years without having to work. The right to social security ensures that persons who are not working are cared for economically. In many states, however, this does not automatically imply that an adequate standard of living is ensured by the state, even though this seems desirable for many. The right to social security includes government benefits (for example retirement benefits in the form of pensions). These are necessary for older persons to guarantee an adequate standard of living.

More appropriate guidance with regard to social security is found in the European Social Charter. It explicitly formulates a right to social protection for older persons in Article 23, including the following issues: 'adequate resources enabling them to lead a decent life and play an active part in public, social and cultural life; . . . to enable older persons to choose their life-style freely and to lead independent lives . . . while respecting their . . . participation in decisions concerning living conditions in the institution'.[93]

The European Social Charter thus clarifies that 'adequate resources' are necessary and goes further by requesting these not only to cover basic needs but also to enable persons to take part in all different aspects of life. Article 27 of the CRC extends this right and grants the right to an adequate standard of living and makes it a prerequisite for the successful 'physical, mental, spiritual, moral and social development' of children.[94] This responsibility is primarily with the parents but needs to be guaranteed by the state if necessary. Many older persons have a legal entitlement to social benefits owing to their prior economic engagement and their contributions to the social security system. However, this does not necessarily guarantee an adequate standard of living as prescribed by Article 27 of the CRC. Furthermore, the responsibility of family members in certain cases (e.g. long-term care) – similar to the CRC – should be considered, whilst the responsibility of the state for those in need still needs to be emphasised.

8.6.8 The right to housing

The right to housing forms part of the right to an adequate standard of living as included in Article 25 of the UDHR. The General Comment No 4 of the CESCR on Adequate Housing provides for specific protection of older persons.[95] The right to housing by far exceeds the mere provision of shelter or the protection from homelessness. It needs to enable everyone to live in 'security, peace and dignity'.[96] Adequate housing means conformity with the legal security of tenure, the availability of services, materials, facilities and infrastructure, affordability, habitability, accessibility, location and cultural adequacy.[97] Children are granted a right to housing by Article 27 of the CRC.[98]

An adequate standard of living and adequate housing are of course of importance to all members of society. For older persons this can however form a particular issue. The requirements of older persons for adequate housing are different from those of younger persons. Older persons may require compatible housing structures (to their physical abilities) and the provision of services for older persons in their home. The aim is to enable older persons to live independently in their own house for as long as possible if they wish to do so.[99]

8.6.9 The right to freedom from violence and abuse

Many older people experience verbal, sexual, psychological and financial abuse.[100] Whilst the right to be free from violence and abuse is not enshrined in most internationally binding treaties, the CRC makes explicit reference to it. Article 19 states that: 'State Parties shall take all appropriate . . . measures to protect the child from all forms of physical or mental violence, injury or abuse, neglect or negligent treatment, maltreatment or exploitation, including sexual abuse . . .'.[101] Children and older persons are both vulnerable groups, often in dependent situations of care. In such situations they are particularly prone to abuse.

UN documents such as the Implementation of the International Plan of Action on Ageing and Related Activities specifically mention a right to freedom from abuse and violence, forming part of the right to dignity.[102] In recent years the protection against abuse, violence and neglect has been made a priority by the UN.[103] Abuse can happen in different settings and accordingly requires targeted approaches. The most common settings for the abuse of older persons might be the institutional setting (physical abuse, misuse of medications, financial abuse), the home setting (isolation, financial abuse, violence) and palliative care (refusal of palliative treatment).[104] Particularly, in these settings there is often a lack of monitoring. These situations often entail dependence from formal and informal carers. Older people are disproportionally likely to require care in one or several of these forms. Therefore, they are exceptionally vulnerable in this respect. Strengthening protection from abuse and violence of older persons requires an effective monitoring system. The need for reporting, investigation and follow-up (with judicial involvement if necessary) is provided for in the CRC. Moreover, it mentions the need for prevention of abuse and violence.[105]

8.7 Third parties and procedural rights

Perhaps the most important lesson to be learned from children's rights law is its focus on the role of third parties, such as parents and legal guardians. Even though the CRC recognises children as autonomous bearers of rights and it is argued that only they have fundamental rights under the CRC, third parties continue to play an important role in their daily lives. The concept of a duty bearer – in classical human rights law the state – is reinterpreted in the CRC and by assigning conditional rights to third parties they are also ascribed certain duties and obligations in order to ensure the full enjoyment of fundamental rights and the best interest of children.[106]

The concept of third parties is an interesting one when elaborating on the rights of older persons. Whilst the CRC emphasises the aspect of 'capability' in accordance 'with the age and maturity of the child'[107] and therefore expects a development towards full capability in decision-making, older persons often see a reverse development. Many cognitive impairments are age-related and can affect older persons in a way that the support of a legal guardian becomes inevitable. The inclusion of the rights and duties of third parties is therefore of particular interest when looking at a possible convention on the rights of older persons. A guiding principle – similar to the CRC – is the idea of the bearers of fundamental rights (the older persons) and the bearers of conditional rights (third parties). The CRC cannot be used as a one-to-one guideline[108] but should rather serve as an inspiration for the involvement of those persons who play a particular role in the lives of older persons and can influence their decisions or take decisions on their behalf. A line on the extent of their conditional role will be difficult to draw and will certainly provoke fruitful discussions in future.

The involvement of third parties also becomes – similar to childcare – visible when looking at the need for care that many older persons have. Within Europe the legal obligation for families to take care of their older family members differs.[109] Informal care within families still plays an important role. Nonetheless, a steady shift towards formal care and alternative forms of care for older persons can be observed.[110] The variety of approaches to care contributes to the difficulty in defining clear responsibilities of third parties. It should, however, not be neglected that there is a risk of an abuse of conditional rights – furthering the current abuse of rights as previously mentioned.

One way to move forward is to pay attention to the procedural rights to be exercised either by the older persons or by those representing them. After the question of *what rights*, the question of *how to exercise* them needs to be addressed, preferably in the same convention. We recall that in children's rights law this second question, not put forward in the CRC, has been taken up by the Council of Europe in the 1996 European Convention on the Exercise of Children's Rights.[111]

This Convention contains useful distinctions regarding the capacity of children, clarifies the roles of parents and the duties of judicial authorities and 'representatives' (a person, such as a lawyer, or a body appointed to act before a judicial authority on behalf of a child), in particular when conflicts arise between children and parents. A similar exercise is needed for older people. This group of people does not become dependent at once, so subtle distinctions and mechanisms are needed to balance and make possible as much autonomy as possible while growing more dependent. Equally, there is the presence of informal and formal carers, both indispensable *and* sources of tension and abuse. Again, subtle legal mechanisms are needed to frame both sides of the coin and a middle ground will have to be found between leaving carers out of the human rights picture or putting them too central, to the detriment of the older care receivers.

8.8 Conclusion: following the example of children's rights law but with improvements that could then be picked up in children's rights law

The group of older persons by now is too populous to be considered a demographic minority. However, it is a group that is often marginalised. One of the ideas brought forward by human rights law is that vulnerable groups require specific protective measures.[112] The CRC is considered successful in the struggle for rights of vulnerable groups, and can serve as an inspiration for a possible convention on the rights of older persons. This chapter has given an overview of the advances in the area of the rights of older persons in order to elaborate on the possibilities of cross-fertilisation of the well-established rights of children and the continually developing rights of older persons.

Both age groups, children and older persons, have many things in common – even though their differences might be more obvious at first sight. One of the main challenges both groups face is a general perception of often being limited in their decision-making abilities. In contributing to a lack of self-determination, this is an issue that clearly makes them vulnerable groups. The CRC, with its innovative proposals concerning the involvement of third parties and participation, is an interesting example of the development towards the personification of human rights. We are certainly arguing in favour of following this path of personification towards a convention on the rights of older persons, a process that seems far from being finalised. The inspiring example of children's rights can serve us as a fruitful source of new ideas to revive and advance this process. In this contribution we have highlighted important contributions of children's rights law to human rights law in general that should serve as reference points: enhanced monitoring and reporting practices; principles in addition to rights; rights that are specifically targeted rather than general; and attention to third parties and to procedural rights.

Whereas it is very apparent to see the CRC as an inspirational source for the rights of older persons, it may seem less obvious the other way around. The struggle for the rights for older people is ongoing; there are legal gaps in the protection of older persons and a specific comprehensive convention is lacking. Hence, there is no level playing field in human rights law between children and older persons. Nonetheless, we have demonstrated that the source of intergenerational inspiration also lies precisely in the struggle to develop a new and comprehensive rights framework for older persons. The path toward a convention for the rights of older persons beholds an opportunity to re-evaluate the effectiveness of existing models, both in terms of content as well as mechanisms of implementation, dialogue and monitoring. Such reflections may lead to adjustments or the creation of synergies from which also the CRC may benefit.

Moreover, the development of human rights standards for older persons can also be a stimulus for new developments in the context of children's rights. The issue of age-based discrimination does not seem to play a major role when it comes to children's rights. We are, however, convinced that this can provoke a fruitful discussion – as could the consideration of an approach based on equal treatment rather than one based purely on the idea of non-discrimination.

Notes

1 United Nations, Department of Economic and Social Affairs, Population Division, *World Population Prospects: The 2015 Revision, Key Findings and Advance Tables* (Working Paper No ESA/P/WP.241 2015) 2.

2 R Muenz, *Aging and Demographic Change in European Societies: Main Trends and Alternative Policy Options* (SP Discussion Paper No 0703 SPTW Bank 2007). Population ageing is strongly visible in Europe as a result of its declining fertility rates and increasing life expectancy. Nearly 18% of the population of the European Union is currently aged 65 years and over (Eurostat, *Key Figures on Europe. 2014 Edition* (Eurostat pocketbooks 2014)). By 2050, this percentage is expected to increase to nearly 30%. A particularly strong shift will be observed in the oldest old people, meaning that about 10% of the population will be part of this age group (Eurostat, Eurostat Regional Yearbook 2014: Population (2014)). In most industrialised states, children or young adults do not therefore represent the majority of the population any longer.

3 F Breyer, S Felder, 'Life expectancy and health care expenditure: a new calculation for Germany using the costs of dying' (2006) 75 *Health Policy* 178. See more in general E Mordini, P De Hert (eds), *Ageing and Invisibility* (Series: Ambient Intelligence and Smart Environments IOS Press 2010) 224.

4 K-L Tang, J-J Lee, 'Global social justice for older people: the case for an international convention on the rights of older people' (2006) 36 *British Journal of Social Work* 1135.

5 P de Hert, E Mantovani, 'Specific human rights for older persons? The inevitable coloring of human rights law' (2011) 4 *European Human Rights Law Review* 398.

6 United Nations General Assembly (UNGA), Convention on the Rights of the Child (CRC) (1989) UN Doc A/RES/44/25.

7 UNGA, 'Declaration of Old Age Rights' (1948) UN Doc A/RES/213. http://research.un.org/en/undhr/ga/thirdcommittee (last accessed 12 December 2016).

8 UNGA, 'Argentinian draft resolution on the Declaration of Old Age Rights' (1948) UN Doc A/C.3.213.

9 ibid.

10 Declaration of Old Age Rights (n 7).

11 United Nations World Assembly on Ageing, 'Vienna International Plan of Action on Aging' (1983) http://www.un.org/en/events/elderabuse/pdf/vipaa.pdf (last accessed 12 December 2016).

12 See Tang and Lee (n 4).

13 United Nations World Assembly on Ageing (n 11).

14 UNGA, 'United Nations Principles for Older Persons' (1991) UN Doc A/RES/46/91.

15 ibid.

16 UNGA, 'Proclamation on ageing' (1992) UN Doc A/RES/47/5.

17 United Nations Second World Assembly on Ageing, 'Political declaration and Madrid International Plan on Action of Ageing' (2002) www.un.org/en/events/pastevents/pdfs/Madrid_plan.pdf (last accessed 12 December 2016).

18 See Tang and Lee (n 4).

19 United Nations Second World Assembly on Ageing (n 17) art 5.

20 M Murphy, 'International human rights law and older people: gaps, fragments and loopholes' (Help Age International 2012) www.helpage.org/download/502e5b41e7b30 (last accessed 12 December 2016).

21 UNGA, 'Social development report of the Third Committee' (2010) UN Doc A/65/448 and UNGA, 'Follow up to the Second World Assembly on Ageing' (2011) UN Doc A/RES/65/182. It was the first forum of this kind installed by

the UN for older persons. Its task is to examine the international framework and it is established 'for the purpose of strengthening the protection of the human rights of older persons by considering the existing international framework of the human rights of older persons and identifying possible gaps and how best to address them, including by considering, as appropriate, the feasibility of further instruments and measures'.

22 United Nations Human Rights Council, 'The human rights of older persons' (2013) UN Doc A/HRC/RES/24/20.

23 ibid.

24 Committee of Ministers of the Council of Europe, 'Recommendation CM/Rec (2014) of the Committee of Ministers to Member States on the promotion of human rights of older persons' (2014) https://www.coe.int/t/dghl/standardsetting/hrpolicy/Publications/cmrec_2014_2en.pdf (last accessed 12 December 2016).

25 A Hoefmans, 'Naar een universeel verdrag voor de rechten van ouderen' in N Van Leuven and P De Hert (eds), *Fundamentele Rechten van Ouderen* (Intersentia 2011). P De Hert, E Mantovani, 'De rechten van de ouderen in het tijdperk van mensenrechten. Naar een ouderenverdrag?' in N Van Leuven, P De Hert (eds), *Fundamentele Rechten van Ouderen* (Intersentia 2011).

26 Compare with De Hert and Mantovani, 'De rechten van de ouderen' (n 25) and D Rodrigues-Pinzón, C Martin, 'The international human rights status of elderly persons' (2003) 18 *American University International Law Review* 915.

27 A Hoefmans, G De Beco, *The UN Convention on the Rights of Persons with Disabilities: an Integral and Integrated Approach to the Implementation of Disability Rights* (Federal Public Service Social Security 2010).

28 More generally, a more proactive policy of reciprocal inspiration between human rights treaties would also help appease concerns of this evolution of personification of human rights in their relationship to the covenants. Opponents of the proliferation of UN human rights treaties point to the need to invest more energy and resources in the implementation of the general human rights framework laid down by the two covenants. Subsequent treaties have therefore deflected attention from that core framework and dilute the potential to bring about real improvement to the human rights of all persons. We argue, on the contrary, that the development of subsequent treaties has reflected a real need and is therefore inevitable and justified. With the proliferation of human rights treaties comes, however, the responsibility to continually evaluate the effectiveness of the treaties and their respective monitoring systems and to adjust where necessary.

29 Compare 'The protection of economic and social rights of older persons also seems to be insufficient. The situation of older persons is perfect evidence of the unity and interdependence of all human rights. Their example allows us to observe how the rights of all generations permeate, and how a violation of any of them entails a violation of others. For instance, no respect for economic and social rights leads to being unable to fully exercise the personal and social rights, and the other way round'. See B Mikolajczyk, 'Is the ECHR ready for global ageing?' (2013) 17(4) *International Journal of Human Rights* 523.

30 G De Beco, A Hoefmans, 'National structures for the implementation and monitoring of the UN Convention on the Rights of Persons with Disabilities' in G De Beco (ed), *Article 33 of the UN Convention on the Rights of Persons with Disabilities* (Martinus Nijhoff Publishers 2013).

31 Ageing is often considered a 'social problem'. Older persons are typically likened to children insofar as they are a separate group from the working population that (often) determine politics as well as public opinion. Consequently, there is segregation between older persons and the rest of society. The negative view of older persons described above includes the idea that their retirement (perceived

as economic unproductivity) renders this group unable to contribute effectively to society. This is invoked as an argument to legitimise marginalisation. See M Fredvang, S Biggs, *The Rights of Older Persons: Protection and Gaps under Human Rights Law* (Social Policy Working Paper 2012); J Angus, P Reeve, 'Ageism: a threat to "ageing well" in the 21st century' (2006) 25 *Journal of Applied Gerontology* 137; L Tornstam, 'The quo vadis of gerontology: on the scientific paradigm of gerontology' (1992) 32 *Gerontologist* 318; J E Thornton, 'Myths of ageing or ageist stereotypes' (2002) 28 *Educational Gerontology* 301; M B Holstein and M Minkler, 'Self, society, and the "new gerontology"' (2003) 43 *Gerontologist* 787. The assumption given with the term 'active and healthy ageing' that ageing successfully necessitates good health excludes those who are not healthy at an older age, in particular those who cannot influence their health status. Although the concept of successful ageing can mark a shift away from the stereotypes of weak and dependent older persons, in their place it creates new stereotypes and demands that can burden rather than empower this group. See Holstein and Minkler (ibid) 787.

32 Keeping in mind the selective approach to the scope of rights which we will mention later on, it is interesting to return to the *travaux préparatoires* on the drafting of the CRC to recall that the initial proposals contained a mere ten articles with substantive provisions. The same can be said of the initial proposals for a UN Convention on the Rights of Persons with Disabilities. The end result for both conventions, however, turned out to encompass practically all human rights.

33 Resolution 67/139 seems to indicate that a selective approach would be preferable should a consensus arise on adopting a legal instrument and requests the Open-ended Working Group on Ageing 'to present a proposal containing, inter alia, the main elements . . . which are not currently addressed sufficiently by existing mechanisms and therefore require further international protection'. So far the working group has not managed to table a proposal due to the underlying disagreement on the need for a legal instrument.

34 UNGA, 'Follow-up to the Second World Assembly on Ageing' (2011) UN Doc A/66/173 www.ohchr.org/Documents/Issues/SForum/SForum2014/A.66.173_en.pdf (last accessed 12 December 2016).

35 S Detrick, *A Commentary on the United Nations Convention on the Rights of the Child* (Martinus Nijhoff Publishers 1999).

36 In their endeavours to increase the effectiveness of and adherence to existing UN human rights treaties, the committees could seek similar avenues of a clustered and selective approach. This could equilibrate the relationship with the Covenants and it would enhance the impact of the treaties on states parties' policies.

37 M O'Flaherty, 'Reform of the UN treaty human rights body system: locating the Dublin Statement' in G Gilbert, F Hampson and C Sandoval (eds), *The Delivery of Human Rights: Essays in Honour of Professor Sir Nigel Rodley* (Routledge 2011). N Bernaz, 'Continuing evolution of the United Nations treaty bodies system' in S Sheeran and Sir N Rodley (eds), *Routledge Handbook of International Human Rights Law* (Routledge 2014).

38 See on the many reservations to the CRC, including on the reporting provisions by countries such as Malaysia, P Van Weerelt, 'Voorbehouden bij mensenrechtenverdragen: een nieuw dieptepunt' (1995) 20 *NJCM-Bulletin* 996.

39 United Nations International Human Rights Instruments, 'Compilation of Guidelines on the form and content of reports to be submitted by State parties to the international human rights treaties' (2009) UN Doc HRI/GEN/2/Rev.6.

40 E Verhellen, 'The Convention on the Rights of the Child: reflections from a historical, social policy and educational perspective' in W Vandenhole, E Desmet, D Reynaert and S Lembrechts (eds), *Routledge International Handbook of Children's Rights Studies* (Routledge 2015).

41 CRC Committee, 'General Comment No 12: The Right of the Child to be Heard' (2009) UN Doc CRC/C/GC/12.

42 On the balance of the CRC between principles and the (extensive) catalaogue of protected rights see J M Pobjoy, 'The best interests of the child principle as an independent source of protection' (2015) 64(2) *International Comparative Law Quarterly* 327, with references therein.

43 M Freeman, 'Article 3: The Best Interests of the Child' in A Alen, J Vande Lanotte, E Verhellen, F Ang, E Berghmans, M Verheyde and B Abramson (eds), *A Commentary of the United Nations Convention on the Rights of the Child* (Brill Nijhoff 2007); W Vandenhole, 'Children's rights from a legal perspective: children's rights law' in W Vandenhole and others (eds), *Routledge International Handbook of Children's Rights Studies* (Routledge 2015).

44 CRC Committee, 'CRC Treaty Specific Reporting Guidelines, harmonised according to the common core document' UN Doc CRC/C/58/Rev.2 (1 October 2010).

45 Convention on the Rights of Persons with Disabilities (CRPD) (2006) art 3: 'The principles of the present Convention shall be: (a) Respect for inherent dignity, individual autonomy including the freedom to make one's own choices, and independence of persons; (b) Non-discrimination; (c) Full and effective participation and inclusion in society; (d) Respect for difference and acceptance of persons with disabilities as part of human diversity and humanity; (e) Equality of opportunity; (f) Accessibility; (g) Equality between men and women; (h) Respect for the evolving capacities of children with disabilities and respect for the right of children with disabilities to preserve their identities'.

46 Indeed, previous treaties limit such general clauses to the obligation of states parties to adopt all appropriate legislative, administrative and other measures for the implementation of the rights of the convention. However, states parties have to implement the Convention as a whole and the reporting procedure also takes into account the principles.

47 H Morten Haugen, 'Human rights principles: can they be applied to improve the realization of social human rights?' (2011) 15 *Max Planck Yearbook of United Nations Law* 419.

48 A Sen, *Commodities and Capabilities* (Oxford University Press 1987); M Nussbaum, *Women and Human Development: The Capabilities Approach* (Cambridge University Press 2000).

49 R Dixon, M Nussbaum, 'Children's rights and the capabilities approach: the question of special priority' (2012) 97 *Cornell Law Review* 549.

50 Compare M Nussbaum, 'Women and equality: the Capabilities approach' (1999) 138 *International Labour Review* 227 with Nussbaum, *Women and Human Development – The Capabilities Approach* (n 48) and Dixon and Nussbaum (n 49) 48.

51 See Nussbaum (n 48) 78.

52 ibid.

53 An older person in the South surrounded by carrying family members cannot be compared with an older, isolated person in the North in need of health, care and so much more.

54 Not all rights and principles essential for children should be employed for older persons. A CRC principle such as the 'best interests of the child', if needed in the context of older persons, is evidently in need of rephrasing. Inspiration for identifying these principles can be found in the 1991 UN Principles for Older Persons (independence, participation, care, self-fulfilment and dignity) (see our discussion in section 1) or can also be found in art 25 of the Charter of Fundamental Rights of the European Union (the rights of older persons), stating that the Union 'recognizes and respects the rights of the older persons to lead

a life of dignity and independence and to participate in social and cultural life'. European Parliament, the Council and the Commission, 'Charter of Fundamental Rights of the European Union' (2010) C83 *Official Journal of the European Union* 389.

55 Compare for example with CRC arts 17 and 24.

56 Compare for example with CRC art 6.

57 Violations of the rights of older persons are common and can be found in a range of contextual settings. Rights are violated within the family and the community but also under the care of institutions. This is not only due to the fact that some older persons are no longer capable of asserting their rights.

58 CRC Committee, 'General Comment No 12: The Right of the Child to be Heard' UN Doc CRC/C/GC/12, paras 2–3.

59 On the importance of this right and the legal deficit at this point see Mikolajczyk, 'Is the ECHR ready for global ageing?' (n 29) 520.

60 M Liebel, 'From evolving capacities to evolving capabilities: contextualizing children's rights' in D Stoecklin, J-M Bonvin (eds), *Children's Rights and the Capability Approach. Challenges and Prospects* (Springer 2014).

61 Recital (e) stipulates that disability is an evolving concept.

62 A Parkes, *Children and International Human Rights Law: The Right of the Child to be Heard* (Routledge 2013).

63 CRC art 1.

64 Compare for example with Eurostat, Eurostat Regional Yearbook 2014: Population (2014).

65 World Health Organization (WHO), 'Definition of an older or elderly person at health statistics and information systems' (2016) www.who.int/healthinfo/survey/ageingdefnolder/en/ (last accessed 12 December 2016).

66 See Hoefmans, 'Naar een universeel verdrag voor de rechten van ouderen' (n 25). This is of course different for those texts focusing specifically on older persons. Non-discrimination is in these specific instruments employed as an angle to approach the rights of older persons (see more in detail, P De Hert and E Mantovani, 'De rechten van de ouderen' (n 25)). It is therefore not surprising that when it comes to specific acts of discrimination on grounds of age we find that there are already some provisions prohibiting it, whilst binding international human rights treaties do not refer to age specifically.

67 UNGA, Universal Declaration of Human Rights (UDHR) (1948) art 2 'Everyone is entitled to all the rights and freedoms set forth in this Declaration, without distinction of any kind, such as race, colour, sex, language, religion, political or other opinion, national or social origin, property, birth or other status. Furthermore, no distinction shall be made on the basis of the political, jurisdictional or international status of the country or territory to which a person belongs, whether it be independent, trust, non-self-governing or under any other limitation of sovereignty'.

68 The other monitored human rights treaties of a general nature also do not specifically rule out age-based discrimination. These core treaties are the International Convention on the Elimination of All Forms of Racial Discrimination, the International Covenant on Civil and Political Rights (ICCPR), the 1966 International Covenant on Economic, Social and Cultural Rights (ICESCR), the Convention against Torture (CAT), the Convention on the Elimination of all forms of Discrimination against Women (CEDAW), the International Convention on the Elimination of all forms of Racial Discrimination (CERD), the CRC, the International Convention on the Protection of the Rights of all Migrant Workers and Members of their Families (ICMW), the International Convention for the Protection of all Persons from Enforced Disappearances (CDEP) and the CRPD. The lack of the inclusion of age as a forbidden ground is excused with

the fact that the demographic transition was not yet obvious at the time of drafting these treaties. See Committee on Economic Social and Cultural Rights, 'General Comment No 6: The Economic, Social and Cultural Rights of Older Persons' (1995) UN Doc E/1996/22. Only the more recent 1990 UN International Convention on the Protection of the Rights of All Migrant Workers and Members of their Families includes a specific reference to age. This convention is, however, too specific in its scope to be applicable to older persons in general.

69 Committee on Economic Social and Cultural Rights, 'General Comment No 6' (n 68): 'This is not determinative of the matter, however, since the prohibition of discrimination on the grounds of "other status" could be interpreted as applying to age. The Committee notes that while it may not yet be possible to conclude that discrimination on the grounds of age is comprehensively prohibited by the Covenant, the range of matters in relation to which such discrimination can be accepted is very limited'. These limited cases can include retirement ages and access to certain forms of education (ibid).

70 Both the Treaty on the Functioning of the European Union (TFEU) (Consolidated Version of the Treaty on the Functioning of the European Union [2010] OJ C83/47) (art 10) and the Charter of Fundamental Rights of the European Union (CFREU) (art 21) have an explicit provision on age-based discrimination.

71 Charter of Fundamental Rights of the European Union (2010) OJ C83/389 art 21. Emphasis added.

72 Compare art 2 CRC with W Vandenhole, 'Children's rights from a legal perspective: children's rights law' (n 43) 32: 'Compared to non-discrimination clauses in other (older) human rights treaties, the CRC's non-discrimination provision is broader in that it also offers protection against discrimination on the basis of status, activities, expressed opinions, or beliefs of a child's parents, legal guardians or family members. Moreover, it explicitly lists the parent's or legal guardian's race, and the children's ethnic origin and disability as prohibited grounds . . . In line with general human rights law, the prohibition of discrimination in the field of economic, social and cultural rights can be argued not to be limited by article 4 CRC, and to be of immediate effect'.

73 A good example is art 34 of EU Charter of Fundamental Rights. This provision on social security and social assistance stresses the need to offer these goods to specific vulnerable groups (old age being one of them).

74 See Mikolajczyk, 'Is the ECHR ready for global ageing?' (n 29) 523.

75 See J Gerards, 'The discrimination grounds of Article 14 of the European Convention on Human Rights' (2013) 13(1) *Human Rights Law Review* 99. An (open) system of equal treatment law is said to allow better to take into account the intricate reasons and grounds that may underlie differences in treatment, and is therefore better geared to the complexity of discrimination cases in modern society and to assess cases related to economic matters or social rights.

76 See Breyer and Felder (n 3).

77 G Backman and others, 'Health system and the right to health: an assessment of 194 countries' (2008) 372 *The Lancet* 2047.

78 This right is formulated in art 35 of the EU Charter of Fundamental Rights: 'Everyone has the right of access to preventive health care and the right to benefit from medical treatment under the conditions established by national laws and practices. A high level of human health protection shall be ensured in the definition and implementation of all the Union's policies and activities'. The right to health care is thus conferred to all groups on an equal basis. The scope of this Charter covers EU legislation and the implementation of it by Member States.

79 UNGA, 'International Covenant on Economic, Social and Cultural Rights' (General Assembly Resolution 2200A (XXI) 1966).

80 ibid art 12. General Comment No 14 of the Committee on Economic, Social and Cultural Rights illustrates art 12 of the ICESCR to clarify that the right to health is not equal to a right to be healthy. It rather covers several entitlements, one of them access to health care. See United Nations Committee on Economic Social and Cultural Rights (CESCR) 'General Comment No 14: The Right to the Highest Attainable Standard of Health' (2000) UN Doc E/C.12/2000/4, para 9. In the context of the legal obligations to respect, protect and fulfil, equal access to adequate facilities has to be guaranteed with regard to art 12 (ibid paras 30–37).
81 CRC art 24.1.
82 CRC art 24.2.
83 See De Hert and Mantovani, 'Specific human rights for older persons?' (n 5).
84 CRC art 32.
85 ibid.
86 Compare for example with Dhaval Dave, Inas Rashad and Jasmina Spasojevic, 'The effects of retirement on physical and mental health outcomes' NBER Working Paper No 12123 (2008) 1(1) *Journal of European Law* J0.
87 CRC art 28.
88 International Covenant on Economic, Social and Cultural Rights (n 78) art 13.
89 CESCR, 'General Comment No 6' (n 68).
90 UDHR (n 67) arts 22 and 25.
91 ibid.
92 Article 25 of the CRC grants children the right to social security. Without having the opportunity of being economically active, children are dependent on their parents or guardians. If those are not able to economically provide for them, the right to social security, and thus an obligation of the state to care for the children in an economic sense, is of utmost importance.
93 Council of Europe, European Social Charter (1996).
94 CRC art 27.1.
95 UN Committee on Economic Social and Cultural Rights, 'General Comment No 4: The Right to Adequate Housing' E/1992/23 (art 11(1) of the Covenant 1991).
96 ibid 7.
97 ibid.
98 CRC art 27.
99 See De Hert and Mantovani, 'Specific human rights for older persons?' (n 5).
100 Help Age International, *Strengthening Older People's Rights: Towards a UN Convention. A Resource for Promoting Dialogue on Creating a New UN Convention on the Rights of Older Persons* (2010).
101 CRC art 19.
102 UNGA, *Implementation of the International Plan of Action on Ageing and Related Activities* (1991).
103 Compare for example with UNGA, 'Follow-up to the Second World Assembly on Ageing' (n 34).
104 See Murphy (n 20).
105 CRC art 19.
106 B Howe, 'Do parents have fundamental rights?' (2001) 36 *Journal of Canadian Studies* 61.
107 CRC art 12.
108 Compare for example with art 14 CRC. The rights and duties of parents and legal guardians with regard to providing direction to children in the exercise of their religion are of low importance for older persons who are unlikely to need religious education.

109 G Sundström and others, 'Family care for elders in Europe: policies and practices' in M Szinovacz, A Davey (eds), *Caregiving Contexts. Cultural, Familial and Societal Implications* (Springer 2008).
110 ibid.
111 Council of Europe, European Convention on the Exercise of Children's Rights (25 January 1996) ETS 160. See S Demars, 'L'enfant et la justice dans les travaux du Conseil de l'Europe' in M T Meulders-Klein (ed), *Familles & justice: justice civile et evolution du contentieux familial en droit comparé* (Bruylant 1997) 577–600.
112 See Rodrigues-Pinzón and Martin (n 26).

Part III

The interplay between children's rights law and human rights law in thematic areas

9 Towards an integrated approach to intra-family relations under the CRC and CEDAW: some reflections

Titia Loenen

9.1 Introduction

Over the past decades, international human rights law has witnessed a tremendous growth. In addition to the Universal Declaration of Human Rights (UDHR) and the two core covenants on civil and political rights and on economic, social and cultural rights a number of more focused and specialised conventions have been adopted. The latter provide an elaboration of the more general human rights standards contained in the former. As such, all these instruments do not exist in isolation, but can be seen as part of a developing body of law. From this perspective the human rights standards laid down in the various human rights conventions should reinforce each other and the specific underlying principles of each of them be integrated further to develop international human rights law as a cohesive whole.

Such an integrated approach to international human rights law is the starting point for this contribution. It will explore the (potential) interplay between the specific gender-based approach underlying the Convention on the Elimination of All Forms of Discrimination against Women (the Women's Convention or CEDAW) and the child-based approach of the Convention on the Rights of the Child (CRC) regarding intra-family relations. More specifically, I will focus on the triangular relationship between mother, father and child.

This kind of exploration seems particularly interesting because of the close connection between women's rights and children's rights: for both women and children their position in the family is of crucial importance; women's role in the family is a core issue to be addressed in any policy to empower them and improve their position; worldwide, the huge majority of primary carers of children is female; historically, both women and children were lumped together as lacking legal subjectivity and now both are being emancipated into rights bearing individual subjects; both women and children constitute a vulnerable group, that is they are in danger of suffering from sustained and structural violations of their human rights. Interestingly, the emancipation of women and children into rights bearers provides space for the articulation of their individual needs and interests for enjoying a dignified life. The Women's Convention and the CRC are part of this articulation.

My contention will be that where intra-family relations are concerned, in elaborating the CRC standards the Committee on the Rights of the Child could draw much more inspiration from the gender-based approach underlying CEDAW than it seems to have done so far. Whereas the Women's Convention pays explicit attention to the rights of the child by giving a prominent place to the child's best interests in several of its core provisions, the CRC is silent about women's rights except where the protection of mothers in their biological role is concerned. The need for integrating a gender perspective in all human rights instruments has been generally acknowledged.[1] As far as the CRC is concerned, integrating a gender perspective is clearly visible in the attention the Committee on the Rights of the Child pays to the specific, gendered position and treatment of 'the girl child'. A highlight in this respect is the joint general comment of this Committee and the Committee on the Elimination of All Forms of Discrimination against Women (CEDAW Committee) on harmful practices.[2] What seems to be attracting less attention so far, however, is the gendered position and roles of parents within the family and their consequences for the realisation of children's rights.

To corroborate this contention, I will start by exploring the ways in which intra-family relations are addressed in the Women's Convention and in the general recommendations of its supervisory body (section 2). Similarly, I will explore the same matter in the context of the CRC (section 3). Subsequently, I will take a closer look at how the approaches towards intra-family relations under the two conventions relate to each other and indicate what, in my view, a more integrated approach towards intra-family relations under the two conventions would imply (section 4). I will round off by some concluding remarks (section 5).

Some caveats are in order here. To start with, focusing on the triangular relationship between mother–father–child is not to be interpreted as an essentialising approach to the many ways in which family relations can be shaped. In addition, as this is a first exploration only, I am trying to paint an overall picture rather than providing a fleshed out and comprehensive analysis; no exhaustive comparison has been possible or envisaged. Research has been limited to the texts of both conventions, the authoritative interpretation and elaboration of the standards they provide as laid down in the General Comments or Recommendations of their supervisory bodies and relevant scholarly literature on the topic.[3]

9.2 Intra-family relations in the Women's Convention

9.2.1 General aspects

For fully understanding the approach to intra-family relations in the Women's Convention the genesis of the Convention and its general characteristics and principles are crucial. To start with, the reasons for having a separate convention for women's rights lies in the worldwide and continuing inequality experienced by women, notwithstanding the promise of equality and equal rights in the basic international human rights documents such as the UDHR, the International Covenant on Civil and Political Rights and the International Covenant on Economic, Social and Cultural Rights.[4] This inequality is closely related to women's role in the family. Historically, women have been perceived and treated first and foremost in their role of mother and put under the control of men. As the CEDAW Committee puts it: 'Inequality in the family underlies all other aspects of discrimination against women'.[5]

The Women's Convention elaborates the human rights standards necessary for achieving women's equality.[6] Ending women's inferior position in society and their subordination to men as wives, mothers or daughters lies at the heart of the approach taken by the convention. The power imbalance between men and women and its wide-ranging consequences in all areas of life and society is a central concern. This is borne out by the Women's Convention's starting points and the main obligations it puts on states parties.

First of all, the asymmetrical focus of the Women's Convention stands out. Contrary to the approach taken in the other human rights conventions, the problem to be addressed is not formulated in sex-neutral terms as the eradication of discrimination 'on grounds of sex'.[7] The Women's Convention addresses the real issue head on by focusing on the eradication of discrimination *against women*. It thereby acknowledges that, generally speaking, where gender relations are concerned men are on the whole not in need of specific protection.

Secondly, the broad scope of the obligations to eradicate discrimination against women must be born in mind. States parties are to embody the principle of the equality of men and women in their legislation and to ensure the practical realisation of this principle (Article 2(a) CEDAW) and to prohibit all discrimination against women (Article 2(b) CEDAW). In addition to the obligation to refrain from engaging in any act or practice of discrimination in whatever area (Article 2(d) CEDAW) a state party also has to take all appropriate measures to eliminate discrimination against women by any person, organisation or enterprise, thus bringing discrimination in the private sphere within the scope of the Convention (Article 2(e) CEDAW).

As the CEDAW Committee has emphasised in its General Comment on Article 2, the wide-ranging obligations flowing from this provision should be read together with the obligations under Articles 3, 4, 5 and 24.[8] In the context of this contribution, Article 5 is of special relevance as it entails obligations to address the root causes of the inequality and discrimination suffered by women. The more structural and ingrained patterns of conduct of men and women have to be modified, including the roles of men and women in the family. In addition, for the purposes of this contribution two other articles dealing explicitly with the role of women in the family merit closer attention: Article 11 (on employment-related matters) and Article 16 (on matters relating to marriage and family relations as such).[9]

9.2.2 Intra-family relations in the Women's Convention

9.2.2.1 Article 5 CEDAW

Article 5(a) CEDAW requires states parties to take all appropriate measures

> [t]o modify the social and cultural patterns of conduct of men and women, with a view to achieving the elimination of prejudices and customary and all

> other practices which are based on the idea of the inferiority or the superiority of either of the sexes or on stereotyped roles for men and women.

As has been emphasised time and again, the far-reaching modification of the traditional roles of men and women this provision calls for is truly transformative in nature. It includes, for example, the elimination of both direct and indirect as well as systemic discrimination and challenging patriarchal power relationships that are foundational for most if not all societies in the world.[10]

Article 5(b) CEDAW addresses the more specific position of women in the family as mothers. It requires States Parties to also take all appropriate measures

> [t]o ensure that family education includes a proper understanding of maternity as a social function and the recognition of the common responsibility of men and women in the upbringing and developments of their children, it being understood that the interest of the children is the primordial consideration in all cases.

Taken together Article 5(a) and 5(b) direct attention to the core problem that has to be addressed to achieve women's equality with men: the inequality of women within the family. At the same time, Article 5 recognises the need to keep in mind the interests of the child at any time.

As mentioned above, inequality in the family is identified by the CEDAW Committee as underlying all other aspects of discrimination against women. As it observed in General Recommendation No 23, historically women have been confined to the private sphere of the home and to their reproductive and child-rearing roles, whereas men have dominated the public sphere with its broad range of activities.[11] The resulting positions of men and women in society are intimately linked to this asymmetrical division of gender roles, as activities in the public sphere bring much more social, economic and political power and are generally considered superior to those in the private sphere. In turn, the underlying cause of the asymmetry mentioned is identified by the Committee as basically similar worldwide:

> In all nations, the most significant factors inhibiting women's ability to participate in public life have been the cultural framework of values and religious beliefs, the lack of services and men's failure to share the tasks associated with the organisation of the household and with the care and raising of children. In all nations, cultural traditions and religious beliefs have played a part in confining women to the private spheres of activity and excluding them from active participation in public life.[12]

Given the importance of the interplay between participation in the public sphere and the division of labour in the private sphere it is not surprising that the Women's Convention addresses the position of women as workers and as parents in more detail in Articles 11 and 16.

9.2.2.2 Article 11 CEDAW

Article 11 addresses several issues concerning mothers in the area of employment. To start with, states parties have 'to eliminate discrimination against women in the field of employment in order to ensure, on a basis of equality of men and women, the same rights' and in particular 'the right to health and to safety in working conditions, including the safeguarding of the function of reproduction (Article 11(1)(f) CEDAW).

In addition, Article 11(2) CEDAW requires states to prevent discrimination against women 'on the grounds of marriage or maternity' and to ensure 'their effective right to work'. To this end states have to take a range of measures that are important for women in their parental role.

Firstly, states parties are to protect women from the adverse effects of becoming a parent on job opportunities. They are to prohibit dismissal on the grounds of pregnancy or of maternity leave and to outlaw discrimination in dismissals on the basis of marital status (Article 11(2)(a) CEDAW). They are also required to ensure women do not lose their jobs because they are away from work to give birth by taking appropriate measures 'to introduce maternity leave with pay or with comparable social benefits without loss of former employment, seniority or social allowances' (Article 11(2)(b) CEDAW).

Secondly, states parties have to facilitate the combination of paid work and participation in public life on the one hand and the caring and family responsibilities of parents on the other. They should do so by encouraging 'the provision of the necessary supporting social services . . . in particular through promoting the establishment and development of a network of child-care facilities' (Article 11(2)(c) CEDAW).

A more specific provision requires states parties to give special protection to women during pregnancy in types of work that could be harmful (Article 11(2)(d) CEDAW).

9.2.2.3 Article 16 CEDAW

Article 16 is the most important and extensive article in the convention dealing with intra-family relationships – and by far the most contested provision of the Convention in view of the many and wide-ranging reservations made to it.[13] The CEDAW Committee considers these reservations invalid 'as they are incompatible with the object and purpose of the Convention'.[14] This assessment shows the core importance attached by the Committee to equality in the family.

Article 16 requires the elimination of discrimination against women 'in all matters relating to marriage and family relations' and to ensure women the same rights on a basis of equality of men and women (Article 16(1)).

To start with this includes the relationship between the spouses as such, for example regarding their rights to enter marriage; to own, acquire and manage property during marriage; and on the dissolution of the marriage. When elaborating on the financial and economic aspects of marriage and family relations, the

Committee has a clear eye for the way in which gendered family roles and parenting affect women much more than men in a negative way.[15] Female-headed households are likely to belong to the poorest segments of society. Economically and financially, women are generally much worse off than men in and after dissolution of the relationship.[16] Their role as primary carer affects their economic opportunities in many ways. In most cases, the value and indirect contribution of care taking activities to the overall welfare of the household is not acknowledged. Thus, post-dissolution financial arrangements often favour men, regardless of whether laws are formulated in a sex-neutral manner. In this context, the Committee reaffirms the importance of providing for substantive as well as formal equality between spouses:

> Formal equality may be achieved by adopting gender-neutral laws and policies, which on their face treat women and men equally. Substantive equality can be achieved only when the States parties examine the application and effects of laws and policies and ensure that they provide for equality in fact, accounting for women's disadvantage or exclusion.[17]

In addition, and as importantly, the elimination of all discrimination against women in all matters relating to marriage and family relations also includes the rights of the spouses as parents towards their children. According to Article 16(d), states parties shall take all appropriate measures to ensure 'the same rights and responsibilities as parents, irrespective of their marital status, in matters relating to their children; in all cases the interests of the children shall be paramount'. Of particular interest in this specific formulation is the reference to the responsibility the parents share. Guaranteeing equal rights is not sufficient. In its general recommendations the Committee emphasises the importance of the shared responsibility of parents for the care, protection and maintenance of children, both inside and outside formal marriage. It calls on states parties to enforce shared rights and responsibilities at law.[18]

Article 16(d) also explicitly draws attention to the rights of the child in this respect by giving pride of place to the best interest of the child where it states that: 'in all cases the interests of the children shall be paramount'. This obligation is reiterated where the need for equal rights of women in respect of guardianship, wardship, trusteeship and adoption of children is concerned (Article 16(1)(f) CEDAW). Thus, the rights of women and the rights of the child are explicitly linked.

9.2.2.4 Conclusions

Under the Women's Convention the asymmetrical relationship of women and men as spouses and as co-parents is fully acknowledged both in the text of the convention and the work of the CEDAW-Committee. This asymmetrical relationship is perceived as part of the wider and systemic inequality between the sexes and as grounded in fundamental cultural perceptions and views starting from stereotypical notions of proper gender roles and a gender-based division of the public and private sphere.

The Committee clearly links the gendered division of family roles with the overall inferior position of women in society, their economic dependence, poverty and lack of social, economic and political power. It also acknowledges the fact that family and caring responsibilities born by women in the private sphere may create tensions with women's personal development and participation in the public sphere. Women have a life beyond being a mother and family carer, however valuable these roles may be. To enable women to enjoy this broader life, men will have to take up a larger part of the responsibilities parents share. In essence, as Freeman has put it, by combining the recognition of the family as the natural and fundamental group unit of society in its preamble with the requirement of equal treatment of women the Women's Convention makes clear that protection of the family may no longer be realised 'at the expense of its female members'.[19] In this regard, it is telling that Article 16(1)(g) on the equal right of husband and wife to choose a profession and an occupation, instead of being included in Article 11 on employment, is addressed in the context of the rights of women in the family.[20]

At the same time, the Women's Convention explicitly recognises the crucial importance of the 'best interests of the child' principle in Articles 5 and 16. In this way it integrates this fundamental principle of children's rights as part of the standards that have to be taken into account in addressing intra-family relations. However, this recognition does neither detract from its gender-based approach to parental roles nor from the obligations of the states parties to eliminate discrimination and achieve (substantive) equality of women in the family.

9.3 Intra-family relationships in the CRC

9.3.1 General aspects

As is the case regarding the Women's Convention, for fully understanding the approach to intra-family relationships under the CRC it is first necessary briefly to address its genesis and the fundamental principles it is based on. The CRC is a landmark in the changing perception of the child: from object to subject, that is to a rights-bearing individual. There is a clear parallel here with the changing position of women. This new approach to the child is manifested in two of the overarching general principles governing the CRC that have been identified by the Committee on the Rights of the Child.[21]

The first is the principle that the views of the child shall be given due weight 'in accordance with the age and maturity of the child' (Article 12(1)). This principle voices the notion that the increasing autonomy and agency of children when they grow up have to be taken into account at all times. The Committee adheres to this principle also if children are very young. They are as much as older children 'holders of all rights enshrined in the Convention'.[22]

The second is the principle that the best interests of the child shall be a primary consideration in all actions concerning children (Article 3(1)). This principle is of special importance for this contribution because it is also explicitly included as a standard to be adhered to in the Women's Convention. Article 3(1) does not mention parents as such, but Article 18(1) does by stating that the best interests of the child 'will be their basic concern'.

The principle of the best interests of the child is a highly flexible and context-dependent principle. This malleability is often perceived as both its strength and its weakness.[23] The CRC Committee distinguishes three aspects of this principle; it is a substantive right as well as a fundamental, interpretative legal principle and a procedural rule.[24] If a conflict occurs between the best interests of the child and the rights of others, for example the parents, the starting point should be to find a solution on a case-by-case basis. First of all, the possibility of harmonising the competing claims or interests should be explored. Only if this turns out to be impossible the stage is reached of balancing the rights and interests at stake. In weighing rights, however, high priority must be given to the child's interests and the latter should not be approached as just one among others: 'a larger weight must be attached to what serves the child best'.[25]

The reason for the priority position of the best interests of the child is explained by the Committee by reference to its vulnerability and lack of power:

> The expression 'primary consideration' means that the child's best interests may not be considered on the same level as all other considerations. This strong position is justified by the special situation of the child: dependency, maturity, legal status and, often, voicelessness. Children have less possibility than adults to make a strong case for their own interests and those involved in decisions affecting them must be explicitly aware of their interests. If the interests of children are not highlighted, they tend to be overlooked.[26]

In this way the Committee confirms it puts the child as a rights bearer at the centre of the CRC.

Taking a closer look at the way in which the CRC deals with intra-family relations it is useful to distinguish two aspects thereof. Firstly, the approach under the CRC to the triangular relationship of state–parents–child in general and, secondly, the approach to the parental roles of mothers and fathers as distinct and gendered categories in relation to the child.

9.3.2 The approach under the CRC to the triangular relationship of state–parents–child in general

According to the preamble to the CRC the family is seen as the fundamental unit of society 'and the natural environment for the growth and well-being' of children. The general framework for the triangular relationship of state–parents–child can be found in Article 5 and Article 18. Article 5 provides the starting point by requiring that the state shall

> [r]espect the responsibilities, rights and duties of parents . . . to provide, in a manner consistent with the evolving capacities of the child, appropriate

direction and guidance in the exercise by the child of the rights recognized in the present Convention.

The provision thus identifies parents as leading in taking care of their children. Only if they do not fulfill their duties and responsibilities the CRC requires states parties to intervene. Of course, the crucial question this raises is when exactly this will be the case. The dangers of too much state control over parental authority was hotly debated in the drafting process and still is a bone of contention, child rights often being perceived by its critics as a challenge to parental autonomy as such.[27]

Whatever the merits of this position, despite this seemingly deferential stance towards parents the CRC is pretty demanding of parents as is borne out by the often detailed and myriad ways in which the Committee has articulated the content of the rights included in the Convention and the obligations they bring along.[28] As parents bear the primary responsibility for realising the rights of children, they are de facto the primary duty bearers even if formally, of course, the CRC can only bind the states parties to it.

To ease the burdens placed on the shoulders of parents, Article 18(2) provides for state support to parents in fulfilling their responsibilities by requiring the state to 'render appropriate assistance to parents' and to 'ensure the development of institutions, facilities and services for the care of children'. In a similar way, Article 27(3) requires states to assist parents in implementing the child's right to an adequate standard of living.

Thus, the state figures in two distinct capacities that may not always sit together easily: as a provider of all kinds of support for parents, but also as the ultimate authority in deciding whether parents live up to their responsibilities and with the power to intervene to protect the child if they do not.

9.3.3 The approach of the CRC to the parental roles of mothers and fathers as distinct and gendered categories

Overall the CRC approaches the parents in a sex-neutral way. Almost nowhere does it differentiate between maternal and paternal roles, except where biological, reproductive differences between the sexes and/or the care for infants are concerned. The latter subjects will be addressed in the next section.

Importantly, the shared responsibility of the parents for the upbringing of their children is explicitly acknowledged in Article 18 CRC. Article 18(1) requires states 'to ensure recognition of the principle that both parents have common responsibilities for the upbringing and development of the child'. It also provides that 'the best interest of the child will be their basic concern'. The Committee regards this shared responsibility generally as in the best interest of the child.[29]

It is apparent that the division of responsibilities between parents lies at the heart of gender relations. However, taking a look at its general comments the Committee hardly ever addresses the gendered dimensions of the shared responsibility of parents in an explicit way. This is also the case where the parental rights and obligations as formulated in the CRC and elaborated by the Committee may clearly and de facto impact men and women differently in their responsibility for taking care of children. Several examples may illustrate this point.

The first example is General Comment No 7 on early childhood (2005).[30] In this general comment the Committee recognises the crucial importance of this period for the development and future of the child. It also acknowledges the special intensity of parental responsibilities in this phase:

> Early childhood is the period of most extensive (and intensive) parental responsibilities related to all aspects of children's well-being covered by the Convention: their survival, health, physical safety and emotional security, standards of living and care, opportunities for play and learning, and freedom of expression. Accordingly, realizing children's rights is in large measure dependent on the well-being and resources available to those with responsibilities for their care.[31]

If anything, in this period the responsibilities of primary carers, and thus mothers rather than fathers, stand out, given the worldwide phenomenon of mothers usually being the primary carers of infants and young children. Nevertheless, nowhere in its general comments does the Committee explicitly recognise this except where the biological role of mothers is concerned and nowhere does it explicitly connect this issue with empowering women/mothers to be able to shoulder their role as the primary carer.

Similarly, in relation to the Committee's concerns about millions of children being raised in (utter) poverty and the urgent need to reduce poverty[32] no links are established with the need for improving the position of women as one of the best poverty reduction strategies.[33]

A second example regards General Comment No 17 on Article 31.[34] In everyday practice, the high and detailed standards the Committee sets for realising the right to leisure and play will put the quite heavy burden these entail mainly on the primary carer. However, the General Comment nowhere specifically recognises this point and does not provide guidance on how to address this.

A third example deals with parental roles and relations after termination of the relationship. The right of the child 'who is separated from one or both parents to maintain personal relations and direct contact with both parents on a regular basis' is provided for in Article 9(3). In this context the Committee emphasises the equal position of both parents. It also explains what the best interests of the child principle means in this setting. According to the Committee it is contrary to the best interests principle 'if the law automatically gives parental responsibility to either or both parents. In assessing the child's best interests, the judge must take into consideration the right of the child to preserve his or her relationship with both parents, together with the other elements relevant to the case'.[35]

Although this makes sense from the perspective of the rights of the child taken in isolation, the Committee does not consider the question whether any of the parents would also have some priority position. Specifically, there is no indication that the interests of the primary carer should be given special attention. First of all, this would seem relevant because the primary carer has a proven track record of taking genuine responsibility for the child. Secondly, this would seem relevant because the primary carer often has invested much more of (mostly her) life in the care of the child, often foregoing many more opportunities for participation in public life than the other parent. It can be argued such interests of the primary carer as an individual rights bearer should also have some extra weight in the balance instead of being taken into account solely through the principle of 'the best interests of the child'. In short, the Committee's lack of attention for the actual responsibility taken by the parents for their children before disruption of the relationship does not seem to do justice to the often gendered dimensions of parental roles and reflects a formal rather than substantive equality approach as far as the equal position of parents is concerned.[36]

A final example concerns the goal of educating and guiding parents on children's rights and on their proper role. In its General Comment on general measures of implementation the Committee points to the importance of this issue and urges states parties to 'take all appropriate measures to enhance parents' understanding of their role in their children's early education'.[37] Similarly, in General Comment No 15: 'The Committee encourages States to adopt and implement a comprehensive strategy to educate children, their caregivers, policymakers, politicians and professionals working with children about children's right to health, and the contributions they can make to its realization'.[38] Although in many respects educating parents may be a sensible and important goal, here again, as long as women figure much more prominently as the primary carers they will bear the heavier burden of achieving such goals. In addition, given the often thin line between well intended education or guidance and uncalled for 'disciplining', such policies entail the risk of paternalistic interventions that will affect primary carers and thus mothers much more than fathers.

9.3.3.1 Motherhood as a biological function

In one respect female parents figure explicitly in the CRC, that is in their biological and reproductive role. Given the close relationship between biological motherhood and the health (and life) of the child this is not surprising.

Maternity protection is included in the CRC itself in Article 24 on the child's right to health. It provides that states parties shall take all appropriate measures 'to ensure appropriate pre-natal and post-natal health care for mothers' (Article 24(2)(d)).

The importance of maternity protection is pointed out in several general comments, and especially in General Comment No 15, devoting a separate part to Article 24(2)(d). The poor health of the mother and suboptimal breastfeeding practices are linked to a high number of infant deaths.[39] The Committee also notes that preventable maternal mortality and morbidity are grave violations of the human rights of women and girls and a serious threat to their and children's right to health.[40] Here, women figure as rights-bearing subjects in their own right.

The Committee demands that the state should provide essential health services for pregnant women and children 'irrespective of their ability to pay'.[41] When it comes to meeting the criteria of *availability* and *accessibility* of children's health services, the Committee explicitly addresses children, pregnant women and mothers together by holding that health facilities must be available and accessible for 'all children, pregnant women and mothers'.[42]

The CRC also explicitly mentions breastfeeding. Article 24(2)(e) speaks about 'the advantages of breastfeeding' and the obligation of states parties to make health related information on this topic widely available and to support the use of that information. In several general comments a lot of concern is directed at breastfeeding, which is to be promoted in view of the child's right to health. The General Comment on the right to health requires states to 'pay particular attention to ensuring full protection and promotion of breastfeeding practices'.[43] The Committee links the state's obligations in this area to the framework adopted by the World Health Assembly.[44] In addition, '[s]pecial measures should be taken to promote community and workplace support for mothers in relation to pregnancy and breastfeeding and feasible and affordable childcare service'.[45]

Whatever the support generated for mothers to enable them to breastfeed, the demands made on mothers in this respect are quite considerable. Ideally, breastfeeding should continue for up to two years:

> Exclusive breastfeeding for infants up to 6 months of age should be protected and promoted and breastfeeding should continue alongside appropriate complementary foods preferably until two years of age, where feasible.[46]

The Committee does not address the question of how such long periods of breastfeeding impact on gender relations and the 'equal position' of parents in the daily reality of women and men's lives. It is clear that an extended period of breastfeeding may pose difficulties with paid work, especially if this takes place away from the home.[47] Mothers seem to appear here in a rather instrumental way only.

9.3.4 Conclusions

Where intra-family relations are concerned, the CRC approaches parents as equally responsible for their children and the Committee stresses the importance of this shared responsibility in its general comments. In doing so, however, the Committee hardly ever addresses the gendered roles of parents and their consequences for achieving children's rights. Although the Committee often implicitly acknowledges the crucial role of the primary carer for the rights and welfare of the child, it does so mostly in sex-neutral language and without explicitly linking this to gendered parental roles. The General Comment on early childhood is a good example.

Only where motherhood as a biological function is concerned does the Committee clearly differentiate between the role of mothers and fathers.

It recognises the crucial role mothers play in the right to life and health of the child. The way in which it addresses this issue, however, runs the risk of instrumentalising women and reducing them to objects instead of rights-bearing subjects in their own right. The strong position the Committee takes on breastfeeding is a case in point. The Committee requires states parties to promote breastfeeding for at least six months and preferably up to two years without addressing the impact this has on the gendered nature of parental roles and on the position of women in the family and in society at large.

9.4 Towards a more integrated approach to intra-family relations

The discussion above has clarified how intra-family relations are approached under the Women's Convention in terms of the gendered roles of men and women in society, including their roles as spouses and parents. The inequality of women in the family has been identified by CEDAW as the core issue to be addressed to realise the rights of women. To achieve this will require a far-reaching modification of fundamental patterns of social and cultural conduct of men and women all over the world. The discussion has also shown that in the context of intra-family relations, attention for the best interest of the child has not been neglected, but has been integrated as a compelling standard in the Women's Convention. In this way the intimate relation and interplay between the rights of women and the rights of the child have been explicitly acknowledged without sacrificing one for the other.

The other way round the CRC is much less explicit about the interplay between women's rights and children's rights, except where the reproductive and biological role of mothers is concerned. The neglect of gender is pointed out by Karin Arts as 'one of the most glaring examples' of important aspects of children's lives that are not explicitly covered in the text of the CRC.[48] In its general comments, the Committee tends to pay attention to this matter in a specific way only. Although it regularly addresses the special vulnerabilities of the girl child, it hardly problematises the gendered dimensions of parental roles and the underlying structural inequality between men and women in an explicit manner.

A remarkable exception to this is provided by the General Comment on harmful practices already mentioned in the introduction and which the Committee has issued in tandem with the supervisory committee to the Women's Convention.[49] The gender perspective adopted in this General Comment is not entirely limited to paying attention to the specific position and vulnerability of the girl child, but includes a more general and overall analysis of the impact of gender relations on the occurrence of harmful practices. It shows a clear eye for the underlying, multidimensional and structural causes of harmful practices, including male-dominated power structures and stereotyped gender roles:

> The Committee on the Elimination of Discrimination against Women and the Committee on the Rights of the Child consistently note that harmful

> practices are deeply rooted in social attitudes according to which women and girls are regarded as inferior to men and boys based on stereotyped roles. They also highlight the gender dimension of violence and indicate that sex- and gender-based attitudes and stereotypes, power imbalances, inequalities and discrimination perpetuate the widespread existence of practices that often involve violence or coercion.[50]

In line with this analysis the General Comment calls for a holistic approach to change those underlying systemic and structural root causes of harmful practices and reminds states parties that they 'have an obligation to challenge and change patriarchal ideologies and structures that constrain women and girls from fully exercising their human rights and freedoms'.[51] In fact, explicit attention is paid to the need for the 'empowerment of women and girls' under a separate heading.[52] To achieve change it is fully acknowledged that the commitment and support of men is indispensable.[53]

This broader gender perspective could provide inspiration for the CRC Committee to develop a gender-based approach to intra-family relations that would address the gendered nature of parental roles. This could be achieved specifically by taking into account some of the following points when addressing intra-family relations.

To start with it should be acknowledged that in the contemporary setting the well-being and realisation of the rights of children is indeed closely intertwined with improving the well-being and rights of women. Improving the position of the one will generally benefit the position of the other and vice versa.[54]

Additionally, it should be fully understood that empowering women and eliminating structural and systemic gender discrimination are key to improving the position of both to start with: 'neither children's rights nor the rights of women can be realised in an environment of structural discrimination in gender relations'.[55] In this respect it is crucial to acknowledge that gender relations are structurally asymmetrical, be it in or outside the family, with overall men wielding much more power over women than vice versa. Worldwide women tend to bear the main burden of the day-to-day care for children and other family members, with all its consequences for their disadvantaged and inferior position in society. As a consequence, it would seem important for the Committee to pay more attention to the gendered nature of parental roles and to empowering women within the family to create a better balance between men and women in their parental roles, as the CRC requires.

As with rights,[56] shared responsibilities should not be 'theoretical or illusory' but 'practical and effective'. To promote this, parental rights towards children should be balanced with actual responsibilities. This could mean, for instance, that absent fathers are not given parental rights that enhance their power over the mother unless they actually share the responsibility for the child. In this respect, caring responsibilities of parents should come first, rights later.

Another point to be borne in mind concerns the consequences of a demanding level of obligations to realise the rights of the child as developed by the CRC

Committee in its General Comments. Generally speaking, demanding standards impact on women much more than men in their parental roles. This is not to call for a lowering of the standards to be set, but it does call for open and clear reflections by the Committee on such effects and how to overcome them.

This brings me to another point. Although the interests of women/mothers and children run to a large extent parallel and improving the position of the latter will benefit the former and vice versa, it would be naïve to ignore the tensions that may arise between women's rights and children's rights.[57] Women have a life beyond motherhood and they may have personal needs, wishes and ambitions that need not always run parallel with those of their children. Such interests are to be respected as women are not to be reduced (again) to their role as mothers. To sacrifice their rights and interests to the rights of children as a matter of principle would undo their emancipation into becoming rights-bearing subjects. Of course, sacrificing the rights of children to women's rights is similarly unacceptable to take as a starting point. In fact, both categories can claim prioritising of their rights and interests as both are vulnerable groups meriting specific protection.[58]

Given this situation, according to Erica Burman the relation between women's rights and children's rights should be approached 'as neither adversarial, nor equivalent, but as allied – albeit as necessarily structured in tension and contest'.[59]

9.5 Concluding remarks

Women's rights and children's rights are closely intertwined and cannot be realised without profound modifications in the gendered nature of intra-family relations. As such, it is very important to develop an integrated approach to the realisation of the human rights of both groups.

Bringing the gender-based approach of the Women's Convention and the child-based approach of the CRC together, my conclusion would be that taking children's rights seriously cannot be achieved without taking women's rights seriously and the other way round. The Women's Convention has explicitly acknowledged this by including the best interests of the child as a compelling standard in Articles 5 and 16. So far, the CRC and its supervisory body have addressed the interplay between women's rights and children's rights in a limited way only, being primarily focused on the specific vulnerabilities of the girl child and the biological role of mothers. This limited approach to integrating a gender perspective will not suffice to improve the position of women and children structurally and fully realise their rights. To be effective, the much broader problem of the gendered nature of intra-family relations has to be addressed, that is, including the relations between parents. The CRC Committee could play a leading role in this respect by taking up the broader gender perspective that is envisaged above in its work. The references to this broader perspective in its joint general comment with CEDAW provide a promising starting point for such an endeavour.

Notes

1 See e.g. the UN *Manual on Human Rights Monitoring*, available on the website of the Office of the High Commissioner for Human Rights, ch 15: 'Integrating gender into human rights monitoring' www.ohchr.org/Documents/Publications/Chapter15-20pp.pdf (last accessed 13 December 2016).
2 UN Committee on the Elimination of Discrimination against Women (CEDAW Committee) and Committee on the Rights of the Child (CRC Committee), 'Joint General Recommendation/General Comment No 31 of the Committee on the Elimination of Discrimination against Women and No 18 of the Committee on the Rights of the Child on harmful practices' (2014) CEDAW/C/GC/31-CRC/GC/18. All general comments/recommendations of the treaty bodies are available through the website of the Office of the High Commissioner of Human Rights www.ohchr.org/EN/HRBodies/Pages/HumanRightsBodies.aspx (last accessed 13 December 2016).
3 A very interesting and in-depth study of the way in which the CRC Committee has dealt with the gendered roles of parents in its 'concluding observations' has been conducted by Marjolein van den Brink, *Moeders in de mainstream. Een genderanalyse van het werk van het VN-Kinderrechtencomité (Mothers in the mainstream. A gender analysis of the work of the UN Committee on the Right of the Child)* (Wolf Legal Publisher 2006). Regretfully, this dissertation is only available in Dutch and as it was published in 2006 it only covers the first 15 years of the Committee's work. Nevertheless, it has been a great inspiration for this contribution.
4 cf the preamble of the Women's Convention: 'Concerned, however, that despite these various instruments extensive discrimination against women continues to exist'.
5 CEDAW Committee, 'General Recommendation No 29 on Article 16: Economic consequences of marriage, family relations and their dissolution' UN Doc CEDAW/C/G/GC/29, section 2.
6 For a comprehensive analysis see M A Freeman, C Chinkin and B Rudolf (eds), *The UN Convention on the Elimination of All Forms of Discrimination against Women: A Commentary* (Oxford University Press 2012).
7 See e.g. art 2 UDHR, art 26 ICCPR and art 2.2 ICESCR.
8 CEDAW Committee, 'General Recommendation no 28 on the Core Obligations of States Parties under Article 2 of the Convention on the Elimination of All Forms of Discrimination against Women', UN Doc CEDAW/C/2010/47/GC.2, section 7.
9 Of the other provisions addressing intra-family relations in some way arts 9, 12 and 14 do so in a limited way only. Article 9 deals with discrimination against women regarding nationality. In addition to requiring the eradication of discrimination in respect of the acquisition or loss of nationality upon marriage by women themselves, it requires states to 'grant women equal rights with men with respect to the nationality of their children' (CEDAW art 9(2)). Article 12 covers non-discrimination in the field of health care and requires states parties to ensure, on a basis of equality of men and women, access to – among others – family planning (CEDAW art 12(1)). As far as pregnancy, confinement and the post-natal period are concerned, states are obligated to ensure 'appropriate services . . . granting free services where needed' as well as 'adequate nutrition during pregnancy and lactation' (CEDAW art 12(2)). Article 14 pays specific attention to the position of rural women and requires attention for their 'significant roles . . . in the economic survival of their families' (CEDAW art 14(1)) and to ensure they participate in and benefit from development and have access to 'services in family planning' (CEDAW art 14(2)(b)).

10 See for a fuller analysis R Holtmaat, 'Article 5' in M A Freeman, C Chinkin and B Rudolf (eds), *The UN Convention on the Elimination of All Forms of Discrimination against Women: A Commentary* (Oxford University Press 2012) 141.
11 CEDAW Committee, 'General Recommendation No 23 on Article 7 (Political and Public Life)' (1997), para 8.
12 ibid para 10.
13 M A Freeman, 'Article 16' in Freeman, Chinkin and Rudolf (eds), *The UN Convention on the Elimination of all Forms of Discrimination against Women: A Commentary* (Oxford University Press 2012) 441.
14 CEDAW Committee, 'General Recommendation no 29 on Article 16' (n 5), para 3.
15 ibid.
16 ibid paras 43–47.
17 ibid para 8.
18 CEDAW Committee, 'General recommendation No 21: Equality in Marriage and Family Relations' (1994) paras 19, 20.
19 See Freeman 'Article 16' (n 13) 411.
20 ibid 432.
21 CEDAW Committee, 'General Comment No 5: General Measures of Implementation of the Convention on the Rights of the Child' (2003) UN Doc CRC/C/GC/5/Rev. 1, para 12. In addition to the two principles discussed here the CRC Committee has identified art 2 (non-discrimination) and art 6 (right to life) to have the status of general principles providing guidance for the interpretation of the CRC as a whole.
22 CEDAW Committee, 'General Comment No 7: Implementing Child Rights in Early Childhood' (2005) UN Doc CRC/C/GC/7/Rev.1, para 1.
23 J Zermatten, 'The best interest of the child principle: literal analysis and function' (2010) 18 *International Journal of Children's Rights* 483, 494.
24 This and the following has been elaborated in CEDAW Committee, 'General Comment No 14: The Right of the Child to Have his or her Best Interests Taken as a Primary Consideration (art 3 para 1)' (2013) UN Doc CRC/C/GC/14.
25 ibid para 39.
26 ibid para 37.
27 See for some of these fears and an argument they are unfounded J Doek, 'What does the Children's Convention require?' (2006) 20 *Emory International Law Review* 199.
28 The extensive and detailed CEDAW Committee, 'General Comment No 17: The Right of the Child to Rest, Leisure, Play, Recreational Activities, Cultural Life and the Arts (art 31)' (2013) UN Doc CRC/C/GC/17 is a case in point.
29 CRC Committee, 'General Comment No 14' (n 24), para 67.
30 CRC Committee, 'General Comment No 7' (n 22).
31 ibid para 20.
32 ibid para 26.
33 See e.g. the approach by the UN Development Project which does elaborate this point www.undp.org/content/undp/en/home/ourwork/povertyreduction/focus_areas/focus_gender_and_poverty.html (last accessed 13 December 2016).
34 CRC Committee, 'General Comment No 17' (n 28).
35 CRC Committee, 'General Comment No 14' (n 24), para 67.
36 cf Van den Brink (n 3) 229–230.
37 CRC Committee, 'General Comment No 5 General Measures of Implementation of the Convention on the Rights of the Child' (2003) UN Doc CRC/C/GC/5/Rev. 1, para 29.

38 CRC Committee, 'General Comment No 15: The Right of the Child to the Enjoyment of the Highest Attainable Standard of Health (art 24)' (2013) UN Doc CRC/C/GC/15, para 93.
39 ibid para 18.
40 ibid para 51.
41 ibid para 94.
42 ibid paras 113, 114.
43 ibid para 35. See also CEDAW Committee, 'General Comment No 17' (n 28), para 27.
44 For an overview of the standards developed in this context and their relation with other international and human rights standards see George Kent, 'Breastfeeding: a human rights issue?' (2001) 44 *Development* 94.
45 CEDAW Committee, 'General Comment No 15' (n 38), para 44.
46 ibid.
47 cf J Evans, 'Guest editorial: women's rights and children's rights: challenges and opportunities' (2001) 44 *Development* 7.
48 K Arts, 'Twenty-five years of the United Nations Convention on the Rights of the Child: achievements and challenges' (2014) 61 *Netherlands International Law Review* 267, 272.
49 CEDAW Committee and CRC Committee, 'Joint General Recommendation/ General Comment No 31 of the Committee on the Elimination of Discrimination against Women and No 18 of the Committee on the Rights of the Child on harmful practices' (n 2).
50 ibid para 6.
51 ibid para 61.
52 ibid paras 61–67.
53 ibid para 65.
54 cf e.g. J Todres, 'Women's rights and children's rights: a partnership with benefits for both' (2004) 10 *Cardozo Women's Law Journal* 603; S Goonesekere, R de Silva-de Alwis, 'Women's and children's rights in a human rights based approach to development', Working Paper for UNICEF division of policy and planning 2005 www.wcwonline.org/pdf/asia2007conf/Women%27s%20and%20Children%27s%20Rights%20in%20a%20Human%20Rights%20Based%20Approach.pdf (last accessed 13 December 2016).
55 S Goonesekere, 'Realizing human rights of women and children: some reflections on law and policy' (2001) 44 *Development* 15, 18.
56 As the European Court of Human Rights has reiterated many times see e.g. *ECtHR Airey v Ireland* (1979–80) 2 EHRR 305 (9 October 1979) Series A no 32, para 24.
57 For an overview of the ways in which the rights and interests of women and children may run parallel and deviate see the special issue on women's rights and children's rights (2001) 44(2) *Development*. For a more theoretical and conceptual analysis see M Minow, 'Rights for the next generation: a feminist approach to children's rights' (1986) 9 *Harvard Women's Law Journal* 1 and F Olsen, 'Children's rights: some feminist approaches to the United Nations Convention on the Rights of the Child' (1992) 6 *International Journal of Law and the Family* 192.
58 In this respect the way in which General Comment No 3 on the best interests of the child discussed in para 3.1 formulates the 'larger weight' that must be attached to the child's interests if it conflicts with the rights of others resembles the 'very weighty reasons' test applied by the European Court of Human Rights where the protection of the rights and interests of vulnerable groups such as women is concerned in the context of art 14 ECHR. The 'very weighty reasons' test in

the context of sex discrimination was already developed by the Court in ECtHR (28 May 1985) *Abdulaziz, Cabales and Balkandali v UK* Application no 9214/80; 9473/81; 9474/81, Series A no 77.

59 Erica Burman, 'Beyond "Women vs. Children" or "WomendandChildren": engendering childhood and reformulating motherhood' (2008) *International Journal of Children's Rights* 16, 177–94.

10 Children's rights and LGBTI persons' rights: some thoughts on their 'integration'

Ivana Isailovic

10.1 Introduction

In this chapter I consider whether or not 'integration' – defined by the editors as the 'deliberate effort' to incorporate the specific concepts or norms of children's rights into the LGBTI[1] 'branch' or 'regime' – is desirable.

Any reflection on this question will need to take into account the analysis of Wouter Vandenhole in this volume. He argues that the uniqueness of some of the Convention on the Rights of the Child's (CRC) characteristics may be exaggerated and that some of the initial legal innovations have in fact been mainstreamed in other human rights regimes. He further points to the numerous weaknesses and limitations of the CRC's concepts and norms and warns us against 'naive attempts' to incorporate them in other human rights regimes.[2]

I pursue some of these reflections concerning the integration of the two 'branches' and the incorporation of CRC's provisions in the LGBTI human rights 'branch'. In doing so, I strive to take into account LGBTI people's experiences and needs on the ground but also how rights are interpreted and may be deployed by different legal actors: policy makers, scholars, activists and other domestic and global decision-makers, including human rights bodies, to take into account, address and regulate LGBTI people's experiences. Asking whether or not concepts and ideas need to be integrated supposes – I believe – a simultaneous discussion about the experiences individuals face and the variety of rights' effects on LGBTI individuals' everyday life.

I argue that some of the distinctive provisions of the CRC, as currently interpreted, are ill-suited to respond to the challenges individuals who self-identify as LGBTI or are perceived as LGBTI face. It follows that integrating some of these provisions in the LGBTI human rights branch will not improve the situation of LGBTI individuals on the ground and may even have the opposite effect. I suggest how some of these provisions may be interpreted or amended in light of both LGBTI individuals' experiences and universal human rights instruments' interpretations by other human rights bodies. It follows that these interpretations may in fact serve as inspiration for the CRC. In order to illustrate these points, I will focus on three provisions: the right to participation (Article 12 of the CRC), the 'best interests of the child' clause (Article 3.1 of the CRC) and the right to education (Article 29 of the CRC).

In the first case, I argue that while the right to participation may be seen as crucial for addressing the distressing situation of intersex children, the current interpretation of this right does not allow to challenge abusive medical practices LGBTI children are subject to. Secondly, I show that the 'best interests of the child' clause may be a problematic provision because of its indeterminacy: while it can be used to promote LGBTI children's and adults' rights, it may also have the opposite effect and be used to impede rights of gays and lesbians and their families. Finally, I show the limits of the right to education provision and suggest that the interpretation of the right to education could be updated in light of LGBTI individuals' specific experiences at school and the need to tackle the abuses individuals may face throughout the school system.

Before developing these arguments, I want to offer some preliminary remarks explaining why answering the editors' initial question, whether there is 'integration', 'inspiration' or 'isolation' when considering the interplay between LGBTI and children's rights may be difficult because of the very characteristics of the rights regime protecting LGBTI persons.

10.2 Preliminary remarks

Unlike other historically marginalised communities, such as women, there are no specific conventions or specific human rights bodies that deal with LGBTI individuals' rights. Thus, there is no specific LGBTI human rights *branch* – as understood by the editors of this volume – which can easily be identified. Rather, LGBTI individuals' rights regime is made of a number of universal and identity-based human rights treaties and norms, and their interpretations by a variety of global and local actors.

This analysis of LGBTI individuals' rights protection is consistent with the one found in the UN documents, such as, for instance, the 'Born Free and Equal' booklet crafted by the UN Human Rights Office of the High Commissioner in 2012. The document is a comprehensive description of how UN human rights bodies have been applying core obligations states have towards LGBTI persons and is intended to guide activists and various rights-users. According to this document, LGBTI rights are not *specific* because: 'the protection of people on the basis of their sexual orientation or gender identity . . . requires enforcement of the universally applicable guarantee of nondiscrimination in the enjoyment of all rights'.[3]

The drafters of the Yogyakarta Principles on the Application of International Human Rights Law in relation to Sexual Orientation and Gender (2006) also adopted a similar position.[4] According to Michael O'Flaherty – who served as Rapporteur and was the member of the group of human rights experts who developed these principles – these principles do not seek to create new special rights but, to propose a 'consistent understanding of the comprehensive regime of international human rights law and its application to issues of sexual orientation and gender identity' and to clarify 'State obligations under existing international human rights law, in order to promote and protect all human rights for all persons on the basis of equality and without discrimination'.[5] In the remainder of the chapter I use the term *LGBTI individuals' rights* to denote these universal and identity-based human rights applicable to persons who self-identify or are perceived as LGBTI.

In addition, the concept of *LGBTI rights* and particularly discrimination on the basis of *sexual orientation* and *gender identity* are new categories in human rights law. This can make the kind of inquiry proposed by the editors more challenging as we are grappling to make sense of the new field's practical and normative effects. LGBTI persons' rights have only recently come to the forefront of the global human rights agenda to address abuses LGBTI individuals face on the streets, at school, in health services or on the job market and legal evolutions have accelerated in the last 20 years.

In 1994, in its case *Toonen v Australia*, the Human Rights Committee decided for the first time that the criminalisation of same-sex private activity between consenting men was contrary to the International Covenant on Civil and Political Rights (hereinafter ICCPR) and for the first time, interpreted the Covenant to cover discrimination on the ground of *sexual orientation*.[6] That same year Amnesty International published a major report on the question of gay and lesbians' human rights violations entitled *Breaking the Silence: Human Rights Violations Based on Sexual Orientation*[7] and launched a couple of years later in 1998 a campaign entitled 'Gay Rights are Human Rights'.

In 2011, the UN released its first report on the question of discrimination practices individuals face because of their sexual orientation and gender identity[8] and around that same time and since then, various UN Committees and human rights bodies have addressed questions related to the ill-treatment LGBTI people face.[9] In September 2015, for the first time, 12 UN entities released a joint call for an end to the discrimination and violence LGBTI adults, adolescents and children face.[10]

The Committee on the Rights of the Child (CRC Committee) has also addressed the issue of LGBTI individuals' rights protection and the protection of children raised by LGBTI families in its General Comments and Concluding Observations to the States. For instance, in its General Comment No 3 on HIV and AIDS the Committee stresses the role of discrimination on the basis of sexual orientation in heightening children's vulnerability.[11] Another example is its General Comment No 13 on the right of the child to freedom from all forms of violence. The Committee seems to refer to 'gay, lesbian, transgender and transsexual' children as particularly vulnerable groups for the first time, adding *gender identity* to discrimination on the basis of sexual orientation.[12]

Recently in its Concluding Observations to Russia the Committee highlighted its concerns regarding laws prohibiting 'unconventional sexual relationships' stressing that the laws encourage 'discrimination and stigma' against LGBTI people, including children and LGBTI families.[13] The Committee made similar remarks in its recent Concluding Observations concerning the reports of Poland where it notes that it is concerned that 'there is no comprehensive law on prohibition of discrimination on all grounds, in all aspects of life and forms, including multiple forms of discrimination' in particular that '. . . lesbian, gay, bisexual and transgender children face discrimination and may become targets of hate crimes'.[14] Accordingly, it recommends that the state amend its law on equal treatment so that 'it covers the issue of discrimination on the basis of gender and sexual orientation . . . in the fields of education, health care, social protection, housing and private and family life . . .'.[15]

Finally, thinking about the interplay between LGBTI rights and children's rights may seem counter-intuitive. Historically, the main human rights question pertaining to LGBTI individuals or those who identify as such was and still concerns *the decriminalisation of adult consensual sexual intercourse.*[16] LGBTI rights did not concern *children* but *adults* and, more specifically, their *sexuality.* In the same vein, recent struggles for marriage rights and marriage equality domestically and internationally reinforce *adults'* rights and protect *their* relationships.[17] The emergence of children's rights may signal a new direction the human rights field is taking in this respect. This shift is also illustrated in the Yogyakarta Principles, which broadened the scope of LGBTI persons' rights to address issues of children's protection because of both their identity and the identity of their family members.[18]

In the remainder of this contribution, I examine the main unique provisions from the Convention on the Rights of the Child and I show what their limits are, and how they could be amended to take LGBTI children's experiences into account.

10.3 The right to be heard and the right to participation

The right of the child to be heard (Article 12 CRC) is a distinctive provision of the CRC and is considered to be one of its overarching principles. Although – as pointed out by Vandenhole – the principle may be criticised because of its lack of child-specificity and the lack of proper theoretical and legal grounding, it could be used to foster the protection intersex children are currently deprived of in most domestic jurisdictions.[19] The right of the child to be heard along with the need to take children's best interests into account in decisions affecting them[20] adds to the universally guaranteed rights such as the right to equality, right to life or health in challenging current medical practices infringing upon intersex children's rights.

This provision may, however, as currently interpreted, be ill-suited for tackling this question for two reasons: firstly, the General Comment on the right of the child to be heard and express its views in all matters – including children's health – does not mention the specific situation of intersex children. Secondly, because the provision essentially deals with *procedural* requirements, it does not impose on the state or private actors the obligation to obtain the informed consent of the child prior to any medical intervention.

Intersex children's bodies do not easily fall into the male or female gender categories enforced across different sectors of society. In most cases, therefore, they undergo 'normalising' cosmetic and reassignment surgeries, which are not always necessary and are prescribed hormone therapy so as to conform to the gender assigned to them by the medical personnel at their birth, without them (or sometimes their parents) having been consulted. These procedures have a series of harmful effects as intersex children may experience serious health complications having life-long consequences, including sterilisation, infection in urinary tract, removal of natural hormones and life-long dependence upon medication.[21] In addition, their present or future gender expression and identity might not match the sex they were assigned at birth, leading to a discrepancy between their legal documents and their gender expression and identity.

These medical interventions – often hidden from the intersex child – reinforce societal widespread understanding of binary gender identity norms and lead to the stigmatisation of intersex people who do not conform to these categories. This in turn may cause feelings of shame and distress for intersex individuals. Moreover, these medical practices may be seen as infringing upon intersex individuals' fundamental rights: rights to physical integrity, the right to health and the right to equality.

The CRC Committee has addressed the question of intersex children in its Concluding Observation to Switzerland in relation to the prohibition of all forms of violence against the child. The Committee notes that 'it is deeply concerned at':

> [c]ases of medically unnecessary surgical and other procedures on intersex children, without their informed consent, which often entail irreversible consequences and can cause severe physical and psychological suffering, and the lack of redress and compensation in such cases.

The Committee further urges the state to:

> [e]nsure that no one is subjected to unnecessary medical or surgical treatment during infancy or childhood, guarantee bodily integrity, autonomy and self-determination to the children concerned, and provide families with intersex children with adequate counselling and support.[22]

Moreover, in its General Comment on the right of the child to the enjoyment of the highest attainable standard of health, the Committee notes that:

> [c]hildren's right to health contains a set of freedoms and entitlements. The freedoms, which are of increasing importance in accordance with growing capacity and maturity, include the right to control one's health and body including sexual and reproductive freedom to make responsible choices.[23]

The right to be heard may further add to the realisation of intersex children's rights and could be reinterpreted in light of these specific needs and experiences of intersex individuals to guarantee substantively the right to control one's health and body that the Committee mentions in its concluding remarks. This is not, however, how the Committee currently interprets Article 12 although, it may be argued that the application of the right to be heard to the situation of intersex children could be inferred from the Committee's emphasis on the right to non-discrimination[24] which – as mentioned earlier – has been already interpreted by the Committee to include gender identity.

It seems more likely, however, that the Committee did not consider the needs and experiences of intersex children even in the context of health services. The Committee stresses in its General Comment on the rights to be heard that the 'realization of the provisions of the Convention requires respect for the child's right to express *his* or *her* views' (emphasis added)[25] emphasising the gender binary, which does not apply to intersex children. It moreover notes that children should be 'provided with information' that states need to ensure that children have access to 'confidential medical counselling and advice without parental consent' and that 'physicians and health care facilities should provide clear and accessible information to children'[26] failing to address the abusive unnecessary and mandatory medical practices performed without very young children's or their parents' knowledge.

Another obstacle to an interpretation of Article 12, which takes into account the actual needs and experiences of intersex children, is its *procedural* and vague nature ill-adapted to intersex children.

According to the Committee, the right of the child to be heard is the central element of the participation processes in which the child may express its views and perspectives that should be considered in decision-making, policy-making and all measures affecting the child and his or her evaluation. This right is essentially *a procedural one* to the extent that the state has no obligation to give the child *a veto power* or to implement their views *substantively*. The right to be heard only implies that the child who is 'capable of forming his or her own views' has the right to express those views freely in all matters affecting it, 'the views of the child being given *due weight* in accordance with *the age* and *maturity* of the child' (emphasis added).

The Committee has also emphasised the connection between the right to be heard and the duty for the state to make child's best interest a primary consideration in all measures that affect them. Here the 'best interest of the child' is a 'procedural right', which obliges the states to '*introduce steps into the action process* to ensure that the best interests of the child are taken into consideration' (emphasis added). It is, the Committee notes, a mandatory step.[27]

There are at least two limitations of this procedural requirement. As such, the right to be heard does not seem to enforce any substantive norm. The procedural requirements may have a range of practical applications and effects: the child may be informed of the negative impacts of the medical interventions, they may express their concerns and views, while these may nonetheless be performed. Secondly, although the Committee emphasised that the clause should not be read as a 'limitation',[28] considering that in most of the cases medical procedures are performed on very young children, the interpretation of the clause may be problematic in practice.

It follows that Article 12 does not expressly mandate that medical surgeries concerning intersex children be performed only if the child has previously given a fully informed consent to them. This silence may be explained by the fact that LGBTI rights are relatively new and that, because of that, LGBTI persons' specific experiences were simply not taken into account or that the interplay between health care and acts constitutive of violence has not been considered by the Committee when drafting the Comment. The Committee's recent emphasis on self-determination and control over one's body may, however, imply that imposing from states and private actors to obtain a prior full, free and informed consent of the child is precisely the policy which is needed.

The CRC could then be updated by integrating within the Convention the interpretations of universal human rights applicable to LGBTI individuals. One source of inspiration could be the Yogyakarta Principles No 18 on Medical Abuses, which seems already to incorporate some of the CRC's provisions. The provision ties together the full, free and informed consent of the child, in accordance with the age and maturity of the child, and the child's best interests in order to impose on states the need to constrain the use of gender reassignment surgery and make respect for gender identity the leading thread in policies that concern intersex children.

According to this principle, states shall:

> [t]ake all necessary legislative, administrative and other measures to ensure that no child's body is irreversibly altered by medical procedures in an attempt to impose a gender identity without the full, free and informed consent of the child in accordance with the age and maturity of the child and guided by the principle that in all actions concerning children, the best interests of the child shall be a primary consideration.[29]

In this part I argued that the right to participate – as currently interpreted by the Committee – fails to address the situation of intersex children. However, as explained above, the Committee's remarks on health and the elimination of any forms of violence may lead us to think that a re-interpretation of the Committee's views on this point may be justified and needed. The Yogyakarta Principles could then be used in order to further guide this endeavour.

10.4 The best interests of the child

The best interests of the child clause (Article 3(1) CRC) – which imposes on states that in all actions concerning children, the best interests of the child shall be a primary consideration – is one of the distinctive features of the CRC. I argue, however, that its transplantation to other regimes may be very problematic because of its indeterminacy. As Wouter Vandenhole rightly points out in this volume, 'the meaning of best interests of the child has remained indeterminate and opaque, so that it tends to be invoked from different sides to justify sometimes opposing decisions'.[30] In this part I highlight some of the concerns and tensions in connection to LGBTI individuals' rights and show that, because of its undetermined character, this clause may be – and has been – used to hinder the rights of LGBTI individuals.

The Committee is careful not to propose any substantive definition of the 'best interests of the child'. In its General Comments it insists on the concept's 'flexibility', 'adaptability' and a need to consider its meaning on a case-by-case basis, in light of 'the particular situation' of the child concerned. According to the Committee: 'the concept of the child's best interest is complex and its content must be determined on a case by case basis . . . . Accordingly, the concept of the child's best interest is flexible and adaptable. It should be adjusted and defined on an individual basis, according to the specific situation of the child or children concerned . . .'.[31]

Although avoiding the rigidity of formal rules and enabling the decision-maker to tailor a legal solution that is 'responsive to the situation of an individual child'[32], the Committee also warns about potential misuses of the concept. According to the Committee, the clause 'may [also] leave room for manipulation' and it stresses that it 'has been abused by Governments and other State authorities to justify racists policies, for example, or by parents to defend their own interests'.[33] It provides illustrations of these instances of manipulation, using what seems to be a non-exhaustive list of specific examples but failing to provide any guidelines for helping us – policy-makers, scholars and other decision-makers – to draw the line between those interpretations of the provision that may be problematic and those that correspond to the goals and the spirit of the CRC.

This indeterminacy is particularly problematic in cases in which children's rights have been or are mobilised to limit LGBTI individuals' right to private and family life. I will highlight two of these instances: the connection between the *child's best interest* and *him or her being raised by a gender differentiated family* and, secondly, the emphasis on 'biology' and 'biological bonds'. Both understandings of the child's best interests delegitimise LGBTI – but also non-conventional and alternative – kin structures and families.

In the first case, states have used arguments based on the child's best interests to justify both the discrimination against LGBTI individuals and limitations to their right to private and family life. *Fretté v France*, decided by the European Court of Human Rights (ECtHR), illustrates this point. In this case, the ECtHR had to decide whether the French authorities' refusal to grant an adoption to a single gay person was contrary to the plaintiff's right to family life interpreted in conjunction with the prohibition of discrimination on the ground of sexual orientation.[34] Although the decision was subsequently partly reversed in *EB v France*,[35] the case – I believe – is still interesting because it shows how the child's best interests can be connected to the claim that a *gender-differentiated household* is crucial for the child's development, and how this claim succeeded in the transnational context.

French authorities rejected the plaintiff's demand for adoption, arguing that his lifestyle did not provide sufficient safeguards 'from a child-rearing, psychological and family perspective'. In assessing whether this decision was legal, the Government Commissioner argued before the French Conseil d'État – the supreme court in administrative law matters – that it was unclear whether negative consequences ensued for children raised by single gay persons and that in any case protecting a child's interests may, in the field of adoption, set a limit to the scope of the prohibition of discrimination on the ground of sexual orientation. According to her:

> [t]he question whether a child is in danger of being psychologically disturbed by his relationship with an adult who cannot offer him or her the reference point of a distinct father and mother, in other words a model of ***sexual difference***, is a very difficult one which divides psychiatrists and psychoanalysts . . . [T]here is no agreement on the answer to that question. If there is any consensus it lies instead in the growing awareness that the rights of the child set the limits of the right to have children and that the child's interests cannot always be reconciled with current developments . . . (emphasis added).

Before the ECtHR, the French Government essentially brought forward these same arguments claiming that the contested measure was adopted in order to protect the child's best interests, and that the lack of a maternal role and the absence of scientific evidence regarding the consequences for children being raised by gay parent(s) justified the refusal to authorise adoption.[36]

It is interesting to note that the Court does not challenge at all the French substantive understanding of best interests of the child. The Court emphasises that the measure is taken having in mind the best interests and the health of the children to be adopted and notes that '[t]he justification for the decision (i.e. not to authorise adoption) lay in the paramountcy of the child's best interests, which formed the underlying basis for all the legislation that applied to adoption'. The Court further observes that '(t)he criteria applied for that purpose had been both objective and reasonable' and that it has no doubt that 'the decisions to reject the applicant's application for authorisation pursued a legitimate aim'. Finally, it stresses – following state's arguments – that scientific uncertainties may explain why the refusal to grant adoption may be consistent with the respect for children's best interests. According to the Court:

> [t]he difference in treatment stemmed from the doubts that prevailed, in view of what was currently known about the subject, about the development of a child brought up by a homosexual and deprived of a dual maternal and paternal role model. There was no consensus about the potential impact of being adopted by an adult who openly affirmed his homosexuality on a child's psychological development and, more generally, his or her future life, and the question divided both experts on childhood and democratic societies as a whole.[37]

By doing so, the Court accepts that the children's best interests may be defined in connection to the protection of gender-differentiated families, which inevitably at the practical and symbolic level induces both the stigmatisation of LGBTI parents and children they are raising (but also single-parent families) and limits LGBTI individuals' right to private life.

As regard the tension between children's rights and LGBTI individuals' rights, the Court highlights how children's best interests clash with the interest of the plaintiff. Nevertheless, it stresses again the absence of consensus of the scientific community on the question of adoption by single gay parents in Europe and notes the 'measured and detailed submission' of the Government. Finally, it concludes by observing that '[i]f account is taken of the broad margin of appreciation to be left to states in this area and the need to protect children's best interests to achieve the desired balance, the refusal to authorise adoption did not infringe the principle of proportionality'.[38]

The *Fretté* case exemplifies thus how in practice governments can use 'the child's best interest' to limit the rights of LGBTI parents and how this argument is given support in the global human rights regime.

Another illustration of how the invocation of children's best interests may be deployed to delegitimise and limit the rights of LGBTI families is the recent mention of *biological bonds* in connection with human rights.[39]A recent ECtHR case addressing the regulation of international surrogacy agreements and their effects in the intending parents' state of origin illustrates this tension.

In the *Mennesson v France* case,[40] the ECtHR had to decide whether the French refusal to recognise the filiation between children born out of surrogacy in the US and their intending French opposite-sex parents was constitutive of a breach of the Convention. In finding that this was the case, the Court emphasised the pivotal role played by children's best interests to see their filiation recognised in France. More specifically, the Court defined the interests of the child in relation to the children's *biological ties* with their genetic father and stressed that these ties are crucial for children's identity.[41] Not recognising the biological filiation between the intending father and his children is therefore particularly detrimental to children's right to family life and their best interests.

The Court does not consider in this case the situation of LGBTI parents but it is easy to understand how this reasoning may be problematic in situations in which intending parents are gay: would the certificate listing them as parents be recognised in the name of children's best interests? Or will the child's best interests be only understood to mandate the recognition of the 'biological filiation'? What if there is no such biological bond? These questions are traditionally seen as falling within the scope of private international law and, in this field, some scholars have recently justified the partial recognition of the foreign filiation by foregrounding the importance of the 'genetic relationship'.[42] One can easily understand how the decision in *Mennesson v France* could reinforce a biological understanding of parenthood and, as a consequence, deprive the non-genetic parent(s) of his/her/their rights.[43]

Best interests of the child are therefore capacious enough to embrace a variety of understandings on how kinship should be regulated in a given jurisdiction, and may in particular have the effect of marginalising legally and socially those whose families do not conform to the biological or gender-differentiated model that some may advocate in the name of children's best interests.

10.5 The CRC and the right to education

A final point concerns the right to education (Article 29 CRC). Self-identified LGBTI children or children perceived as LGBTI face numerous challenges throughout the educational system. According to the last survey done by the European Fundamental Rights Agency, 80 per cent of respondents have witnessed negative behaviour while in school, because a schoolmate was perceived to be LGBT.[44] In this context, various human rights bodies stressed that states have the obligation to enact comprehensive non-discrimination legislative and other measures, including grounds of sexual orientation and gender identity, to prohibit and prevent discrimination in private spheres and diminish attitudes that cause and perpetuate discrimination.[45] In particular, this includes the obligation of states to address bullying, harassment[46] and hate-speech in the educational setting.[47]

In this part, I argue that the interpretation of the Article 29 of the CRC – which does not explicitly concern LGBTI children or children of LGBTI parents – could and should be amended to address specific challenges children and adults may face.

Bullying, intimidation, the perpetuation of negative stereotypes and hate speech directly bear upon the right to education, which is guaranteed under the CRC, but also other human rights instruments.[48] In its General Comment, the Committee has observed that Article 29.(1) 'underlines the individual and subjective right to a specific quality of education'. It stresses that the core message of Article 29.1 is 'child-centred education', which means that the key goal of education is 'the development of the individual child's personality, talents and abilities, in recognition of the fact that every child has unique characteristics, interests, abilities, and learning needs'.[49] This means, for instance, that the 'curriculum must be of direct relevance to the child's social, cultural, environmental and economic context and to his or her present and future needs and take full account of the child's evolving capacities'.[50]

Moreover, the Committee stresses the need to combat discrimination, which can have exactly the same effect as preventing children from accessing the school system. According to the Committee, discrimination on the basis of the prohibited ground 'offends the human dignity of the child and is capable of undermining or even destroying the capacity of the child to benefit from educational opportunities'.[51] The Committee goes on to refer to discrimination on the basis of gender, disability and HIV, and also addresses the connections between Article 29.1 and the struggle against 'racism, xenophobia and related intolerance'.[52]

The Committee does not examine the situation of LGBTI children in relation to this specific provision, even though this reading could be inferred from its interpretations of the Convention. The Committee's subsequent definition of discrimination and the incorporation of gender identity and sexual orientation under the discrimination clause of the CRC point to that interpretation. Moreover, the Committee stresses that education should promote values such as 'respect for differences' and should challenge 'all aspects of discrimination and prejudices',[53] which may also refer to discrimination towards LGBTI persons. One could also infer for instance that problematic curricula or policies and practices that create, tolerate or contribute to the creation of a hostile environment can be challenged using the Committee's observation in relation to gender equality. In the General Comment, the Committee notes that:

> [g]ender discrimination can be reinforced by practices such as a curriculum which is inconsistent with the principles of gender equality, by arrangements which limit the benefits girls can obtain from the educational opportunities offered, and by unsafe or unfriendly environments which discourage girls' participation.[54]

The Article, however, does not refer *explicitly* to LGBTI children or adults and does not tackle issues such as sexual education, or the respect for the sexual orientation and gender identity of the parents or children's teachers. A more explicit affirmation of these principles is warranted and may be found in the interpretations to the universal right to education and the right to the highest attainable standard of physical and mental health given by various human rights bodies[55] – in particular the findings of the Special Rapporteur of the right to education, the European Committee for Social Rights and the Yogyakarta Principles. These interpretations may be used to enrich the CRC and address some of its current shortcomings.

For instance, in connection with sexual education, the Special Rapporteur on the right to education has called upon states to implement the right to comprehensive sexual education, which both reflects diversity and is non-discriminatory. More particularly, the Special Rapporteur on the right to education has emphasised that:

> In order to be comprehensive, sexual education must pay special attention to the issue of diversity since everyone has the right to deal with his or her own sexuality without being discriminated against on grounds of sexual orientation or gender identity. Sexual education is the basic tool for ending discriminations against persons of diverse sexual orientations.[56]

In that respect, the European Committee of Social Rights has found in its landmark case *International Center for the Legal Protection of Human Rights (INTERIGHTS) v Croatia*[57] that parties to the European Social Charter were required to provide sexual education to young people on a non-discriminatory basis without promoting and entrenching stereotypes and prejudices concerning sexual orientation. According to the Committee, sexual education:

> [s]hould also not be used as a tool for reinforcing demeaning stereotypes and perpetuating forms of prejudice which contribute to the social exclusion of historically marginalised groups and others that face embedded discrimination and other forms of social disadvantage which has the effect of denying their human dignity.[58]

In light of this, it found that the Croatian curriculum[59] contained statements that stigmatise gay people and are 'based upon negative, distorted, reprehensible and degrading stereotypes about the sexual behaviour' of all gay persons.[60]

Finally, the Yogyakarta Principles dealt comprehensively with the question of the right to education, here again directly incorporating expressions and provisions of the CRC, and adapting it to the specific situation of LGBTI children and adults. According to Principle No 16:[61] '[e]veryone has the right to education, without discrimination on the basis of, and taking into account, their sexual orientation and gender identity'. The principle further clarifies the different state obligations, emphasising the 'equal treatment of students, staff and teachers within the education system' and similarly to Article 29(1) provides that 'education is directed to the development of each student's personality, talents, and mental and physical abilities to their fullest potential, and responds to the needs of students of all sexual orientations and gender identities'. Regarding the education methods, curricula and resources it states the need to 'enhance understanding of and respect for, inter alia, diverse sexual orientations and gender identities'.[62]

Unlike the CRC, the Principle No 16 also addresses the issue of LGBTI parenting when stating that states need to ensure that 'education is directed to the development of respect for human rights, and of respect for each child's parents and family members, cultural identity, language and values, in a spirit of understanding, peace, tolerance and equality, taking into account and respecting diverse sexual orientations and gender identities'.[63] In addition, it also addresses the question of prohibition of violence towards teachers, staff and students and urge states to 'ensure that laws and policies provide adequate protection for students, staff and teachers of different sexual orientations and gender identities against all forms of social exclusion and violence within the school environment, including bullying and harassment'.[64]

In this part, I have reflected on the limitations of the right to education as interpreted by the Committee and how interpretations and norms provided by other human rights bodies could be used to address these shortcomings.

10.6 Conclusion

This contribution has put forward some reflections regarding the integration of LGBTI rights and the CRC. It makes two contributions: it shows that the distinctive rights and concepts guaranteed by the CRC may not be adequate for tackling the specific challenges self-identified LGBTI children or adults, or children and adults perceived as LGBTI face, despite the fact that in recent years the CRC has focused on the situation of LGBTI persons. Secondly, it demonstrates that the interpretation of the CRC could in fact integrate the knowledge built by other human rights bodies – and, more particularly, the expertise on discrimination based on gender identity and sexual orientation which informs the Yogyakarta Principles – to update the scope of children's rights.

Notes

I would like to thank Eva Brems, Ellen Desmet and Wouter Vandenhole for asking me to contribute to this edited volume and for the constructive discussions on the earlier versions of this chapter. All errors are mine.

1 In this contribution, *gay* refers to an individual who identifies as male and is emotionally and sexually attracted to other individuals who identify as male, *lesbian* refers to a person who identifies as a woman and is emotionally and sexually attracted to another person of her gender, *bisexual* refers to a person who is emotionally and sexually attracted to persons of different genders. *Trans* is the umbrella term used to describe individuals whose gender expression and identity differ from the one attached to the gender (male or female) they were assigned at their birth and encompasses a wide range of gender identities. *Intersex* is also an umbrella term used here to describe individuals whose characteristics do not match the medically and socially defined gender binary. I also use in this contribution gender neutral pronouns they/them/their.
2 W Vandenhole, 'Distinctive characteristics of children's human rights law', ch 1 in this volume.
3 United Nations High Commissioner for Human Rights (UNHCHR), 'Born free and equal', www.imdb.com/title/tt2149175/ (last accessed 13 December 2016).
4 Although not formally a binding treaty, the Yogyakarta Principles is said to be the most 'authoritative statement' of states' obligations having a significant legal impact on national, regional and international levels. See M O'Flaherty, 'The Yogyakarta Principles at 10' (2015) 33 *Nordic Journal of Human Rights Law* 280, 281, 287–94 (internal quotation omitted).
5 ibid 283 (internal quotation omitted).
6 *Toonen v Australia* Communication No 488/1992 (1994), UN Doc CCPR/C/50/D/488/1992. A similar finding was made in 2002 by the European Court of Human Rights in *Dudgeon v UK* Application no 7525/76 (ECtHR, 22 October 1981).
7 Amnesty International, *Breaking the Silence: Human Rights Violations based on Sexual Orientation* (Amnesty International 1995).
8 UNHCHR, 'Discriminatory laws and practices and acts of violence against individuals based on their sexual orientation and gender identity' (2011) UN Doc A/HRC/19/4; see also the updated report: UNHCHR, 'Discrimination and violence against individuals based on their sexual orientation and gender identity' (2015) UN Doc A/HRC/19/4.
9 See e.g. Committee against Torture (CAT), 'General Comment No 2: Implementation of article 2 by states parties' (2008) UN Doc CAT/C/GC/2, para 21, noting that 'State parties must ensure that . . . their laws are in practice applied to all persons, regardless of . . . gender, sexual orientation, transgendered identity'; Committee on Economic, Social and Cultural Rights (CESCR), 'General Comment No 20: Non-discrimination in economic, social and cultural rights' (2009) (art 2 para 2 of the International Covenant on Economic, Social and Cultural Rights) UN Doc E/C.12/GC/20, para 32, noting that: '"(o)ther status" as recognised in article 2, paragraph 2, includes sexual orientation. States parties should ensure that a person's sexual orientation is not a barrier to realizing Covenant rights, for example, in accessing survivor's pension rights. In addition, gender identity is recognized as among the prohibited grounds of discrimination; for example, persons who are transgender, transsexual or intersex often face serious human rights violations, such as harassment in schools or in the workplace'; CEDAW, 'General Recommendation No 28: Core Obligations of States Parties under Article 2 of the Convention on the Elimination of All Forms

of Discrimination against Women' (2010) UN Doc CEDAW/C/GC/28, para 18, noting: 'The discrimination of women based on sex and gender is inextricably linked with other factors that affect women, such as . . . sexual orientation and gender identity.'

10 UN Joint Statement, 'Ending violence and discrimination against lesbian, gay, bisexual, transgender and intersex people' www.ohchr.org/Documents/Issues/Discrimination/Joint_LGBTI_Statement_ENG.PDF (last accessed 13 December 2016).

11 CRC Committee, 'General Comment No 3: HIV/AIDS and the Rights of the Child' (2003) UN Doc CRC/GC/2003/1, para 6.

12 CRC Committee, 'General Comment No 13: The Right of the Child to Freedom from all Forms of Violence' (2011) UN Doc CRC/C/GC/13, para 72(g). See also CRC Committee, 'General Comment No 15: the Right of the Child to the Enjoyment of the Highest Attainable Standard of Health' (art 24) (2013) UN Doc CRC/C/GC/15 para 8,noting that: 'States parties have an obligation to ensure that children's health is not undermined as a result of discrimination' and that 'discrimination on the basis of sexual orientation and gender identity is included under the non-discrimination clause of the Convention'.

13 CRC Committee, 'Concluding Observations on the Combined Fourth and Fifth Periodic Reports of the Russian Federation' (2014) UN Doc CRC/C/RUS/CO/4-5, paras 24–25.

14 CRC Committee, 'Concluding Observations on the Combined Third and Fourth Periodic Reports of Poland' (2015) UN Doc CRC/C/POL/CO/3-4, para 16.

15 ibid para 17.

16 *Toonen v Australia* Communication No 488/1992 (1994), UN Doc CCPR/C/50/D/488/1992; see also *Dudgeon v UK* Application no 7525/76 (ECtHR, 22 October 1981).

17 Robert Wintmute, 'From "sex rights" to "love rights"' in Nicholas Bamforth (ed), *Sex Rights: The Oxford Amnesty Lectures 2002* (Oxford University Press 2005), describing the progress of LGBT rights as a transition from basic rights (right to life) to sex rights (prohibition of the criminalisation of sodomy) and love rights (recognition of same-sex partnership including marriage rights).

18 See Yogyakarta Principle No 13(b) (the right to social security and other social protective measures: 'States shall . . . (e)nsure that children are not subject to any form of discriminatory treatment within the social security system or in the provision of social or welfare benefits on the basis of their sexual orientation or gender identity, or that of any member of their family)', Principle No 15(d) (the right to adequate housing: 'States shall . . . (e)stablish social programmes, including support programmes, to address factors relating to sexual orientation and gender identity that increase vulnerability to homelessness, especially for children and young people, including social exclusion, domestic and other forms of violence, discrimination, lack of financial independence, and rejection by families or cultural communities, as well as to promote schemes of neighbourhood support and security); Principle No 18(b): 'States shall . . . [t]ake all necessary legislative, administrative and other measures to ensure that no child's body is irreversibly altered by medical procedures in an attempt to impose a gender identity without the full, free and informed consent of the child in accordance with the age and maturity of the child and guided by the principle that in all actions concerning children, the best interests of the child shall be a primary consideration'); Principle No 24(c), (d) (the right to found a family: 'States shall . . . [t]ake all necessary legislative, administrative and other measures to ensure that in all actions or decisions concerning children, whether undertaken by public or private social welfare institutions, courts of law, administrative authorities or legislative bodies, the best interests of the child shall be a primary

consideration, and that the sexual orientation or gender identity of the child or of any family member or other person may not be considered incompatible with such best interests; (d) In all actions or decisions concerning children, ensure that a child who is capable of forming personal views can exercise the right to express those views freely, and that such views are given due weight in accordance with the age and maturity of the child').

19 ibid.

20 CRC Committee, 'General Comment No 14: The Right of the Child to Have his or her Best Interests Taken as a Primary Consideration' (2013) UN Doc CRC/C/GC/14 art 3, para 1.

21 Commissioner for Human Rights, Human Rights and Intersex People, Issue Paper (2015) 14 https://wcd.coe.int/com.instranet.InstraServlet?command=com.instranet.CmdBlobGet&InstranetImage=2768767&SecMode=1&DocId=2282716&Usage=2 (last accessed 13 December 2016). See also FRA, 'The fundamental rights situation of intersex people' Fra Focus (2015) http://fra.europa.eu/sites/default/files/fra-2015-focus-04-intersex.pdf (last accessed 13 December 2016).

22 CRC Committee, 'Concluding observations on the combined second to fourth periodic reports of Switzerland' (2015) UN Doc CRC/C/CHE/CO/2-4, para 43.b.

23 CRC Committee, 'General Comment No 12: The Right of the Child to be Heard' (2009) UN Doc CRC/C/GC/12, para 24.

24 ibid para 75.

25 ibid para 98.

26 ibid.

27 ibid para 70.

28 ibid para 20. This means that the child is presumed to have the capacity to form his/her/their own opinion.

29 Yogyakarta Principle No 18.

30 See Vandenhole (n 2).

31 CRC Committee, 'General Comment No 14' (n 20), para 14.

32 ibid para 34.

33 ibid.

34 *Fretté v France* Application no 36515/97 (ECtHR, 22 May 2002).

35 *EB v France* Application no 43546/02 (ECtHR, 22 January 2008).

36 *Fretté v France* (n 34) para 35.

37 ibid para 36.

38 ibid para 42.

39 I will here focus on one specific case to illustrate this point. Whether or not the 'biological question' becomes a prominent one in the global human rights field would, however, mandate further investigation.

40 *Mennesson v France* Application no 651/92 (ECtHR, 26 June 2014).

41 ibid para 100.

42 See e.g. S Bollée, 'La gestation pour autrui en droit international privé' (2014) *Travaux du Comité Français du Droit International Privé*. See also a comparative approach to the different solutions at the domestic level in K Trimmings, P R Beaumont (eds), *International Surrogacy Arrangements: Legal Regulation at the International Level* (Hart Publishing 2013).

43 See, however, a recent judgment of the Federal Supreme Court of Germany, which rejected this interpretation of *Mennesson v France* upheld by lower courts. It consequently recognised the parental rights of the two men listed on the foreign birth certificate as parents of the child born out of surrogacy. Bundesgerichtshof, decision of 10 December 2014 (No XII ZB 463/13).

44 FRA, *EU LGBT Survey, European Union Gay, Lesbian, Bisexual and Transgender Survey* (European Union Agency for Fundamental Rights 2013) 18.
45 United Nations Human Rights Council, 'Discrimination and violence against individuals based on their sexual orientation and gender identity' (2015) UN Doc A/HRC/29/23, para 16.
46 ibid para 17.
47 See for instance in the European context *Vejdeland and Others v Sweden* Application no 1813/07 (ECtHR, 9 February 2012).
48 CRC art 29.1:

1. States Parties agree that the education of the child shall be directed to:

(a) The development of the child's personality, talents and mental and physical abilities to their fullest potential;
(b) The development of respect for human rights and fundamental freedoms, and for the principles enshrined in the Charter of the United Nations;
(c) The development of respect for the child's parents, his or her own cultural identity, language and values, for the national values of the country in which the child is living, the country from which he or she may originate, and for civilisations different from his or her own;
(d) The preparation of the child for responsible life in a free society, in the spirit of understanding, peace, tolerance, equality of sexes, and friendship among all peoples, ethnic, national and religious groups and persons of indigenous origin;
(e) The development of respect for the natural environment.

See also International Covenant on Social and Economic Rights art 13. CRC adds new elements when compared with the ICSER such as respect for one's parents, cultural identity, national values and different civilisations and respect for the natural environment.
49 CRC Committee, 'General Comment No 1: Article 29(1): The Aims of Education' UN Doc CRC/GC/2001/1, para 9.
50 ibid.
51 ibid para 10.
52 ibid para 11.
53 ibid para 11.
54 ibid para 9.
55 United Nations General Assembly (UNGA), 'Report of the United Nations Special Rapporteur on the right to education' (2010) UN Doc A/65/162, paras 10–15.
56 ibid para 21.
57 *International Center for the Legal Protection of Human Rights (INTERIGHTS) v Croatia* Complaint No 45/2007 (ECSR, 30 March 2009).
58 ibid para 48.
59 ibid.
60 ibid paras 60–61.
61 Principle No 16 reads as follows:
Everyone has the right to education without discrimination on the basis of, and taking into account, their sexual orientation and gender identity.
States shall:

(a) Take all necessary legislative, administrative and other measures to ensure equal access to education, and equal treatment of students, staff and teachers within the education system, without discrimination on the basis of sexual orientation or gender identity;

(b) Ensure that education is directed to the development of each student's personality, talents, and mental and physical abilities to their fullest potential, and responds to the needs of students of all sexual orientations and gender identities;

(c) Ensure that education is directed to the development of respect for human rights, and of respect for each child's parents and family members, cultural identity, language and values, in a spirit of understanding, peace, tolerance and equality, taking into account and respecting diverse sexual orientations and gender identities;

(d) Ensure that education methods, curricula and resources serve to enhance understanding of and respect for, inter alia, diverse sexual orientations and gender identities, including the particular needs of students, their parents and family members related to these grounds;

(e) Ensure that laws and policies provide adequate protection for students, staff and teachers of different sexual orientations and gender identities against all forms of social exclusion and violence within the school environment, including bullying and harassment;

(f) Ensure that students subjected to such exclusion or violence are not marginalised or segregated for reasons of protection, and that their best interests are identified and respected in a participatory manner;

(g) Take all necessary legislative, administrative and other measures to ensure that discipline in educational institutions is administered in a manner consistent with human dignity, without discrimination or penalty on the basis of a student's sexual orientation or gender identity, or the expression thereof;

(h) Ensure that everyone has access to opportunities and resources for lifelong learning without discrimination on the basis of sexual orientation or gender identity, including adults who have already suffered such forms of discrimination in the educational system.

62 Principle 16(d).
63 Principle 16(c).
64 Principle 16(e).

11 Undocumented migration: integrating the children's rights concept of nuanced vulnerability in human rights law

Julie Ryngaert and Wouter Vandenhole

11.1 Introduction

This chapter studies the interplay between children's rights law and human rights law in the context of undocumented migration. It will proceed in two stages. Firstly it maps the state of affairs as to the relation between children's rights law and human rights law in the area of undocumented migration. It demonstrates how children's rights law and human rights law apply their own notions of vulnerability by and large in isolation. Secondly, and more importantly, it argues for an integration of the nuanced approach to vulnerability that characterises children's rights law in the area of (undocumented) migration.

Both children's rights law and human rights law often use the concept of vulnerability. Nonetheless, the way both frameworks do it differs. Contrary to human rights law, children's rights law imbues the concept of vulnerability with various nuances. We argue that the latter is the better approach. Although the concept of vulnerability offers strong leverage for contributing to the legal protection of individuals and groups, strong reliance on it may enhance the actual vulnerability of individuals and groups. A nuanced vulnerability concept reduces these risks.

This chapter will explore the potential contribution of a nuanced vulnerability concept to the framing of the human rights of undocumented migrants. Firstly it explains the most important principles of a nuanced vulnerability concept as used in children's rights law. Secondly, it looks at the current vulnerability approach to undocumented migrants through the (quasi-)jurisprudence of the UN Committees, the European Court of Human Rights (ECtHR) and the European Committee of Social Rights (ECSR). The current vulnerability approach employed in general human rights law is rather limited and abstract. Hence, in the current state of affairs, children's rights law and human rights law appear to employ their own understanding of vulnerability in isolation from each other.

In the next section, we argue in favour of the integration in human rights law of a more nuanced vulnerability concept for all undocumented migrants, drawing on the approach characteristic to children's rights law. We spell out in particular the conceptual and practical value that such a nuanced vulnerability concept may add to the analysis of the human rights of undocumented migrants.

11.2 The nuanced vulnerability concept in children's rights law

Both human rights law and children's rights law use the notion of vulnerability in order to pay particular attention to individuals or groups who suffer more than others. Because of their vulnerability, they are believed to be entitled to priority treatment and enhanced protection. The *way* in which the vulnerability concept is framed is, however, of crucial importance in order to avoid that the labelling as 'vulnerable' creates or reinforces their vulnerability, inequality or exclusion.

Children's rights law, as reflected in the interpretation of the Convention of the Rights of the Child (CRC), generally adopts a more nuanced approach to vulnerability, and hence to children's humanity. Three important elements have been introduced into the children's rights vulnerability concept. Firstly, the CRC's child image combines vulnerability with autonomy. A child is never exclusively autonomous nor vulnerable. Contextual elements determine how much autonomy or vulnerability prevails. The Committee on the Rights of the Child (CRC Committee) too links up vulnerability with autonomy, capacities or agency (section 2.1). Secondly, the understanding of vulnerability is relational or contextual. Vulnerability is the result of both inherent, individual characteristics (being a child), and external factors or structures that cause or reinforce vulnerability. Hence, vulnerability is a layered concept owing to varying degrees of internal and external factors. It is not a label that is tagged on children simply because of their age (section 2.2). Thirdly, the CRC Committee pays attention to the diversity within children as a vulnerable group, so as to avoid generalisations about children and their vulnerability (section 2.3).

11.2.1 Central image of the child: vulnerability and agency

Which characteristics are attributed to children as fully-fledged human beings is rather complex.[1] It was not until the adoption of the CRC in 1989 that human rights doctrine paid attention to the question of how a child was perceived. Before, to the extent that provisions of the general human rights treaties addressed children in particular, they did so from an exclusively protectionist agenda, and often by protecting the family.[2]

Two schools of thought on children, i.e. child protection and child liberation theories, have to some extent influenced the CRC. Child protection theorists mainly emphasise the welfare and special needs of the child. From this paternalistic point of view, children are approached as irrational and dependent individuals, on whose behalf decisions should be made by rational autonomous adults. Child liberation theorists, on the other hand, predominantly draw attention to children as autonomous individuals and 'fully-fledged beneficiaries of human rights'.[3] This strand of thinking acknowledges that children do possess a competence for rational thought by means of which informed choices can be made. Moreover, the lack of competence in decision-making on the part of children is not of overriding importance to exclude them from participation in decision-making.[4]

The approach adopted by the CRC stands midway between a protection and liberation approach.[5] A child is considered as 'an initially highly vulnerable person in need of protection, nurturing and care who under parental guidance gradually prepares for an independent life in a social setting of rights and duties when reaching eighteen'.[6] Two general principles frame the characteristics of the child as constructed by the CRC, as reflected in Article 3 and Article 12 CRC. On the one hand, there is the state obligation to take the child's 'best interests' into account as a primary consideration in all matters affecting the child (Art 3 CRC). From this perspective, the child tends to be seen as a dependent human being in need of protection against harm. At the same time, the CRC recognises the agency of children through the right to voice, to be heard and to participation (Article 12 CRC).[7] These two principles forge a balanced image of the child, namely that of a vulnerable child yet with agency.[8] The degree of agency and vulnerability differs from child to child and arises from the interaction of multiple factors. In some cases, children may be (considered) especially in need of protection. In other cases, children themselves can best judge what they really want or need.

11.2.2 Relational or contextual vulnerability of the child

From a children's rights perspective, the vulnerability of children is not merely and automatically based on personal and inherent factors, i.e. the simple fact of age, of 'being a child'. Other factors too may reinforce or reduce personal vulnerability.

The CRC Committee often frames the vulnerability of children as relational or contextual.[9] It emphasises the relationship between the child and the circumstances that cause or increase vulnerability, as well as the situations in which a child happens to be vulnerable. Frequently, the Committee explains *why* a child is vulnerable in that particular circumstance.[10] Vulnerability of children is hence not determined only by fixed and inherent characteristics (i.e. of being a child), but also by variable external (social, societal, historical) structures, events or contexts that cause, reduce or reinforce vulnerability.[11] Vulnerability is a layered concept rather than a label tagged onto each child.[12]

11.2.3 Heterogeneity within the vulnerable group of children

Whenever the CRC Committee refers to vulnerable groups of children, it does so in a careful way. It either refers to their vulnerability in a hypothetical way ('may be more vulnerable', 'can be rendered vulnerable') or in carefully chosen language ('in many cases forms of multiple discriminations increase the vulnerability', 'girls with disabilities are often more vulnerable') or wording ('the best interests of a child in a specific situation of vulnerability will not be the same as those of all the children in the same vulnerable situation') that allow for diversity within the vulnerable group.[13]

11.2.4 Undocumented migrant children

Quite remarkably, the nuanced vulnerability concept has not yet been systematically integrated by the CRC Committee in its approach to undocumented migrant children. There may be several explanations. First of all, undocumented migrant children as a group are not frequently mentioned by the Committee in its General Comments and Concluding Observations. When they are mentioned, the notion of vulnerability is not often explicitly mobilised.

However, if and when the CRC Committee *does* invoke the vulnerability of undocumented migrant children, it does so in a nuanced way. It contextualises their vulnerability by focusing on situations which make them vulnerable.[14] It also allows for heterogeneity of undocumented migrant children who are in a vulnerable situation: 'The best interests of a child in a specific situation of vulnerability will not be the same as those of all the children in the same vulnerable situation. Authorities and decision-makers need to take into account the different kinds and degrees of vulnerability of each child, as each child is unique and each situation must be assessed according to the child's uniqueness. An individualised assessment of each child's history from birth should be carried out, with regular reviews by a multidisciplinary team and recommended reasonable accommodation throughout the child's development process'.[15]

In sum, children's rights law in general employs a nuanced vulnerability concept. Surprisingly, that general approach is not systematically followed by the CRC Committee with regard to undocumented migrant children. Let us now turn to human rights law.

11.3 The vulnerability approach to undocumented migrants in human rights law

The vulnerability approach to undocumented migrants in human rights law contrasts with the general nuanced vulnerability approach in children's rights law. In what follows, we introduce the approach taken by the UN human rights treaty bodies, the ECtHR and the ECSR.

11.3.1 UN human rights treaty bodies

The UN human rights treaty bodies pay particular attention to the vulnerability of undocumented migrants. However, they have so far failed to develop a coherent and layered understanding of vulnerability: they use different concepts to denote vulnerability, and it is not clear which criteria are to be met in order to be considered 'vulnerable'.

11.3.1.1 The Committee on Migrant Workers and the Committee on the Elimination of Discrimination against Women

The Committee on Migrant Workers (CMW Committee) and the Committee on the Elimination of Discrimination against Women (CEDAW Committee) come closest to the CRC Committee's general vulnerability approach.[16] Both Committees understand the vulnerability of undocumented migrants sometimes from a relational and contextual perspective.[17] They focus on the relationship between the undocumented migrant and his vulnerability. The circumstances that make undocumented migrants (more) vulnerable are explained (albeit rather summarily) as well as those for which these migrants may be vulnerable in a given context. The CMW Committee, for example, points out that the lack of a valid residence or labour permit exposes female migrant workers to abuse and exploitation.[18] With regard to underage migrant workers, that Committee has highlighted their young age, isolation, separation from their families and dependence on the employer as factors that may increase their vulnerability for human rights violations.[19]

Both Committees sometimes use careful and rather hypothetical phrasing ('may be more vulnerable', 'can be rendered vulnerable'), which avoids generalisations and allows for diversity within the vulnerable group of (female) migrant workers.[20] However, no explicit link is made with autonomy, agency or capabilities.

11.3.1.2 Other committees

The Committee on the Elimination of Racial Discrimination and the Human Rights Committee sometimes address the human rights of undocumented migrants, but they have so far not identified this group as vulnerable.[21] The Committee Against Torture (CAT) and the Committee on Economic, Social and Cultural Rights (CESCR) do consider undocumented migrants as a vulnerable group, but do not pay attention to nuances.[22]

11.3.2 European Court of Human Rights

Although the ECtHR regularly includes the notion of vulnerability in its case-law, it does not seem to have a clear theoretical understanding of the concept. For sure, the Court has explicitly denoted several groups, such as Roma, mentally disabled persons, persons with HIV and asylum-seekers, as vulnerable groups in need of special protection.[23] It remains unclear, however, exactly what makes them a vulnerable group.[24] Since the Court usually uses the expression '*particularly* vulnerable groups' (emphasis added), it seems to suggest that persons belonging to such a group or being in such a situation are *more* vulnerable than others.[25]

With regard to children, the ECtHR has invoked the notion of vulnerability in several cases in which the detention conditions, reception conditions and treatment of (undocumented) migrant children were assessed in light of Article 3 (prohibition of torture, inhuman or degrading treatment) and Article 5 (right to liberty).[26] With regard to adults, the ECtHR has employed the notion of inherent vulnerability of an asylum-seeker, in the case of *MSS v Belgium and Greece* and *Tarakhel v Switzerland*.[27] The Court uses different notions to point out their vulnerability, and it is not clear whether these notions are mutually interchangeable. For undocumented migrant children, it tends to refer mainly, but not exclusively, to the vulnerable *situation* in which they are or in which they tend to be,[28] whereas for adult asylum-seekers, it focuses on their *membership* of a vulnerable group.[29]

The ECtHR recognises the (extremely) vulnerable situation of undocumented migrant children, because of their 'age', their 'illegal' status in a foreign country, their personal situation and their traumatic experiences, and stresses their need for special protection.[30] It emphasises the positive state obligation to protect children and other vulnerabe groups under Article 3 of the European Convention on Human Rights (ECHR) and underlines that the situation of extreme vulnerability is paramount to and takes precedence over the status as an (undocumented) foreigner.[31] Central to the Court's assessment whether their detention and living conditions are in violation of Article 3 ECHR is their vulnerability. In almost all cases, the Court has held that a violation had taken place because the state did not take into account the particular vulnerability of the applicant as migrant child.[32]

In the case of *Tarakhel v Switzerland*, the Court considered prospectively that the removal in the absence of certain assurances would violate Article 3 ECHR.[33] In all cases, the Court, taking into account the causes of vulnerability, emphasises the impact that the state's failure to take their particular vulnerability into account has on their already vulnerable situation.[34] It thus increases the protection level to be guaranteed by the state to the specific vulnerable group of migrant children.

The ECtHR also applies, inter alia,[35] because of the vulnerability of underage migrants, stricter rules for the permissibility of deprivation of liberty under Article 5 ECHR. Deprivation of liberty is only allowed in an exhaustive list of situations. Article 5(1)(f) ECHR allows for 'the lawful arrest or detention of a person to prevent his effecting an unauthorised entry into the country or of a person against whom action is being taken with a view to deportation or extradition'. In case of adult migrants, the Court requires that the deprivation of liberty is proportionate.[36] In case of migrant children, the Court is stricter: because of their (extreme) vulnerability, absolute necessity is to be demonstrated.[37]

The ECtHR does not mention the vulnerability of undocumented adult migrants. This may create the impression that it does not consider them as vulnerable. The implications of this approach are particularly visible in the case of undocumented *families.* Concerning the children, the Court takes the obligation to protect children, because of their vulnerability, against torture and inhuman or degrading treatment as the starting point and typically finds that the living conditions in detention violate Article 3 ECHR.[38] With regard to the parents, the Court considers on the other hand that their detention may have created feelings of powerlessness, anxiety and frustration, but that the fact that they were not separated from their children during the detention must have provided some degree of relief from those feelings, so that it typically concludes that the threshold required for a violation of Article 3 has not been reached.[39] The Court equally refrains from examining the impact of the parents' own detention and that of their children on the formers' mental health.

The Court also distinguishes between children and their parents to assess the permissibility of their deprivation of liberty in light of Article 5(1) ECHR.

Since it requires absolute necessity with regard to the children, because of their vulnerable situation, it typically finds a violation of Article 5(1) ECHR as far as the children are concerned.[40] The parents' detention is typically found not to be in violation of Article 5(1) ECHR, because no necessity standard is applied in their regard.[41] Exceptionally, in one judgment, the Court qualified the mother's detention as arbitrary because of her protracted unlawful detention in a place that was manifestly inappropriate to house a family and in conditions that amounted to a violation of Article 3 with regard to her children.[42]

Since the case of *MSS v Greece*, the Court has identified a particular category of foreigners, i.e. asylum-seekers, as vulnerable.[43] In this case, the Court accepted that the applicant, who was an adult asylum-seeker, was a vulnerable person because of his past traumatic experiences ('because of everything he had been through during his migration and the traumatic experiences he was likely to have endured previously')[44] but it also more generally indicated that vulnerability is an inherent characteristic of *asylum-seekers*.[45] Hence, it attached considerable importance to the applicant's status as an asylum-seeker, and thus as a member of a vulnerable group in need of special protection, in the examination of his case in the light of Articles 3 and 5 ECHR. The Court ruled that his detention circumstances were unacceptable ('taken together, the feeling of arbitrariness and the feeling of inferiority and anxiety often associated with it, as well as the profound effect such conditions of detention indubitably have on a person's dignity, constitute degrading treatment contrary to article 3 of the Convention') and that 'the applicant's distress was accentuated by the vulnerability inherent in his situation as asylum-seeker'.[46]

Concerning the living conditions, more specifically whether the situation of extreme material poverty amounted to a violation of Article 3 ECHR, the Court again attached considerable importance to the applicant's status as an asylum-seeker, and, therefore, as a member of a vulnerable group in need of special protection.[47] Although the Court made it clear that Article 3 could not be interpreted as implying a state obligation to provide everyone within his jurisdiction with a home or a general obligation to give refugees financial assistance to enable them to maintain a certain standard of living,[48] it referred to the broad consensus at the international and European level concerning the need for special protection for the vulnerable group of asylum-seekers, 'as evidenced by the Geneva Convention, the remit and activities of the UNHCR and the standards set out in the Reception Directive'.[49]

Since Greece had not taken into account the applicant's vulnerability as an asylum-seeker nor met its obligations (shelter, material aid etc) under the Reception Directive, the applicant had found himself in a situation of extreme poverty, 'living on the street, with no resources to sanitary facilities, and without any means of providing for his essential needs'.[50] In taking into account the positive obligations under the EU directive, the Court increased the protection level that states parties that are also a Member State of the EU have to offer to the group of asylum-seekers.

Compared to the key principles of a nuanced vulnerability concept as used in children's rights law, the jurisprudence of the ECtHR shows some parallel developments, but at the same time ignores certain nuances. The ECtHR approaches the vulnerability of migrants from a relational perspective. It flags the relationship between the applicant and the circumstances that cause the applicant's vulnerability. For example, it has pointed out the vulnerability of being an asylum-seeker because of past traumatic experiences[51] and the (extreme) vulnerability of undocumented migrant children because of their age, their illegal status in a foreign country and their personal and past experiences. In both cases, the ECtHR emphasised the aggravating impact of the inaction of the state party on the already existing vulnerable situation.

However, with regard to asylum-seekers, the ECtHR does not interpret vulnerability as a layered concept that results from both individual and external factors, but rather as a label that is tagged on and inherent to the situation of asylum-seekers. Nor does the ECtHR make any mention of autonomy, capacities and agency. It recalls, for example, the situation of extreme vulnerability of a child which is paramount to and takes precedence over the status as a foreigner, but does not clarify the rationale for that wording, nor does it contextualise the vulnerability of children within the agency that they may also have. Undoubtedly, in the detention cases at stake, considering the situation of (extreme) vulnerability of the children concerned as paramount was absolutely warranted. Nonetheless, the one-sided emphasis on extreme vulnerability is reductionist and disempowering, as it reflects only one dimension of the child image.

From a children's rights perspective, it would have been more appropriate to take the balanced image of a child as starting point: a child is regarded as being vulnerable and endowed with agency at the same time. The degree of agency and vulnerability depends on the interaction between multiple factors. Certainly, in the particular cases under discussion, the outcome would have been the same, since they hardly enjoyed any autonomy and their vulnerability was blatant.[52] The ECtHR has adopted the same reductionist approach with regard to the group of (adult) asylum-seekers in the case of *MSS v Belgium and Greece*, by considering them as *inherently* vulnerable.[53]

In sum, the ECtHR seems to emphasise unilaterally the vulnerability of children and asylum-seekers *as a group*, and tends to overlook the diversity within these vulnerable groups.[54] Not all persons belonging to a vulnerable group have the same vulnerabilities, experiences or needs. Whenever children's rights law refers to vulnerable groups, it acknowledges the heterogeneity within the group, typically by using hypothetical and carefully chosen language (e.g. 'girls with disabilities are often more vulnerable', 'the best interests of a child in a specific situation of vulnerability will not be the same as those of all the children in the same vulnerable situation'). This emphasis on the unique characteristics of a person in a concrete situation avoids essentialising vulnerable groups. As already mentioned, it is important not to minimise the agency of individuals who do belong a priori to a certain predefined category of vulnerable persons, nor to downplay the vulnerability of persons who do not belong a priori to a predefined category of vulnerable groups. In recognising the inherent vulnerability of asylum-seekers[55] and systematically excluding the vulnerability of undocumented migrants, the ECtHR gives the wrong impression that persons belonging to vulnerable groups are always vulnerable, while those who do not belong to a vulnerable group will never be vulnerable.[56]

11.3.3 European Committee of Social Rights

The ECSR too has mobilised the vulnerability concept in a couple of cases on the economic, social and cultural (ESC) rights of undocumented migrants. Different notions circulate, such as 'vulnerable groups',[57] 'vulnerable category of persons',[58] 'categories of vulnerable people'[59] or 'vulnerable situation'.[60] The ECSR clearly considers undocumented migrant children as a vulnerable group.[61] Its position with regard to the vulnerability of undocumented adult migrants remains implicit if not ambiguous: although it has recently found violations of the right to shelter with regard to undocumented adult migrants too, in line with earlier cases regarding children, it has not explicitly drawn on vulnerability language.[62]

The ECSR makes in particular use of the vulnerability concept in order to exceptionally extend the personal scope of the (Revised) European Social Charter to persons or groups who textually do not come within the personal scope of the Charter.[63] The Committee has done so when the restriction of the personal scope would deprive vulnerable groups of the protection of the most basic rights enshrined in the Charter or impair their fundamental rights, such as the rights to life or physical integrity or the right to human dignity.[64] Whereas the ECSR has relatively recently extended the personal scope of the Charter to undocumented adult migrants too, it has refrained to explicitly draw on vulnerability language with regard to the latter.[65]

The ECSR seems to take a similar approach to the child image of undocumented migrant children as general children's rights law does in its nuanced approach to vulnerability.[66] In the case of *DCI v Belgium*, in which the lack of shelter for undocumented migrant children was complained of, the ECSR referred to their condition as 'children' and to their specific situation as 'unlawful', characterising them as combining vulnerability and limited autonomy.[67] By combining these two features, the ECSR indicates that children are not inherently vulnerable, that their agency and vulnerability interact, but that in the particular case of undocumented children vulnerability prevails over agency. Owing to their limited autonomy, according to the ECSR, they are not able do decide themselves whether to stay or to leave, and cannot therefore be held genuinely responsible for their place of residence.[68] Furthermore, the ECSR considers that 'the situation of unaccompanied minors, becomes even more vulnerable and the stay should be managed entirely by the State, which has a duty to care for children living within its territory and not to deprive them of the most basic protection on account of their "unlawful" migration status'.[69]

The ECSR, however, does not elaborate in depth why migrant children are vulnerable or why unaccompanied minors are even more vulnerable. The lack of a relational and contextual perspective on the concept of vulnerability frequently reappears. The ECSR takes the vulnerable situation of undocumented children as a starting point, but does not explain why.[70] Finally, the ECSR does not seem to be aware of the diversity within the group of migrant children, nor does it take into account the individual characteristics of minors who belong to the vulnerable group of migrant children.[71]

The ECSR considers both undocumented migrant children and adults as vulnerable groups, but with regard to the latter, it does so in a rather implicit and unclear way. It seems to impose stricter conditions on states parties for migrant children, however, presumably because their fundamental rights are more likely to be violated given their vulnerability and limited autonomy.[72] This may explain why the ECSR in the case of *FIDH v France* was of the opinion that the limited access to medical treatment in case of emergencies or other life-threatening conditions did not violate the rights of undocumented migrant adults under Article 13 European Social Charter (right to social and medical assistance), whereas the same limited access was considered to be in violation of Article 17 (right of children and young persons to protection) (revised) European Social Charter as regards undocumented migrant children.[73]

11.4 Arguments in favour of the integration of a nuanced vulnerability concept in human rights law

The previous sections illustrate the discrepancy between children's rights law and human rights law in their approach to undocumented migrants. First of all, the concept of vulnerability is not applied to all undocumented migrants. The UN committees tend to consider both undocumented migrant children and adults as vulnerable. Within the Council of Europe, the vulnerability of both is not so unequivocally acknowledged. The ECtHR accepts the (extreme) vulnerability of undocumented migrant children, but has refrained from accepting the vulnerabilty of undocumented migrant adults. An exception has been made for (adult) asylum-seekers, to be distinguished from ***undocumented*** migrants. The ECSR considers undocumented migrant children as a vulnerable group, but has not yet accepted explicitly the vulnerability of undocumented adults.

By explicitly adopting the vulnerability concept for undocumented migrant children but not for undocumented adult migrants, a dichotomy has been created, which creates tension between both groups. General human rights law, especially as reflected in the case law of the ECtHR and to a lesser degree in that of the ECSR, appears to take an abstract human and child image as a starting point regarding undocumented migrant adults and children. It creates the impression that undocumented migrant children are only, automatically and inherently vulnerable, whereas adults' agency and absence of vulnerability is considered to be a given. In practice, the lack of nuance results in a separate regime for children and adults, where minors enjoy a certain priority, isolated from adults, concerning their rights to liberty as well as to the enjoyment of socio-economic rights.

Compared to the nuanced vulnerability approach in children's rights law, general human rights law applies conceptual developments with regard to undocumented migrant children insufficiently and inaccurately at times. Of the UN treaty bodies, only the CMW and the CEDAW apply a nuanced vulnerablity approach that is analogous to that of the CRC Committee. In the Council of Europe, both the ECtHR and the ECSR have incorporated some nuances regarding undocumented migrant children similar to those introduced by the CRC Committee.

The aforementioned observations do not seek to question the vulnerability of undocumented minor migrants, but want to problematise the use of a rather one-sided notion of vulnerability that does not serve vulnerable groups nor those who do not belong to these a priori vulnerable groups at all. Based on the key principles of a nuanced vulnerabily concept as used in children's rights law, we seek to demonstrate that the use of the nuanced vulnerability concept is defendable and desirable for undocumented migrant *adults* too, and that a more nuanced and refined vulnerability approach would strongly alleviate the tension between undocumented migrant adults and children.

11.4.1 Nuanced vulnerability as an appropriate concept for undocumented migrants

11.4.1.1 Intricate connection between autonomy or agency and vulnerability

Children's rights law adopts a balanced image of the child, namely that of a vulnerable child yet with agency. It does not portray a child as exclusively vulnerable or autonomous. The degree of agency and vulnerability of a child depends on contextual, situational and personal factors.

The ECSR recognises this intricate connection between autonomy and vulnerability of minors, also when they are undocumented migrants,[74] but not of undocumented migrant adults. The fact that the ECSR does not apply the concept of vulnerability to undocumented migrant adults could be understood to mean that the ECSR sees them as purely autonomous agents who are making their own free choices. This interpretation may be concluded from the statement of the ECSR on the vulnerability and limited autonomy of undocumented migrant children: 'As a result of their lack of autonomy children cannot be genuinely responsible for their place of residence. Children are not able to decide themselves whether to stay or to leave'.[75] A contrario, adults may be suggested to be genuinely responsible for their place of residence.

The ECtHR does not mention the vulnerability of undocumented migrant adults at all. Concerning undocumented migrant children, the Court emphasises their (extreme) vulnerability, rather than taking the inextricable connection between their vulnerability and agency as a starting point. Owing to their extreme vulnerability – the combined result of their age, 'illegal' status, personal situation and the past traumatic experiences – enhanced legal protection needs to be offered. By considering undocumented migrant adults a priori as not vulnerable, and undocumented migrant minors as vulnerable, a differentiation of legal protection between both age categories is introduced. An explanation for this differentation may be found in the Court's view that undocumented migrant adults not only are autonomous agents who are able to make their own free choices of stay and can be held responsible for their decisions, but also that they can cope with traumatic or stressful experiences in their country of origin or the host country. Migrant children are assumed not to have that resilience, what renders them (extremely) vulnerable.[76] The fact that the ECtHR considers the specific group of (adult) asylum-seekers to be vulnerable, contrary to the group of undocumented migrant adults, may be explained by the fact that it accepts for this category of migrants that the past experiences are more traumatic and that the choice to leave their country of origin was more forced and less voluntary.

However, from a children's rights law perspective, the approach of the ECSR and ECtHR, namely the one-sided emphasis on either the vulnerability or the agency of a person along age lines, is reductionist as it only reflects one dimension of a person. This deficiency is particularly visible in the jurisprudence of the ECtHR because the Court does not only focus on the extreme vulnerability of undocumented migrant children, it also does not make any effort to examine or understand the vulnerability of undocumented adults.

Research and legal doctrine have shown that the portrayal of exclusive vulnerability of undocumented minors or the exclusive autonomy of adult migrants is at odds with reality. Several studies have demonstrated undocumented migrant children's agency and resilience, despite the precarious situation in which they find themselves.[77] In the same way as migrant adults, they sometimes choose to leave their country of origin, looking for a better future. The majority of the group of non-accompanied migrants is between 15 and 18 years old. At this age, one can suppose that they are capable to plan things, to use networks and resources to flee. The Special Rapporteur on the human rights of migrants has urged to see minors as independent agents and not as 'objects' or only 'victims of cirumstances'.[78]

Research has equally illustrated that migrant adults, despite their autonomy to make free choices, can also be vulnerable in certain situations or unable to cope with stressful circumstances. Furthermore, several reports of the Special Rapporteur on the human rights of migrants have pointed out the vulnerability of undocumented migrants. He refers, among other aspects, to the special vulnerability of undocumented migrants to detention and to different factors that increase their vulnerability, such as not being able to speak the language; gender (women in detention are vulnerable to sexual violence); age (unaccompanied elderly people); physical and mental health condition (persons suffering from mental disorders, persons with physical disabilities, persons with HIV, victims of torture).[79] With regard to health, it has been argued that '[m]igrants may be more vulnerable to poor health by virtue of their often low socioeconomic status, the process of migration and their vulnerability as non-nationals in the new country'.[80] Similarly, challenges in accessibility and the security of tenure with regard to the right to adequate housing have been attributed to migrants' vulnerable status as non-nationals.[81]

11.4.1.2 Contextual or relational vulnerability

Children's rights law frames the vulnerability of the child not only within the relation between the child and the circumstances that cause or even increase vulnerability, but refers also to personal and external factors that cause, limit or increase vulnerability. It points to the interaction between different sorts of factors. The ECSR, in contrast, does not define the concept of vulnerability. It makes mention of vulnerable groups, but does not elaborate on the concept. For example, in the case of *DCI v Belgium*, it presumes that all children, particularly undocumented migrant children, are vulnerable, but does not clarify the rationale for that wording. The ECtHR does contextualise and frame the vulnerability of vulnerable groups by attributing vulnerability to inherent (e.g. being a child, being an asylum-seeker) as well as external factors (e.g. traumatic experiences in the country of origin, migration trajectory). Unfortunately, there is the mistaken claim by the ECtHR, of inherent, personal or automatic vulnerability of a child or an asylum-seeker. Owing to the status of 'being a child' or 'being an asylum-seeker', it is assumed that children or asylum-seekers need special attention. This notion of vulnerability is based on personal factors only, i.e. the simple fact of being a child or being an asylum-seeker.

Several studies, for example, the STEPS Consulting Study and the DEVAS-project, have shown that the vulnerability of undocumented migrants in the detention context must be understood as a mechanism governed by the interaction of internal and external factors.[82] A study by STEPS Consulting Social, commissioned by the European Council, examined in particular the detention conditions of third country nationals.[83] In that study, 'vulnerability' was said to arise from three sets of factors: personal factors, environmental factors and risk factors. Personal factors result from the specific conditions of a person, such as physical and mental conditions, age, genetic composition and knowledge. Environmental factors are defined as experiences of migrants after their arrival in Europe. Risk factors concern more specifically characteristics or circumstances that, if present, reduce the chance of a positive outcome, such as past experiences (in the country of origin or as a consequence of migration).

The DEVAS-project[84] concerning the process of vulnerability in detention, draws the same conclusion, namely that 'vulnerability can be conceptualised as a concentric circle of personal (internal), social and environment (external) factors that may strengthen or weaken an individual's personal condition'.[85] The study shows that (the degree of) vulnerability of undocumented migrants to negative influences of detention – or in other words, the extent to which the migrant is capable of coping with his detention – depends not only on personal characteristics (e.g. sex, age, family condition, personal financial means, being aware of the migration and asylum and detention policy, language skills, personal expectations, health condition), but that environmental (e.g. length and circumstances of detention) and social (e.g. family, connection to the outside world, connection with lawyers or non-governmental organisations (NGOs)) factors play an important role in the 'coping strategy' of undocumented migrants to deal with the situation of detention.[86]

11.4.1.3 Diversity within the group of undocumented migrants

Children's rights law tries to avoid an over-emphasis on the homogeneity of the group of minors by attaching importance to the individual and unique characteristics of each person belonging to the vulnerable group. It avoids generalisation and essentialisation of the group of minors. Furthermore, it allows flexibility: those who belong to a vulnerable group are not automatically considered vulnerable while those who do not belong to a vulnerable group, are not automatically considered not vulnerable. This approach is reflected in the language that is used: vulnerable groups of children are referred to in a hypothetical way or in carefully chosen language that allows for diversity within the vulnerable group. By contrast, the ECSR and the ECtHR seem to recognise only certain predefined categories or classes of vulnerable persons, such as minors and asylum-seekers, but tend to ignore the diversity within these groups.

Taking into account the aforementioned studies which consider vulnerability as a result of the interaction between different external and internal factors and thus differing from one person to another, every person can be in a vulnerable situation. Monitoring bodies should pay more attention to individualised vulnerability of undocumented migrant adults. They should realise that undocumented adults, although they do not belong to the predefined category of vulnerable groups, can be (extremely) vulnerable as an individual migrant because of the interplay of internal and external factors.

11.4.2 Added value of a nuanced vulnerability concept for the analysis of the situation of undocumented migrants

A nuanced vulnerability concept not only offers strong conceptual leverage for contributing to the legal protection of individuals and groups, but also reflects a less one-dimensional way of understanding someone's humanity, without having recourse to essentialising and stigmatising these individuals and groups.

On the other hand, a less or insufficiently nuanced vulnerability concept has several conceptual and practical shortcomings. The conceptual shortcomings in the (quasi-)jurisprudence have to do above all with a lack of nuance or refinement in the understanding of the humanity of undocumented migrant children and adults. General human rights law, especially as reflected in the case law of the ECtHR and to a lesser degree in that of the ECSR, appears to take an abstract human and child image as a starting point regarding undocumented migrant children and adults. It creates the impression that undocumented migrant children are automatically and inherently vulnerable, contrary to undocumented migrant adults of whom the agency and non-vulnerability is considered to be a given.

In practice, this lack of nuance results in a separate regime for children and adults, where minors enjoy a certain priority, isolated from adults, concerning their right to liberty as well as to the enjoyment of socio-economic rights. The question is whether an undocumented migrant child really benefits from this isolation in practice. Would it help undocumented children, for example, if states could no longer detain them, while they would be able to continue to do so with regard to their parents? Obviously, such a practice would be highly problematic in light of the right to family life. Or, what about the right of an undocument migrant child to material aid that can only be realised in a return centre? The dichotomy between undocumented children and adults results not only in essentialising both groups, but also in underestimating the agency and capacities of migrant children and the vulnerability of migrant adults.

The added value of a nuanced vulnerability approach to the analysis of the human rights of undocumented migrants may be twofold: theoretical and practical. The incorporation and application of a more nuanced vulnerability concept does not necessarily make an equally important contribution to both levels, however. A solid contribution of a nuanced vulnerability approach not only requires the elimination of the conceptual deficiencies but also effective legal protection of undocumented migrants in practice.

The *conceptual* value that a nuanced vulnerability approach can add to the analysis of human rights of undocumented migrants lies in a less reductionist and a more nuanced approach of the humanity of undocumented migrants. A nuanced vulnerability approach as used by children's rights law, takes the interaction of autonomy and vulnerability of all undocumented (adult and minor) migrants for granted and makes the degree of vulnerability and agency dependent on several factors, and not only and exclusively on internal (inherent) factors (such as 'being a child' or 'being an asylum-seeker'). In the nuanced vulnerability approach, every undocumented migrant may find himself in a vulnerable situation, but may be able to cope with difficult traumatic experiences as well. Another conceptual added value of the vulnerability approach lies in the incentive for acknowledging the diversity within a vulnerable group and for taking the individual vulnerability of persons more into account, including those who do not belong to a predefined vulnerable group. The integration and application of a nuanced vulnerability concept in both children's and human rights law, is also likely to reduce the tensions between both frameworks, since the rights of children will no longer be pitted against those of adults. The binary distinction between children on the one hand and adults on the other hand will give way to a continuum of vulnerability accross the board.

The *practical* value that the incorporation and application of a nuanced vulnerability approach may have in the analysis of the situation of undocumented migrants, builds on the conceptual contribution. By moving beyond a dichotomy between minors and adults in which children enjoy special treatment, isolated from adults, the legal protection of all undocumented migrants, regardless of age, may be strengthened. In such an 'equalising up' approach, the ECtHR and the ECSR would need to justify their interpretation in a more nuanced and less one-sided way, to the benefit of all undocumented migrants.

11.5 Conclusions

This chapter has outlined the relationship between children's rights law and human rights law in the area of undocumented migration. It has shown how children's rights law and human rights law apply their notions of vulnerability by and large in isolation: whereas the former uses a nuanced vulnerability concept that draws on internal and external factors and acknowledges that agency and vulnerability can coexist, the latter mainly employs a binary distinction between undocumented children who are said to be exclusively vulnerable, and adults who are considered to be autonomous and hence responsible for their situation.

This chapter has argued in favour of an integration in the area of migration of the nuanced approach to vulnerability that characterises children's rights law. That integration would not only be a welcome conceptual development, but it would also avoid that children's rights are pitted against human rights, or undocumented children against undocumented adults. The introduction of a nuanced vulnerability concept in which attention is paid to both internal and external factors in a case-specific analysis does not allow for equalising down the legal protection that undocumented children currently enjoy, but rather urges to equalise up the legal protection of undocumented adults.

Beyond the case of undocumented migrants, the added value of a nuanced vulnerability approach to human rights law may lie not only in offering strong conceptual leverage for contributing to the legal protection of vulnerable individuals and groups, but also in reflecting a less one-dimensional way of understanding someone's humanity, without having recourse to essentialising and stigmatisation of individuals and groups.

Notes

1 We take a non-essentialist approach: see O Nieuwenhuys, 'Editorial: the ethics of children's rights' (2008) 15 *Childhood* 4.
2 See e.g. ICESCR art 10.
3 N Cantwell, 'The origins, development and significance of the United Nations Convention on the Rights of the Child' in S Detrick (ed), *The United Nations Convention on the Rights of the Child: A Guide to the* Travaux Préparatoires (Martinus Nijhoff 1992) 27.
4 C Breen, *Age Discrimination and Children's Rights* (Martinus Nijhoff 2006) 2–8.
5 ibid 8; W Vandenhole, 'A children's rights perspective on poverty' in W Vandenhole, J Vranken and K De Boyser (eds), *Why Care? Children's Rights and Child Poverty* (Intersentia 2010) 19.
6 A Eide, 'Article 27: the right to an adequate standard of living' in A Alen, J Vande Lanotte, E Verhellen, E Berghmans and M Verheyde (eds), *A Commentary on the United Nations Convention on the Rights of the Child* (Martinus Nijhoff 2006) 3.
7 J Bhabha, 'The child: what sort of human?' (2006) 121 *The Humanities in Human Rights: Critique, Language, Politics* 1526–35.
8 For further elaboration, see D Archard, M Skivenes, 'Balancing a child's best interests and a child's views' (2009) 17 *International Journal of Children's Rights* 1, 1–21.
9 This is particularly visible in the General Comments of the CRC Committee; see e.g. CRC Committee, 'General Comment No 3: HIV/AIDS and the Rights

of the Children' UN Doc CRC/BC/2003/3, para 30; CRC Committee, 'General Comment No 4: Adolescent Health and Development in the context of the Convention on the Rights of the Child' UN Doc CRC/GC/2003/4, paras 6 and 8; CRC Committee, 'General Comment No 6: The Treatment of Unaccompanied and Separated Children outside of their Country of Origin' UN Doc CRC/GC/2005/6, paras 23 and 50; CRC Committee, 'General Comment No 7: Implementing Child Rights in Early Childhood' UN Doc CRC/C/GC/7/Rev 1, paras 18 and 36; CRC Committee, 'General Comment No 9: The Rights of Children with Disabilities' UN Doc CRC/C/GC/9, paras 8–10; CRC Committee, 'General Comment No 11: Indigenous Children and their Rights under the Convention' UN Doc CRC/C/GC/11, para 64. The Concluding Observations of the CRC Committee do not often use the relational approach of the vulnerability concept.

10 F Luna, 'Elucidating the concept of vulnerability: layers not labels' (2009) 2 *International Journal of Feminists Approaches to Bioethics* 1, 129.

11 CRC Committee, 'General Comment No 3' (n 9) para 30; CRC Committee, 'General Comment No 4', paras 6 and 38; CRC Committee, 'General Comment No 6' (n 9) paras 23 and 50; CRC Committee, 'General Comment No 7: Implementing Child Rights in Early Childhood' UN Doc CRC/C/GC/7/Rev.1 paras 18 en 36; CRC Committee, 'General Comment No 9: the Rights of Children with Disabilities' UN Doc CRC/C/GC/9 paras 8–10; CRC Committee, 'General Comment No 11: Indigenous Children and their Rights under the Convention' UN Doc CRC/C/GC/11, para 64.

12 Luna (n 10).

13 Zie e.g. Committee, 'General Comment No 4' (n 11), para 38; CRC Committee, 'General Comment No 9' (n 11) paras 8 and 10; CRC Committee, 'Day of General Discussion on Children without Parental Care' UN Doc CRC/C/153 paras 670–672.

14 See e.g. CRC Committee, 'General Comment No 14 on the Right of the Child to Have his or her Best Interests Taken as a Primary Consideration (art 3, para 1)' UN Doc. CRC/C/GC/14, para 54: 'An important element to consider is the child's situation of vulnerability, such as . . . being a refugee or asylum seeker'; CRC Committee, 'Concluding Observations (Honduras, 2007)' UN Doc CRC/C/HND/CO/3, para 18: 'children in situations of vulnerability, including unaccompanied, migrant and asylum-seeking children', paras 70–71: 'are particularly vulnerable to becoming victims of exploitation and abuse'.

15 CRC Committee, 'General Comment No 14' (n 14) para 76.

16 CMW, 'General Comment No 1: Migrant Domestic Workers' UN Doc CMW/C/GC/1; CMW, 'General Comment No 2: The Rights of Migrant Workers in an Irregular Situation and Members of their Families' UN Doc CMW/C/GC/2; CEDAW, 'General Recommendation No 26: Women Migrant Workers' UN Doc CEDAW/C/2009/WP.1/R.

17 CEDAW, 'General Recommendation No 26' (n 16) paras 4, 10, 12 and 22; CMW, 'General Comment No 1' (n 16) paras 7, 11, 14, 21, 24 and 43.

18 CMW, 'General Comment No 1' (n 16) para 7.

19 ibid para 14.

20 CEDAW, 'General Recommendation No 26' (n 16) paras 10 and 19; CMW, 'General Comment No 1' (n 16) paras 7, 11, 21, 24 and 43.

21 Both committees focus on the group of undocumented migrants, but do not mention their vulnerability or membership to a vulnerable group. E.g. CERD, 'General Recommendation No 30: Discrimination Against Non-citizens' UN Doc CERD/C/64/Misc.11/rev 3; HRC (30 April 1997) 'A. v Australia' UN Doc CCPR/C/59/D/560/1993; HRC (13 November 2002) 'C. v Australia'

UN Doc CCPR/C/76/D/900/1999; HRC (29 October 2003) 'Bakhtiyari v Australia' UN Doc CCPR/C/79/D/1069/2002.

22 CAT, 'Concluding observations (The Netherlands, 2007)' UN Doc CAT/C/NET/CO/4 para 7; CAT, 'Concluding observations (Finland, 2011)' UN Doc CAT/C/FIN/CO/5-6 para 17; CESCR, 'Concluding observations (France, 2008)' UN Doc E/C.12/FRA/CO/3, para 47; CESCR, 'Concluding observations (Belgium, 2008)' UN Doc E/C.12/BEL/CO/3, para 35; CESCR, 'Concluding observations (Argentina, 2011)' UN Doc E/C.12/ARG/CO/3, para 20.

23 For a discussion of vulnerable groups in the case law of the ECtHR see L Peroni, A Timmer, 'Vulnerable groups: the promise of an emerging concept in European human rights convention law' (2013) 11 *International Journal of Constitutional Law* 4, 1056–85; A Timmer, 'A quiet revolution: vulnerability in the European Court of Human Rights' in M Fineman, A Grear (eds), *Vulnerability: Reflections on a New Ethical Foundation for Law and Politics* (Ashgate 2013) 147–70.

24 ibid.

25 Peroni, Timmer (n 23) 1064.

26 *Mubilanzila Mayeka and Kaniki Mitunga v Belgium* Application no 13178/03 (ECtHR, 12 October 2006) para 55 (art 3 EVRM) and paras 103–105 (art 5 ECHR); *Muskhadzhiyeva and Others v Belgium* Application no 41442/07 (ECtHR, 19 January 2010) paras 55–56 (art 3 ECHR) and paras 73–74 (art 5 ECHR); *Rahimi v Greece* Application no 8687/08 (ECtHR, 5 April 2011) paras 81–86 (art 3 ECHR); *Kanagaratnam and Others v Belgium* Application no 15297/09 (ECtHR, 13 December 2011) paras 61–67 (art 3 ECHR) and paras 86–88 (art 5 ECHR); *Popov v France* Application nos 39472/07 and 39474/07 (ECtHR, 19 January 2012) paras 84–103 (art 3 ECHR) and para 119 (art 5 ECHR).

27 *MSS v Belgium and Greece* Application no 30696/09 (ECtHR, 21 January 2011) paras 249–64.

28 *Mubilanzila Mayeka and Kaniki Mitunga v Belgium* (n 26) para 55 ('vulnerable situation', 'highly vulnerable members of society'); *Rahimi v Greece* (n 26) paras 62 and 82 (*'des enfants et autres personnes vulnerables'*; *'une situation d'extrême vulnérabilité'*); *Kanagaratnam and Others v Belgium* (n 26) paras 61–67 ('des enfants et autres personnes vulnerables'; 'une situation d'extrême vulnérabilité')); *Popov v France* (n 26) paras 91, 102 and 119 ('la situation d'extrême vulnérabilité').

29 *MSS v Belgium and Greece* (n 27) paras 251 and 263 ('vulnerable population group', 'vulnerability as an asylum seeker').

30 *Mubilanzila Mayeka and Kaniki Mitunga v Belgium* (n 26) para 55 ('her very young age, the fact that she was an illegal immigrant in a foreign land and the fact that she was unaccompanied by her family')); *Muskhadzhiyeva and Others v Belgium* (n 26) para 86 (*'. . . que le requérant, en raison de son âge et de sa situation personnelle, se trouvait en une situation d'extrême vulnérabilité'*); *Kanagaratnam and Others v Belgium* (n 26) para 67 (*'Il faut donc partir de la presumption que les enfants étaient vulnerable tant en raison de leur qualité d'enfants que de leur histoire personnelle'*); *Tarakhel v Switzerland* Application no 29217/12 (ECtHR, 4 November 2014) para 119.

31 *Mubilanzila Mayeka and Kaniki Mitunga v Belgium* (n 26) paras 53–55; *Muskhadzhiyeva and Others v Belgium* (n 26) paras 53–58; *Rahimi v Greece* (n 26) paras 62 and 87; *Kanagaratnam and Others v Belgium* (n 26) paras 61–62; *Popov v France* (n 26) para 91; *Tarakhel v Switzerland* (n 30) paras 99 and 119.

32 *Mubilanzila Mayeka and Kaniki Mitunga v Belgium* (n 26) paras 58–59; *Muskhadzhiyeva and Others v Belgium* (n 26) paras 59–63; *Rahimi v Greece* (n 26) paras 86 and 92–95; *Kanagaratnam and Others v Belgium*, Application no 15297/09 (ECtHR, 13 December 2011) paras 66–69; *Popov v France*, Application nos 39472/07 and 39474/07 (ECtHR, 19 January 2012) paras 102–103.

33 *Tarakhel v Switzerland* (n 30) para 122.
34 This can indirectly be concluded from all the above-mentioned cases, given the causes of their vulnerability, and is explicitly mentioned in *Popov v France* (n 26) para 102: '*Les deux enfants . . . se trouvaient dans une situation de particulière vulnérabilité, accentuée par la situation d'enfermement. Ces conditions de vie ne pouvaient qu'engendrer pour eux une situation de stress et d'angoisse et avoir des conséquences particulièrement traumatisantes sur leur psychisme*'.
35 In addition, the ECtHR also accepts the primacy of the best interests of the child. See e.g. *Rahimi v Greece* (n 26) para 108; *Popov v France* (n 26) para 140.
36 *Saadi v United Kingdom* Application no 13229/03 (ECtHR, 29 January 2008) para 70; *Muskhadzhiyeva and Others v Belgium* (n 26) para 74; *Popov v France* (n 26) para 120.
37 *Mubilanzila Mayeka and Kaniki Mitunga v Belgium* (n 26) paras 103–105; *Muskhadzhiyeva and Others v Belgium* (n 26) paras 73–75; *Kanagaratnam and Others v Belgium* (n 26) paras 86–88; *Popov v France* (n 26) paras 119–21.
38 *Kanagaratnam and Others v Belgium* (n 26) paras 61–69; *Popov v France* (n 26) paras 91–103.
39 *Muskhadzhiyeva and Others v Belgium* (n 26) paras 64–66; *Kanagaratnam and Others v Belgium* (n 26) paras 70–72; *Popov v France* (n 26) paras 104–105.
40 *Muskhadzhiyeva and Others v Belgium* (n 26) paras 69–75; *Popov v France* (n 26) para 121.
41 *Muskhadzhiyeva and Others v Belgium* (n 26) para 74; *Popov v France* (n 26) para 120.
42 *Kanagaratnam and Others v Belgium* (n 26) paras 89–95.
43 *MSS v Belgium and Greece* (n 27) para 225: 'The Court deems it necessary to take into account the circumstances of the applicant's placement in detention and the fact that in spite of what the Greek Government suggest, the applicant did not, on the face of it, have the profile of an "illegal immigrant". On the contrary, following the agreement on 4 June 2009 to take charge of the applicant, the Greek authorities were aware of the applicant's identity and of the fact that he was a potential asylum-seeker'.
44 ibid para 53.
45 ibid para 233 ('the applicant's distress was accentuated by the vulnerability inherent in his situation as asylum seeker'); para 251 ('the applicant's status as an asylum seeker, and as such, a member of a particularly underprivileged and vulnerable population group in need of special protection'). Compare *Tarakhel v Switzerland* (n 30) paras 98 and 118.
46 *MSS v Belgium and Greece* (n 27) para 251.
47 ibid para 251.
48 ibid para 249.
49 ibid para 251.
50 ibid paras 263–64.
51 ibid para 53.
52 *Mubilanzila Mayeka and Kaniki Mitunga v Belgium* (n 26) paras 55, 103–105; *Muskhadzhiyeva and Others v Belgium* (n 26) paras 55–56 and paras 73–74; *Rahimi v Greece* Application no 8687/08 (ECtHR, 5 April 2011) paras 62 and 86–87; *Kanagaratnam and Others v Belgium* (n 26) paras 61–62, 67 and 87; *Popov v France* (n 26) paras 91, 102–103 and 119. See also J Ryngaert, W Vandenhole, 'Mainstreaming children's rights in migration litigation: *Muskhadzhiyeva and Others v Belgium*' in E Brems (ed), *Diversity and European Human Rights. Rewriting Judgments of the ECHR* (Cambridge University Press 2013) 68–92.
53 *MSS v Belgium and Greece* (n 27) para 233.
54 The ECtHR defines explicitly the groups of asylum seekers as vulnerable group. With regard to migrant children, it underlines particularly their vulnerable

situation. See e.g. *Muskhadzhiyeva and Others v Belgium* (n 26) para 56; *Rahimi v Greece* (n 26) para 86; *Kanagaratnam and Others v Belgium* (n 26) para 62.

55 *MSS v Belgium and Greece* (n 27) para 233.

56 See also the 'partly concurring and partly dissenting opinion' of Judge Sajo in the case of *MSS v Belgium and Greece* (n 27) in which he refuses to consider asylum seekers as a vulnerable group, because 'they are not a group historically subject to prejudice with lasting consequences, resulting in their social exclusion'.

57 *Defence for Children International (DCI) v Belgium* Application no 69/2011 (ECSR, 23 October 2012) para 72.

58 *Defence for Children International (DCI) v Netherlands* Application no 47/2008 (ECSR, 20 October 2009) paras 38 and 61.

59 ibid para 46.

60 ibid para 64.

61 The ECSR makes explicit mention of undocumented minors as vulnerable or members of a vulnerable group. See e.g. *Defence for Children International (DCI) v Netherlands* (n 58) para 38; *Defence for Children International (DCI) v Belgium* (n 57) para 37.

62 *Conference of European Churches (CEC) v Netherlands* Application no 90/2013 (ECSR, 1 July 2014); *European Federation of National Organisations working with the Homeless (FEANTSA) v Netherlands* Application no 86/2012 (ECSR, 2 July 2014).

63 See para 1 of the Appendix to the Charter: 'The persons covered by Articles 1 to 4 include foreigners only insofar as they are nationals of other Parties lawfully resident or working regularly within the territory of the Party concerned subject to the understanding that these articles are to be interpreted in the light of the provisions of Articles 18 and 19 of the Charter'. This interpretation would not prejudice the extension of similar facilities to other persons by any of the parties.

64 *Defence for Children International (DCI) v Belgium* (n 57) para 35.

65 *Conference of European Churches (CEC) v Netherlands* (n 64); *European Federation of National Organisations working with the Homeless (FEANTSA) v Netherlands* Application no 86/2012 (ECSR, 2 July 2014).

66 *Defence for Children International (DCI) v Netherlands* (n 58) para 25; *Defence for Children International (DCI) v Belgium* (n 57) para 37.

67 *Defence for Children International (DCI) v Belgium* (n 57) para 37.

68 ibid.

69 ibid.

70 *Defence for Children International (DCI) v Netherlands* (n 58) paras 38, 46 and 64; *Defence for Children International (DCI) v Belgium* (n 57) para 141.

71 *Defence for Children International (DCI) v Netherlands* (n 58) para 47.

72 *Defence for Children International (DCI) v Belgium* (n 57) para 37.

73 *International Federation of Human Rights Leagues (FIDH) v France* Application no 14/2003 (ECSR, 8 September 2004) paras 32–38.

74 *Defence for Children International (DCI) v Netherlands* (n 58) para 25.

75 *Defence for children International (DCI) v Belgium* (n 57) para 37.

76 ibid para 37: 'Moreover, the risk of impairing fundamental rights is all the more likely where children are at stake. This is due to their condition as "children" and their specific situation as "unlawful" migrants, combining vulnerability and limited autonomy. As a result, in particular, of their lack of autonomy children cannot be held genuinely responsible for their place of residence. Children are not able to decide themselves whether to stay or to leave'.

77 See e.g. M Vervliet, *The Trajectories of Unaccompanied Refugee Minors: Aspirations, Agency and Psychosocial Well-being* (Academia Press 2013).

78 CRC Committee, 'Day of 2012 General Discussion: the Rights of All Children in the Context of International Migration' para 5, www.ohchr.org/Documents/

HRBodies/CRC/Discussions/2012/DGD2012ReportAndRecommendations.pdf (last accessed 14 December 2016).

79 United Nations Human Rights Council (UNHRC), 'Report of the Special Rapporteur on the Human Rights of Migrants, Jorge Bustamante' (2011) UN Doc A/HRC/17/33; UNHRC, 'Report of the Special Rapporteur on the Human Rights of Migrants, François Crépeau' (2012) UN Doc A/HRC/20/24.

80 UNHRC, 'Report Jorge Bustamante' (n 79) para 37.

81 ibid para 41.

82 STEPS Consulting Social, 'The conditions in centres for third country national (detention camps, open centres as well as transit centres and transit xones) with a particular focus on provisions and facilities for persons with special needs in the 25 EU Member States' (European Union Committee on Civil Liberties, Justice and Home Affairs 2007); Philip Amaral (ed), 'DEVAS-project, becoming vulnerable in detention, Civil Society Report on the detention of vulnerable asylum seekers and irregular migrants in the European Union' (Jesuit Refugee Service, European Regional Office 2010).

83 STEPS Consulting Social (n 82).

84 Amaral (n 82).

85 ibid 90.

86 ibid 89–103.

12 Children's rights and media: imperfect but inspirational

Eva Lievens

12.1 Children and the media

The media play a very important part in children's lives.[1] Children watch television on traditional TV sets, look up video clips on YouTube, search things they need to do their homework through Google, play games on tablets or mobile phones and create profiles on (mini)social networks or virtual environments. Sometimes, children are the subject of reports by the press, in general as an important group in society, or in particular when something noteworthy happens to a specific child. Hence, as citizens with rights and responsibilities, children move seamlessly between different roles in the media environment: they are users, subjects and participants.

12.1.1 Children as media users/consumers

A recent report by the independent regulator and competition authority for the United Kingdom communications industry, Ofcom, on children's and parents' media use and attitudes,[2] found that in 2015 children between 8 and 11 consumed on average 14.8 hours of television content per week (compared to 13.2 hours in 2005) and children between 12 and 15 watched on average 15.5 hours of television (compared to 14.7 hours in 2005). The 8–11 year olds consumed 11.1 hours of internet per week (compared to 4.4 hours in 2005), and the 12–15 year olds 18.9 hours (compared to 8 hours in 2005). These statistics show that children's media consumption counts for a significant proportion of their everyday activities. The content which is consumed may range from information to entertainment as well as commercial content. From a global perspective, it has been estimated that one in three internet users worldwide is under the age of 18.[3]

12.1.2 Children as media subjects

Children are often reported about in the press. The shocking image of Aylan Kurdi, the infant refugee who died during a sea crossing, for instance, was put on newspaper front pages worldwide. Such images can be seen as the personification of a societally relevant issue, and often children are (re)presented as a particularly vulnerable group in society. In other cases, specific children are the subject of reports, sometimes because, unfortunately, they are victims of accidents, or, because they have become 'semi-public' persons, owing to their being the offspring of famous parents or to participation in entertainment programmes such as *The Voice Kids*.[4]

12.1.3 Children as media participants

Children also actively participate in media environments, especially as members of social media platforms, where they not only consume, but also create and share content. Research has found that children from as young as seven are present on platforms such as Facebook, Twitter, Instagram and Tumblr. In 2011, the EU Kids Online study found that 38 per cent of 9–12 year olds and 77 per cent of 13–16 year olds in Europe had a social networking services (SNS) profile.[5] A 2013 UK survey found that 30 per cent of children aged 7–11 in the UK had their own Facebook profile.[6] Along the same lines, findings of May 2016 showed that 38 per cent of Flemish 9–12 year olds have a Facebook profile.[7]

Without a doubt, today's media environment, and the different roles that children may take up, ensures that children's access to education, information and entertainment as well as participation in social, cultural and political life can be improved.[8] Moreover, interaction with others through (social) media also enhances children's personal development and contributes to the creation of identity. At the same time, children's rights may be challenged or threatened by certain use or characteristics of and content on platforms, or acts by providers or other users.

12.2 Children, fundamental rights and the media

12.2.1 United Nations

Since the creation of the UNCRC it has been accepted universally that children are entitled to a number of fundamental rights that are important in the media environment, such as the right to freedom of expression (Article 13 UNCRC), the right to be heard (Article 12 UNCRC) and the right to privacy (Article 16 UNCRC). At the same time, children sometimes need to be protected, for instance, from content or behaviour that may harm them (Article 17 UNCRC).

Article 13 UNCRC proclaims the right of children to *freedom of expression*, which 'includes the freedom to seek, receive and impart information and ideas of all kinds, regardless of frontiers, either orally, in writing or in print, in the form of art, or through any other media of the child's choice'.[9] This fundamental right can only be restricted if this is provided by law and necessary 'for respect of the rights or reputations of others, or for the protection of national security or of public order, or of public health or morals' (para 2). The article has a broad scope of application, which extends to traditional, new and even future media.

Article 13 UNCRC is closely linked to Article 12 UNCRC. This article, which is considered to be one of the four 'general principles' of the UNCRC,[10] imposes on states the obligation to ensure that children have the *right to express their views freely in all matters that affect them*, and that these views are given due weight in accordance with their age and maturity. Articles 13 and 12 should not be confused: whereas Article 12 imposes a strict obligation on states to guarantee that children are heard, Article 13 implies that states must refrain from interfering in the expression of a child's view, while protecting the right of access to means of communication and public dialogue.[11] However, the initiatives taken by states under Article 12 may facilitate or strengthen children's exercise of Article 13.

Another crucial article with regard to media content and services is Article 17 UNCRC. This article recognises the important function of the *mass media* and requires states to ensure that children have *access* to 'information and material from a *diversity* of national and international sources, especially those aimed at the promotion of his or her social, spiritual and moral well-being and physical and mental health',[12] since access to a wide diversity of information is a prerequisite for the exercise of other fundamental rights, most importantly the right to freedom of expression.[13] States are thus incited to pursue a proactive policy which stimulates the cultural, educational and informational potential of media with respect to children,[14] by (a) encouraging the mass media to disseminate information and material of social and cultural benefit to the child, (b) encouraging international cooperation in the production, exchange and dissemination of such information and material from a diversity of cultural, national and international sources, (c) encouraging the production and dissemination of children's books, and (d) encouraging the mass media to have particular regard to the linguistic needs of the child who belongs to a minority group or who is indigenous. Finally, Article 17(e) UNCRC encourages the development of guidelines to protect children from harmful material, such as violent, racist or pornographic material.[15] This final element relates to the vulnerability of the child with regard to the impact of certain media content on its development and health and, hence, the necessity to 'protect' the child (see section 3.1).

The exact scope of Article 17(e) has been the subject of debate. According to Sacino, in her detailed analysis of the article, the scope of this paragraph does not concern the protection of children from harmful material by states themselves.[16] She contends that this particular state task is included within the scope of other articles (such as Article 3 UNCRC, related to the protection and care necessary for the well-being of each child) and that Article 17 (e) solely concerns the encouragement of other actors, such as *industry*, to develop the guidelines mentioned in this paragraph.[17]

Article 17(e) also explicitly refers to Article 18 UNCRC, as such clearly pointing to parents as relevant actors, as this article recalls the primary responsibility of *parents* for the upbringing and development of the child. Furthermore, according to Article 18(2), *states* must 'render appropriate assistance to parents and legal guardians in the performance of their child-rearing responsibilities'. An example of this 'assistance' or, otherwise put, the 'duty of care' of the state,[18] could be the provision of adequate information by states to parents about media content to which their children can be exposed.[19] In 2014, the UN Committee on the

Rights of the Child confirmed the duty of states 'to provide adequate training and support to parents and other caregivers . . ., to enhance their technical skills, inform them about the risks and potential harm, learn about how children use technology and be able to support children in using digital media and ICTs in a responsible and safe manner'.[20]

Along the same lines, reference could also be made to Article 5 UNCRC. Article 5 refers to the responsibilities, rights and duties of *parents* (or other persons legally responsible for the child), to offer, in a manner consistent with the evolving capacities of the child, appropriate direction and guidance to the child when exercising his or her rights. This provision could be interpreted as implying that parents have a responsibility to (do their best to) support their children in their approach to (new) media, taking into account the age of their children and their evolving maturity. The United Nations General Assembly has also touched upon the responsibilities of parents in this respect, where it encouraged 'measures to protect children from violent or harmful web sites, computer programmes and games that negatively influence the psychological development of children, taking into account the responsibilities of the family, parents, legal guardians and caregivers'.[21] Ultimately, parents or other *carers* are the only persons who will be able to monitor their children's actual day-to-day media use. However, it should be noted that this responsibility is increasingly being challenged by the growing adoption of smart phones, which are inherently more 'private' devices and which make supervision more and more difficult.

Finally, increasingly important in today's media environment is the child's right to *privacy*, formulated in Article 16 UNCRC. According to this article, children cannot be subjected to any arbitrary or unlawful interference – by state authorities or by others (e.g. private organisations)[22] – with their privacy, family, home or correspondence, nor to unlawful attacks on their honour and reputation. Moreover, it is clearly stated that the law should protect a child against such interference. The right to privacy is directed at the child itself and is to be protected in all situations.[23] In the media environment, privacy issues could, for instance, arise with respect to identification in news reports, the collection of personal data by advertisers or social network providers, and monitoring a child's internet use, email or messenger conversations.

12.2.2 Council of Europe

Children's rights have also been awarded a significant place in the European legislative and policy framework concerning media. The Council of Europe has, over the past decade, issued various documents concerning media and human rights in general, and children's rights in particular.[24] In those documents the importance of the protection of the right to privacy (Article 8 European Convention on Human Rights (ECHR)) and the right to freedom of expression (Article 10 ECHR) of children has always been emphasised.

The European Court of Human Rights (ECtHR) has confirmed that the protection of children against content injurious to their well-being is a legitimate interest on the basis of which national measures can be taken. In the *Handyside* case, the Court was of the opinion that the sanctioning of the publisher of The Little Red Schoolbook on the basis of the UK Obscene Publications Acts did not violate Article 10 ECHR.[25] The Little Red Schoolbook, which was targeted at children from 12 to 18, contained passages with information regarding sexual activities and the taking of drugs. The Strasbourg Court found that the national judges were entitled to think at that moment in time that The Little Red Schoolbook would have 'pernicious effects on the morals of many of the children and adolescents who would read it' para 52.

In *Vejdeland v Sweden* the Court found that a criminal conviction for distributing leaflets that contained hate speech against homosexual individuals in schools constituted no violation of Article 10 ECHR.[26] In its assessment the Court took into account that 'the leaflets were left in the lockers of young people who were at an impressionable and sensitive age and who had no possibility to decline to accept them' (para 56). However, the Court does not only approach the issue of children and media or information from a protective perspective. In another case, their right to receive various types of information, not only news but also cultural expressions as well as pure entertainment, was affirmed.[27] In casu, the applicants' tenancy agreement was terminated because they had installed a satellite dish, contrary to the provisions of that agreement. In their assessment of the case the judges in Strasbourg attached specific significance to the fact that for an immigrant family with three children it was particularly important to receive television programmes in Arabic and Farsi in order to maintain contact with the culture and language of their country of origin. The Court found a violation of Article 10 ECHR, thereby recognising the right to receive or access information, also for children.

With regard to the right to privacy, the Strasbourg Court found a violation of Article 8 ECHR in a case concerning an advertisement that was put on an internet dating site by unknown persons in the name of a 12-year-old boy without his knowledge.[28] This advertisement included the age of the boy, a description of his physical characteristics, a link to his website which contained a picture and a telephone number, and a statement that he was seeking an intimate relationship with a boy. At the time of the occurrence of the facts, it was not possible under Finnish law to obtain the identity of the perpetrator (through the internet provider). This led the Court to conclude that the Finnish Government had failed to protect the right to respect for the applicant's private life as the confidentiality requirement had been given precedence over the child's physical and moral welfare. In its judgment, the Court emphasised that '[c]hildren and other vulnerable individuals are entitled to State protection, in the form of effective deterrence, from such grave types of interference with essential aspects of their private lives' (para 46).

In March 2016, the Council of Europe adopted its third Strategy on the Rights of the Child.[29] In this strategy, 'the rights of the child in the digital environment' is explicitly recognised as one of five priority areas for the next five years.

12.2.3 European Union

The European Union (EU) has included a legal basis for the protection of children's rights in the Charter of Fundamental Rights (Article 24) as well as the Lisbon Treaty, and has developed a EU strategy on the rights of the child.[30] Both the UNCRC as well as the Charter have been referred to by the Court of Justice of the European Union in cases related to the regulation of media in order to protect minors.[31] The 2006 Recommendation on the protection of minors and human dignity and on the right of reply in relation to the competitiveness of the European audiovisual and online information services industry[32] starts with a reference to Article 24 of the Charter. In the 2011 EU Agenda for the Rights of the Child, media and modern technology, and achieving a high level of protection of children in the digital space, in particular, was one of the priorities identified.[33]

12.3 Children's rights in today's information society

A similar theme runs through children's rights documents at all levels: on the one hand, children are active subjects of rights who can invoke and exercise a number of fundamental rights but, on the other, this also entails that sometimes they need to be safeguarded from harmful influences. This balancing act is very much at the heart of current debates about children in today's information society.

Numerous policy documents at European level have emphasised the importance of safeguarding children's rights in today's information society. With regard to social networking sites, for instance, the Council of Europe's Recommendation on the protection of human rights with regard to social networking services articulated in 2012 that these services can significantly advance human rights and fundamental freedoms, in particular the right to 'freedom of expression, to create and to exchange content and ideas'. At the same time, given the increasingly central role that these services play in the lives of children, the recommendation pointed to the fact that this particular group of users should 'be protected because of the inherent vulnerability that their age implies'.[34]

In April 2014, the Committee of Ministers of the Council of Europe, in its guide to human rights for internet users, explicitly included a section targeted at children and young people. According to the guide, children are entitled to special protection and guidance when using the internet, on the one hand, and have the right to freely express their views and participate in society, on the other hand.[35] The 'balance between empowerment and protection of children in the online world' was also a key issue articulated by the Committee on the Rights of the Child in its report on the 2014 day of general discussion on 'Digital media and children's rights', given the vast opportunities to learn, participate, play, work and socialise, on the one hand, and new risks, on the other hand.[36]

This main theme can be framed against the background of the concept of the 'three Ps' that is regularly referred to in the context of the UNCRC: provision, protection and participation.[37] The recurring discourse with regard to children and media, both in research and in policy, largely focuses on the 'balance' between 'protection' and 'participation', and only sparingly refers to the 'provision' part.

12.3.1 Protection

The protection paradigm is, and has always been, omnipresent in the debate related to media and minors. Parental and governmental fears related to the vulnerability of children, as media users or consumers, have appeared with each new medium and its content. Although these fears were often amplified by moral panic, media effects research provided certain evidence for regulating media to protect minors. This research discipline arose during the Interbellum and has since undergone an enormous evolution. Whereas in the first half of the 20th century a large and powerful effect was ascribed to the media,[38] from 1950 onwards research increasingly focused on a limited effects model.[39] This model also applies to children and assumes that they are not passive receivers, but 'active and motivated users of media, who critically evaluate what they are shown'.[40] Currently, however, most media scholars assume that the issue is much more complex and that the effects of the media largely depend on the message, the medium, the audience and the type of effect focused upon.[41]

Throughout the years, innumerable studies have been conducted with the aim of discovering what effect, if there is one at all, particular media have on their users. Following the rise in popularity of movies in the 1920s in the United States, the Payne Fund sponsored a study into the real impact of films on children and adolescents, which found that a bad influence could be distinguished.[42] This 1930s research has been followed by an enormous array of studies, ranging from an analysis of the 'evil of comic books' (by Frederic Wertham),[43] to inquiries into copycat crimes inspired by television programmes,[44] to the many studies on the effects of violent video games.[45]

Among media scholars there seems to be an overall consensus that confrontation with particular types of content at an early age may have negative consequences on a child's development.[46] Hence, restrictions on the publication or distribution of potentially harmful media content have been included in criminal law (e.g. prohibition on distributing material that is considered contrary to public decency, criminalisation of online child pornography) as well as in European and national media and communications law in order to protect minors. Specific provisions that aim to protect minors in traditional television broadcasting as well as in on-demand services have been included in the EU Audiovisual Media Services Directive. These provisions have been implemented in Member States' legislation by means of watersheds or classification/labelling systems, which indicate the age for which programmes are considered appropriate and the type of potentially harmful content that is included (sex, violence, hate speech etc).[47] Similar classification schemes have traditionally also been used in order to regulate films, either imposed by law or as part of self- or co-regulatory mechanisms.

As digital technologies have gained in popularity, concerns regarding the protection of children in the transformed media environment were raised. Within media effects research it was emphasised that it is not possible to straightforwardly apply research straightforwardly on the effects of traditional media to new media, since 'people's response to media content is strongly shaped by the particularities of each medium'.[48] Certainly, 'new' media, such as the internet, social and mobile media, show characteristics that differ from traditional media: not only facilitated access to (more extreme forms of) content, but also the growing element of 'choice' and the lowered threshold for content production (making it possible, for instance, to take pictures with a smartphone and disseminate them across the whole world by uploading them to the internet),[49] the commercialisation of content as well as children's personal data, increased social interaction, the influence of interactive media on children's identities and media multi-tasking.[50]

Children are no longer only passive 'receivers' of content, but are producers, creators and active participants. Hence, 'protecting' them by means of traditional regulation is much less obvious: there are numerous actors involved (content as well as platform providers, internet access providers, users that not only consume/use but also produce/create content), and national/territorial borders are transcended. Hence, policies aimed at a safer internet for children, have over the past 15 years shifted towards the use of alternative regulatory instruments such as self- and co-regulation.[51] Such instruments involve other stakeholders, such as content and platform providers as well as device manufacturers, in efforts to minimise risks for children, for instance by providing reporting mechanisms for illegal and harmful content and conduct, by predefining privacy settings, or by rating or labelling content, such as video games and mobile apps.[52]

Notwithstanding this evolution towards more empowering forms of protection, the 'vulnerability' of the child has very recently come sharply into focus again in the context of the review of the data protection legislation at EU level. Article 8 of the new General Data Protection Regulation (GDPR),[53] which will apply to the processing of personal data from May 2018 onwards, sets out that processing of personal data of a child who is below the age of 16, in relation to the offer of information society services (e.g. setting up a profile on a social networking site, registering on a mobile app) shall be 'lawful only if and to the extent that consent is given or authorised by the holder of parental responsibility over the child'. Even though Member States can choose to lower this age to 13 in their national legislation, this article adopts a paternalistic and anachronistic approach and gives adolescents the impression that they cannot be trusted to make sensible decisions about their internet and mobile media use. Instead of enhancing protection this obligation will much more likely restrict children's rights to interact with friends and have access to valuable content and information, and will effectively decrease their rights to participation as responsible citizens in today's information society.[54]

12.3.2 Participation

Discourse regarding children's participation and media is built around two main strands. A first strand focuses on the fact that media enable and facilitate participation of children in various parts of life. Research by Third and others, for instance, has found that: 'children understand digital media as playing a vital role in enabling them to be informed citizens who can participate meaningfully in their communities, and enabling them to participate in friendship and broader community networks'.[55] A second strand emphasises the importance of participation by children in policy-making about media. Article 12 UNCRC, which attributes to children the right to have a say in matters that concern them, is also thought to include children's participation in decision-making, policy-making, preparation of laws and measures, as well as their evaluation.[56] Although child participation in the development of policies in various domains is said to be important, too often this remains a theoretical aspiration. This is not to say that children's interests are not taken into account, but in governmental policy-making processes these interests are often represented by non-governmental organisation (NGOs), children's ombudpersons or children's rights commissioners. Children themselves are usually not included in the development of policies that may impact them.[57] An illustration thereof is the introduction of Article 8 in the GDPR, discussed above.[58] However, when children are given the actual opportunity to participate, it has been demonstrated that they can provide alternative viewpoints, offer valuable contributions[59] and valuable insights in how they experience, perceive or engage with certain situations, issues or opportunities.

There is little evidence of the participation of children in formulating policies with regard to traditional media. Participation has largely been in the background. One example to the contrary, that did have an actual impact, can be found in a recent amendment of the Flemish Code of Journalistic Ethics of the Flemish Council of Journalism (*Raad voor de Journalistiek*), a self-regulatory body for journalistic ethics. A guideline regarding the principles that journalists must take into account regarding portrayal of children in the media[60] was added to the code in 2015, after close cooperation between the Council, other European press councils (members of the Alliance of Independent Press Councils of Europe) and the Flemish Office of the Children's Rights Commissioner (*Kinderrechtencommissariaat*). Input from children was gathered through questions and experiences that were received by the complaints service of that office and through conversations with children that were portrayed in the press or had taken part in programmes. The guideline focuses on consent by children and/or parents to be portrayed, and on giving children the opportunity to tell their own stories. For instance, the new guideline contains an important new addition with regard to an absolute prohibition of reporting (in an identifiable manner) about minors who are the subject of a measure of the juvenile courts, which is laid down in the Belgian Criminal Code.

According to the new guideline, reporting about such minors may be justified from a deontological perspective in certain circumstances. This may be the case (1) when a report does not concern nor mentions the measure taken by the court, (2) when identification details are published that have been released by the judiciary, the police or Childfocus, for instance in case of a search operation or (3) in exceptional circumstances of significant public interest, for instance in order to allow a minor to give his or her side of the story. This addition finds its origin in the observation by the Children's Rights Commissioner that certain children who are in such a situation explicitly stated that they felt it was unfair that their story could not be told, and that they were prevented from participating in programmes or news stories and expressing their opinions or views.

Following the rise of digital media, awareness about the importance of consulting children with regard to policy-making that affects their media use has been on the increase. The UN Committee on the Rights of the Child recommended, following its day of general discussion on 'Digital media and children's rights', states to promote: 'the exchange and sharing of ideas, information, experiences and good practices, including through the creation of platforms, with all stakeholders, especially children, at the national, regional and international level'.[61] The importance of actual participation is emphasised even more explicitly by requiring states to ensure that: 'children are consulted in order to take into account their views and experiences in developing laws, policies and programmes' and that they are 'actively engaged in the design and implementation of initiatives aimed at fostering safe use of digital media and ICTs [information and communication technologies]'.[62]

Furthermore, the idea is slowly maturing that not only governments should involve children in the shaping of policies, but that businesses that provide media content or services to children should also consult them and incorporate their needs and interests into their strategies. This should be part of their Corporate Social Responsibility (CSR) with regard to respect for human rights.[63] The Guidelines for Industry on Child Online Protection, for instance, were published by the ITU in October 2014. In these guidelines it is recommended that industry draws 'upon internal and external expertise and consult[s] with key stakeholders, including children, on child online safety mechanisms to obtain ongoing feedback and guidance on company approaches'.[64]

Recent participatory research with children regarding their rights in the digital age has shown that children want to be involved in conversations with policy-makers on how to use digital media to support children's rights and want to take responsibility.[65]

In order to implement such truly participatory processes, innovative mechanisms can be adopted, and optimal use can be made of digital communication technologies. One example is the Youth Manifesto,[66] which is an online declaration by European youth on how digital rights and responsibilities should be envisaged. Another illustration is the use of participatory design or co-creation sessions which actively engage children in developing policies at macro- or micro-level. Such sessions may, for instance, involve pupils in developing class- and school-level cyberbullying policies or may address the reformulation of the terms of use of a social networking website aimed at children from their perspective.[67] Other mechanisms that can be used are digital story-telling, citizen journalism[68] and online blogging or collaborative platforms such as the Voices of Youth platform[69] or 'Makerspaces'.[70]

12.3.3 Provision

Although the importance of dissemination of 'diverse information and material of social and cultural benefit to the child' is explicitly mentioned in Article 17 UNCRC, policy documents only sparingly refer to this aspect. This does not mean that no measures are taken in order to achieve this goal. Examples are obligations imposed on public service broadcasters to provide high-quality content for children on television, as well as on their online platforms, or the attribution of subsidies for the creation of serious games. With regard to the digital media environment, the 2012 EU's European strategy for a better internet for children does emphasise that new and higher quality content and services, dedicated to children, must be developed.[71]

One of the pillars of that strategy focuses on stimulating the production of creative and educational online content for children, for which the European Commission, industry as well as Member States should take up their responsibility. A report by the European Youth Panel in the context of the Safer Internet Forum, organised by the Commission in 2015, confirmed that young people feel that they can also play an important role in positive online content creation.[72] The Council of Europe's 2016 Strategy on the rights of the child does explicitly refer to 'provision for children in the digital environment' as well. Under that heading, education with regard to digital citizenship as well as hate speech is put forward as an important priority.[73]

12.4 Exploring the unique characteristics of children's rights in the media environment

Comparing general human rights and children's rights in the media environment, it becomes apparent that the combination of Articles 12, 13 and 17 UNCRC provides for a more elaborate framework than general human rights documents, where the relevant articles are those related to the right to freedom of expression (Article 19 of the Universal Declaration of Human Rights,[74] Article 19 International Covenant on Civil and Political Rights[75] and Article 10 ECHR).[76] Although the wording and scope of Article 19 ICCPR and Article 13 UNCRC are very similar, the additional rights laid down in Article 12 (the right to be heard) and 17 UNCRC (the right to have access to media)[77] provide children with strong claims related to participation, provision *and* protection in the media environment. It has been confirmed in various UN documents that there is a close relationship between these three articles. The Special Rapporteur on the promotion of the right to freedom of opinion and expression, Frank La Rue, stated the following in his report on the right of the child to freedom of expression:

> This right [i.e. the child's right to have access to information, Article 17 UNCRC] is closely related to the right to seek information set out in Article 13 of the Convention, as its exercise aims to enable children to inform themselves and thus be able to participate in social life. The Committee on

> the Rights of the Child has noted that the fulfilment of this right also constitutes a prerequisite for the effective exercise of the right to be heard (art. 12). . . . The Committee has also observed that the media play an important role both in promoting awareness of the rights of children to express their views and in providing opportunities for the expression of such views (see CRC/C/GC/12, para 83).[78]

Article 12 UNCRC has been considered a 'unique' provision in human rights law, as a 'right that only children have, not adults'.[79] Langelaude argues in this context that: '[c]learly adults do not have a general right expressly set out under the ICCPR to express their views in all situations concerning them'.[80]

We have described above that Article 12 imposes a positive obligation on states and holds the key to participation in society in general, and participation in decision-making and policy-making in particular. A more explicit acknowledgement of such a participatory right, however, could also be beneficial for (adult) media users in general. This has been argued by Hasebrink, who stated that '[a]ccountability for media quality and diversity would be significantly improved by expanded public participation in media governance processes'.[81] Therefore, he proposed to not only view media users as 'consumers' of media products, but also as 'owners of rights', meaning 'human beings who have to be protected from harm or biased information' as well as 'citizens' 'who have specific ideas about how the media could and should serve societal needs'.[82] In general human rights law, there is no positive obligation on states to provide such participatory structures, yet in order to guarantee adults' rights in the media environment, inspiration could perhaps be found in the recent increase in efforts to give children a voice in policy-making about (digital) media.

Furthermore, Article 17 UNCRC can also be considered an 'inspirational' provision as it embodies elements of ***provision*** (17(a)/(d): provision of diverse information and material of social and cultural benefit to children (including minorities) to promote their well-being), ***protection*** (17(e): protection from information and material injurious to the child's well-being) as well as ***participation*** (17 para 1: right to have access to information and material, as a prerequisite for the effective exercise of the right to be heard and the right to freedom of expression). As such, this article attributes a positive right to children to have access to information, as well as imposes a positive obligation on states to ensure that socially and culturally beneficial material is created and disseminated. This stands in contrast to general human rights provisions (such as Article 19 ICCPR), which are conceptualised as predominantly 'negative' rights, and do not grant a positive right to have access to information.[83]

However, it could be argued that a positive right to have access to information and media is becoming increasingly important for all citizens, not only children. Although in the context of general human rights law there is no official recognition of a 'right to access (or receive) information' there is a trend towards a growing recognition of the importance of such a right in the case law of the ECtHR with regard to information that is held by governments.[84] In the case of *Youth Initiative for Human Rights v Serbia*,[85] for instance, the Court held that the refusal of the intelligence agency of Serbia to provide factual information concerning the use of electronic surveillance to a youth NGO, which acted as a public watchdog, constituted a violation of Article 10 ECHR.

The same holds true with regard to a 'right to have access to the internet'. Recent participatory research related to digital media has shown that children effectively consider access to digital media a fundamental right.[86] In general human rights documents, access to the internet is not yet recognised as a human right.[87] However, the significance thereof is increasingly emphasised in various policy documents and case law. La Rue, in his capacity as Special Rapporteur on the promotion and protection of the right to freedom of opinion and expression, found that states do have 'a positive obligation to promote or facilitate the right to freedom of expression and the means necessary to exercise this right, which includes the internet'.[88] The ECtHR has held on several occasions that

> in the light of its accessibility and its capacity to store and communicate vast amounts of information, the Internet plays an important role in enhancing the public's access to news and facilitating the dissemination of information in general (see *Ahmet Yıldırım v Turkey* Application no 3111/10, para 48 (ECtHR 2012); *Times Newspapers Ltd v United Kingdom (Nos 1 and 2)* Application nos 3002/03 and 23676/03 para 27 (ECtHR 2009)).[89]

In *Cengiz and Others v Turkey*,[90] a case concerning blocking of access to YouTube in Turkey, the Court recognised that a website such as YouTube constitutes an important means to exercise the right to receive and communicate information and ideas, and also provides a platform for the emergence of citizen journalism. According to the court, the blocking was not prescribed by law and, hence, a violation of Article 10 was found. Although as such this does not yet recognise a truly positive and general right to have access to information or specific media, in future general human rights documents and case law a more positive approach could be inspired on the children's rights' perspective that to really being able to exercise the right to freedom of expression such access, also in developing countries, is indispensable.

A final characteristic in this context, which may provide inspiration for general human rights protection in the media environment, is the explicit recognition of the responsibility of various actors, or a so-called multi-stakeholder approach. The responsibility of *states* with regard to children's rights and media is recognised in Articles 12 and 13, as well as 17 UNCRC. Article 17 also refers to responsibilities of the *media*, as well as to the responsibilities of *parents* (through the reference to Article 18 UNCRC). Although these responsibilities mentioned in the UNCRC are linked to the 'childness of a child' and its evolving capacities,[91] 'third parties' in the media sector, such as journalists, internet service providers, search engines or social network site providers, carry responsibilities vis-à-vis all media users. This is already recognised in various ways, such as through the creation and implementation of self-regulatory mechanisms for journalistic ethics, in references in case law of the ECtHR to the responsibilities of journalists,[92] and in the increasing calls for the integration of human-rights based CSR principles by providers of online content and services providers.[93]

Moreover, it could be argued that in today's information society, adult media users can be considered 'vulnerable' as well. Examples of such vulnerabilities are related to the increasing algorithmisation of media and online content services, threatening media diversity and pluralism, and the often covert collection and selling of personal data of media users, challenging the right to privacy. This should trigger the duty of states to encourage the media and online industry to really take up their responsibilities towards those media users, and offer them not only a higher level of human rights protection, but also the opportunity to actively exercise their agency in relation to their media use.

12.5 Imperfect but inspirational?

Children's rights in the media sector show many *imperfections.* The focus has traditionally been on the protection of 'vulnerable' minors from harmful media content. This protective stance has only recently, and especially in light of the emergence of digital media and the internet, been complemented with a gradual increase in participation. This is visible both at a general level in allowing children to participate in shaping media and internet policy, and at a more practical or implementation level in providing them with skills and tools that empower them and enable them to exercise their agency. Additional imperfections are a predominant focus on Western children's rights and media use – although the voices that call for attention to the situation in the global South are getting louder[94] – and the fact that the provision of high-quality content and access to innovative, educational and diverse online resources for children in various languages could significantly be improved.

Notwithstanding these imperfections, however, our theoretical exploration of the way in which children's rights are conceptualised with regard to media does provide indications that certain principles that have been made explicit in the area of children's rights could also be *inspirational.* The combination of Articles 12, 13 and 17 acknowledges the importance of 'provision', 'protection' and 'participation' in the media environment. Thinking more fundamentally about how these principles could be implemented for all users, for instance by a more explicit recognition of a positive right of access to (digital) media and information, enhanced protection by states *and* third parties with regard to (new media) practices that threaten media users' rights to freedom of expression and privacy, and true participation of all citizens in media policymaking at various levels, could strengthen general human rights protection in the media sector. However, we must remain vigilant that those inspirational elements are not diluted in new regulatory measures that have an impact on children and their participation in today's information society. The adoption of Article 8 GDPR and the reversal to a more paternalistic perspective is in this respect a disheartening development.

Notes

1 The author would like to thank Prof Dr Dirk Voorhoof as well as the other reviewers for their valuable comments on a draft version of this chapter.
2 Ofcom, 'Children and parents: media use and attitudes report' (2015) stakeholders.ofcom.org.uk/market-data-research/other/research-publications/childrens/children-parents-nov-15/ (last accessed 15 December 2016).
3 S Livingstone, J Carr and J Byrne, 'One in three: internet governance and children's rights' (2015) GCIG Paper No 22 Global Commission on Internet Governance Paper Series www.cigionline.org/publications/one-three-internet-governance-and-childrens-rights (last accessed 15 December 2016).
4 *The Voice Kids* is a talent show that is broadcast on television in various countries in which children compete to be the best singer.
5 S Livingstone, K Ólafsson and E Staksrud, 'Risky social networking practices among "underage" users: Lessons for evidence-based policy' (2013) *Journal of Computer-Mediated Communication* 303.
6 NSPCC, 'Younger children and social networking sites: a blind spot' (2013) www.nspcc.org.uk/Inform/resourcesforprofessionals/onlinesafety/younger-children-and-social-networking-sites_wda99104.html (last accessed 30 March 2016).
7 Mediaraven, Linc and MICT, 'Onderzoeksrapport Apestaartjaren 6' (2016) www.apestaartjaren.be/onderzoek/apestaartjaren-6?platform=hootsuite (last accessed 15 December 2016).
8 Livingstone, Carr and Byrne (n 3). See also United Nations General Assembly (UNGA), 'Report of the Special Rapporteur on the Promotion and Protection of the Right to Freedom of Opinion and Expression: Frank La Rue, the right of the child to freedom of expression' (2014) UN Doc A/69/335.
9 The United Nations Committee on the Rights of the Child (CRC Committee) has stressed that it is not sufficient to just include the 'general' right to freedom of expression applicable to everyone in a country's constitution. It is necessary, according to the Committee, to also expressly incorporate the child's right to freedom of expression in legislation. See for instance CRC Committee, 'General Guidelines for Periodic Reports' (1996) UN Doc CRC/C/58: 'States parties are requested to provide information on the measures adopted to ensure that the civil rights and freedoms of children set forth in the Convention, in particular those covered by articles 7, 8, 13 to 17 and 37(a), are recognized by law specifically in relation to children and implemented in practice, including by administrative and judicial bodies, at the national, regional and local levels, and where appropriate at the federal and provincial levels'.
10 CRC Committee, 'General Comment No 12: The Right of the Child to be Heard' (2009) UN Doc CRC/C/GC/12.
11 UNHRC 'Report of La Rue' (n 8); CRC Committee, 'General Comment No 12' (n 10).
12 Emphasis added by the author.
13 S Meuwese, M Blaak and M Kaandorp (eds), *Handboek Internationaal Jeugdrecht* (Ars Aequi Libri 2005).
14 D Voorhoof, 'Media(recht) en kinder(recht)en' in E Verhellen (ed), *Kinderrechtengids (KIDS): Commentaren, regelgeving, rechtspraak en nuttige informatie over de maatschappelijke en juridische positie van het kind* (Mys en Breesch 1994).
15 UNHRC, 'Report of La Rue' (n 8).
16 S W Sacino, 'Article 17: access to a diversity of mass media sources' in A Alen, J Vande Lanotte, E Verhellen, F Ang, E Berghmans, M Verheyde and B Abramson (eds), *A Commentary on the United Nations Convention on the Rights of the Child* (Brill Nijhoff 2012): 'Article 17 is not to be a vehicle for State control of content:

Article 17 does not require or authorize State censorship of the content of mass media communications'.

17 ibid.

18 See Voorhoof (n 13).

19 R Hodgkin, P Newell, *Implementation Handbook for the Convention on the Rights of the Child* (Unicef 2002). Sacino (n 15) finds that this reference deliberately avoids clarifying the relationship between the role of the States and the role of parents in the protection of young people from harmful media content, because there could not be found a consensus on the division of this responsibility.

20 CRC Committee, 'Report of the 2014 Day of General Discussion (DGD) on digital media and children's rights' (2014) www.ohchr.org/Documents/HRBodies/CRC/Discussions/2014/DGD_report.pdf (last accessed 15 December 2016).

21 UNGA, 'Resolution: a world fit for children' (2002) UN Doc A/RES/S-27/2.

22 See Hodgkin and Newell (n 18).

23 ibid. See also Meuwese, Blaak and Kaandorp (n 12).

24 cf for instance Council of Europe, 'Declaration of the Committee of Ministers on protecting the dignity, security and privacy of children on the internet' (2008) search.coe.int/cm/Pages/result_details.aspx?ObjectID=09000016805d3d2d (last accessed 15 December 2016); Council of Europe, 'Recommendation CM/Rec(2009)5 of the Committee of Ministers to member states on measures to protect children against harmful content and behaviour and to promote their active participation in the new information and communications environment' (2009) wcd.coe.int/ViewDoc.jsp?Ref=CM/Rec(2009)5&Language=lanEnglish&Ver=original&Site=CM&BackColorInternet=9999CC&BackColorIntranet=FFBB55&BackColorLogged=FFAC75 (last accessed 15 December 2016).

25 *Handyside v United Kingdom* Application no 5493/72 (ECtHR, 7 December 1976).

26 *Vejdeland v Sweden* Application no 1813/07 (ECtHR, 9 February 2012).

27 *Khurshid Mustafa and Tarzibachi v Sweden* Application no 23883/06 (ECtHR, 16 December 2008).

28 *KU v Finland* Application no 2872/02 (ECtHR, 2 December 2008).

29 Council of Europe, 'Strategy for the Rights of the Child (2016–2021) (2016) wcd.coe.int/ViewDoc.jsp?p=&Ref=CM%282015%29175&Language=lanEnglish&Ver=final&Site=CM&BackColorInternet=C3C3C3&BackColorIntranet=EDB021&BackColorLogged=F5D383&direct=true (last accessed 15 December 2016).

30 EU Commission, 'Towards an EU Strategy on the Rights of the Child' (Communication) COM(2006) 367 final.

31 See e.g. Case C–244/06 *Dynamic Medien Vertriebs GmbH v Avides Media AG* (ECJ, 14 February 2008).

32 Parliament and Council Recommendation 2006/952/EC of 20 December 2006 on the protection of minors and human dignity and on the right of reply in relation to the competitiveness of the European audiovisual and on-line information services industry [2006] OJ L378/72.

33 EU Commission, 'An EU Agenda for the Rights of the Child' (Communication) COM(2011)0060 final: 'The Commission will contribute to empowering and protecting children when they are vulnerable, notably by: . . . supporting Member States and other stakeholders in strengthening prevention, empowerment and participation of children to make the most of online technologies and counter cyber-bullying behaviour, exposure to harmful content, and other online risks namely through the Safer Internet programme and cooperation with the industry through self-regulatory initiatives (2009–2014)'.

34 Council of Europe, 'Recommendation CM/Rec(2012)4 of the Committee of Ministers to member States on the protection of human rights with regard to

social networking services' (2012) wcd.coe.int/ViewDoc.jsp?id=1929453&Site=CM (last accessed 15 December 2016).

35 Council of Europe, 'Recommendation CM/Rec(2014)6 of the Committee of Ministers to member States on a Guide to human rights for internet users' (2014) wcd.coe.int/ViewDoc.jsp?id=2184807 (last accessed 30 March 2016) (emphasis added by the author).

36 CRC Committee 'Report of the 2014 DGD' (n 19). The Committee had already emphasised the same concern the year before, e.g. related to exposure to cyberbullying, pornography and grooming: CRC Committee, 'General Comment No 17: The Right of the Child to Rest, Leisure, Play, Recreational Activities, Cultural Life and the Arts (art 31)' (2013) UN Doc CRC/C/GC/17.

37 CRC Committee, 'General Comment No 12' (n 10).

38 G Sparks, *Media Effects Research: A Basic Overview* (Thomson 2006).

39 P Valkenburg, *Children's Responses to the Screen: A Media Psychological Approach* (Erlbaum 2004).

40 ibid.

41 Sparks (n 37).

42 S Kirsh, *Children, Adolescents and Media Violence: A Critical Look at the Research* (Sage Publications 2006); Sparks (n 37).

43 Kirsh (n 41): 'Wertham claimed that the murder and mayhem illustrated in crime comics and the grisly depictions of death in horror comics were sure to promote deceit and increase antisocial behavior in children'; Sparks (n 37). Wertham's research was widely criticised and found to be exaggerated and unfounded.

44 Sparks (n 37).

45 C Anderson, D Gentile and K Buckley, *Violent Video Game Effects on Children and Adolescents: Theory, Research and Public Policy* (Oxford University Press 2007); Kirsh (n 41).

46 R O'Connell, J Bryce, 'Children and young people in on-line and related off-line environments: promoting well-being and minimising risk of harm: Study commissioned by the Council of Europe', not published.

47 The Dutch *Kijkwijzer* classification system is a good example; see www.kijkwijzer.nl/english (last accessed 15 December 2016).

48 A Millwood Hargrave, S Livingstone, *Harm and Offence in Media Content: A Review of the Evidence* (Intellect 2006).

49 ibid.

50 P Valkenburg, 'Expert opinion Schadelijke media en weerbare jeugd: een beleidsvisie 2005–2010' www.ivir.nl/publicaties/vaneijk/Wijzerkijken.pdf (last accessed 15 December 2016).

51 E Lievens, *Protecting Children in the Digital Era: The Use of Alternative Regulatory Instruments* (Martinus Nijhoff Publishers 2010).

52 See Pan European Game Information PEGI, www.pegi.info/en/index/ (last accessed 15 December 2016).

53 Regulation (EU) 2016/679 of the European Parliament and of the Council of 27 April 2016 on the protection of natural persons with regard to the processing of personal data and on the free movement of such data, and repealing Directive 95/46/EC (General Data Protection Regulation) [2016] OJ L 119/1.

54 See also S Livingstone, 'No more social networking for teens?' (LSE Media Policy Blog, 18 December 2015) http://blogs.lse.ac.uk/mediapolicyproject/2015/12/18/no-more-social-networking-for-young-teens/ (last accessed 15 December 2016);J Savirimuthu, 'EU General Data Protection Regulation Article 8: has anyone consulted the kids?' (LSE Media Policy Blog, 1 March 2016) http://blogs.lse.ac.uk/mediapolicyproject/2016/03/01/eu-general-data-protection-regulation-article-8-has-anyone-consulted-the-kids/ (last accessed 15 December 2016).

55 A Third, D Bellerose, U Dawkins, E Keltie and K Pihl, 'Children's rights in the digital age: a download from children around the world' (2014) www.unicef.org/publications/files/Childrens_Rights_in_the_Digital_Age_A_Download_from_Children_Around_the_World_FINAL.pdf (last accessed 15 December 2016).
56 Special Rapporteur on the promotion and protection of the right to freedom of opinion and expression (n 6); United Nations Committee on the Rights of the Child (n 10).
57 Third, Bellerose, Dawkins, Keltie and Pihl (n 54).
58 Savirimuthu (n 53).
59 Unicef, 'Children's rights and business principles' (2013) www.unglobalcompact.org/docs/issues_doc/human_rights/CRBP/Childrens_Rights_and_Business_Principles.pdf (last accessed 15 December 2016).
60 Flemish Council of Journalism, 'Guideline regarding press and minors' (2015) www.rvdj.be/node/432 (last accessed 15 December 2016).
61 CRC Committee, 'Report of the 2014 DGD' (n 19).
62 ibid.
63 Various initiatives have already been taken to increase awareness within the private sector with regard to human rights and CSR, such as the UN Guiding principles on business and human rights, and, specifically tailored to children's rights, the children's rights and business principles, drafted by the UN Global Compact, UNICEF and Save the Children in 2013. In addition, in 2013 the Committee on the Rights of the Child published a General comment on State obligations regarding the impact of the business sector on children's rights. See also: Council of Europe, 'Recommendation of the Committee of Ministers to member states on human rights and business' (2016) https://wcd.coe.int/ViewDoc.jsp?p=&Ref=CM/Rec%282016%293&Language=lanEnglish&Ver=original&BackColorInternet=DBDCF2&BackColorIntranet=FDC864&BackColorLogged=FDC864&direct=true (last accessed 15 December 2016).
64 ITU, 'Guidelines for industry on child online protection' (2014) www.itu.int/en/cop/Documents/bD_Broch_INDUSTRY0809.pdf (last accessed 15 December 2016) (emphasis added by the author).
65 Third, Bellerose, Dawkins, Keltie and Pihl (n 54). Cf also: European Youth Panel 2015, Report www.betterinternetforkids.eu/documents/167024/491234/YEP_brochure_final.pdf/9c5ea634-4e98-4183-b7ab-77e9e38b580a (last accessed 11 April 2016): 'Having young people participate in events such as these [Safer Internet Forum] is vital because we need to express our opinions and concerns just as much as the adults. Our online safety is important and should be put at the forefront of everyone's actions'.
66 www.youthmanifesto.eu (last accessed 15 December 2016).
67 V Donoso, E Lievens, 'Participatory policy-making as a mechanism to increase the effectiveness of school policies against cyberbullying' (2013) http://emsoc.be/wp-content/uploads/2013/12/D.1.3.1.-Participatory-policy-making-as-a-mechanism.pdf (last accessed 15 December 2016); and V Donoso, M Van Mechelen and V Verdoodt, 'Increasing user empowerment through participatory and co-design methodologies' (2014) http://emsoc.be/wp-content/uploads/2014/09/D1.3.1c_ICRI1.pdf (last accessed 15 December 2016).
68 Livingstone, Carr and Byrne (n 3).
69 www.voicesofyouth.org (last accessed 15 December 2016).
70 European Youth Panel 2015 (n 64).
71 EU Commission, 'European strategy for a better internet for children' (Communication) COM(2012) 196 final.
72 European Youth Panel 2015 (n 64).
73 Council of Europe (n 28).

74 UDHR art 19: 'Everyone has the right to freedom of opinion and expression; this right includes freedom to hold opinions without interference and to seek, receive and impart information and ideas through any media and regardless of frontiers'.

75 ICCPR art 19: '1. Everyone shall have the right to hold opinions without interference. 2. Everyone shall have the right to freedom of expression; this right shall include freedom to seek, receive and impart information and ideas of all kinds, regardless of frontiers, either orally, in writing or in print, in the form of art, or through any other media of his choice. 3. The exercise of the rights provided for in paragraph 2 of this article carries with it special duties and responsibilities. It may therefore be subject to certain restrictions, but these shall only be such as are provided by law and are necessary: (a) For respect of the rights or reputations of others; (b) For the protection of national security or of public order (ordre public), or of public health or morals'.

76 This section of the chapter focuses on the right to freedom of expression, and not the right to privacy, although as demonstrated above, the latter right may also be relevant. However, a comparison of the right to privacy in general human rights and children's rights documents would lead us too far within the current scope, and will be studied in the future, for instance, within the content of the AdLit research project; see www.adlit.be (last accessed 15 December 2016).

77 Special Rapporteur on the promotion and protection of the right to freedom of opinion and expression (n 8).

78 ibid.

79 ibid.

80 S Langelaude, 'Understanding the child's right to freedom of expression' (2010) *Human Rights Law Review* 33.

81 U Hasebrink, 'Giving the audience a voice: the role of research in making media regulation more responsive to the needs of the audience' (2011) *Journal of Information Policy* 321.

82 ibid.

83 Langelaude (n 79).

84 D Voorhoof, 'Freedom of journalistic newsgathering, access to information and protection of whistle-blowers under article 10 ECHR and the standards of the Council of Europe' in Council of Europe, *Journalism at Risk: Threats, Challenges and Perspectives* (Council of Europe 2015).

85 *Youth Initiative for Human Rights v Serbia* Application no 48135/06 (ECtHR, 25 June 2013).

86 Third, Bellerose, Dawkins, Keltie and Pihl (n 54). Cf also United Nations Committee on the Rights of the Child (n 35): 'The UN Committee on the Rights of the Child already emphasised in 2013 that the increasing extent to which information and communication technologies are a central dimension in the lives of children entails that (equal) access to the internet and social media for them is crucial, also for the realisation of other, related, rights, such as the right to leisure, play and culture (article 31 UNCRC)'. See also Special Rapporteur on the promotion and protection of the right to freedom of opinion and expression (n 8).

87 Special Rapporteur on the promotion and protection of the right to freedom of opinion and expression (Frank La Rue), 'Report on key trends and challenges to the right of all individuals to seek, receive and impart information and ideas of all kinds through the internet' (2011) UN Doc A/66/290.

88 ibid. Cf also Council of Europe, 'Internet governance – Council of Europe Strategy 2016–2019' https://search.coe.int/cm/Pages/result_details.aspx?ObjectId=09000016805c1b60 (last accessed 15 December 2016): 'Individuals rely on the Internet for their everyday activities and more and more people have

access to online services. For many, including children and young people, it is their primary source of information and means of expression. The Internet is therefore an invaluable space for the exercise of fundamental rights such as freedom of expression and information'.

89 *MTE v Hungary* Application no 22947/13 (ECtHR, 2 February 2016).

90 *Cengiz and Others v Turkey* Application nos 48226/10 and 14027/11 (ECtHR, 1 December 2015).

91 E Brems, 'Children's rights and universality' in Jan Willems (ed), *Developmental and Autonomy Rights of Children* (Intersentia 2002).

92 D Voorhoof, 'Freedom of expression, the media and journalists: case law of the European Court of Human Rights' in T McGonagle, *IRIS Themes Vol III* (European Audiovisual Observatory 2015).

93 E Lievens, 'Is self-regulation failing children and young people? Assessing the use of alternative regulatory instruments in the area of social networks' in S Simpson, M Puppis and H Van den Bulck, *European Media Policy for the Twenty-First Century* (Routledge 2016).

94 Livingstone, Carr and Byrne (n 3).

13 Out of isolation: a claim for explicit attention for children in the movement towards recognition of an environmental right

Danielle van Kalmthout

13.1 Introduction

The debate on the interrelations between human rights and the environment started with the Stockholm Declaration in 1972 (Declaration of the United Nations Conference on the Human Environment).[1] To date, however, international human rights law has not recognised a universal human right to a clean and healthy environment. At the same time, some recent international human rights instruments explicitly recognise links between human rights and the environment and the amount of 'green' case law has increased, in particular within the European Court of Human Rights (ECtHR). The number of resolutions of the United Nations on human rights and the environment and the appointment of the Independent Expert on this issue by the Human Rights Council (UNHRC) in 2012 show the importance attached by the international community to the relation between human rights and the environment as well as the complexity to adopt a specific universal environmental right.[2]

This chapter contributes to the discussion of the position of children's rights within this general debate on human rights and the environment. Do children, in the movement towards a general environmental right, need a specific right? When considering the state of the environment today and the knowledge we have of the impact of environmental protection both on human and planetary health, and especially the health of children, the question also arises whether the Convention on the Rights of the Child (CRC) still provides an adequate answer to this general consensus that environmental protection is one of the main challenges of the 21st century? Principle 3 of the 1992 Rio Declaration refers to the 'developmental and environmental needs of present and future generations'. Although today's children are part of tomorrow's generations and they are more vulnerable than adults to environmental degradation and pollution, it seems that the specific needs of these 'future generations' are barely part of the discussions on the links between environmental protection and human rights.

This chapter will illustrate why children, compared to adults and 25 years after the adoption of the CRC, need a separate environmental right in parallel to a general right considering the changed environment in which present and future generations will grow up. In the first part of this chapter it will be illustrated that children will inherit a different environment from the one we are living in today. It will also be argued that children, compared to adults, need an additional level of human rights protection in relation to this changed environment to ensure their right to life *and* development. The second part examines the extent to which human rights law recognises environmental rights for children through an analysis of the current provisions of the CRC, including the most recent General Comments of the Committee.

13.2 New century, new challenges on the 25th anniversary of the Convention on the Rights of the Child

One of the main stated reasons underlying the adoption of a specific convention on children's rights was that: 'children, because of their special vulnerability and immaturity, require a higher standard of protection in some areas of their life than which was found in existing international law'.[3] Today, the provisions of the CRC remain as valid as before but, at the beginning of the 21st century, additional challenges face present and future generations.

The environment in which today's children live, grow and play is dramatically different from that of their grandparents.[4] Today it is widely understood that the environment exerts powerful influence over patterns of health and disease in children.[5] The environment has changed, as have the diseases with which today's children are confronted. A distinction should be made between industrialised countries and the children in low- and middle-income countries. The major causes of morbidity and mortality among children in the world's industrialised developed countries are chronic diseases, such as asthma, birth defects, neurodevelopmental disorders, leukaemia and brain cancer, testicular cancer and child obesity.[6]

Exposure to environmental hazards is known or suspected to be responsible for a series of acute and chronic diseases that, in the industrialised countries, have replaced infectious diseases as the principal causes of illness and death in childhood.[7] It is often said that children in low- and middle-income countries face a double burden of disease from environmental risks because they are exposed to the threats related to under-development (such as scarce food, contaminated water, polluted air, lack of sanitation and garbage disposal, inadequate housing and social violence), as well as to the emerging problems associated with rapid development.[8] More than one-third of the burden of disease among children worldwide is attributable to preventable environmental risk factors.[9]

In addition to the change in environmental health issues, today's children and future generations will also be confronted with other environmental changes. The scale, spread and rate of change of global drivers of environmental change are without precedent; burgeoning populations and growing economies are pushing environmental systems to destabilising limits and are having an impact on human and planetary health at the local, regional and global levels.[10] Together with natural processes, such as earthquakes, solar radiation and volcano eruptions, this will lead to environmental impact and change in the natural capital of the earth's atmosphere, land, water and biosphere.[11]

Humanity will face a range of environmental impacts. Firstly, through climate change the temperature on Earth is likely to rise by more than 3°C compared to pre-industrial levels if no further commitments and action are taken to reduce greenhouse gas emissions.[12] Such a warming level will have consequences at a global scale on, for example, water and food security, health, ecosystems and biodiversity.[13] Climate change has been identified as possibly the biggest global health threat of the 21st century.[14]

The atmosphere also suffers from the depletion of the stratospheric ozone layer.[15] Children are a vulnerable group when affected by climate change. Especially in poor countries, climate change threatens children's basic rights to education, health, clean water and food.[16] Secondly, there are multiple indications of continuing decline in biodiversity.[17] Pressures on biodiversity have remained high or continued to increase, leading to ongoing degradation of ecosystems, reductions in species populations and increasing extinction risks, as well as erosion of genetic variety.[18] No one is immune to the adverse impacts of biodiversity loss and degraded ecosystems but children, as the most vulnerable segment of our society, are more susceptible to the effects of under- and malnourishment, polluted water and infectious diseases that may be unleashed as the web of life frays.[19]

A third driver of environmental change is the pollution and degradation of the planet's natural resources.[20] Today we are collectively exploiting Earth's resources at accelerating rates and the intensities surpass the capacity of its systems to absorb wastes and neutralise the adverse effects on the environment.[21] In fact, the depletion or degradation of several key resources has already constrained conventional development in some parts of the world.[22] Waste and chemicals constitute an additional consequence of environmental change at the local, regional and global levels. The unsound management of waste can lead to mutually reinforcing undesirable effects. It can pollute and contaminate the environment, pose a threat to human health and represent a loss of resources in the form of both materials and energy.[23]

The World Bank states that the increasing amount of municipal solid waste is linked to urbanisation and economic development.[24] This increasing urbanisation will also affect children from an environmental perspective, given that one city dweller in three lives in slum conditions.[25] In addition, global chemical pollution is a serious threat to sustainable development and livelihoods. The problem impacts on both humanity and ecosystems, and includes adverse effects from long-term exposure to low or sub-lethal concentrations of single chemicals or to mixtures of chemicals.[26] A recent study by the World Health Organization (WHO) indicated that 4.9 million deaths were attributable to environmental exposure to chemicals in 2004.[27] For all these reasons, children inherit a different environment compared to the one of previous generations.

Children's rights are a specific part of human rights because it is recognised that children's special vulnerability requires in certain areas a higher standard of protection, as opposed to adults. Compared to the discussions on human rights and the environment, it seems as if the debate on children's rights within the context of the degrading environment is less concrete about the specific needs for children. The following section will first briefly examine the debate on human rights and the environment at the international, regional and national levels to gain a better understanding of the general context. The second section will analyse why children differ from adults in relation to environmental rights.

13.2.1 Human rights and the environment

Almost from the time of the emergence of contemporary international environmental law in the late 1960s, a relationship between international human rights and international environmental law was strongly perceived.[28] At the international level, the Declaration of the United Nations Conference on the Human Environment (Stockholm 1972) established in its preamble and Principle 1 for the first time a link between the environment and human rights.[29] This statement was the start of the debate on the interrelations between human rights and the environment. Following the Stockholm Conference, the 1992 Rio de Janeiro Conference on Environment and Development (UNCED) took a step further and focused on the link that exists between human rights and the environment in procedural terms.[30] However, there was no explicit recognition of a substantive right to a clean and healthy environment. Principle 1 of the 1992 Declaration does not go beyond stating that: '[human beings] are entitled to a healthy and productive life in harmony with nature'. Nor have the later conferences on sustainable development in Johannesburg in 2002 and Rio de Janeiro in 2012 proclaimed a right to a healthy environment.[31]

When it comes to procedural rights, the Aarhus Convention[32] is explicit about ensuring that individuals and groups have the ability to protect their environmental interests. This United Nations Economic Commission for Europe (UNECE) Convention is a result of Principle 1 of the Stockholm Declaration, linking human rights and environmental protection with Principle 10 of the 1992 Rio Declaration, which calls for public participation in decision-making, access to information and access to justice (see Article 1 Aarhus Convention). Both the UNHCR and the UN Environment Programme (UNEP) have been discussing the relationship between human rights and environment.[33] However, it seems that no consensus exists on how to address environmental issues through the concept of human rights.[34] In 2012, the United Nations General Assembly appointed John H Knox as independent expert on human rights and the environment to study 'the enjoyment of a safe, clean, healthy and sustainable environment'.[35] In his preliminary report, Knox concludes that human rights and environmental protection are inherently interdependent: realisation of fundamental human rights depends on the environment and effective environmental protection depends on the exercise of human rights.[36]

While a general environmental right has not been established at the universal level, a growing interaction can be perceived between specific environmental instruments and human rights instruments. Various international human rights instruments recognise links between human rights and the environment, particularly in the contexts of the right to food, the right to health and indigenous rights to property, natural resources and culture.[37]

The themes for which inter-relations between human rights and the environment can be observed are very diverse, as is demonstrated by the following two examples. The International Labour Organization Convention No 169 on Indigenous and Tribal Peoples 1989 specifies that governments shall take measures to protect and preserve the environment of the territories inhabited by indigenous peoples.[38] Another reference to a collective right to protect the environment is Article 55 of Protocol I 1977 to the Geneva Conventions of 1949. While this article applies to the protection of the environment in time of war, it makes clear that 'the use of methods or means of warfare which are intended or may be expected to cause such damage to the natural environment and thereby to prejudice the health or survival of the population' is prohibited. Although no general environmental right has yet been recognised at the universal level, these distinct examples show that, for specific global human rights treaties, a consensus seems to have been reached on environmental protection and human rights.

That environmental rights are not generally part of human rights treaties might be explained by the fact that: 'international environmental regimes necessarily involve a tension between ideals of national sovereignty over natural resources, and the necessity of obligation-backed cooperation to adequately protect the global environment'.[39] Although Principle 21 of the Stockholm Declaration provides that states have the sovereign right to exploit their own resources, other environmental instruments create the obligation on the part of all states to conserve the common heritage resources within their territory, even when they do not cross national boundaries.[40] This tense relationship between the common interests of mankind and the individual interests of states may constitute an important barrier to recognising a general environmental right.

At the national and regional levels, much more progress has been made compared to the global level. Over 90 states have adopted a right to a healthy environment in their national constitutions.[41] The definitions of these rights differ a great deal from state to state and from region to region. Such formulations of the right to environment qualify the phrase by words such as 'healthy', 'safe', 'secure' or 'clean'.[42] At the regional level, Article 24 of the African Charter on Human and Peoples' Rights 1981 contains a specific *substantive* 'right of individuals to a general satisfactory environment favorable to their development', as does Article 11 of the San Salvador Protocol to the American Convention on Human Rights. The revised Arab Charter on Human Rights also contains a right to a healthy environment.[43]

Although the European Convention on Human Rights (ECHR) does not explicitly recognise a substantive right to a clean environment, the ECtHR pronounced for the first time in line with environmental concerns and human rights in the *López Ostra* case.[44] The Court found a violation of Article 8 (right to respect for private and family life) because 'severe environmental pollution may affect individuals' well-being and prevent them from enjoying their homes in such way as to affect their private and family life adversely even though it does not seriously endanger their health'. This was further developed in later case law, in which the European Court also referred to other provisions of the ECHR, such as the right to life (Article 2),[45] the right to a fair trial and to have access to a court (Article 6),[46] the right to receive and impart information and ideas (Article 10),[47] the right to an effective remedy (Article 13)[48] and the right to protection of property (Article 1 Protocol 1).[49]

The closest the Convention comes to creating a substantive human right to the environment is primarily through the case law on Article 8, where it has become well established that serious environmental damage may lead to a violation of this article.[50] The European Committee of Social Rights has interpreted the right to the protection of health (Article 11) under the European Social Charter as including the right to a healthy environment.[51]

13.2.2 Children's specificity and environmental rights

While the discussion of general human rights and the environment in international law continues, there is an increasing body of scientific evidence that demonstrates that children are more vulnerable to environmental degradation, which may impact their right to development. Moreover, awareness is growing that we should protect our environment for current and future generations. This section analyses three reasons why children differ from adults in relation to environmental rights.

The first reason is strongly connected to the right to health,[52] namely that children are particularly vulnerable to environmental pollution possibly leading to death or health effects, potentially later in life.[53] This 'unique susceptibility' of children to environmental hazards is attributable to a number of factors.[54] The greater susceptibility of children to environmental pollution compared to adults has been known since the 1990s, when the assumption that the entire population reacts to environmental contaminants in a similar manner was disproved. Bearer concluded that children should not be treated as 'little adults' in developing environmental policy as children are, because of their unique physical, biological and social characteristics, among the most vulnerable members of the population.[55] Since then, scientific evidence has accumulated and has been disseminated in many reports and declarations.[56] It seems that, because children are particularly vulnerable, they need a more comprehensive level of protection against environmental hazards.

The second reason is that experience and research indicate that children and women are highly vulnerable to economic, demographic and climatic shifts; for children in particular, the repercussions of these shocks may have life-long consequences.[57] The 1994 Ksentini Report on human rights and the environment described for the first time the impact of environmental degradation on vulnerable groups and demanded a legal framework for the preservation of the interests of future generations and mutually to agree on the components of a right to a healthy environment.[58] What Ksentini stressed in her report is that the huge potential of children and youth is jeopardised by the 'mutually reinforcing problems of persistent poverty, rapid population growth and environmental degradation'.

It seems that this spiral makes it very difficult to comply with one of the core principles of the CRC, which is the right to life, survival and development (Article 6 CRC). Children are confronted with environmental degradation that may interfere with their development process of becoming healthy adults. An example is the effect of air pollution on children's health and development. The intra-uterine, perinatal and early childhood periods, during which the lungs are developing and maturing, are very vulnerable times and these are periods when the lungs are susceptible to injury by air pollutants.[59] It can be argued that recognition of environmental rights is needed to ensure the optimum development of the child, both physically and psychologically.

The third reason why children differ from adults in relation to environmental rights is that children are part of tomorrow's generations. This specific relationship between children and the right to a clean environment has been acknowledged for quite some time. The 1987 Brundtland report 'Our common future' states that our generation profits from the already overdrawn environmental resource account, but that our children inherit the losses.[60] This principle of inter-generational equity is embodied in Principle 1 of the Stockholm Declaration, which besides linking human and environmental rights, associates environmental protection with present and future generations. The Rio+20 summit renewed its commitment on inter-generational equity and sustainable development.[61] While a worldwide consensus seems to exist that future generations should be taken care of, there is less consensus on how to implement this in practice. Arguably, the protection of the environmental rights of the members of the future generations who are already among us (i.e. children) is one piece of this puzzle. The concept of inter-generational equity, however, falls outside the scope of this chapter.

13.3 The Convention on the Rights of the Child and the environment

Having established that children are particularly vulnerable to environmental pollution and degradation that may have an impact on their development, the extent to which human rights law actually recognises environmental rights for children will now be examined through an analysis of the current provisions of the CRC. The United Nations Convention on the Rights of the Child[62] explicitly refers to the environment in two articles, namely Article 24 CRC on the right to health and health services and Article 29 CRC on the right to education. Although the Convention does not contain an explicit environmental right, some authors argue that such a right is implicitly embedded in the Convention.

13.3.1 Provisions in the CRC referring to the environment

13.3.1.1 Right to health

'Environmental pollution' is explicitly mentioned in Article 24(2)(c) CRC on the right to health and health care because the article's aim is to combat child mortality owing to malnutrition and the lack of clean drinking water.[63] It was late in the drafting process of the Convention that India proposed to add this provision because it was much concerned about the high child mortality in the poorer sector of the population in developing countries.[64] Austria added the environmental reference.[65] Today, it seems that the specific goal of Article 24(2)(c) CRC is too limited to encompass the current environmental challenges which go far beyond the scope of combating child mortality attributable to malnutrition and clean water. It seems that the Committee on the Rights of the Child also recognised progressively under this heading the importance of a variety of environmental issues.

In the context of the state reporting procedure, in 2000 the Committee linked environmental pollution and access to safe drinking water and adequate sanitation in a recommendation to Jordan.[66] Since then, on many occasions the Concluding Observations of the Committee have referred to different environmental issues as impediments to the right to health.[67] General Comment No 15 of 2013 demonstrates a broader interpretation of the right to health and advocates that states should take measures to address the dangers and risks that local environmental pollution poses to children's health.[68] This General Comment also calls upon states to put children's health concerns at the centre of their climate adaptation and migration strategies, calling this one of the biggest threats to children's health.[69]

Children's health remains threatened by malnutrition and unsafe water supplies through environmental pollution.[70] Additionally, children's health is also exposed to new environmental challenges, such as climate change, biodiversity loss and the unsustainable conservation and management of limited natural resources owing to economic growth and the expanding world population, as described above. Exposure to environmental hazards is known or suspected to be responsible for a series of acute and chronic diseases that, in the industrialised countries, have replaced infectious diseases as the principal causes of illness and death in childhood.[71] Chronic diseases representing a 'new pediatric morbidity' include asthma, childhood cancer, lead poisoning, developmental disorders and endocrine disruption.[72] Urbanisation and pervasive poverty in developing countries aggravate both 'basic' and 'modern' health risks, leading to a double burden in pediatric environmental health.[73] In discussions on sustainable development and the need to protect current and future generations from environmental harm, it is submitted that Article 24 CRC covers part but not all of these environmental challenges.

Thus, Article 24 CRC explicitly mentions the environment in the context of health but is not adapted to today's environmental reality and does not take into account current scientific knowledge that demonstrates that environmental factors have an important impact on children's health and development. Children's health is a matter of unsafe water and malnutrition but also of acute and chronic diseases as well as other environmental threats, such as climate change, biodiversity depletion and unsustainable management of natural resources. General Comment No 15 also recognises that the right to health today encompasses more than combating malnutrition, clean drinking water and sanitation.

13.3.1.2 Right to education

The word 'environment' in relation to 'education' is mentioned in two articles of the convention. Article 24(2)(e) CRC on health education provides that states shall inform, educate and support all segments of society, including parents and children in the use of basic knowledge of 'child health and nutrition, the advantages of breastfeeding, hygiene and environmental sanitation and the prevention of accidents'. It seems that this article specifies in detail what the state's obligation entails in respect of health; children's health is coupled with nutrition and education should be given to prevent as much as possible diseases relating to bad sanitation. Considering that Article 24 CRC no longer meets the additional environmental challenges and that both developing and developed states are increasingly confronted with children's environmental health problems, one may conclude that this paragraph no longer suits today's context either. For example, Article 24(2)(e) CRC obliges states parties to ensure that parents have 'a basic knowledge' to implement the child's right to health. Information on endocrine disrupting chemicals[74] does not fall within the scope of Article 24(2)(e) CRC, which seems to be limited to malnutrition and bad sanitation.

However, when taking into account that (unborn) children are more susceptible to endocrine disrupting chemicals,[75] should states, in both developing and developed countries, not 'inform, educate and support' parents with sufficient 'basic knowledge'? This seems justified because, according to Article 18(1) of the Convention, parents have the primary responsibility for the upbringing and development of the child, with the best interests of the child as their basic concern. Within this context it should be noted that the UN Independent Expert on human rights and the environment concludes in his recent report that the Committee's interpretations of the Convention place responsibility for preventing environmental harms that impact on children's rights on states and government actors.[76]

Article 29(1)(e) CRC on the aims of education specifies in that states agree that children's education shall be directed to 'the development of respect of the natural environment'. General Comment No 1 of the Committee explains that one of the functions of this article is to promote and reinforce the range of specific ethical values enshrined in the Convention, including '. . . respect for the natural environment in an integrated and holistic manner'.[77] To develop this, the Committee makes a link with sustainable development and suggests this should be learnt by children at home, in school and within the community, that it should encompass both national and international problems, and actively involve children in local, regional or global environmental projects.[78]

It may be argued that the objective of Article 24(2)(e) CRC is limited to specific areas of health education and thus establishes no inter-relation between the environment and the right to health. Article 29 CRC on the preparation of children as responsible citizens may give the clearest message in the Convention on environmental rights, although it is restricted to the aims of education. So while the environment is explicitly mentioned, these articles do not seem to be drafted as environmental rights provisions and their scope seems insufficient to deal with the important environmental threats current and future generations face.

13.3.2 Are environmental rights indirectly embedded in the CRC?

Negotiations on the CRC do not suggest that a right to a clean environment was meant to be included.[79] Many human rights bodies and experts take an approach similar to that of the Stockholm Declaration and understand environmental protection as a precondition to the enjoyment of several internationally guaranteed human rights, especially the rights to life and health.[80] For the same reason, according to Fitzmaurice, some authors are of the opinion that environmental, both substantive and procedural, rights for children are already contained in the Convention.[81] Ksentini, for example, calls for special attention for vulnerable groups and children in her recommendations and expresses the opinion that the environmental dimension lies dormant in some of the provisions of the CRC.[82] This section will analyse, with the approach of the Stockholm Declaration in mind, the extent to which specific children's rights provisions implicitly contain environmental rights.

13.3.2.1 Right to life, survival and development

The fact that environmental protection is a precondition to the enjoyment of several human rights would surely apply to one of the four general principles of the Convention:[83] Article 6 on the right to life, survival and development.[84] This fundamental right remains unrealised for some 6.6 million children under five years old who died in 2012, mostly from preventable causes.[85] This child mortality is to a large extent owing to environmental pollution (see section 13.3.1.1). Although children in developing countries are disproportionately hit by the impact of environmental pollution, children in both developing and developed countries are affected. While most deaths attributable to the environment still occur in sub-Saharan Africa, according to the WHO, other regions have higher per capita rates of non-communicable diseases, which could be prevented by lowering environmental exposure.[86]

Article 6 CRC goes further than the right to life and survival because it includes the child's right to development. For children having to cope with disease, one may question whether their right to development, including physical, mental, psychological and social development, is realised 'to their full potential'.[87] This right to development is also reflected in General Comment No 16, which states that childhood is a unique period of development where unsafe products and environmental hazards may have life-long, irreversible and even transgenerational consequences.[88] This General Comment makes an explicit reference to Article 6 CRC, stating that environmental degradation and contamination arising from business activities can compromise children's rights to health, food security and access to safe drinking water and sanitation.[89] Children who contributed to the draft General Comment also called for environmental protection laws that prohibit multi-national companies from polluting the environment.[90]

Compared with other human rights treaties, Article 6(2) CRC adds another new element as it refers explicitly to a positive obligation of parties to the Convention to ensure the survival and development of the child, although this obligation is weakened by the wording 'to the largest extent possible'.[91]

Bearing the above in mind, it seems that the realisation of the right to life and development for children is impeded by the state of the environment and by the effect pollution has on the health of children. Its recent interpretation of Article 6 CRC shows that the Committee attaches importance to the impact of environmental pollution on children's rights.

13.3.2.2 Right to an adequate standard of living

A clean and healthy environment would also be a precondition for realising the child's right to a standard of living adequate for the child's physical, mental, spiritual, moral and social development (Article 27 CRC). Article 27 is based on Article 6 CRC and is very much attached to Article 24 CRC.[92] Although the Convention does not contain a specific reference to poverty, let alone a right to protection against poverty, rights in Article 2 and 27 CRC in particular may be mobilised in a children's rights approach to poverty.[93] However, the terms 'adequate' and 'necessary' used in Article 27 imply that the child's right is to *minimal*, not optimal, living conditions that support holistic development.[94] Moreover, children in poverty can suffer twice as much from multiple and cumulative environmental exposures as their wealthier neighbours, or even more.[95]

The focus in Article 27 CRC goes beyond 'nutrition, clothing and safe housing' as a basic need because the terminology makes it clear that this right is about many aspects of the development of the child.[96] Indeed, the holistic development of the child includes much more than just material resources such as food, clothing and housing.[97] Speaking about the right to development in Article 6 CRC, on which Article 27 CRC is based, one may also question the extent to which the environment is contributing positively to the child's development. Disconnection from nature may have important consequences for children's healthy development and well-being.[98]

Kellert is of the opinion that to play in nature, particularly during the critical period of middle childhood, appears to be especially important for developing the capacities of creativity, problem solving, and emotional and intellectual development.[99] Van den Berg warns of the decline in modern children's direct experience of nature and safe outdoor play, in particular with increasing urbanisation.[100] According to UNICEF, by 2050 over two-thirds of the global population will grow up in cities and towns, where for billions of people the urban experience is one of poverty and exclusion.[101] The state of the environment is a growing factor in determining the right to an adequate standard of living which, in turn, influences children's development, in particular for those living in poverty. Together with the predicted urbanisation and an expected increased disconnection from nature, one may question whether the preconditions for implementing the right stated by Article 27 CRC can be fulfilled.

13.3.2.3 Right to leisure, play and culture

Looking at environmental rights and the development of the child as described in Article 27 CRC, the right to leisure, play and culture also comes into focus (Article 31 CRC). The right to play is a new type of right, which was recognised for the first time in the CRC and thereafter in Article 12 of the African Charter on the Rights and Welfare of the Child.[102] Consensus usually exists in the recognition that play can impact positively on children's physical and psychological development, on their social skills, on learning self-control and autonomy and to develop their creativity.[103] According to David, 'Article 31 may well be the most neglected provision by the CRC Committee since it started its monitoring work in 1991' and is 'often perceived as a luxury in comparison to other rights whose violations bear more cruel, visible and spectacular consequences'.[104] He adds that this perception is relatively persistent, despite wide recognition in and outside child development circles of the crucial role that rest, play, leisure and culture have for the social, cognitive and personal development of the child.

As discussed above, environmental, social and cultural factors lead to children playing less outside and becoming alienated from nature, while the benefits for a child's development of both being in direct contact with nature *and* being able to play outdoors are widely recognised. In 2013, the Committee adopted General Comment No 17 as it was concerned about the poor recognition by states of the rights of Article 31 CRC.[105] The need for children to play outdoors is emphasised in the report with the enumeration of the factors for an optimum environment and the challenge to reverse unsafe and hazardous environments, in particular for the world's poorest children.[106] According to the report, one of the challenges is a lack of access to nature and the pressure for educational achievement resulting in children now spending more time indoors at school leading to less contact with nature.[107] These specific elaborations of the right to play in the General Comment may be further interpreted as if the Committee, besides being worried about the implementation of this right by states, is of the opinion that a clean and healthy environment is needed for children to enjoy this right.

Summing up, it has been argued that Articles 24, 27, 29 and 31 of the CRC are needed to guarantee the enjoyment of the right to life, survival and development of Article 6 of the CRC. Articles 6, 27 and 31 do not explicitly mention the environment. Following the approach of understanding environmental protection as a precondition to the enjoyment of these rights, meaning that these are indirectly embedded in the CRC, it also seems that it is more and more difficult for children actually to enjoy these rights precisely because of the lack of a clean and healthy environment. It is not only children's 'caring environment' in which they grow up that will shape the adults they become but their 'living environment' as well. Children are confronted with environmental degradation that impedes the development process, including their physical, mental, psychological and social development of becoming healthy adults.

It should be noted that Knox, the UN Independent Expert on human rights and the environment, observes in a recent report 'several trends' between the environment and the rights guaranteed under the CRC by the Committee.[108] According to this report, the Committee on the Rights of the Child has recognised and made reference to a wide variety of environmental issues, mostly in the Concluding Observations to States Parties on national environmental threats as well as in recent General Comments. Indeed, such 'trends' may be deduced from the recent General Comments Nos 15, 16 and 17 in which it seems the Committee is seeking to interpret the Convention according to identified additional needs.

13.3.3 General principles of the CRC and Environment: Articles 3 and 12

In addition to the right to life of Article 6 CRC, three other articles of the Convention have been identified by the Committee on the Rights of the Child as general principles: Article 2 (non-discrimination), Article 3 (best interests of the child) and Article 12 (respect for the views of the child). The following section will analyse in more detail the inter-relation between two of the possibly applicable general principles of the Convention and the environment.

13.3.3.1 The best interests of the child

From Article 3(1) CRC it follows that 'every legislative, administrative and judicial body or institution is required to apply the best interests principle by systematically considering how children's rights and interests are or will be affected by their decisions and actions'.[109] According to Freeman, Article 2 CRC which requires states to respect and ensure the rights set forth in the Convention without discrimination, precedes the 'best interests' standard.[110] He concludes that the provisions of the Convention should be applied with the 'best interest of the child' always in mind, whilst this cannot be done without reference to the rights of the child recognised in the Convention.[111] This would mean that if an environmental right is not recognised in the Convention, Article 3 CRC would not apply in environmental matters.

One of the reasons why children's best interests are to be of primary consideration is that, in a world run by adults, there would be a danger that children's interests would be completely ignored.[112] As seen above, some authors are of the opinion that environmental rights are implicitly recognised in the Convention because they constitute a precondition to a number of children's rights. If this is the case, it would imply that 'the best interests of the child' have to be translated into current environmental legislation and policy. To ensure the realisation of Article 3(1) CRC, the Committee on the Rights of the Child requires a child impact assessment and evaluation in legislation and policy development and delivery at all levels of government.[113] This implies that states must carry out a child impact assessment and evaluation for all environmental legislation and policy. One may question the extent to which current environmental legislation and policy takes account of the specificity of children compared to adults. As argued above, children need more protection in comparison with adults because they are more vulnerable to environmental degradation. If the best interests of the child were taken into account, this specific vulnerability would be visibly reflected in environmental policy.

13.3.3.2 Respect for the views of the child

Besides the need for protection because of the vulnerability of children, the Convention gives children participation rights.[114] Article 12 CRC on respect for the views of the child is innovatory because it gives children voice 'in all matters affecting the child'. According to Hart, children's and adolescents' views give an added value to societal debate and decision-making, especially on the community level.[115] Orama concludes at the same time that unfortunately the stage of genuine dialogue has not been reached so far, not even within the professionals' children's rights field; adults still tend to think that it is the adult professionals who know what is really *in the best interests* of children. Also, child participation is strongly criticised, mostly on account of traditionally hierarchical societal structures where children are not seen as subjects of rights but rather as citizens of tomorrow.[116]

One of the most common and cogent criticisms levelled at Article 12 CRC is that it is easy for adults to comply with the various outward signs of consultation and ultimately ignore children's views.[117] Lundy observes that the precise remit of Article 12 CRC is not yet fully understood because the article has two key elements: (i) the right to express a view; *and* (ii) the right to have the view given due weight. The idea of child participation promoted by the Convention requires deep changes in cultural attitudes towards children.[118] When it comes to participation on environmental matters children nowadays are represented at fora from local to international levels.[119] Environmental degradation seems certainly a 'matter affecting the child' in the sense of Article 12 CRC. To what extent, as well as the right to express a view, their views are actually given weight in environmental policy is another question. However, children need not only to be protected from environmental degradation but also to be involved and participate in protecting their future world and that of their children.[120]

The application of the general principles of Articles 3 and 12 CRC could strengthen the position of children in environmental legislation and policy. The implementation of 'the best interests of the child' principle seems the most difficult. If an environmental right were recognised in the provisions of the Convention, the best interests principle would apply to states parties' environmental legislation and policies. It was argued above that the child's interests *are* at stake in environmental matters and that these interests should be of primary consideration because children are disproportionately affected. Concerning Article 12 CRC, children nowadays do have the opportunity to express their views on environmental matters in many fora but more research should be carried out on the results.

13.4 Conclusion: A claim for an additional level of human rights protection for children in the movement towards recognition of a general environmental right

The debate on the recognition of a general environmental right started some decades ago, although no such right has yet come into being. In 2014, the Convention on the Rights of the Child celebrated its 25th anniversary and, while the provisions of the Convention remain very relevant, the world in which children grow up today has changed tremendously, including exposure to new environmental challenges. This chapter has aimed to answer the question of whether children, in the movement towards the recognition of a general environmental right, need in parallel to adults a specific environmental right.

It may be concluded that present and future generations face new environmental challenges of unprecedented size. Moreover, scientific evidence shows that 'children are no little adults' when it comes to the effect of environmental pollution and degradation because of their 'unique susceptibility' possibly leading to death or health effects, potentially later in life. This increasing body of evidence demonstrates that children, compared with adults, are more vulnerable to environmental pollution and degradation. This impedes their development process, including their physical, mental, psychological and social development, of becoming healthy adults. Not only children's 'caring environment', but also the 'living environment' in which they grow up, will shape the adults they become.

Children's rights are a specific part of human rights because the differentiation between adults and children requires additional protection for children in certain areas. The environmental challenges children are exposed to now and in the future also require additional protection. In analysing the current provisions of the CRC and the extent to which they recognise an environmental right for children it seems that, although some provisions refer to environmental matters, they have not sufficiently considered the environmental outlook and today's knowledge of children's environmental health for present and future generations. The approach to understanding environmental protection as a precondition to the enjoyment of several internationally guaranteed human rights, especially the rights to life, development and health may be insufficient for present and future generations; it seems more and more difficult for children actually to enjoy these rights precisely because of the lack of a safe, clean, healthy and sustainable environment.

In the movement towards the recognition of environmental rights as human rights, these specific needs of children and the requirement of an additional level of protection should receive explicit attention. This implies that the debate should include discussions on the relevance of the separate recognition of children's environmental rights. Instead of being isolated in these discussions, children and their needs concerning environmental rights should be fully connected to the main debate.

Notes

1 The author wishes to thank Prof Dr Eva Brems for her constructive comments on earlier drafts of this chapter.
2 United Nations Human Rights Council (UN HRC), 'Human rights and the environment' (2012) UN Doc A/HRC/RES/19/10.
3 G Van Bueren, *The International Law on the Rights of the Child* (Martinus Nijhoff Publishers 1998) 13.
4 P J Landrigan, R A Etzel (eds), *The Textbook of Children's Environmental Health* (Oxford University Press 2014) 103; see also United Nations Secretary-General's High-level Panel on Global Sustainability, 'Resilient people, resilient planet: a future worth choosing' (2012) https://sustainabledevelopment.un.org/index.php?page=view&nr=374&type=400&menu=35 (last accessed 5 October 2016); see also Intergovernmental Panel on Climate Change Fifth Assessment Report (WGII AR5), 'Climate Change 2014: impacts, adaptation and vulnerability' www.ipcc.ch/report/ar5/wg2/ (last accessed 16 December 2016).
5 ibid 10; see also A Prüss-Üstün, C Corvalán, 'Preventing disease through healthy environments: towards an estimate of the environmental burden of disease' (World Health Organization 2006) www.who.int/quantifying_ehimpacts/publications/preventingdisease.pdf (last accessed 16 December 2016).
6 ibid 5: 'Today, in the aftermath of the epidemiological transition, and despite the ever-present threats of tuberculosis, HIV/AIDS, and newly emerging infections, the principal causes of illness, disability, and death among children in the United States, Japan and Western Europe are no longer infectious diseases'.
7 J Pronczuk-Garbino (ed), *Children's Health and the Environment: A Global Perspective* (World Health Organization 2005) 7.
8 Landrigan and Etzel (n 4) 103–104.
9 ibid 103.
10 United Nations Environment Programme (UNEP), *The Global Environment Outlook 5 (GEO-5)* (UNEP 2012) Figure 1: The GEO-5 DPSIR conceptual framework 4.
11 ibid xx.
12 Potsdam Institute for Climate Impact Research and Climate Analytics, 'Turn down the heat: Why a 4°C warmer world must be avoided' Report for the World Bank (2012) xiii.
13 ibid ix and xiii; see also Intergovernmental Panel on Climate Change Fifth Assessment Report (WGII AR5), Climate Change 2014: impacts, adaptation, and vulnerability (n 4).
14 A Costello, M Abbas, A Allen, S Ball and others, 'Managing the health effects of climate change' (2009) 373 *The Lancet* 1693.
15 P Birnie, A Boyle and C Redgwell, *International Law and the Environment* (3rd edn, Oxford University Press 2009) 336.
16 UNICEF, 'UNICEF UK Climate Change Report 2013' www.unicef.org.uk/Documents/Publication-pdfs/unicef-climate-change-report-2013.pdf (last accessed 5 October 2016) 1; S Bartlett, 'Climate change and urban children: impacts and implications for adaptation in low- and middle-income countries' (2008) *Environment and Urbanization* 501.
17 The world leaders committed in 2002, through the Convention on Biological Diversity, to 'achieve by 2010 a significant reduction of the current rate of biodiversity loss'; see The Global biodiversity Outlook (GBO-3), a periodic report prepared by the Secretariat of the Convention on Biological Diversity, concluding that this target has not been met.
18 UNEP, *GEO-5* (n 10) 162.

19 UNEP, UNDP Conference, 'Role of biodiversity, healthy ecosystems in supporting child health', 30 April 2010, New York; see also Landrigan and Etzel (n 4) 190–92.

20 For Birnie, Boyle and Redgwell (n 15) 586, the term 'natural resources' covers both living and non-living resources: the former are distinguished from the latter by the fact that they are renewable if conserved and destructible if not whereas the latter include non-renewable minerals such as oil, gas, coal and minerals mined commercially on land and at sea, sometimes to the point of virtual exhaustion, for human purposes.

21 UNEP, *GEO-5* (n 10) xviii.

22 ibid.

23 ibid 175.

24 The World Bank, 'What a waste: a Global review of solid waste management' (2012) The World Bank sitesources.worldbank.org/INTURBDEVELOPMENT/Resources/336387-1334852610766/What_a_Waste2012__Final.pdf (last accessed 5 October 2016).

25 UNICEF, *The State of the World's Children: Children in an Urban World* (UNICEF 2012) 2.

26 UNEP *GEO-5* (n 10) 168.

27 A Prüss-Ustün, Carolyn Vickers, Pascal Haefliger and Roberto Bertollini, 'Knowns and unknowns on burden of disease due to chemicals: a systematic review' (2011) 10(9) *Environmental Health* 9.

28 D K Anton, D L Shelton, *Environmental Protection and Human Rights* (Cambridge University Press 2011) 118.

29 United Nations Conference on the Human Environment, 'Declaration of the United Nations Conference on the Human Environment, Stockholm 1972' (1973) UN Doc A/CONF.48/14/Rev.1, 3.

30 In particular Principle 10 on access to information, public participation and access to justice, see Council of Europe, *Manual on Human Rights and the Environment* (2nd edn, Council of Europe Publishing 2012) 11.

31 United Nations General Assembly (UNGA), 'Report of the Independent Expert John H Knox on the issue of human rights obligations relating to the enjoyment of a safe, clean, healthy and sustainable environment' UN Doc A/HRC/22/43 (24 December 2012) 6.

32 UNECE, 'Convention on Access to Information, Public Participation, in Decision-making and Access to Justice in Environmental Matters' (25 June 1998) www.unece.org/fileadmin/DAM/env/pp/documents/cep43e.pdf (last accessed 16 December 2016).

33 UN Human Rights Sub-Commission on Prevention of Discrimination and Protection of Minorities, 'Draft principles on human rights and the environment' (1994) http://hrlibrary.umn.edu/demo/HRandEnvironment_Ksentini.pdf (last accessed 5 October 2016); UNEP, High Level Expert Meeting on the New Future of Human Rights and Environment, Nairobi 2009 http://www.unep.org/environmentalgovernance/Events/HumanRightsandEnvironment (last accessed 5 October 2016); UN HRC res 16/11 adopted 7 June 2011, 'Human rights and the environment', UN HRC Res 19/10, adopted 22 March 2012, 'Human rights and the environment' (see also n 2).

34 Daniel Bodanksky, Jutta Brunnée and Ellen Hey (eds), *The Oxford Handbook of International Environmental Law* (Oxford University Press 2007) 664–79.

35 See UN HRC, 'Human rights and environment' (n 2) (2 April 2012, confirmed by A/HRC/25/L.31 (24 March 2014). The mandate was further extended in March 2015 for another three years as a Special Rapporteur www.ohchr.org/EN/issues/Environment/IEEnvironment/pages/IEenvironmentindex.aspx (last accessed 16 December 2016).

36 UNGA, 'Knox Report'(n 31) 4.
37 UNEP and CIEL, 'Compendium on human rights and the environment: selected international legal materials and cases' (Advance version, United Nations Environmental Programme and Center for International Environmental Law 2014) 10.
38 ILO Convention 169, Article 7.
39 UNEP Compendium (n 37) 20.
40 ibid 20–21.
41 UNGA, *Report of Knox* (n 31) 5.
42 Dinah Shelton, 'Draft paper on human rights and the environment: past, present and future linkages and the value of a Declaration' George Washington University Law School, High Level Expert Meeting on the New Future of Human Rights and the Environment: Moving the Global Agenda Forward (Nairobi, 30 November–1 December 2009) 3 www.unep.org/environmentalgovernance/LinkClick.aspx?fileticket=vmj6UL3O5Ho%3d&tabid=2046&language=en-US (last accessed 16 December 2016).
43 Arab Charter on Human Rights Art 38 (22 May 2004).
44 See *López Ostra v Spain* (1994) Series A no 303-C.
45 Article 2 of the ECHR lays down a positive obligation on states to take appropriate steps to safeguard the lives of those within their jurisdiction. Article 2 has been applied where certain activities endangering the environment are so dangerous that they also endanger human life. ibid 9, 35. See eg *Öneryildiz v Turkey* ECHR 2004-XII.
46 See e.g.*Taşkin and others v Turkey* ECHR 2004-X.
47 See e.g. *Vides Aizsardzîbas Klubs v Latvia* App no 57829/00 (ECtHR, 27 May 2004).
48 See e.g. *Öneryildiz v Turkey* ECHR 2004-XII.
49 See e.g. *Fredin v Sweden* (1991) Series A no 192.
50 Ole W Pedersen, 'European environmental human rights and environmental rights: a long time coming?' (2008) 21 *Georgetown International Environmental Law Review* 91.
51 Council of Europe (n 30) 9. See e.g. *Marangopoulos Foundation for Human Rights (MFHR) v Greece* (European Committee of Social Rights, 6 December 2006).
52 Article 24 CRC on the rights to health and health services.
53 WHO Global Plan for Action on Children's Health and the Environment (2010–2015) 1: 'Each year, at least 3 million children under the age of five die due to environment-related diseases' www.who.int/ceh/cehplanaction10_15.pdf?ua=1 (last accessed 16 December 2016).
54 Pronczuk-Garbino (n 7) 3.
55 Cynthia F Bearer, 'Environmental health hazards: how children are different from adults, The future of children' (1995) 5 *Critical Issues for Children and Youths* 11–12; see also Global Diversity Outlook (n 17) 10: 'Three powerful new insights have catalyzed recent growth of children's environmental health: (1) Recognition that children at all ages, and especially in the embryonic and fetal periods, are uniquely vulnerable and exquisitely sensitive to hazardous exposures in the environment; (2) Growing understanding that changes in the environment – positive as well as negative changes – are powerful drivers to health and disease in children; (3) Realization that environmental exposures in early life can influence health and disease not only in infancy and childhood but also across the entire human life span into adult life and even into extreme old age'.
56 See Human Rights and the Environment, Rio + 20 Joint Report OHCHR and UNEP (9 June 2012) www.unep.org/environmentalgovernance/Portals/8/publications/JointReport_OHCHR_HRE.pdf (last accessed 16 December 2016);

see also UNEP Global Environment Outlook 5 (n 22); and WHO website on children's environmental health www.who.int/ceh/en/ (last accessed 16 December 2016).

57 UNICEF, 'Report 2012' (n 25) 61.

58 UN HRC, Sub-Commission on Prevention of Discrimination and Protection of Minorities, UN Economic and Social Council, 'Final Report prepared by Mrs Fatma Zohra Ksentini, Special Rapporteur' E/CN.4/Sub.2/1994/9 (6 July 1994).

59 Regional Office of Europe of the World Health Organization, 'Effect on air pollution on children's health and development: a review of evidence' (2005) WHO Europe 36 www.euro.who.int/__data/assets/pdf_file/0010/74728/E86575.pdf?ua=1 (last accessed 16 December 2016).

60 WCED, 'Report of the World Commission on Environment and Development (WCED): Our common future' A/42/427 (1987), para 25.

61 UNGA, 'The future we want: outcome document adopted at Rio+20' (2012) UN Doc A/CONF.216/L.1, para 86.

62 UN Convention on the Rights of the Child (New York, 20 November 1989) (entry into force 2 September 1990); 195 State Parties www.ohchr.org/EN/HRBodies/CRC/pages/CRCIndex.aspx/indicators.ohchr.org (last accessed 16 December 2016).

63 CRC art 24(1): 'States Parties recognize the right of the child to the enjoyment of the highest attainable standards of health and to facilities for the treatment of illness and rehabilitation of health. States Parties shall strive to ensure that no child is deprived of his or her right of access to such health care services. (2) States Parties shall pursue full implementation of this right and, in particular, shall take the appropriate measures: . . . (c) *To combat disease and malnutrition*, including within the framework of primary health care through, inter alia, the application of readily available technology and *through the provision of nutritious food and clean drinking water*, taking into consideration the dangers and risks of environmental pollution' (emphasis added).

64 S Detrick, *The United Nations Convention on the Rights of the Child: A Guide to the* travaux préparatoires (Martinus Nijhoff Publishers 1992) 353, 405.

65 S Detrick, *A Commentary on the United Nations Convention on the Rights of the Child* (Kluwer Law International 1999) 409; see also E/CN.4/1989/48, para 412 www.ohchr.org/Documents/Publications/LegislativeHistorycrc2en.pdf (last accessed 5 October 2016).

66 CRC Committee, 'Concluding observations on Jordan' UN Doc CRC/C/15/Add. 125 (28 June 2000) 50.

67 United Nations High Commissioner for Human Rights (UNHCHR), 'Mapping human rights obligations relating to the enjoyment of a safe, clean, healthy and sustainable environment: individual report on the United Nations Convention on the Rights of the Child', Report No 5 by John Knox (2013), paras 28–39 http://srenvironment.org/ (last accessed 16 December 2016).

68 CRC Committee, 'General Comment No 15: The Right of the Child to the Enjoyment of the Highest Attainable Standard of Health (art 24)' (2013) UN Doc CRC/C/GC/15, para 49.

69 General Comments are prepared by the Committee on the Rights of the Child and make an interpretation the Convention's articles, see http://tbinternet.ohchr.org/_layouts/treatybodyexternal/TBSearch.aspx?Lang=en&TreatyID=5&DocTypeID=11 (last accessed 16 December 2016).

70 OHCHR, 'Report on the right of the child to the enjoyment of the highest attainable standard of health' (2013) www.ohchr.org/EN/Issues/Children/RightHealth/Pages/righttohealthindex.aspx (last accessed 16 December 2016).

71 Pronczuk-Garbino (n 7) 7–10. See also EEA-JRC, *Environment and human health: Joint EEA-JRC report* (European Environment Agency 2013); 'Non communicable diseases represent the greatest burden of mortality and morbidity in the EU. Exposure to air pollution, noise, poor quality water, chemicals, radiation, biological agents, and otherwise degraded environments are important components' www.who.int/topics/environmental_health/en/ (last accessed 16 December 2016).
72 See Pronczuk-Garbino (n 7) 7–10.
73 ibid.
74 See Landrigan and Etzel (n 4) 325 'Endocrine disrupting chemicals are synthetic chemicals that act upon the body's natural system of hormone-responsive tissues. In many cases, endocrine-disrupting chemicals (EDCs) have a chemical structure similar to that of naturally occurring hormones, such as the sex steroid hormones estrogen and testosterone, and thus can mimic, block, or alter normal hormonal signaling'.
75 Åke Bergman, Jerrold J Heindel, Susan Jobling, Karen A Kidd and R Thomas Zoeller (eds), *State of the Science of Endocrine Disrupting Chemicals 2012, Summary for Decision-makers* (WHO/UNEP 2013) www.who.int/ceh/publications/endocrine/en (last accessed 16 December 2016).
76 UNHCHR (n 67) para 110.
77 CRC Committee, 'General Comment No 1: Article 29(1): The Aims of Education' UN Doc CRC/GC/2001/1, para 13.
78 ibid.
79 S Brice, 'Convention on the Rights of the Child: using a human rights instrument to protect against environmental threats' (1995) 7 *Georgetown International Environmental Law Review* 587, 591.
80 See Shelton, 'Human rights and the environment' (n 42).
81 M Fitzmaurice, 'The right of the child to a clean environment' (1999) 23 *Southern Illinois University Law Journal* 611, 634 and 635.
82 Brice (n 79) 599.
83 CRC Committee, 'General Guidelines regarding the form and content of initial reports to be Submitted by States Parties under Article 44', paragraph 1(b) of the Convention on the Rights of the Child, UN Doc CRC/C/5/Rev. 2, para 23; the four general principles of the CRC are arts 2 (Non-discrimination), 3 (Best interest of the child), 6 (Right to life, survival and development) and 12 (Respect for the views of the child).
84 CRC art 6 provides that: '(1) States Parties recognize that every child has the inherent right to life; (2) States Parties shall ensure to the maximum extent possible the survival and development of the child'.
85 UNICEF, *Every Child Counts: The State of the World's Children 2014* (UNICEF 2014) www.unicef.org/sowc2014/numbers/ (last accessed 16 December 2016).
86 A Prüss-Ustün, J Wolf, C Corvalán, R Bos and M Neira, 'Preventing disease through health environments: a global assessment of the burden of disease from environmental risks' (World Health Organization 2016) 89–91, http://apps.who.int/iris/bitstream/10665/204585/1/9789241565196_eng.pdf?ua=1 (last accessed 16 December 2016).
87 CRC Committee, 'General Comment No 5: General Measures of Implementation of the Convention on the Rights of the Child (arts 4, 42 and 44, para 6)' UN Doc CRC/GC/2003/5, para 12 making clear that development is not restricted to physical development.
88 CRC Committee, 'General Comment No 16: State Obligations Regarding the Impact of the Business Sector on Children's Rights' UN Doc CRC/C/GC/16.
89 Children's rights may be violated by corporate activities through child labour where children may be exposed to environmental risks associated with dangerous

work. See e.g. Save the Children, 'Doing good work for us children: children and adolescent's contributions to the draft General Comment on Child Rights and Business Sector' (2012); ILO, *Children in Hazardous Work: What We Know, What We Do* (International Labour Organization 2011) www.ilo.org/ipec/informationresources/WCMS_156475/lang--en/index.htm (last accessed 16 December 2016).

90 See e.g. Save the Children (n 89) 13.

91 M Blaak, M Kaandorp, S Meuwese (eds), *Handboek Internationaal Jeugdrecht*, (Defense for Children 2012) 199.

92 A Eide, 'Article 24: the right to health' in A Alen, J Vande Lanotte, E Verhellen, F Ang, E Berghmans, M Verheyde and B Abramson (eds), *A Commentary on the United Nations Convention on the Rights of the Child* (Brill Nijhoff 2006).

93 W Vandenhole, J Vranken and K De Boyser (eds), *Why Care? Children's Rights and Child Poverty* (Intersentia 2010) 26–27.

94 A Bowers Andrews, N Hevener Kaufman, *Implementing the UN Convention on the Rights of the Child: A Standard of Living Adequate for Development* (Praeger Publishers 1999) 7.

95 WHO Europe, 'Environment and health risks: a review of the influence and effects of social inequities' Background document prepared for the Fifth Ministerial Conference on Environment and Health, Parma, Italy (10–12 March 2010).

96 Blaak and others (n 91) 425.

97 Jan C M Willems (ed), *Developmental and Autonomy Rights of Children: Empowering Children, Caregivers and Communities* (Intersentia 2002) 78: 'Holistic refers to both physical and psychological (i.e. emotional, social, moral and intellectual) development of the child, taking account of the child's cultural context'.

98 H Little, S Wyver, 'Outdoor play: does removing the risks reduce the benefits?' (2008) 33 *Australian Journal of Early Childhood* 33. See also Health Council of the Netherlands and the Dutch Advisory Council for Research on Spatial Planning, Nature and the Environment, 'Nature and health: the influence of nature on social, psychological and physical well-being' (2004) Health Council of the Netherlands and RMNO https://www.gezondheidsraad.nl/sites/default/files/Nature_and_health.pdf (last accessed 16 December 2016).

99 Stephan R Kellert, 'Nature and childhood development' in S Kellert, *Building for Life: Designing and Understanding the Human-Nature Connection* (Island Press 2005) 63–89.

100 A E van den Berg, C G van den Berg, 'A comparison of children with ADHD in a natural and built setting' (2011) 37 *Child: Care, Health and Development* 430–39 www.agnesvandenberg.nl/publicaties.html (last accessed 16 December 2016).

101 UNICEF, *The State of the World's Children* (n 25) 1, 3.

102 P David, 'Article 31: the right to leisure, play and culture' in Alen and others, *A Commentary on the United Nations Convention on the Rights of the Child* (Brill Nijhoff 2006), paras 5, 55.

103 ibid 23–24; see also J Van Gils, 'The child's right to play: the right to be a child' in A Alen, H Bosly, M De Bie, J Vande Lanotte, F Ang, I Delens-Ravier, M Delplace, C Herman, D Reynaert, V Staelens, R Steel and M Verheyde (eds), *The UN Children's Rights Convention: Theory Meets Practice* (Intersentia 2007) 363.

104 ibid para 42.

105 CRC Committee, 'General Comment No 17: The Right to Rest, Leisure, Play, Recreational Activities, Cultural Life and the Arts (article 31)' (2013)

UN Doc CRC/C/GC/17. In CRC Committee, 'General Comment No 7: Implementing Child Rights in Early Childhood' (2006) UN Doc CRC/C/GC/7, the Committee had already recognised that the right to play space is especially at risk in urban environments.

106 ibid part VI.

107 ibid part VI, B.

108 UNHCR, 'Knox Report' (n 67) paras 107–110.

109 CRC Committee, 'General Comment No 5' (n 87).

110 M Freeman, 'Article 3: the best interests of the child' in Alen and others, *A Commentary on the United Nations Convention on the Rights of the Child* (Brill Nijhoff 2006) 8.

111 ibid 9; see also Blaak and others (n 91) 145: 'The best interest of the child is one of the general principles which are fundamental for the implementation and interpretation of *all the other substantive articles of the CRC*'. Emphasis added. However, Detrick assumes that Article 3(1) is applicable in conjunction with each of the CRC's substantive provisions as well as with respect for actions that are not covered by express obligations pursuant to the CRC; see Detrick (n 65) 90.

112 ibid 40.

113 CRC Committee, 'General Comment No 5' (n 87), para E.

114 Articles 12 (Respect for the views of the child), 13 (Freedom of expression), 14 (Freedom of thought, belief and religion), 15 (Freedom of association), 16 (Right to privacy) and 17 (Access to information from mass media) CRC.

115 See also Hart's ladder of participation in R A Hart, 'Children's participation: from tokenism to citizenship' (Innocenti Essays No 4, United Nation's Children Fund 1992). Hart proposes 'The ladder of participation' representing eight levels of young people's participation in projects.

116 K Orama, 'Child-led organizations and the role of adult professionals: a quest for dialogue', Written contribution to Working Group 9: 'Child-led organizations: listened to and taken seriously?' for the Institute of Human Rights, Abo Akademi University (4 September 2009) on the occasion of the celebration of the 20th anniversary of the adoption of the CRC, Geneva (8–9 October 2009).

117 L Lundy, '"Voice" is not enough: conceptualising Article 12 of the United Nations Convention on the Rights of the Child' (2007) 33 *British Educational Research Journal* 927. Lundy proposes a model: 'Space, voice, audience and influence', which conceptualises the distinct facets of Article 12.

118 F Ang (ed), *Participation Rights of Children* (Intersentia 2006) 23.

119 UN Major Group for Children and Youth; the MGCY is the official voice for anyone under 30 in the sustainability negotiations. They are engaging with people from across the world to share their voices at the UN http://childrenyouth.org (last accessed 16 December 2016).

120 Roger A Hart, *Children's Participation: The Theory and Practice of Involving Young Citizens in Community Development and Environmental Care* (UNICEF/Earthscan 2002) 141–50.

14 Children's rights in business and human rights: from the sidelines to the centre field?

Gamze Erdem Türkelli

14.1 Introduction

We often speak of the human rights of children or 'children's human rights'[1] as a synonym for children's rights. In fact, the area of children's rights is best considered as a specialised field of human rights law to underscore its inherent place within the broader human rights landscape. However, normative discussions and developments in this broader landscape may not always find pathways into children's rights. This contribution focuses on the human rights and business aspect of the debate on transnational human rights obligations[2] in order to analyse and appraise whether the relationship between normative developments in the broader human rights landscape, on the one hand, and in the children's rights field, on the other, can be characterised by isolation, inspiration or integration.

The first section of the chapter presents the limited attention that children's rights have received in the broader debate on the human rights obligations of business enterprises, especially within the recent multilateral frameworks. Section 14.2 focuses on normative developments in children's rights and business that were inspired by the general human rights field as attested by the Children's Rights and Business Principles (CRBPs) initiative and the General Comment No 16 of the UN Committee on the Rights of the Child (CRC Committee). Section 14.3 tackles the issues of operationalisation of the recent frameworks and implementation of standards, both within the broader human rights landscape and within the specific area of children's rights, which occur often in isolation from one another. Section 14.4 focuses on the challenges and opportunities presented by normative developments in the field of business and human rights more broadly and children's rights specifically, as well as on the way forward. Section 14.5 concludes.

14.2 Situating children's rights in the business and human rights debate

The ever-expanding web of global economic, social and political transactions and connections, routinely termed 'globalisation', presents both practical and normative challenges to the way in which we conceptualise human rights. The challenges posed by globalisation are of course not confined to the field of human rights. The critical international relations theorist Robert W Cox has argued that globalisation is fuelled by the global economy, and the global production this economy depends on 'is able to make use of the territorial divisions of the international economy, playing off one territorial jurisdiction against another so as to maximize reductions in costs, savings in taxes, avoidance of anti-pollution regulation, control over labour, and guarantees of political stability and favour'.[3]

Even in the absence of a purposive manipulation of territorial jurisdictions by actors in the global economy, rights holders may still find themselves faced with serious legal difficulties when attempting to pursue the addressees of their human rights claims, in other words the human rights duty-bearers. Because globalisation has made it more convenient and at times more profitable for companies to set up different entities in different legal jurisdictions, it is not always clear at which level or by which entity a decision has been taken or to enforce claims against entities involved in cross-border transactions. These difficulties may often become insurmountable for those individuals, such as children, who are disadvantaged owing to de jure or de facto restrictions to exercise their rights even in the absence of challenges brought about by globalisation.

The characterisation of human rights law essentially as an interaction between an individual or a group and the relevant state on whose territory the individual or the group is found has become both outdated and conceptually untenable. Confining human rights obligations to territorial boundaries and to state actors serves to widen existing gaps in human rights protection.[4] As the International Law Association's Non-state Actors Committee concluded, albeit somewhat cautiously:

> Whether the attributes of international actors are called rights/obligations or expectations/claims, there is a need for clarity to improve understanding of the appropriate roles of all actors, state and non-State, active in the international legal plane and to improve their responsibility/accountability to the international community as a whole.[5]

In response to the recognition of 'an increasing need to attach *public law duties to ostensibly private actors*',[6] a growing number of scholars have been drawing attention to the necessity of widening the scope of international human rights law to include actors beyond territorial states.[7] Scholarship has mostly developed around issues and solutions from a general human rights perspective, while children's rights have remained relatively isolated on the sidelines.[8]

This multi duty-bearer framework would bring together the different state and non-state actors, including states in a territorial or extraterritorial capacity, international organisations and business enterprises as human rights duty-bearers.[9] In Koh's words, there is an attempt at least conceptually to 'organize the activities and relations of myriad transnational players, not simply nation-states, with the goal not of reflecting parochial state [and private[10]] interests, but of advancing an enlightened global system dedicated to the promotion of human dignity'.[11] This attempt of 'linking human rights with ethics and globalization'[12] has taken many forms, including numerous initiatives within international organisations and academic networks that gave birth to several soft law frameworks on transnational human rights obligations.[13]

Transnational human rights obligations as an overarching legal concept is relatively novel but global efforts seeking to regulate the behaviour of private actors, including most notably multi-national corporations (MNCs), are not. In fact, some of the most significant developments within the broader transnational human rights debate have taken place within the area of business and human rights. The early products of these regulatory efforts, the ILO Tripartite Declaration[14] and the OECD Guidelines for Multinational Enterprises,[15] date from the 1970s. Riding on the waves of anti-colonisation and development, these initiatives sought to shape business behaviour more towards developing states than as regards individuals.[16]

Respect for human rights was introduced in the process with the Draft Code of Conduct on Transnational Corporations (TNCs)[17] in the 1980s. However, it was not until the 1990s that the 'question of human rights responsibilities of TNCs [was] spectacularly revived'.[18] Although this revival coincides with the first decade of the Convention of the Rights of the Child (CRC), the major soft law frameworks born out of this revival have not integrated children's rights in any explicit way. In fact, children and their rights are comprised directly or indirectly by these frameworks but in a limited and non-specified fashion.

The following is an analysis of the extent to which and the grounds on which children and their rights feature in the two most widely referenced soft law frameworks on business and human rights, namely the UN Framework with its accompanying UN Guiding Principles (UNGPs) and the OECD Guidelines, as well as the business and human rights related statements of UN treaty bodies that do not exclusively focus on children's rights.[19]

14.2.1 UN Guiding Principles on Business and Human Rights

Unanimously endorsed by the UN Human Rights Council, the UN Framework and UN Guiding Principles on Business and Human Rights (UNGPs) have become important baseline references in the domain of business and human rights. The references in the UN Framework and the UNGPs to children or their rights are few and far between. The UN Framework does not refer explicitly to children or children's rights. The only reference to children's issues is found in a footnote to paragraph 83 of the Framework, which refers to treaty body recommendations to States on investigating and prosecuting corporate human rights abuses.[20] The related footnote refers to the recommendation of the CRC Committee to state parties to 'take measures, where appropriate and, subject to national law, to establish criminal, civil or administrative liability of legal persons for treaty offences' for domestic or transnational offences resulting in violations as set out under Article 3(4) of the Optional Protocol on the Sale of Children, Child Prostitution and Child Pornography (OPSC).[21]

Upon the presentation of the UN Framework, the Human Rights Council had requested the former Secretary-General's Special Representative for Business and Human Rights (SRSG) Ruggie also to 'integrate a gender perspective throughout his work and to give special attention to persons belonging to vulnerable groups, in particular children'.[22] The resulting UNGPs do not refer to children's rights directly but refer to children among 'individuals from groups or populations that may be at heightened risk of becoming vulnerable or marginalized'[23], who may require special attention in the implementation of the guidelines.[24] Under the Commentary to paragraph 3 on state duty to protect, there is a call on states to provide 'guidance to business enterprises on respecting human rights, . . . recognizing the specific challenges that may be faced by [inter alia] . . . children'.[25] Paragraph 12 on business responsibility to respect internationally recognised human rights entails the possibility (in its commentary) that additional standards may be applicable to business enterprises depending on circumstances. As such, other UN instruments on the rights of vulnerable groups, including children, such as the CRC, are implicitly referred to.[26] The UNGPs, however, do not include the almost universally ratified CRC among minimum contents of the business responsibility to respect human rights (Principle 12).[27]

Unlike previous initiatives at the UN such as the Draft Code of Conduct and the UN Norms, the UNGPs were able to achieve an inherently difficult consensus among states in the Human Rights Council over the minimum content and the scope of the regulation of corporate action with regards to human rights.[28] This accomplishment does not preclude that further reflection and critique are needed, for 'putting in place a robust framework regarding the human rights obligations of companies'.[29] The UN Framework and UNGPs are especially limited in three ways. Firstly, they fall short of reflecting the current state of international law and the most recent developments as regards state obligations in regulating the extraterritorial activities of business in their jurisdiction or domiciled in their territory.[30] Such obligations in fact exist under different international legal frameworks such as the CRC-OPSC (Article 3) and the Convention against Torture (Articles 4–9). Secondly, considering the UNGPs as 'the authoritative global reference point for business and human rights'[31] unduly constrains the public debate on direct business obligations by shying away from framing business duties as legal obligations and discounting that business may have a broader range of obligations than to respect human rights. Thirdly, the scope and content of relevant human rights obligations in the UNGPs fall short of reflecting human rights protection and realisation standards for persons or groups that may be disadvantaged, including children.

The UNGPs represent a milestone but not the last word on human rights obligations of business, as evidenced by the statement of the Government of Ecuador[32] and the subsequent proposal for an internationally binding instrument.[33] The highly divided vote by which the resolution for the elaboration of such an instrument was adopted points to tensions among the UN member states about the future of the business and human rights debate.[34] The concurrent acceptance of a more widely supported rival resolution in the Human Rights Council aiming to support the UNGPs[35] means that the inter-governmental work on the elaboration of an internationally binding instrument will run simultaneously with the implementation of the UNGPs.

14.2.2 OECD Guidelines for Multinational Enterprises

The OECD Guidelines for Multinational Enterprises, originally dating from 1976, have been called the 'only multilaterally agreed and comprehensive code of responsible business conduct that governments have committed to promoting'.[36] Non-binding in nature, the OECD Guidelines address multinational business enterprises that are operating in or from the territory of adhering States. The OECD Guidelines underwent their latest revision in 2011, introducing among other things a new chapter on human rights that incorporates the approach of the UN Framework and UNGPs. The OECD Guidelines' treatment of children's rights and children-related issues is considerably broader than that of the UNGPs.

The OECD Guidelines' new Chapter IV on Human Rights, paragraph 40 accepts that enterprises can have an impact on virtually the entire spectrum of internationally recognised human rights and that 'some human rights may be at greater risk than others in particular industries or contexts, and therefore will be the focus of heightened attention'.[37] Children are considered by the Guidelines to be among the more vulnerable persons whose rights may be at greater risk and who are protected through relevant UN human rights instruments.[38] In line with the UNGPs, the OECD Guidelines also stipulate that additional standards may be needed for 'specific groups or populations that require particular attention' including children.[39]

The OECD Guidelines additionally contain standards on child labour, calling on enterprises to 'contribute to the effective abolition of child labour, and take immediate and effective measures to secure the prohibition and elimination of the worst forms of child labour as a matter of urgency'.[40] Although the OECD Guidelines do not explicitly refer to children's rights, they do not limit the scope of children-related issues to child labour and children as vulnerable persons. In the Commentary to Chapter VIII on Consumer Interests, children are recognised as 'becoming increasingly significant forces in the market' and business enterprises are called on to 'apply fair business, marketing and advertising practices and to ensure the quality and reliability of the products that they provide'.[41] Indirectly, the chapeau of Chapter VIII on Consumer Interests evokes the right to health of adult and child consumers alike. The OECD Guidelines are far more explicit than the UNGPs in integrating children's rights into their general business and human rights framework. They are also more comprehensive in terms of the broader scope of the child-business relationship they recognise, extending beyond the emphasis on children as members of society with special or increased protection needs to include both child labour and children as consumer issues.

14.2.3 UN treaty bodies

UN treaty bodies have been illuminating different aspects of the business–human rights relationship for over two decades without specifically integrating children's rights. For instance, in its General Comment No 12 on the right to food (1999), the UN Committee on Economic, Social and Cultural Rights (ESCR Committee) concluded that different non-state actors including the 'private business sector' are responsible for the realisation of the right to adequate food alongside states.[42] General Comment No 12 also placed upon both the national and transnational private business sector the responsibility to 'pursue its activities within the framework of a code of conduct conducive to respect of the right to adequate food'.[43] The following year, the ESCR Committee published General Comment No 14 on the right to highest attainable standard of health, which noted that 'the private business sector [also] ha[s] responsibilities regarding the realization of the right to health'.[44] This General Comment mentioned the right to health of children in the context of the 'obligations of actors other than states parties' to flag the important role UNICEF plays in this regard.[45]

The ESCR Committee has most recently adopted General Comment No 23 on the right to just and favourable conditions of work (Art. 7 ICESCR). The General Comment notes that the 'prohibition of . . . social and economic exploitation of children and young persons' is included in the normative content of Article 7 ICESCR.[46] The General Comment goes on to note that specific legal measures such as increasing minimum ages for entry into employment in line with ILO Convention No 138 should be considered in order to protect the health and safety of young workers.[47]

14.3 A Specific business and children's rights focus

The children's rights sub-area of human rights is a relative newcomer to the thematic area of transnational human rights. Despite the obvious shortcomings of the UN Framework and UNGPs, as discussed above, they have created a hitherto unseen impetus fuelling further reflection on the human rights obligations of business. Keeping up the momentum, the children's rights obligations of business have moved from intermittent and highly limited presence in the public debate to the centre field. The need for a children's rights specific viewpoint on human rights obligations of business has been particularly well explained by the CRC Committee:

- Childhood is a unique period of physical, mental, emotional and spiritual development and violations of children's rights . . . may have life-long, irreversible and even trans-generational consequences.
- Children are often politically voiceless and . . . reliant on governance systems, over which they have little influence, to have their rights realised. . . .
- It is generally challenging for children to obtain remedy – whether in courts or other mechanisms – when their rights are infringed upon, even more so by business enterprises. . . .[48]

The developments in the broader human rights field have served as inspiration for initiatives on children's rights and business to counteract the long-term and possibly inter-generational effects of children's rights violations by business, given the relative disadvantage children experience when asserting their rights and seeking remedies.

14.3.1 Children's Rights and Business Principles

The Children's Rights and Business Principles (CRBPs) were launched by UNICEF, UN Global Compact and Save the Children on 12 March 2012. They respond to the absence of a 'child rights perspective [that is] explicitly addressed' in the business and human rights agenda.[49] By using children's rights and human rights of children as synonyms, the CRBPs seek to mainstream children's rights within the broader heading of human rights. The process culminating in the UNGPs heavily inspired the development of the CRBPs. In fact, an approach similar to the one taken by SRSG Ruggie was adopted, whereby a multi-stakeholder consultation process was undertaken, lasting over three months and involving not only business, civil society, experts, and government representatives but also children.[50] Once the multi-stakeholder consultation process and research culminated in the draft CRBPs, these draft principles were opened up for written and online consultation, again following a similar trajectory to the public consultation processes launched by the SRSG on the draft Framework and the draft UNGPs. The major difference between the two processes was the inclusion of children directly as stakeholders in the multi-stakeholder consultation process for the CRBPs. On the basis of a child participation strategy developed by Save the Children and Plan International, over 400 children between the ages 7 and 17 in nine countries were consulted.[51]

The CRBPs draw heavily on the normative content of the UN Framework and UNGPs, both in terms of the so-called 'differentiated but complementary responsibilities' of States and business enterprises and in terms of the proposed recommendations to business enterprises. Clearly inspired by the UN Framework and UNGPs, the CRBPs depart from the notion that states have the primary duty to protect, respect and fulfil children's rights at all levels and go on to state that 'all societal actors, including business, must comply with applicable national law and respect international standards on children's rights'.[52] The CRBPs reference the ILO Conventions No 138 on Minimum Age and No 182 on the Worst Forms of Child Labour in addition to the CRC and its Optional Protocols as documents embodying these international standards. [53] The CRBPs explicitly reiterate, echoing the UNGPs, that they reflect the internationally recognised human rights of children and do not impose new international legal obligations.[54]

The 10 principles of the CRBPs are depicted in a circular fashion, centred on the first principle relating to children's rights integration. Principle 1 on children's rights integration starts out by specifying the 'core principles underpinning children's rights', namely 'the best interests of the child, non-discrimination, child-participation, and survival and development'.[55] Around this core, children's rights at the workplace,[56] the marketplace[57] and within the community and environment[58] are situated. Consequently, the CRBPs showcase the broader scope of the child–business relationship beyond the important but very limited aspect of child labour.[59] The concepts of 'policy commitment', 'human rights due diligence' and 'remediation' are directly imported from the UNGPs.[60] They denote the type of policies and processes incumbent on all business enterprises in meeting their respective responsibilities under the principle of children's rights integration. In the context of the CRBPs, a 'policy commitment' clarifies the business's responsibility to respect human rights including children's rights along with expectations from personnel, business partners and other business liaisons.[61] It is interesting that the policy commitment does not extend to the development and implementation of a child protection code of conduct, which is listed among voluntary actions under Principle 4.

Human rights due diligence as a broader concept was laid out by the UNGPs[62] and is modified by the CRBPs as 'a business's ongoing processes for assessing its actual and potential human rights impact, including on children's rights'.[63] This impact analysis entails the following measures: identifying and assessing actual or potential adverse impact on children's rights, integrating these findings across all relevant internal functions and processes and ceasing/preventing/mitigating adverse impact, and monitoring and tracking the effectiveness of the business responses.[64] The CRBPs do not specify what actions amount to effective due diligence for adverse impacts but urge companies to consider such options as 'performance contracts and reviews, surveys and audits (self-assessments or independent audits) on a periodic basis'.[65]

In the event that a business enterprise is found to have caused adverse children's rights impacts, it should act to 'counteract, or make good' these impacts, through 'effective operational level grievance mechanisms or judicial mechanisms'.[66] The CRBPs refer to the UNGPs for non-judicial grievance mechanism effectiveness criteria.[67] Remediation should additionally be based on 'child-sensitive processes'.[68]

The CRBPs organise business action with respect to children's rights in two categories: the corporate responsibility to respect, and the corporate commitment to support.[69] The corporate responsibility to respect is a minimum requirement incumbent on businesses and is applicable to a business's own activities as well as dealings with other parties regarding its operations, products or services. In this way, global supply chains as well as value chains are incorporated into the framework. As in the case of the UNGPs, the corporate responsibility to respect children's rights and human rights is defined in a negative way as avoiding infringement on the human rights of others, including children, and addressing any adverse impacts that business activities might cause. The corporate commitment to support comprises voluntary actions to support children's rights through 'core business activities, strategic social investments and philanthropy, advocacy and public policy engagement, and working in partnership and other collective action', which 'are strongly encouraged even if not required'.[70]

The distinction between the corporate responsibility to respect and the corporate commitment to support may be viewed as a scale of involvement.

As such, the commitment to support in the CRBPs goes beyond refraining from doing harm, entails more active involvement and may include what are deemed 'positive obligations'. The portrayal of this more active involvement not as a responsibility but as a commitment of voluntary nature strongly echoes the UNGPs, which state that companies 'may have additional responsibilities' complementing the baseline expectation to respect when 'they have undertaken additional commitments voluntarily'.[71] Although the CRBPs do not advance business obligations by framing positive involvement as a voluntary 'commitment', the notion of 'support' nonetheless goes beyond the responsibility to respect in the UNGPs. The CRBPs are a clear indication that children's rights have taken inspiration from the general human rights field and integrated many of its concepts, such as due diligence, policy commitment and remediation, in developing a children's rights-centred approach.

14.3.2 CRC Committee General Comment No 16

During roughly the same time period as the launch of the CRBPs and building on the same momentum, the CRC Committee was working on a general comment on the issue of business and children's rights. A decade before releasing this general comment, the CRC Committee had invoked children's rights and responsibilities of non-state actors at its 2002 General Day of Discussion, referring to the ESCR Committee's General Comment No 14. The CRC Committee concluded that the 'responsibilities to respect and ensure the rights of children extend beyond the State, including individuals, parents, legal guardians and other non-state actors'.[72]

The Committee issued its General Comment No 16 on state obligations regarding the impact of the business sector on children's rights on 17 April 2013. General Comment No 16 has given further institutional legitimacy to the move of children's rights to the forefront of the business and human rights debate, given that over the years the legal status of general comments 'has grown beyond a mere technical recommendation into an authoritative source of interpretation'.[73]

The Committee is only mandated to address state parties but General Comment No 16 nonetheless speaks to the question of direct obligations of business enterprises by underlining that businesses have duties and responsibilities to respect children's rights, even in the absence of a specific treaty to that effect.

At this juncture, there is no international legally binding instrument on the business sector's responsibilities vis-à-vis human rights. However, the Committee *recognises* that duties and responsibilities to respect the rights of children extend in practice beyond the state and state-controlled services and institutions and apply to private actors and business enterprises.[74] Therefore, all businesses must meet their responsibilities regarding children's rights and states must ensure they do so. In addition, business enterprises should not undermine the states' ability to meet their obligations towards children under the Convention and the Optional Protocols thereto.[75]

The Committee calls on States to 'require businesses to undertake child-rights due diligence . . . [to] identify, prevent and mitigate their impact on children's rights including across their business relationships and within global operations'.[76] Like the CRBPs, the General Comment gives a children's rights context to the due diligence requirement borrowed from the UN Framework. General Comment No 16 reaches further than both the UNGPs and the CRBPs, holding that states should impose stricter due diligence and monitoring requirements on business where there is a high risk of involvement in children's rights violations.[77] General Comment No 16 also concludes that large businesses should be encouraged and even required publicly to disclose their children's rights impact assessments as a part of their due diligence efforts.[78]

General Comment No 16 makes an overture by underlining that the 'Convention does not limit a State's jurisdiction to "territory"',[79] thus allowing a response to impacts caused by transnational operations of business that may not be attributable to a single legal entity located in a single jurisdiction. By accommodating the extraterritorial application of state obligations, General Comment No 16 defines a state's obligation to respect, protect and fulfil to encompass all children in its territory as well as all subject to its jurisdiction.[80] General Comment No 16 specifies, for instance, that extraterritorial criminal jurisdiction is envisaged under Article 3 of the CRC-OPSC.[81] It recognises that it may be difficult for states parties to discharge of their duties to respect, protect and fulfil children's rights when businesses are legally separated, incorporated in one jurisdiction and operating in yet another.[82] The General Comment designates host states as primary duty-bearers that are required to regulate all business enterprises (domestic or transnational) within their borders to prevent adverse impacts by business enterprises.[83] Accordingly, home states of transnational business enterprises too are duty-bearers as regards the extraterritorial activities of business enterprises, provided that there is a 'reasonable link' between the state and the business it is seeking to regulate.[84]

General Comment No 16 points to the complex business networks on the global scale, noting that business impacts on children's rights are 'rarely the result of the action or omission of a single business unit, whether it is the parent company, subsidiary, contractor, supplier or other'.[85] The document also underscores the need for child-sensitive procedures for remediation, given the difficulties that children and their families might face when attempting to access remediation processes in a context of complex global operations undertaken by transnational corporations.[86]

Like the CRBPs, the CRC Committee's General Comment No 16 reflects the influence of developments in the general human rights field on the normative frameworks informing children's rights. However, whereas the CRBP's relationship to the UNGPs ranges between inspiration and integration, the CRC Committee's General Comment represents a critical appraisal of the UNGPs and a differentiated outlook on business obligations, based specifically on the CRC and its Optional Protocols. The CRC Committee's legal interpretation of the business and human rights landscape is more attuned to the human rights challenges that business' activities present on the ground, including the need for child-sensitive procedures and processes and the questions of extra-territoriality.

14.4 Operationalising business obligations

Neither international human rights commitments nor soft law norms set through various frameworks have tangible value unless they are translated into action. Without operationalisation and consequent implementation, human rights standards cannot provide human rights protection in an effective and meaningful way. Reporting requirements under international human rights treaties, the elaboration of General Comments and Concluding Observations by human rights treaty bodies, the establishment of individual communications procedures and, finally, the establishment of international courts and tribunals all point to the indispensability of upholding principles through operationalisation and implementation. This is especially important in the case of voluntary commitments and non-binding principles such as the UNGPs and CRBPs that 'do not themselves create a system of monitoring and enforcement. As such, businesses do not necessarily have to accept the comprehensive standards they establish, and are not required to report on the extent to which they do or do not abide by [these] norms'.[87]

Owing to the differences in authorship, audience and ownership, the implementation of the frameworks on business and human rights and on business and children's rights respectively, take place in isolation from one another. In fact, even within the general human rights field and within the children's rights field, the different frameworks are not implemented in a coordinated fashion. Both the UNGPs and the OECD Guidelines were authored within intergovernmental organisations and subsequently endorsed by states. The implementation therefore rests largely on state action, with guidance and facilitation of the relevant organisation. General Comment No 16 too is addressed to state parties and the CRC Committee, as its author, acts as a point of reference and guidance. The CRBPs, on the other hand, are born out of a private initiative of a UN agency, an NGO and a business platform and address businesses directly. As such, their implementation is spearheaded by UNICEF and supported by the UN Global Compact and Save the Children, and will depend on the willingness of business partners.

14.4.1 Operationalising the general business and human rights frameworks

14.4.1.1 UN Guiding Principles

The United Nations Working Group on the issue of human rights and transnational corporations and other business enterprises (UN WG) was established in June 2011[88] for the implementation of the UNGPs.[89] The UN WG is tasked with, inter alia:

- promot[ing] the effective and comprehensive dissemination and implementation of the Guiding Principles
- identif[ying], exchang[ing] and promot[ing] good practices and lessons learned on the implementation of the Guiding Principles
- provid[ing] support for efforts to promote capacity building and the use of the Guiding Principles.[90]

The UN WG also liaises with national bodies in order to contribute to the development of national action plans to implement the UNGPs. The UN WG published its guidance to states in the preparation of national action plans (NAPs) in December 2014.[91] The UN WG specified four essential criteria for effective NAPs:

1. NAPs need to be founded on the UN Guiding Principles
2. NAPs need to be context-specific and address the country's actual and potential adverse corporate human rights impacts
3. NAPs need to be developed in inclusive and transparent processes
4. NAP processes need to regularly be reviewed and updated.[92]

The guidance, like the UNGPs, situates children within the broader list of groups more vulnerable to corporate human rights abuses.[93] It calls on states to invite representatives of these groups, including children, as stakeholders in the process of the elaboration of the NAPs.[94] In addition to their participation as stakeholders, the guidance recommends that states support processes within UN bodies aimed at strengthening the rights of these groups[95] and guarantee the same level of legal protection to these groups and their representatives when providing remedies through state-based judicial mechanisms.[96] The UN WG also invites states to eliminate legal barriers to effective remedy inter alia by providing 'tailored assistance' specifically to children.[97] In addition, it states that governments should consider 'ensuring that the national legal framework requires business enterprises to respect children's rights' including the CRC Committee's General Comment No 16 to address gaps in domestic legal frameworks.[98] Through the Guidance of the UN WG, children's rights have made their way into the implementation of the UNGPs, at least nominally.

The elaboration of NAPs in response to the UNGPs has been a relatively slow process thus far. Fewer than 35 states have prepared or are in the process of preparing NAPs. The existing NAPs vary considerably in terms of their specific content and format. An initial analysis of the NAPs with regards to how they invoke children's rights reveals that children are generally mentioned either within the context of groups who are more vulnerable to violations and marginalisation[99] or in reference to child labour.[100] The CRBPs are also invoked in the context of initiatives on business and human rights with possibilities of incorporation into the broader framework provided by the UNGPs.[101] The Italian NAP lists 'children's rights' as an international priority area of the country[102] and explicitly incorporates a sub-heading of 'Children's Rights' under 'Labour and Equal Opportunities

Policies' of the NAP.[103] In its NAP, Finland has committed to reporting on the implementation to the CRC Committee, as well as to providing Finnish and Swedish translations of General Comment No 16 for public use with a summary to be distributed inter alia to business enterprises.[104] The NAP of Sweden highlights the work of the Ombudsman for Children in Sweden, based on monitoring compliance with the CRC.[105] The NAP of Lithuania is the only one without any references to children, child labour or children's rights.[106] Notwithstanding the UN WG guidance, the content and scope of the NAPs are ultimately left to the discretion of the UN member states.

There are other avenues being explored within the UN system for the implementation of the UNGPs besides the NAPs. On the practical side, the UN Office of the High Commissioner for Human Rights (OHCHR) published a guide in 2012 providing extensive guidance on the practical meaning of each principle in a business context all the while recognising that further work should go into preparing operational guidelines, which 'will vary depending on the sector, operating context and other factors'.[107] The UN Global Compact and the OHCHR responded to the need for a general familiarisation tool for businesses by creating the human rights and business learning tool. This tool is a web-based course consisting of five modules and a self-assessment test for company managers and personnel to understand the importance and relevance of human rights to their work.[108]

The longer term vision centres on incorporating the business and human rights agenda in the 'broader mainstreaming of human rights in the United Nations system'.[109] The major hurdle in realising this vision is the 'lack of capacity [not just in the UN system but also] among States, business enterprises, national human rights institutions and other actors' to implement the business and human rights agenda.[110] To overcome this challenge, UN institutions and agencies such as the OHCHR, the Food and Agriculture Organization of the United Nations (FAO) and UNICEF have been working on enhancing their human resources for internal capacity-building purposes.[111] Furthermore, the Secretary-General has tabled the idea for the establishment of a global fund on business and human rights to meet the financial challenges of capacity building at the stakeholder level.[112]

A study on the feasibility of such a global fund for capacity building was undertaken at the request of the Human Rights Council, exploring the practicalities relating to multi-stakeholder engagement, governance models and funding options for the proposed fund.[113] Based on stakeholder views as well as a review of existing UN voluntary funds,[114] with a particular focus on the more recent ones,[115] the study drew attention to convergence among stakeholders on the usefulness of the proposed fund and the importance of adequate safeguards for legitimacy and independence (transparency of donations and allocation of funds to projects).[116] There were, however, visible differences of opinion on the 'fund's mandate, criteria for eligibility and governance models'.[117] The Human Rights Council has mandated the OHCHR to engage in consultations with States and relevant stakeholders to inform the final decision on the creation of the proposed fund.[118]

14.4.1.2 OECD Guidelines

The OECD Guidelines require adhering states to set up national contact points (NCPs), which are tasked with implementing the guidelines, including through awareness raising and promotional activities, handling of enquiries and acting as a grievance mechanism for the non-observance of the guidelines.[119] The grievance mechanism requires that the NCPs resolve issues arising from the implementation of the OECD Guidelines 'in a manner that is impartial, predictable, equitable and compatible with the principles and standards of the Guidelines'.[120] Communications can be brought before the NCPs by the business community, worker organisations, non-governmental organisations (NGOs) and other stakeholders.[121] As a rule of procedure, the NCPs are required to assess whether the instances 'merit further examination' and if so, to 'offer good offices to help the parties involved to resolve the issues'.[122] Since 2000, when the NCP mechanism was established, human rights-related instances have made up 27 per cent of the total instances (around 360) submitted to NCPs.[123] The children's rights related instances have thus far included issues such as child and forced labour[124] and the sale of powdered milk to developing countries.[125]

While the implementation of the UNGPs has concentrated on state regulation through NAPs, the OECD has been focusing on developing sector-specific initiatives to complement its Guidelines. The OECD 'Due Diligence Guidance for Responsible Supply Chains of Minerals from Conflict-affected and High-risk Areas' was developed to assist companies in due diligence reporting in the specific area.[126] This voluntary guidance includes several references to the importance of due diligence in ascertaining that sourcing of minerals does not contribute to abusive practices including the worst forms of child labour.[127] The 'OECD Due Diligence Guidance for Meaningful Stakeholder Engagement in the Extractives Sector' (oil, gas, mining) was approved by the OECD Investment Committee and OECD Working Party for Responsible Business Conduct on 4 December 2015.[128] This document calls for the 'prioritization of most severely impacted and vulnerable groups in stakeholder engagement activities (e.g. women, children, indigenous peoples)' as they are less likely to have opportunities to influence decision-making.[129] The document also recognises that overlapping vulnerabilities to adverse impacts may result for indigenous children or female children as a result of belonging to more than one group at risk of marginalisation.[130]

A similar note on indigenous children is included in the joint 'FAO-OECD Guidance for Responsible Agricultural Supply Chains', which was adopted in March 2016.[131] In addition, this joint FAO–OECD Guidance refers to the effective abolition of child labour in the agricultural sector.[132] At the same time, OECD has been working on developing guidance for responsible supply chains and due diligence in the garment and footwear sector.[133] This initiative has resulted in a draft 'Due Diligence Guidance for Responsible Supply Chains in the Garment and Footwear Sector', which concentrates heavily on the prevention of child labour that is hazardous or in its worst forms.[134]

14.4.2 Operationalising business and children's rights frameworks

14.4.2.1 Children's Rights and Business Principles

The UNICEF Corporate Social Responsibility team acts as the focal point for the operationalisation of the CRBPs. UNICEF's patronage for the implementation of children's rights and business standards contained in the CRBPs has benefits over setting up an ad hoc or project-based institution: UNICEF is a highly specialised and permanent organisation and lends the initiative not only credibility but also a stable network of institutional partners, specialist staff and adequate infrastructure. As such, UNICEF has the potential to become the 'one stop shop' for governments, local civil society organisations and businesses in the implementation of children's rights and business standards.

The CRBPs are directly addressed to companies and therefore, unlike the UNGPs, their operationalisation is not linked to state action. To respond to practical challenges of implementation, UNICEF has developed a toolkit for companies looking to incorporate the CRBPs in collaboration with several non-profit organisations. In this effort, '45 companies from 25 countries' participated in the pilot of the toolkit.[135] The toolkit includes a workbook on operationalising the principles, a guide on conducting children's rights impact assessments, a guide on children's rights in sustainability reporting, a guide for integrating children's rights into the policies and codes of conduct and a guide on stakeholder engagement.[136] The impact assessment tool fleshes out a total of 58 'primary criteria' under each of the principles and the actions that need to be taken in order for the criteria to be fulfilled.[137]

The guide on sustainability reporting uses the Global Reporting Initiative (GRI) tools as benchmarks to report and disclose on children's rights since 'reporting and disclosure on children's rights-related issues (beyond child labour) is significantly underdeveloped'.[138] In this way, another 'external' tool, this time not from the broader human rights field but from the sustainability field, is integrated into the CRBPs.[139] The guide on policy commitments for children's rights identifies under each of the principles how businesses can integrate children's rights into their general human rights commitments in existing policies and codes of conduct.[140] The final tool provides guidance to companies on how to engage stakeholders on children's rights.[141] UNICEF has started directly engaging companies in five priority sectors including extractives, ICT, travel and tourism, food and beverages, and consumer goods.[142]

Another proposed initiative of UNICEF is called the UNICEF Corporate Lab, which aims to bring together businesses, children's rights and sustainability experts as well as government representatives in support of the implementation of the CRBPs. The proposed platform will allow companies 'to develop guidance and metrics that will enable a wider roll-out and implementation' of the CRBPs globally and also undertake country-based work 'to drive measurable results for children on issues and in countries and/or regions of interest to Corporate Lab participants'.[143] UNICEF's existing partners will be prioritised in the selection of participating companies, which are to represent various industries, sub-sectors and countries.[144] The platform is expected to be instrumental in the development of industry-specific guidance for companies operating in different sectors[145] as well as 'business-led action plans to address the most material child rights challenges', including key performance indicators for monitoring the progress and impact of specific projects.[146]

UNICEF's partners in the development of the CRBPs have also taken steps to assist in their implementation. Save the Children issued a guidebook for civil society organisations, whose involvement is deemed crucial in ensuring the effectiveness of the principles. Accordingly, civil society organisations should focus their work in four areas: guidance, enforcement, monitoring and advancement of the CRBPs, while promoting the participation of children in all matters that relate to them.[147] The UN Global Compact, on the other hand, released best practice examples for each principle for putting the CRBPs into practice.[148]

14.4.2.2 General Comment No 16

Concluding observations of the CRC Committee in response to state reporting are the main venue for putting General Comment No 16 into practice. Since its release, several concluding observations have explicitly referenced General Comment No 16 under the section on 'Children's rights and the business sector'.[149] In fact, the CRC Committee had integrated the UN Protect, Respect, Remedy Framework into its concluding observations even before the release of the General Comment.[150] It has raised concerns in its concluding observations about the violation of human rights and children's rights by companies abroad,[151] about children's right to health being adversely affected by coal emissions[152] and lead poisoning[153] and about the impacts of extractive industries and forestry on children in the absence of adequate impact assessments.[154] In addition to the work of the CRC Committee, UNICEF has published two documents in partnership with NGOs to make General Comment No 16 more accessible. The first document addresses state parties aiming to put General Comment No 16 into practice,[155] whereas the second one is a so-called 'plain language' version of the General Comment for the general public.[156]

14.5 The challenges, the opportunities and the future

14.5.1 General human rights frameworks

The debate about the human rights obligations of business is far from resolved. The ongoing exploration on a binding treaty signals that the normative assertions of the UN Framework and UNGPs effectively discounting the existence of binding business obligations are being contested not only by civil society and academics but also by a number of states. This contestation will be pivotal in evaluating whether the UN Framework 'underestimates (. . . intentionally or not) what is required to push corporate responsibility for human rights beyond due diligence processes and the redress of individual grievances'.[157] Clearly, the business obligations debate will be a highly divided one, with the proponents of a binding treaty on one side and those in favour of implementing the UNGPs as existing standards on another.

Even for those in favour of the existing standards, the coordinated and uniform implementation of the UNGPs across different states is an apparent challenge. Although former SRSG Ruggie has welcomed the work of different stakeholders and institutions on the operationalisation of the UNGPs, he also flagged the potential hazard of divergent interpretations that could undermine the convergence attained with the UNGPs.[158] This hazard is also present in the implementation of the OECD Guidelines, especially with regard to the outcome of specific instances at different NCPs. As underscored by Larry Catá Backer, '[a]t some point it will be necessary to order this heterodox and polycentric operation – not necessarily to unify it, but to ensure substantial coordination with a necessary flexibility'.[159] Given the different directions states have taken with the NAPs, it is questionable whether this coordination can ever be achieved.

The process of crafting a binding treaty on business and human rights, no matter the outcome, will be crucial in determining the direction in which the current debate evolves. The danger of the UN Framework 'becom[ing] the basis for a lukewarm, even counter-productive, set of practices around business and human rights'[160] can only be thwarted if the normative groundwork on business and human rights, including the human rights of children, is further strengthened. In this rapidly changing area of the law, challenging the former SRSG's 'principled pragmatism'[161] may in fact serve to clarify the existing human rights obligations of business and achieve a more inclusive vision on business obligations that incorporates the rights of disadvantaged persons and groups.

14.5.2 Children's rights specific frameworks

Two important studies by the Global Child Forum on children's rights and the corporate sector[162] carried out following the release of the CRBPs have identified a number of challenges in putting children's rights and business initiatives into practice. Firstly, child labour is still the first and sometimes only aspect of the business–children relationship taken into account by business enterprises.[163] Secondly, although companies have become more attuned to demands on general human rights, children's rights do not in any prominent way feature in their current thinking.[164] Thirdly, business enterprises cite international labour standards and the UN Global Compact principles in lieu of international human rights conventions when referencing international standards on children's rights.[165] Fourthly, even though international human rights treaties and principles such as the CRBPs are not well known, the UN Global Compact, UNICEF and Save the Children – the three organisations that developed the CRBPs – enjoy a degree of familiarity with business enterprises and investors.[166]

There are two alternative interpretations for these findings. The more cynical perspective would dictate that the lack of a holistic view of children's rights on the part of the business enterprises and the limited focus on children's rights is attributable to a lack of interest on the part of these businesses to meaningfully engage with children's rights. Similarly, equating international standards on children's and human rights to the UN Global Compact principles and ILO conventions would be deemed a move to circumvent international human rights law in order to be held to less comprehensive standards.

From a more optimistic perspective, on the other hand, one might consider the focus on child labour as the 'first step through the door' and an opportunity for introducing businesses to children's rights in a comprehensive fashion. Similarly, perceiving international labour standards and principles of the UN Global Compact as international standards on human rights may simply amount to a knowledge gap on the part of managers and personnel of business enterprises, perpetuated by a business culture that places emphasis solely on tasks related to corporate performance in terms of profits and production or services outputs. In addition, companies may employ legal personnel who are experts in corporate law, trade law or tax law but who may lack a perspective of public international law and human rights law, thereby creating a de facto omission of these fields in corporate legal exercises. The reality is most likely a mixture of the more cynical and the more optimistic interpretations. Accordingly, there are opportunities to be seized and dangers to be avoided when operationalising frameworks on business and human rights, including those on the rights of children.

14.5.3 The way forward

Children's rights were on the sidelines of the debate on the human rights obligations of business until recently. Developments in the broader business and human rights agenda have acted as inspiration, creating a momentum and interest in bringing children's rights into the centre field. The infusion of norms and standards from the broader human rights field into children's rights has not gone without critical and selective appraisal. In reality, the process of introducing children's rights to the debate on the human rights obligations of business has been a mixture of inspiration and integration. While children's rights initiatives have retained what are deemed to be the distinctive features of children's rights, including its general principles, some tools and concepts from the broader human rights field such as due diligence, policy commitment, impact assessment requirements and stakeholder engagement have been integrated directly, without modification.

The momentum on children's rights and business has not yet been translated into a tangible integration of children's rights into the broader human rights discussions on transnational obligations in a meaningful way. Going forward, the debate on the human rights obligations of business should seek to incorporate insights and guidance from children's rights (and other specialised fields of human rights) for conceptual, policy and implementation reasons. As the proposal and the preparations for elaborating an internationally binding instrument on the human rights obligations of business enterprises demonstrate, the tensions surrounding the debate on business obligations for human rights are far from resolved. Conceptually, human rights are a broader umbrella, including the rights of more disadvantaged persons or groups such as children, the disabled, indigenous peoples and others. Given the 'in progress' nature of the transnational human rights obligations landscape, the explicit incorporation of the special entitlements and enhanced protection requirements for these persons or groups in the broader human rights framework will create synergies for effectively realising their rights. For instance, children's rights, if meaningfully integrated in the broader human rights field, may lead to new opportunities for business action going beyond the 'do no harm' axiom.

Guidance of the CRC Committee about the duties of private actors, as set out in its General Comments, Concluding Observations and General Days of Discussion, could be instrumental in clarifying the human rights obligations of the private sector. This guidance may act, in turn, as inspiration for the general human rights field in conceptualising obligations beyond state borders and the regulation of extraterritorial activities of business enterprises.[167] Furthermore, human rights principles such as the right to meaningful participation and the prohibition of discrimination are important in the articulation of the rights of all, especially those, including children, who are at risk of marginalisation. It is all the more crucial that conceptual integration takes place while the field is proverbially still under construction, inter alia through negotiations on a binding treaty, the development of jurisprudence and scholarship.

The existing norms and frameworks on business and human rights will continue to be at the heart of policy-making and implementation efforts, despite the fact that the normative debate has not reached finality. From a policy perspective, integration of children's rights principles and tools in the business and human rights frameworks would provide further clarity for rights-holders and create expediency effects for duty-bearers. Rights holders, children and adults alike would be able to advance their human rights claims with regards to business activities and operations using a common framework and shared implementation mechanisms. Thus far, children's rights have integrated insights and tools from the broader human rights field. It may be time to reverse the trend and feature children's rights in the general human rights frameworks more prominently. In practical terms, this would amount to recognising children's rights explicitly within state policies on business regulation including through NAPs or through the work of NCPs and within business' own human rights policies, for instance, in a separate sub-section. General Comment No 16, the CRBPs and guidance documents on these two frameworks should serve to illuminate how children's rights can be practically incorporated into existing policies or upcoming policy-making processes on human rights and business.

By the same token, incorporating children's rights tools and principles in human rights impact assessments, due diligence and reporting procedures would reduce transaction costs for companies, avoid duplication and allow for a more comprehensive analysis of the human rights and children's rights effects of business activities. Such implementation tools would accordingly also focus on the entire range of children's rights, moving beyond addressing only child labour. In addition, remediation procedures would be crafted in child-sensitive ways to ensure that children are not de facto or de jure barred from these processes based on their age, and that their best interests are taken into account.[168] If children's rights principles and tools are not incorporated in the broader human rights and business framework, this may result in divergent interpretations and applications in the two fields. Further complicating the outlook is the peril of a 'pick and choose' approach to implementation.

Frameworks such as the UNGPs, the OECD Guidelines and the CRBPs – by virtue of their expressly voluntary nature – already present the danger that what should be considered human rights obligations would dissolve into corporate social responsibility schemes. A more holistic approach to the human rights obligations of business, one that integrates insights, principles and tools from children's rights to provide children's rights-sensitive implementation and child-sensitive procedures, is both a functional necessity and a moral responsibility for empowering children alongside adults as rights holders.

Notes

1 UNICEF, The Global Compact and Save the Children, 'Children's Rights and Business Principles (CRBPs)' (2012) 12 www.unicef.org/csr/css/PRINCIPLES_23_02_12_FINAL_FOR_PRINTER.pdf (last accessed 17 December 2016).

2 Transnational human rights obligations are defined for the purposes of this chapter as the human rights obligations of actors other than the domestic/territorial state and thus include the human rights obligations of extraterritorial states and non-state actors.

3 R W Cox, 'Global perestroika' (1992) 28 *Socialist Register* 26, 30.

4 Maastricht Principles enumerate these gaps as follows:

- the lack of human rights regulation and accountability of transnational corporations (TNCs)
- the absence of human rights accountability of intergovernmental organisations (IGOs), in particular international financial institutions (IFIs)
- the ineffective application of human rights law to investment and trade laws, policies and disputes
- the lack of implementation of duties to protect and fulfil ESCRs abroad, inter alia through the obligations of international cooperation and assistance (ETO Consortium, 'Maastricht Principles on Extraterritorial Obligations in the area of Economic, Social and Cultural Rights' (2011) www.etoconsortium.org/nc/en/library/maastricht-principles/?tx_drblob_pi1[downloadUid]=23 (last accessed 17 December 2016)).

5 Non-state Actors Committee, *First Report of the Committee, Non-state Actors in International Law: Aims, Approach and Scope of Project and Legal Issues* (2010) International Law Association 24 www.ila-hq.org/download.cfm/docid/7EFF9EAA-D573-441E-A40C8D2FB7740C6A (last accessed 17 December 2016).

6 H H Koh, 'Is there a "new" New Haven School of International Law?' (2007) 32 *Yale Journal of International Law* 559, 569 (original emphasis).

7 See inter alia R Higgins, *Problems and Process: International Law and How We Use It* (Oxford University Press 1994); S Skogly, *The Human Rights Obligations of*

the World Bank and IMF (Cavendish 2001); N Jägers, *Corporate Human Rights Obligations: In Search of Accountability* (Intersentia 2002); P Alston (ed), *Non-state Actors and Human Rights* (Oxford University Press 2005); A Clapham, *Human Rights Obligations of Non-state Actors* (Oxford University Press 2006); O de Schutter (ed), *Transnational Companies and Human Rights* (Hart 2006); M E Salomon, A Tostensen and W Vandenhole (eds), *Casting the Net Wider: Human Rights, Development and New Duty-bearers* (Intersentia 2007); H J Steiner, P Alston and R Goodman (eds), *International Human Rights in Context: Law, Politics, Morals* (3rd edn, Oxford University Press 2008); D D Bradlow, D B Hunter (eds), *International Financial Institutions and International Law* (Kluwer 2010); A McBeth, *International Economic Actors and Human Rights* (Routledge 2010); A Clapham (ed), *Human Rights and Non-state Actors* (Edward Elgar 2013); M Gibney, W Vandenhole (eds), *Litigating Transnational Human Rights Obligations: Alternative Judgments* (Routledge 2014).

8 There is nevertheless noteworthy scholarship attempting to highlight children's rights issues, especially as regards their economic, social and cultural rights; see e.g. W Vandenhole, 'Economic, social and cultural rights in the CRC: is there a legal obligation to cooperate for development?' (2009) 17 *International Journal of Children's Rights* 23; M N Wabwile, *Legal Protection of Social and Economic Rights of Children in Developing Countries: Reassessing International Cooperation and Responsibility* (Intersentia 2010).

9 Other duty-bearers may be intergovernmental organisations, armed groups, NGOs and individuals. See W Vandenhole, G E Türkelli and R Hammonds, 'Reconceptualizing human rights duty-bearers' in A Mihr, M Gibney (eds), *The SAGE Handbook of Human Rights* (SAGE 2014) 1035–7.

10 Added by the author.

11 Koh (n 6) 572.

12 M Robinson, 'Ethics, human rights and globalization' (Second Global Ethic Lecture, University of Tubingen Germany, 21 January 2002) www.weltethos.org/1-pdf/20-aktivitaeten/eng/we-reden-eng/speech_Robinson_eng.pdf (last accessed 17 December 2016).

13 These frameworks include those concentrating on a particular actor such as business (UN Framework and Guiding Principles on Business and Human Rights, the OECD Guidelines for Multinational Enterprises) or international financial institutions (the Tilburg–GLOTHRO Principles on World Bank, IMF and Human Rights) to those focusing on a particular sub-field of rights such as economic, social and cultural rights (the Maastricht Principles on Extraterritorial Obligation of States in the area of Economic, Social and Cultural Rights). Previous attempts at the UN include the Draft Code of Conduct on Transnational Corporations (1990) and the UN Norms on the Responsibilities of Transnational Corporations and other Business Enterprises with Regard to Human Rights (2002).

14 The ILO Tripartite Declaration of Principles concerning Multinational Enterprises and Social Policy was adopted in 1977 and last revised in 2006.

15 The OECD Guidelines for Multinational Enterprises were adopted in 1976. Their latest revision, which took place in 2011, introduced a chapter on human rights and incorporated the UN Protect, Respect, Remedy Framework and its Guiding Principles into the document.

16 O de Schutter, 'The challenge of imposing human rights norms on corporate actors' in O de Schutter (ed), *Transnational Corporations and Human Rights* (Hart Publishing 2006) 2.

17 The 1990 Draft of the Code, which was ultimately not adopted, stated: 'Transnational corporations should/shall respect human rights and fundamental freedoms in the countries in which they operate. In their social and industrial

relations, transnational corporations should/shall not discriminate on the basis of race, colour, sex, religion, language, social, national and ethnic origin or political or other opinion. Transnational corporations should/shall conform to government policies designed to extend equality of opportunity and treatment.' ('UN Draft Code of Conduct on Transnational Corporations' in UNCTAD, *International Investment Instruments: A Compendium, Vol 1 Multilateral Instruments*, UNCTAD/DTCI/30 (Vol I 1996) para 13 http://unctad.org/en/Docs/dtci30vol1_en.pdf (last accessed 17 December 2016)).

18 See de Schutter (n 16) 9.

19 Thus excluding the work of the CRC Committee.

20 UN Human Rights Council (UNHRC), 'Protect, respect and remedy: a framework for business and human rights' [UN Framework] UN Doc A/HCR/8/5 (2008) 22, para 83.

21 UN Framework (n 20) 22, para 83 footnote 49.

22 UN HRC, 'Resolution 8/7: Mandate of the Special Representative of the Secretary-General on the issue of human rights and transnational corporations and other business enterprises' UN Doc A/HRC/RES/8/7 (2008), para 4(d).

23 These include indigenous peoples, women, national or ethnic minorities, religious and linguistic minorities, persons with disabilities, and migrant workers and their families. See UN OHCHR, 'UN Guiding Principles on Business and Human Rights' (2011) (UNGP) UN Doc HR/PUB/11/04, 1.

24 UNGP (n 23) Principles 3 and 12, Commentary.

25 UNGP (n 23) Principle 3, Commentary.

26 UNGP (n 23) Principle 12, Commentary.

27 In fact, while Principle 12 refers to the business responsibility to respect 'internationally recognized human rights', it also makes the qualification that these are to be 'understood, at a minimum, as those expressed in the International Bill of Rights and the principles concerning fundamental rights set out in the International Labour Organization's Declaration on Fundamental Principles and Rights at Work'. Furthermore, the Commentary of the Principle refers to the International Bill of Human Rights and the eight ILO core conventions as the 'authoritative list of the core internationally recognized human rights'. (UNGP (n 23) Principle 12.)

28 J H Knox, 'The Ruggie rules: applying human rights law to corporations' in R Mares (ed), *The UN Guiding Principles on Business and Human Rights: Foundations and Implementation* (Martinus Nijhoff 2012) 79–80.

29 S Deva, D Bilchitz (eds), *Human Rights Obligations of Business: Beyond the Corporate Responsibility to Respect* (Cambridge University Press 2013) 4.

30 Castan Centre for Human Rights Law, Monash University Melbourne, 'Submission to the Secretary General's Special Representative on Business and Human Rights on Proposed Guiding Principles for Business and Human Rights' www.law.monash.edu.au/castancentre/policywork/cc-submission-business-human-rights-principles.pdf (last accessed 17 December 2016). Wabwile showcases the different regimes under which states may have extraterritorial obligations in M N Wabwile, 'Universal human rights and states' international responsibility' in Mihr and Gibney (eds), *The SAGE Handbook of Human Rights* (n 9) 1001–1002.

31 Upon the universal endorsement of the UNGP by the UN Human Rights Council, the former SRSG John Ruggie concluded that the Council's endorsement establishes the Guiding Principles as the 'authoritative global reference point for business and human rights' UN Office of the High Commissioner for Human Rights (OHCHR), 'New Guiding Principles on Business and Human Rights endorsed by the UN Human Rights Council' www.ohchr.org/en/NewsEvents/Pages/DisplayNews.aspx?NewsID=11164 sthash.Sav6831Q.dpuf (last accessed 17 December 2016).

32 'Statement on behalf of a Group of Countries at the 24th Session of the Human Rights Council, September 2013' business-humanrights.org/sites/default/files/media/documents/statement-unhrc-legally-binding.pdf (last accessed 17 December 2016). (A number of NGOs supported this initiative with a petition: 'Statement to the Human Rights Council in support of the initiative of a group of states for a legally binding instrument on transnational corporations' (13 September 2013) www.stopcorporateimpunity.org/?p=3830 (last accessed 17 December 2016)).

33 UN HRC, 'Draft resolution: elaboration of an international legally binding instrument on transnational corporations and other business enterprises with respect to human rights' (2014) UN Doc A/HRC/26/L.22/Rev. 1.

34 'Joint Statement: call for an international legally binding instrument on human rights, transnational corporations and other business enterprises' (27 May 2014) http://viacampesina.org/en/index.php/actions-and-events-mainmenu-26/stop-transnational-corporations-mainmenu-76/1612-joint-statement-call-for-an-international-legally-binding-instrument-on-human-rights-transnational-corporations-and-other-business-enterprises (last accessed 17 December 2016). (The supporting organisations have since formed the Treaty Alliance: http://www.treatymovement.com/ (last accessed 17 December 2016)).

35 UN HCR, 'Draft resolution: human rights and transnational corporations and other business enterprises UN Doc A/HRC/26/L.1 (2014) www.business-humanrights.org/media/documents/norway_resolution_23_06_14.doc (last accessed 17 December 2016). (The resolution called for issuing a 3-year extension of the mandate of the UN Working Group on Business and Human Rights (UN WG) and requesting the UN WG 'to explore and facilitate the sharing of legal and practical measures to improve access to remedy . . . for victims of business-related abuses, including the benefits and limitations of a legally binding instrument' (para 8).)

36 OECD, *OECD Guidelines for Multinational Enterprises* (OECD Publishing 2011) 3. http://dx.doi.org/10.1787/9789264115415-en (last accessed 17 December 2016).

37 OECD (n 36) ch IV, para 40.

38 ibid.

39 ibid.

40 ibid ch V: 'Employment and industrial relations', para 1(a) (As in the case of the ILO Tripartite Declaration, the OECD Guidelines refer to the ILO Convention No 182 on the Worst Forms of Child Labour.)

41 ibid ch VIII, paras 83–84.

42 UN Committee on Economic, Social and Cultural Rights (ESCR Committee), 'General Comment No 12: The Right to Adequate Food (Art 11)' UN Doc E/C.12/1999/5.

43 ESCR Committee, 'General Comment No 12' (n 42) para 20.

44 ESCR Committee, 'General Comment No 14: The Right to the Highest Attainable Standard of Health (Art 12)' UN Doc E/C.12/2000/4, para 42.

45 ibid para 63.

46 ESCR Committee, 'General Comment No 23: The Right to Just and Favourable Conditions of Work (Art 7)' UN Doc E/C.12/GC/23, para 6.

47 ibid para 47(b).

48 CRC Committee, 'General Comment No 16: State Obligations regarding the Impact of the Business Sector on Children's Rights' (2013) UN Doc CRC/C/GC/16, para 4.

49 Website of the Children's Rights and Business Principles Initiative, 'Overview' http://childrenandbusiness.org/?page_id=12 (last accessed 17 December 2016).

50 A number of consultation reports are available online through Business & Human Rights Resource Centre: http://business-humanrights.org/en/development-pre-launch-consultation (last accessed 17 December 2016).
51 UN Global Compact, 'Development of the Children's Rights and Business Principles' www.unglobalcompact.org/Issues/human_rights/childrens_principles/development.html (last accessed 17 December 2016).
52 UNICEF, The Global Compact and Save the Children, Children's Rights and Business Principles [CRBPs], preamble, http://unglobalcompact.org/docs/issues_doc/human_rights/CRBP/Childrens_Rights_and_Business_Principles.pdf (last accessed 17 December 2016).
53 The accompanying workbook prepared by UNICEF on the CRBPs also highlights ILO Conventions No 156 on equal opportunities and equal treatment for men and women workers, and workers with family responsibilities, No 183 on Maternity Protection and No 77 on Medical examination of children and young persons for fitness for employment in industry, as well as the 1998 ILO Declaration on Fundamental Principles and Rights at Work as relevant conventions. (UNICEF 'Children are everyone's business: Workbook 2.0 – A guide for integrating children's rights into policies, impact assessments and sustainability reporting' (2013) 9 www.unicef.org/csr/css/Workbook_2.0_231213_Web.pdf (last accessed 17 December 2016).
54 CRBPs (n 52) preamble.
55 ibid Principle 1(a) (original emphasis). These concepts and others employed in the CRBPs are defined in a glossary section of the Principles.
56 Principles 2, 3 and 4 are on child labour, decent work, protection and safety in business activities and facilities.
57 Principles 5 and 6 are on product safety, and marketing and advertising.
58 Principles 7 to 10 are on environment, land acquisition and use, security arrangements, emergencies, and collaboration with governments and communities.
59 Accordingly, children are not only child labourers but also potential future adult employees of businesses, dependents of company employees, consumers, members of broader communities in which businesses operate and, more generally, stakeholders.
60 These concepts are introduced in Principle 15 of the UNGP and further elaborated in Principles 16–22.
61 CRBPs (n 52) 14.
62 UNGP (n 23) Principles 17–21 and related Commentary.
63 CRBPs (n 52) principle 1.b(ii).
64 UNICEF and the Danish Institute for Human Rights have published an impact assessment tool for business use, in order to guide companies on how to assess their children's rights impact. The tool includes 58 primary criteria as well as a number of secondary criteria for businesses to use – upon further elaboration – to determine the actual or potential range of their impact on children's rights. See UNICEF and the Danish Institute for Human Rights (DIHR), 'Children's rights in impact assessments: a guide for integrating children's rights into impact assessments and taking action for children' (2013) 8 www.unicef.org/csr/156.htm (last accessed 17 December 2016).
65 UNICEF and DIHR (n 64) 8.
66 CRBPs (n 52) Principle 1(b)(iii).
67 Principle 31 of the UNGP sets out the effectiveness criteria as legitimate, accessible, predictable, equitable, transparent, rights-compatible and a source for continuous learning. Operational-level grievance mechanisms are subject to the same criteria and are also to be based on engagement and dialogue (UNGP (n 23)).
68 This term is not defined in the CRBPs but the UNICEF Workbook notes that the remediation channels should be accessible to children and that companies should

take care that instances of child sexual abuse do not go unreported. The grievance mechanisms do not all have to be managed by the company but the company is required to ascertain that they are in place locally. See UNICEF, 'Children are everyone's business: pilot workbook' 36 www.unicef.org/csr/css/Workbook_A4_LR_low_res.pdf (last accessed 17 December 2016)).

69 See Annex I for an overview of what the 'corporate responsibility to respect' and the 'corporate commitment to support' entails for each principle.

70 CRBPs (n 52) 5.

71 The UN Framework additionally states that companies performing public functions also may have these additional responsibilities (UN Framework (n 20), para 24).

72 CRC Committee, 'General Day of Discussion 2002 on the Private Sector as Service Provider and its Role in Implementing Child Rights Recomm. 6' UN Doc CRC/C/121, 153, para 653(6).

73 P Gerber, J Kyriakakis and K O'Byrne, 'General Comment 16: State Obligations Regarding the Impact of the Business Sector on Children's Rights: What is its standing, meaning and effect?' (2013) 14 *Melbourne Journal of International Law* 1, 9.

74 Emphasis added.

75 CRC Committee, 'General Comment No 16' (n 48), para 8.

76 ibid para 62.

77 ibid.

78 ibid para 65.

79 ibid para 39.

80 ibid.

81 ibid para 40.

82 ibid para 38.

83 ibid para 42.

84 A 'reasonable link' is said to exist when 'a business enterprise has its centre of activity, is registered or domiciled or has its main place of business or substantial business activities in the state concerned'; see CRC Committee, 'General Comment 16' (n 48) para 43.

85 ibid para 38.

86 ibid para 67.

87 Save the Children, *How to Use the Children's Rights and Business Principles: A Guide for Civil Society Organizations* (2nd edn 2014) 14.

88 UN OHCHR website, 'WG on HR and transnational corporations and other business enterprises' www.ohchr.org/EN/Issues/Business/Pages/WGHRandtransnationalcorporationsandotherbusiness.aspx (last accessed 17 December 2016).

89 The initial mandate of the UN WG was extended a further three years in June 2014. See UN HRC, 'Resolution 26/22 on human rights and transnational corporations and other business enterprises' (2014) UN Doc A/HRC/RES/26/22, para 10.

90 UN HRC, 'Resolution 17/4 on human rights and transnational corporations and other business enterprises' (2011) UN Doc A/HRC/RES/17/4, para 6 (a, b, c).

91 UN Working Group on Business and Human Rights (UN WG), 'Guidance on National Action Plans on Business and Human Rights: Version 1.0' (2014) UN OHCHR.

92 UN WG, 'Guidance on NAPs' (n 91) ii.

93 ibid 4, 6, 20, 27, 28, and 29.

94 ibid 4.

95 ibid 27.

96 ibid 29.

97 ibid 30.
98 ibid 19.
99 The UK NAP refers to children once, under new government actions planned in the context of 'raising awareness and tackling the negative impacts of business activity, including on the human rights of groups', including children. See UK HM Government, 'Good business: implementing the UN Guiding Principles on Business and Human Rights' (2013) 'New actions planned', vi. The NAP of Italy underscores the links between environmental pollution, right to health and the stronger effects on women and children. See Government of Italy, 'The foundations of the Italian Action Plan on the United Nations "Guiding Principles on Business and Human Rights"' (2014) 23. The Spanish NAP includes a commitment on the part of public authorities to keep existing regulation updated, especially as it regards groups vulnerable to rights violations, including children. See Gobierno de España, 'Plan de Empresa y Derechos Humanos' (2014) 14.
100 For instance, the term 'child' is mentioned five times in the Dutch NAP and each of these references relates to child labour (the prevention of child labour, universal ratification of the ban on child labour and its elimination). There is no mention of children's rights specifically. See Netherlands, 'NAP on Business and Human Rights' (2013), 2, 4, 6, 7. The Danish NAP references children twice; one of these references is on the compliance of Danish domestic law with international labour standards, including those on child labour (Denmark, 'Danish National Action Plan – implementation of the UN Guiding Principles on Business and Human Rights' 26).
101 UK, 'Good business' (n 99); Italy, 'The foundations of the Italian Action Plan' (n 99) 80; Government Offices of Sweden, 'Action Plan for Business and Human Rights' (2015) 13.
102 Italy, 'The foundations of the Italian Action Plan' (n 99) "The bases for future action".
103 Italy, 'The foundations of the Italian Action Plan' (n 99) 31–32.
104 Finland, 'National Action Plan on the Implementation of the UN Guiding Principles on Business and Human Rights' (2014) 15.
105 Sweden, 'Action Plan for Business and Human Rights' (n 101) 15 and 17.
106 Lithuania, 'Lithuania's Action Plan on the implementation of the UN Guiding Principles on Business and Human Rights' (2015).
107 UN OHCHR, 'The corporate responsibility to respect human rights: an interpretive guide' (HR/PUB/12/02 2012) 3, www.ohchr.org/Documents/Publications/HR.PUB.12.2_En.pdf (last accessed 17 December 2016).
108 The UN Global Compact, 'Human rights and business learning tool' http://human-rights-and-business-learning-tool.unglobalcompact.org/site/overview/ (last accessed 17 December 2016); Module 1: Introduction to human rights, Module 2: Respecting human rights, Module 3: Supporting human rights, Module 4: Complicity and Module 5: Remedy.
109 UN HRC, 'Report of the Secretary-General on Contribution of the United Nations system as a whole to the advancement of the business and human rights agenda and the dissemination and implementation of the Guiding Principles on Business and Human Rights' UN Doc A/HRC/21/21 2012, para 28.
110 UN HRC, UN Doc A/HRC/21/21 (n 109) para 60.
111 ibid paras 23 and 24.
112 ibid para 101.
113 UN HRC, 'Resolution 21/5 on Contribution of the United Nations system as a whole to the advancement of the business and human rights agenda and the dissemination and implementation of the Guiding Principles on Business and Human Rights' UN Doc A/HRC/RES/21/5 2012 para 11.

114 UN HRC, 'Report of the Secretary-General on the challenges, strategies and developments with regard to the implementation of the resolution 21/5 by the United Nations system, including programmes, funds and agencies – Addendum 1: Study on the feasibility of a global fund to enhance the capacity of stakeholders to implement the Guiding Principles on Business and Human Rights' UN Doc A/HRC/26/20/Add.1 (2014) Section II.

115 These include the United Nations Democracy Fund (UNDEF), United Nations Peacebuilding Fund, the Fund for Gender Equality, United Nations Voluntary Trust Fund for Victims of Trafficking in Persons, Especially Women and Children and the Rana Plaza Donors Fund.

116 UN HRC, UN Doc A/HRC/26/20/Add.1 (n 114), para 49.

117 ibid para 51.

118 UN HRC, 'Human rights and transnational corporations and other business enterprises' UN Doc A/HRC/26/L.1 (2014) para 17.

119 OECD Guidelines (n 36) 68.

120 OECD Guidelines, 'Procedural guidance' (n 36) 72.

121 ibid 72.

122 ibid.

123 OECD, 'Database of specific instances' https://mneguidelines.oecd.org/database/ (last accessed 24 January 2017).

124 *German Watch, Global March and Coordination gegen Bayer-Gefahren v Bayer CropScience* (Germany NCP, 11 October 2004); *Global Witness v Afrimex* (UK NCP, 20 July 2007); *ECCHR v Ecom Agroindustrial Corp. Ltd* (Switzerland NCP, 3 May 2010); *SHERPA and ECCHR v Devcot* (France NCP, 22 October 2010); *ECCHR v Otto Stadtlander GmbH* (Germany NCP, 25 October 2010); *ECCHR v Cargill Cotton Ltd* (UK NCP, 1 December 2010); *ECCHR v ICT Cotton Ltd* (UK NCP, 7 December 2010); *ECCHR v Louis Dreyfus Commodities Suisse SA* (Switzerland NCP, 23 December 2010).

125 *Mellemfolkeligt Samvirke (ActionAid Denmark) v Arla Foods* (Denmark NCP, 9 July 2014).

126 OECD, *OECD Due Diligence Guidance for Responsible Supply Chains of Minerals from Conflict-affected and High-risk Areas* [*DDG for Responsible Supply Chains*] (2nd edn, OECD Publishing 2013).

127 ibid 21, 59, 60.

128 OECD, *OECD Due Diligence Guidance for Meaningful Stakeholder Engagement in the Extractive Sector* [*DDG for Meaningful Stakeholder Engagement*] (Provisional Version) (2016).

129 ibid 18 and 34.

130 ibid 77 and 84, respectively.

131 OECD, *OECD–FAO Guidance for Responsible Agricultural Supply Chains* (2016) 74.

132 ibid 25 and 35.

133 OECD website, 'Responsible supply chains in the garment and footwear sector' http://mneguidelines.oecd.org/responsible-supply-chains-textile-garment-sector.htm (last accessed 17 December 2016).

134 OECD, *OECD Due Diligence Guidance for Responsible Supply Chains in the Garment and Footwear Sector* (Draft Version) (February 2016).

135 UNICEF, 'Children's rights and business: innovation and action' (2013) www.unicef.org/csr/css/Child_Rights_and_Buisness_Innovation_and_Action_Programme.pdf (last accessed 17 December 2016). (The companies and partners include many large corporations, industry organisations and consultancies such as Arcor, Aviatur, Banco Popular, BSR, Cisneros, Confederation of Indian Industry, Danish Institute for Human Rights, DTAC, Enodo Rights, Etipres, Grupo ICE, HCL Technologies, IKEA, ING, Kuoni, Mercantil Banco Universal,

Nissan, Nomogaia, Nordic Choice Hotels, Novo Nordisk, Pyramid Consulting, Rosy Blue, Sanoma, Sansiri, Sime Darby, Srinivasan Services Trust, Svenska Cellulosa Aktiebolaget SCA, Telefonica, Telenor, Telenor Pakistan, TwentyFifty, Two Tomorrows, Unilever, Vision Banco and Zynergy Projects & Services Private Limited (UNICEF, 'Children are everyone's business' (n 68) 2).

136 UNICEF, 'Children are everyone's business: Workbook 2.0' (n 53); UNICEF and Danish Institute for Human Rights (DIHR), 'Children's rights in impact assessments' (2013); UNICEF, *Children's Rights in Sustainability Reporting* (2nd edn, 2014); UNICEF and Save the Children, 'Children's rights in policies and codes of conduct: a tool for companies' (2013); UNICEF, 'Engaging stakeholders on children's rights' (2014).

137 UNICEF and DIHR (n 136) 4.

138 Ernst Ligteringen, 'Forward', in UNICEF, 'Children's rights in sustainability reporting' (n 136) 3.

139 GRI is focused on voluntary sustainability reporting by private entities. The initiative has been developing and disseminating guidelines to be used for sustainability reporting since 1997, when it was founded to monitor investment compliance with principles for responsible environmental conduct developed by the Coalition for Environmentally Responsible Economies (CERES) (GRI, 'About GRI' www.globalreporting.org/information/about-gri/gri-history/Pages/GRI's%20history.aspx#sthash.TW8jiDsf.dpuf (last accessed 17 December 2016).

140 UNICEF and Save the Children, 'Children's rights in policies and codes of conduct' (n 136) 4.

141 UNICEF, *Engaging Stakeholders on Children's Rights: A Tool for Companies* (1st edn 2014) www.unicef.org/csr/css/Stakeholder_Engagement_on_Childrens_Rights_021014.pdf (last accessed 17 December 2016).

142 UNICEF website, 'An industry approach' www.unicef.org/csr/433.htm (last accessed 17 December 2016).

143 UNICEF, 'UNICEF corporate lab concept note for consultation at the UNICEF global workshop on children's rights and business' (2013) 2 www.unicef.org/csr/css/CSR_CORPORATE_LAB_Concept_Note.pdf (last accessed 17 December 2016).

144 UNICEF, 'UNICEF corporate lab concept note' (n 143) 4.

145 The UNICEF corporate lab concept note includes a focus on four industries: consumer goods (including retail, apparel, luxury goods, consumer staples), information and communication technologies (including internet, telecom and consumer electronics), travel and tourism, and financial services (including banking and insurance).

146 UNICEF, 'UNICEF corporate lab concept note' (n 143) 3. (According to the concept note, country-level action plans are planned for the UK, Sweden, the US, Brazil, Argentina, Kenya, South Africa, India, Bangladesh, Indonesia, Malaysia, Viet Nam and China, which were chosen as priority countries.)

147 Save the Children, 'How to use the Children's Rights and Business Principles' (n 87) 20.

148 UN Global Compact, 'Children's Rights and Business Principles – good practices per principle' (2014) www.unglobalcompact.org/docs/issues_doc/human_rights/CRBP/GoodPracticesPerPrinciple.pdf (last accessed 17 December 2016).

149 CRC Committee, 'Concluding observations on the combined third and fourth periodic reports of China' UN Doc CRC/C/CHN/CO/3-4 (2013), paras 23–24; CRC Committee, 'Concluding observations on the combined third and fourth periodic reports of Germany' UN Doc CRC/C/DEU/CO/3-4 (2014) paras 22–23; CRC Committee, 'Concluding observations on the combined second to fourth periodic report of the Congo' UN Doc CRC/C/COG/

CO/2-4 (2014), paras 26–27; CRC Committee, 'Concluding observations on the fourth periodic report of the Netherlands' UN Doc CRC/C/NDL/CO/4 (2015), paras 22–23.

150 See CRC Committee, 'Consideration of reports submitted by states parties under Article 44 of the convention: concluding observations: Australia' UN Doc CRC/C/AUS/CO/4 (2012); CRC Committee, 'Concluding observations on the combined third and fourth periodic report of Canada' UN Doc CRC/C/CAN/CO/3-4 (2012), paras 28–29.

151 CRC Committee, 'Concluding observations – Germany' (n 149), para 22 and 'Concluding observations – the Netherlands' (n 149), para 22.

152 CRC Committee, 'Concluding observations – Germany' (n 149), para 22.

153 ibid para 23.

154 CRC Committee, 'Concluding observations – Congo' (n 149), para 26.

155 UNICEF and International Commission of Jurists (ICJ), 'Obligations and actions on children's rights and business: a practical guide for states on how to implement the UN Committee on the Child's General Comment No 16' (2015).

156 UNICEF and Save the Children, 'Children's rights and business explained: a plain-language version of the UN Committee on the Rights of the Child's General Comment No16' (2015).

157 C Parker, J Howe, 'Ruggie's diplomatic project and its missing regulatory infrastructure' in R Mares (ed), *The UN Guiding Principles on Business and Human Rights: Foundations and Implementation* (Martinus Nijhoff 2012) 274.

158 J Ruggie, 'The shift from principles to practice' www.shiftproject.org/article/shift-principles-practice-0 (last accessed 17 December 2016).

159 L Catá Backer, 'From institutional misalignments to socially sustainable governance: the guiding principles for the implementation of the United Nation's "Protect, respect and remedy" and the construction of inter-systemic global governance' (2011) 25(1) *Pacific McGeorge Global Business & Development Law Journal* 101, 158.

160 See Parker and Howe (n 157) 274.

161 UN OHCHR, 'Principled pragmatism: the way forward for business and human rights' (7 June 2010) www.ohchr.org/EN/NewsEvents/Pages/PrincipledpragmatismBusinessHR.aspx (last accessed 17 December 2016).

162 The first study was a benchmarking study conducted with more than 1000 publicly listed companies (Global Child Forum (GCF) and Boston Consulting Group (BCG), 'Children's rights and the corporate sector: setting a benchmark' (2014)). The other was a study on investors' perspectives, which surveyed 195 European and North American asset owner institutions that are signatories to the UN supported voluntary Principles for Responsible Investment (GCF and GES, 'Investor perspectives on children's rights' (2014)).

163 GCF and GES, 'Investor perspectives on children's rights' (n 162) 4 and 7.

164 GCF and BCG, 'Children's rights and the corporate sector: setting a benchmark' (n 162) 5.

165 ibid 16.

166 ibid 19.

167 CRC Committee, 'General Comment No 16' (n 48), paras 42–43.

168 ibid paras 66–72; CRBPs (n 52) Principle 1(b)(iii).

Index

Aarhus Convention 254
abduction 40, 45
academics/scholars 111, 192, 274–5; general principles and advancement of children's rights: perspective of 60–1
accessibility 28, 64, 65, 113–14, 120, 159, 184, 221–2
accountability 61, 86, 139
adoption 27, 178, 199–200
advertising 102
advocates for children 123–4
African Charter on Human and Peoples' Rights 255
African Charter on the Rights and Welfare of the Child 262
African Commission: Working Group on Indigenous Populations/ Communities 131
age-based discrimination 124–5, 148, 155–6, 158, 162
agriculture 286
AIDS 194
American Convention on Human Rights 255
Amnesty International 194
Annan, Kofi 109
Arab Charter on Human Rights 255
armed conflict 96, 120
assisted reproduction 40–1
asylum 41–2, 46, 93
austerity 43
autonomy 95, 123, 181; adults' reproductive 41; family 82; indigenous peoples 133; individual 28, 40, 42, 43, 47, 54, 60, 73, 77, 86, 95, 96, 97, 98–9, 102, 103, 104, 125, 179; older persons 149, 157, 161; progressive *see* evolving capacities; women 95, 96, 97, 98–9
available resources; CRC 23, 114, 153; CRPD 23, 111, 112, 114, 119, 122; older persons 153
awareness raising 100, 101, 104

Ban Ki-Moon 151
best interests: of the child *see* best interests of the child; revisiting capacity: status, functionality, best interests and supported decision-making 116, 122–6
best interests of the child 3–4, 26–7, 32, 37–8, 46–7, 181; adults, interests of 40, 45–6; capacity and decision by child 125; CEDAW 174, 178, 179, 185, 187; child-specificity, upholding 38–9; Children's Rights and Business Principles (CRBPs) 279; CRC Art 3(1): *a* primary consideration 27, 45; CRC Art 21: in adoption the paramount consideration 27; CRPD Art 7(2) 27, 37, 65, 111; decision-making, opaque 42–5; environment 263–4; general principle of CRC 27–8, 52, 53–5, 56, 57–9, 60, 62, 152–3, 179–80, 263–4; heard, right to be 197; interdependency 46; interpretative legal principle 26, 37, 57, 180; LGBTI persons' rights 192, 193, 195, 197, 198–201; migration, undocumented 212; 'paramount' importance 27, 37, 38, 40, 41, 58, 178, 200; parents' right to oversee limited and functional 73–4, 75, 76, 81; procedure, rule of 26, 37, 57, 180, 197; relational theory 46; specific express principle 61; substantive right 26, 37, 57, 180; supported decision-making model

and 125; termination of relationship: preserve relationship with both parents 182–3; UK State Party report (2014) 58–9; United States 79; universalism, avoiding artificial and sterile 39, 40–2; work, right to work in 132
biodiversity 135, 258
breastfeeding 184, 185
Brundtland Report 257
bullying 202, 204; cyber- 240
Bush, George H.W. 22
business and human rights 30, 273; challenges, opportunities and future 288–92; Children's Rights and Business Principles (CRBPs) 273, 279–81, 283, 284, 287–8, 289, 292; media 240; operationalising business obligations 283–8; situating children's rights 273–8; specific business and children's rights focus 278–83

capabilities approach 47, 153–4
capacity 115, 125, 126, 161; CRPD: status, functionality, best interests and supported decision-making 115, 116, 122–6; *Gillick v West Norfolk and Wisbech AHA* 125; *see also* evolving capacities
capital punishment 25, 57
Carter, Jimmy 22
characteristics of children's human rights law, distinctive 2, 21–32, 192; best interests of the child 26–7, 32; general principles 27–9, 32; indivisibility of civil, political, economic, social and cultural rights 22–4; new substantive norms or elements 24–6; third parties as duty-holders beyond state, inclusion of 29–31, 32
child abuse 79, 160
child development theories 136
child labour 79, 96–7, 109, 132, 158, 277, 279, 286, 289, 290
child soldiers 109
child-care facilities 177, 184
Children's Rights and Business Principles (CRBPs) 273, 279–81, 283, 284, 287–8, 289, 292
Children's Rights Information Network (CRIN) 60
circumcision 120
civil, political, economic, social and cultural rights 94; CRPD 65, 110–11, 114, 121–2; indivisibility of 22–4
civil society (organisations (CSOs)) 62, 81, 151, 288; general principles and advancement of children's rights: perspective of 60
civilisations, respect for different 25
clinical trials 140
clothing 30
coal emissions 288
code of conduct 280
collective/group rights 101, 139, 141, 255
Committee on Economic, Social and Cultural Rights (CESCR) 23, 25, 26, 30, 31, 93, 159, 214, 278, 281
Committee on the Elimination of Discrimination against Women (CEDAW) 100–1, 102; gender perspective: intra-family relations 176, 177–9, 185; harmful practices 93, 174, 185–6, 187; joint General Recommendation/Comment with CEDAW committee 93, 174, 185–6, 187; migration, undocumented 213–14, 220; reservations against Art 16 177; violence against women 97
Committee on the Elimination of Racial Discrimination (CERD) 130, 139–40, 214
Committee on Migrant Workers (CMW Committee) 213–14, 220
Committee on the Rights of the Child (CRC) 21, 84, 151, 152; 'becoming' rather than 'being', children as 25; best interests of the child 26, 27, 37, 57, 180, 181, 182–3, 197, 199; breastfeeding 184, 185; business and children's rights 30, 273, 275, 278, 281–3, 284, 285, 288, 291; consent 140; cultural change 102–3; early childhood 182; education 202–4; environment 258, 259, 261, 262, 263; ESC rights: progressive realisation 23–4; gender perspective: intra-family relations 173–4, 181–4, 185–7; general principles of CRC 27–9, 52, 53–8, 61, 64, 66, 67, 152–3, 179; girl child 174, 185, 187; health, right to 31; individual and collective right to be heard 139; international cooperation 31; intersex

children 196–8; joint General Recommendation/Comment with CEDAW Committee 93, 174, 185–6, 187; LGBTI individuals' rights 194–5, 196–8, 202–4; maternity protection 183–4; media 233–4, 240; migration, undocumented 212, 213; non-state actors, responsibilities of 30; state obligations 102–3, 104
Committee on the Rights of Persons with Disabilities (CRPD) 28, 65–6, 115, 122, 152
consent: children 138, 140, 141, 157, 197–8; indigenous peoples: free, prior and informed 138, 139–40, 141; older persons 157
constructions of indigenous peoples and children, Western 134–7
consultation 140; indigenous peoples 138–9, 141; persons with disabilities 116, 118–19; *see also* participation, right to
consumer interests 277
Convention against Torture 22, 276
Convention on the Elimination of All Forms of Discrimination against Women (CEDAW) 23, 37, 62, 66, 95, 104; Art 2: policy measures 99, 100, 175; Art 5: social and cultural change 94, 99–102, 103, 104, 175–6, 179, 187; Art 5 as basis for general principle 62–3, 104; Art 11: employment 177, 179; Art 16: marriage 177–8, 179, 187; intra-family relations under CRC and CEDAW *see separate entry*
Convention on the Elimination of All Forms of Racial Discrimination (CERD) 23, 62, 66; Art 2(e) and Art 4 as basis for general principles 63
Convention on the Exercise of Children's Rights 161
Convention on preventing and combating violence against women and domestic violence 103–4
Convention on the Rights of the Child (CRC) 24, 38–9, 47, 81–2, 83–4, 86, 93, 98, 115, 120, 125, 147, 162, 236; Preamble 180; Art 1: definition of child 131, 155; Art 2: equality and non-discrimination 27, 53–5, 56–8, 60, 61, 111, 118, 156, 261; Art 3: best interests of the child 26, 27, 37, 45, 52, 53–5, 56, 57–9, 60, 62, 111, 179–80, 192, 193, 198, 212, 233, 263–4; Art 3(2) 72–3, 74; Art 3(3) 72, 74; Art 4: available resources 23, 24, 31, 52, 54, 56, 104, 114, 153, 154; Art 5: third-party duty-holders 25, 54, 56, 61, 71, 72, 73, 74, 76, 82, 83, 84, 118, 132, 180–1, 234; Art 6: right to life, survival and development 27, 52, 53–6, 57–8, 60, 61, 257, 260–1, 262; Art 7: registration after birth 31; Art 8: preserve identity 118; Art 9: separation from parents 117, 182; Art 11: illicit transfer 31; Art 12: views of child/right to participation 27, 52, 53–5, 56, 57–8, 59, 60–1, 62, 67, 102, 114, 121, 132, 138, 152, 154, 155, 179, 192–3, 195–8, 212, 232–3, 239, 241–2, 243, 244, 264; Art 13: freedom of expression 54, 55–6, 232–3, 241, 243, 244; Art 14: freedom of thought, conscience and religion 24, 25, 54, 71, 75–6, 77–8, 81–2; Art 16: privacy, family, home or correspondence 54, 119, 234; Art 17: mass media 31, 54, 233, 241–2, 243, 244; Art 18: child-rearing responsibilities 29, 71, 72, 74, 76, 82, 83, 84, 180, 181, 233, 243, 259; Art 19: protection from violence or abuse 118, 120, 160; Art 20: state care 72, 118; Art 21: adoption 27, 31, 72; Art 22: refugees 31; Art 23: disabled children 25, 31, 111–12, 115, 118, 119; Art 24: health 31, 55, 103, 157, 183, 184, 257–8, 259, 261, 262; Art 27: standard of living 29, 30, 31, 72, 74, 159, 181, 261–2; Art 28: education 25, 26, 31; Art 29: education 25, 55, 61, 202, 259, 262; Art 31: leisure and play 182, 262; Art 34: sexual exploitation 31; Art 35: abduction 31; Art 37(a): prohibition of capital punishment and life imprisonment 25; Art 39: recovery and reintegration 56, 120; Art 41 151; Art 42: make provisions widely known 60; Art 45: international cooperation 31; becoming/developing child 21–2; international relations 22; intra-family relations under CRC and CEDAW *see separate*

entry; migration, undocumented 211; paradigm shift 21–2; US campaign to ratify CRC: children's rights/parental rights dichotomy 72, 78–81, 86; *see also* Committee on the Rights of the Child
Convention on the Rights of Persons with Disabilities (CRPD) 21, 23, 95, 98, 104, 110, 126, 155; Preamble 111, 113; Art 1: purpose 110; Art 3: general principles 28, 61, 64–6, 116, 120–1, 153, 155; Art 4: general obligations 65, 110, 111, 114, 116, 118–19, 122; Art 5: non-discrimination 65, 66; Art 7: children 65, 111, 116, 117; Art 7(2): best interests 27, 37, 65, 111; Art 7(3): views of children 111, 114; Art 8(2)(b): foster respect in education system 116, 119; Art 9: accessibility 65, 120; Art 10: right to life 120; Art 11: situations of risk and humanitarian emergencies 120; Art 12: equality before the law 122–4; Art 13: access to justice 121; Art 16: freedom from exploitation, violence and abuse 85, 110, 116, 118; Art 17: protecting integrity 120; Art 18: liberty of movement 121; Art 19: living independently 65, 121; Art 20: personal mobility 121; Art 21: freedom of expression 121–2; Art 23: home and family life 116, 117, 118, 119; Art 24: education 117, 119; Art 25: health 117, 119; Art 30: play, recreation and sporting facilities 117, 119; extending and reconfiguring existing rights 120–2; inclusion of 'third parties' 85–6; new rights for all 119–20; new rights for children with disabilities 116–19; optimistic reading 112–16; pessimistic reading 109–12; revisiting capacity: status, functionality, best interests and supported decision-making 122–6
corporal and physical punishment 60, 84–5, 103
corporate commitment to support 280–1
corporate responsibility to respect 280–1
corporate social responsibility (CSR) 240
Council of Europe 113, 149, 161, 219, 220, 234–5, 236, 241
CRC Committee *see* Committee on the Rights of the Child
criminal justice 42
criminal law 135, 137, 195, 275
crucifixes 77
cultural change 95, 99–104, 175–6, 185; harmful cultural practices 93, 101, 103, 109, 174, 185–6, 187
cultural context 202; older persons 155–6; and scope of children's rights law 132
cultural identity 25, 204
cultural, social, economic, civil and political rights 94; CRPD 65, 110–11, 114, 121–2; indivisibility of 22–4
culture, play and leisure 262
cyberbullying 240

deaths 183, 253, 260
Declaration on the Rights of the Child (1959) 37
definitions: child 130–2, 134; indigenous peoples 130–1, 132, 133–4; integration, inspiration and isolation 1–2, 192; older persons 155–6
deportation of parents 46
detention 120
developing countries 101, 103, 122, 258; development assistance 31
difference, respect for 28, 64, 65
dignity 25, 28, 47, 61, 64, 148, 157, 202, 274; right to work in 132
disabilities 95, 133, 140, 149, 150; best interests 26, 37, 43, 65, 111, 116, 117, 118, 122–6; blind children 117; capacity 115, 116, 122–6; consultation 116, 118–19; Convention on the Rights of Persons with (CRPD) *see separate entry*; deaf children 117; deafblind children 117; general principle 118; girl children with 117, 212, 217; identities, preserve 116; inclusion of 'third parties' 85–6; non-discrimination 25; social attitudes 113; social model 113, 125, 126; vote, right to 113–14
disaster relief 31
discrimination *see* non-discrimination
dismissal 100, 177

dissolution of marriage 177–8
domestic violence 40, 100; Convention on preventing and combating violence against women and 103–4
due deference principle 61
due diligence 30, 280, 281, 282, 286, 288–9, 290, 291

economic, social, cultural, civil and political rights 94; CRPD 65, 110–11, 114, 121–2; indivisibility of 22–4
education 31, 44, 84, 102, 104, 109, 183; CEDAW 62, 99, 100, 101, 176; compulsory schooling 79; CRPD: foster respect in education system 116, 119; CRPD: right not to be excluded from general education system 117, 119; health 157, 259; Islamic headscarf 76; LGBTI persons' rights 192, 193, 202–4; older persons 157, 158; religious 76–7, 84; right to 24, 25, 26, 75, 158, 192, 193, 202–4, 259–60; sexual 203–4
elderly *see* older persons
emancipation rights 93–5; crucial emancipation tool: Art 5 CEDAW 99–102; lessons for children's rights 102–4; women's rights and children's rights as 96–9
employment *see* work
end-of-life decision making 38
environment 25, 120, 251–65; children's specificity and environmental rights 256–7; CRC and the environment 257–64; human rights and 254–6; indigenous peoples 135, 136–7
environmental law 28
equality 61, 97, 98, 99, 162; before the law 121, 122–3, 124; of capabilities 154; economic inequality 85; intersex children 196; night work 96; older persons 156; of opportunity 28, 64, 65; reasonable accommodation: substantive 65; women 174, 176, 177, 178, 179, 182, 184, 185; *see also* non-discrimination
ethic of care 47
eugenic practices 118
European Committee of Social Rights 203, 256; migration, undocumented 210, 218–19, 220, 221, 222, 223, 224
European Convention on Human Rights (ECHR): Art 2: right to life 256; Art 3: torture 214, 215, 216; Art 5: liberty 214, 215–16; Art 6: fair trial 256; Art 8: private and family life 41–2, 45, 46, 199, 200, 234, 235, 255–6; Art 9: freedom of thought, conscience and religion 75, 77; Art 10: information 234, 235, 241, 242–3, 256; Art 13: effective remedy 256; Art 14: discrimination 156; Prot No 1, Art 1: property 256; Prot No 1, Art 2: religious education 76–7; Prot No 2: discrimination 156
European Court of Human Rights 251; best interests of the child 27, 45, 199–201; education and religion 77; environment 255–6; LGBTI rights 199–201; media 234–5, 242–3; migration, undocumented 210, 214–18, 219, 220–1, 222, 223, 224; religious freedom 75
European Social Charter 159, 203–4, 219, 256; Revised (RESC) 21, 218
European Union 202, 241; best interests 27; Charter on Fundamental Rights 21, 27, 155, 156, 157, 236; Commission 96, 241; Court of Justice 96, 236; General Data Protection Regulation (GDPR) 238, 239, 244; night work 96; older persons 155, 156
evolving capacities 24, 25, 56, 98, 132, 155, 202, 234, 243; CRPD 28, 64, 65, 116, 118, 155; freedom of religion 76, 77, 78; parents' rights limited by 73, 75, 81; principle of 61
extractive industries 288

female genital mutilation (FGM) 109
feminism 96
Food and Agriculture Organization (FAO) 285, 286
food, right to 278
footwear sector 286
forestry 288
freedom of expression 54, 55–6, 232–3, 241, 243, 244; CRPD (Art 21) 121–2; ECHR (Art 10) 234, 235, 241, 242–3, 256

Fretté v France 199–201
fulfilment, obligations of 25

garment sector 286
gender identity 193–4, 196, 197, 198, 202, 203, 204
general principles of CRC 4–5, 27–9, 32, 52–67, 104, 114, 121, 123, 152–3, 154, 179–80; contribution to advancement of children's rights 58–61; environment 263–4; implications for other areas of human rights law 61–6; term 'principles' 54; *see also individual principles under* Convention on the Rights of the Child
general principles of CRPD 28, 61, 64–6, 116, 118, 120–1, 153, 155
genetic heritage 41
Geneva Conventions (1949) 255
Gillick v West Norfolk and Wisbech AHA 125
Global Child Forum 289
Global North 101, 103
Global Reporting Initiative (GRI) 287
Global South/developing states 101, 103, 122
globalisation 273–5
group/collective rights 101, 139, 141, 255
guardianship 135, 178

harassment 202, 204; sexual 102
hate speech 202, 235, 237, 241
hazardous materials 139
health (care) 60, 184; CEDAW 62, 177; consent 140, 157, 197–8; CRPD 116, 117, 118, 119, 120; environmental pollution 253, 256, 265; intersex children 195–6, 197–8; lack of capacity and best interests principle 38, 43–4; LGBTI children 193, 195–6, 197–8; older persons 146, 156–7; reproductive health 100, 116, 118; reproductive technologies 40–1; right to health 30, 31, 156–7, 177, 183, 196, 257–8, 288
heard, right to be *see* participation, right of/views of child
HIV 194, 202, 221
housing 30, 44, 159–60
humanitarian assistance 31

idealised constructions 141; of children 135, 136, 137; of family life 80; of indigenous peoples 135, 136, 137
immigration 41–2, 46, 59
indigenous peoples 93, 95, 98, 129–41, 255, 286; participation and consent 138–41; personal scope of children's rights law and rights law of 129–34; self-identification 130, 131, 132, 133; Western constructions 134–7
individual claims and public international law 115
indivisibility of civil, political, economic, social and cultural rights 22–4
infanticide 57
inspiration 15; best interests principle 2, 3–4, 9, 32, 38–47; business and human rights 273, 279, 281, 282, 290, 291; disabilities, persons with 3, 5, 8–9, 11, 66, 119, 120, 121–2, 125–6; draw inspiration from other branches of human rights law 1, 6, 8–11, 94, 102–4, 119, 120, 121–2, 125–6, 129, 132, 138, 139, 140, 141, 151, 162; general principles 2, 3, 5, 29, 32, 63, 66–7; holistic approach: civil, political, economic, social and cultural rights 9, 11, 24, 121–2; indigenous peoples 9–10, 11, 129, 132, 138, 139, 140, 141; LGBTI persons 193; meaning of 1–2; media 14, 16, 242–4; older persons 3, 10, 11, 147, 151, 152, 154, 157, 161, 162; race discrimination 63, 66; source of 1, 2–6, 14–15, 24, 32, 38–47, 63, 66–7, 72, 85, 86, 147, 152, 154, 157, 161, 162, 244; third parties as duty-holders 2–3, 6, 32, 72, 85, 86, 161, 162; women 7–8, 11, 63, 66, 94, 102–4
insurance: private health insurance companies 30
integration 15; best interests principle 2, 4, 27, 32, 38–47, 179, 193, 198, 201; business and human rights 13, 14, 16, 275, 276, 277, 278, 279–80, 281, 282, 287, 288, 290–2; distinctive characteristics of children's human rights law 2, 21, 24, 27, 29, 32; environmental rights 13–14, 15, 251–2, 265; LGBTI persons 12–13, 16–17, 192, 193, 195, 198, 201, 202, 204; meaning of 1–2, 192;

migrants, undocumented 14–15, 16, 210, 213, 219–24, 225; women 12, 15–16, 173–4, 179, 185–7
integrity: capabilities approach and bodily 154; physical 196; respect for physical and mental 120
Inter-American Court of Human Rights 134, 139
inter-generational equity 257
interdependency 46, 124, 154
interests of the child 26; best *see separate entry*
intergenerational conflict 79
international assistance and cooperation 31
International Center for the Legal Protection of Human Rights (INTERIGHTS) v Croatia 203–4
International Covenant on Civil and Political Rights (ICCPR) 21, 26, 77, 174, 194, 241, 242
International Covenant on Economic, Social and Cultural Rights (ICESCR) 21, 25, 26, 157, 158, 174, 278
International Labour Organization (ILO) 96, 97, 275, 278, 279, 290; indigenous peoples 130, 138–9, 255
International Law Association 274
international organisations 30, 130, 274, 275; *see also individual organisations*
international relations 22
intersectionality 93
intersex children 193, 195–8
intra-family relations under CRC and CEDAW 173–87; CEDAW 174–5, 178–9, 185–6, 187; (Art 5) 175–6, 187; (Art 11) 177; (Art 16) 177–8, 187; CRC 179–80, 184–7; (approach to parental roles of mothers and fathers as distinct and gendered categories) 181–3; (approach to state–parents–child relationship) 180–1; (motherhood as biological function) 183–4; towards more integrated approach 185–7
Islamic headscarf 76
Islamic Shariah 78
isolation 173; best interests principle 38–47; business and human rights 13, 273, 274, 283; distinctive characteristics of children's human rights law 21, 32; LGBTI and children's rights 193; meaning of 2; migrants, undocumented 210, 224, 225

juvenile justice 60, 135, 137; best interests of the child 27, 59

Ksentini Report (1994) 256, 260

lead poisoning 288
legal aid 44
leisure, play and culture 262
LGBTI persons' rights and children's rights 192–204; best interests of the child 198–201; CRC and right to education 202–4; intersex children 193, 195–8; preliminary remarks 193–5; right to be heard and right to participate 195–8
LGBTI rights 95; integration: children's rights and 192–204
libertarianism 43
life, right to (CRPD) 120
life, survival and development, right to 24, 25, 260–1; general principle of CRC 27–8, 52, 53–6, 57–8, 60, 61
life-long learning 158
local non-indigenous communities 133–4

Madrid International Plan of Action on Ageing (2002) 148, 149
mainstreaming 25, 26, 31, 93, 117, 192, 279
margin of appreciation 42
marketplace 280
marriage 177–8, 195
mass media organisations 30
maternity 96, 98, 99, 176, 177, 181–5, 187
media 104, 231–44; CRC Committee 103; CRPD 121; fundamental rights, children and 232–6; information society: children's rights 236–41; sexist stereotypes 102; unique characteristics of children's rights in media environment 241–4
Mennesson v France 201
mental (in)capacity 38, 43–4
migrant workers 23, 93, 133; best interests 26

migration, undocumented 210–25; best interests of the child 26; integration of nuanced vulnerability concept in human rights law 219–24; nuanced vulnerability concept in children's rights law 211–13; vulnerability approach in human rights law 213–19
Millennium Development Goals (MDGs) 109
minorities 93, 95, 133
Muslim legal tradition 132

national security 41
national values 25
neuroscience 132
night work 96
non-discrimination 62, 66, 156, 162, 291; CERD 23, 62, 63, 66; Children's Rights and Business Principles (CRBPs) 279; CRC 24, 25, 27–8, 53–5, 56–8, 60, 61, 66, 111, 118, 156; CRPD 25, 28, 64, 65, 111, 123, 124; disability 25, 28, 64, 65, 111, 123, 124, 125, 156, 202; gender identity 193, 197; race 23, 62, 63, 66, 156, 202; sex 23, 28, 37, 62–3, 64, 65, 66, 94–5, 98, 99–102, 103, 104, 105, 156, 175–9, 186; sexual orientation 140, 156, 193, 194–5, 199–200, 202, 203–4; social model of childhood 125–6; structural discrimination 94–5; *see also* age-based discrimination; equality
non-governmental organisations (NGOs) 62, 84–5, 118, 126, 223, 239, 286, 288; general principles and advancement of children's rights: perspective of 60, 61
non-state duty-bearers 30
'not-yet' human beings 135
nutrition 30

OECD Guidelines for Multinational Enterprises 275, 277, 283, 286, 289, 292
older persons 25, 95, 98, 146–62; adding principles to listed rights 152–4; best interests 26; carers 160, 161; general principles 29; highlighting specific principles and rights 154–60; monitoring of human rights: making it smarter 151–2; movement towards convention for 147–9; new treaty: double opportunity if scope controlled 149–51; procedural rights 160–1, 162; selective or cluster approach 150–1; third parties 86, 160–1, 162

paediatric research 140
parents 5–6, 40, 71–86, 160–1; best interests principle and interests of 39, 40–1, 45–6; child contact and residence disputes 39, 40; conciliation between children's rights and rights, duties and responsibilities of 72, 81–4, 85, 86; definitions 71; deportation of 46; duties of 74, 78, 81, 82–3, 84, 86, 98, 102, 161; functional rights 73–4, 75, 76, 81, 86; legal analysis of Arts 3(2) and (3), 5 and 18 CRC 72–5; limited rights 73–4, 75, 76, 81, 86; other human rights law: third party inclusion 84–6, 86; respect for 25; responsibility of 29–30, 73–4, 81, 82, 83–4, 86, 181, 182, 186, 233, 243; 'right' to parent 40–1; rights, duties and responsibilities of parents and child's right to freedom of religion 75–8; rights of 73–4, 75, 76, 78–81, 82, 83, 84, 86, 93, 102, 161, 186, 259; US campaign to ratify CRC: children's rights/parental rights dichotomy 72, 78–81, 86
participation, right to/views of child 24, 44, 97, 98, 102–3, 140–1, 162; Art 12 CRC 27, 52, 53–5, 56, 57–8, 59, 60–1, 62, 67, 102, 114, 121, 132, 138, 152, 154, 155, 179, 192–3, 195–8, 212, 232–3, 239, 241–2, 243, 244, 264; business and children's rights 279, 291; Children's Rights and Business Principles (CRBPs) 279; CRPD: Art 7(3) 111, 114; environment 264; general principle of CRC 27–8, 52, 53–5, 56, 57–8, 59, 60–1, 62, 67, 152, 154, 264; general principle of CRPD 64, 120–1, 154–5; indigenous peoples 133, 138, 140–1; individual and collective right to be heard 139; intersex children 192–3, 195–8; LGBTI persons' rights and

children's rights: integration 192–3, 195–8; media 238–40; older persons 154–5; United States 79; *see also* consent; consultation
paternalism 4, 21–2, 38, 42, 43, 44, 47, 96, 97, 104, 132, 136, 183, 244
patriarchy 79, 176, 186
pensions 159
pharmaceutical companies 30
Plan International 279
play: areas 120; leisure and culture 262; in nature 261
political, civil, economic, social and cultural rights 94; CRPD 65, 110–11, 114, 121–2; indivisibility of 22–4
pornography 275
poverty 151, 179, 182, 256, 261; best interests of the child 26
power relationships 140, 176, 185–6
pregnancy 98, 177, 184
prison 25, 101
privacy 54, 81, 119, 234; home and family life (Art 23 CRPD) 116, 117, 118, 119; private and family life (Art 8 ECHR) 41–2, 45, 46, 199, 200, 234, 235, 255–6
private health insurance companies 30
problem child 135, 137
professionals: perspective on general principles and advancement of children's rights 59–60
progressive realisation: ESC rights 23–4
prostitution 275
protection, right to 24, 237–8
provision, right to 24, 241
public policy 41–2, 46
public space 135

race discrimination 23, 62, 63, 66, 156, 202
rape 100
Reagan, Ronald 22
refugees 41–2, 93
relational theory 46
religion, freedom of 81–2; rights, duties and responsibilities of parents and child's right to 75–8
reproductive: health 100, 116, 118; technologies 40–1
researchers 30
respect 25, 61, 116, 119
retirement age 158, 159
Rio Declaration (1992) 251, 254
romanticised/idealised constructions 141; of children 135, 136, 137; of family life 80; of indigenous peoples 135, 136, 137

Save the Children 60, 67, 279, 283, 288, 289
sentimentalism 136
sex discrimination 23, 28, 37, 62–3, 64, 65, 66, 94–5, 98, 99–102, 103, 104, 105, 156, 175–9, 186
sexual harassment 102
sexual orientation discrimination 140, 156, 193, 194–5, 199–200, 202, 203–4
smoking 103
social, cultural, economic, civil and political rights 94; CRPD 65, 110–11, 114, 121–2; indivisibility of 22–4
social exclusion 204, 261
social isolation 158
social model of childhood 125–6
social movement 79
social security, right to 158–9
sociology of childhood 136
sperm donors: anonymity 41
standard of living 83; Art 27 CRC 29, 30, 31, 72, 74, 159, 181, 261–2; older persons 158–9, 160; retirement age 158, 159
state(s) 29–30, 38, 72–3, 74–5, 78, 81–3, 84–5, 86, 93, 180–1; beyond the domestic 31, 32; breastfeeding 184, 185; business and human rights 275; CEDAW 99–102, 175–6, 179; CRPD 85–6, 104, 110, 111, 114, 116, 117–19, 123, 124; cultural change 99–104; freedom of religion and 76, 78; general principles and advancement of children's rights: perspective of state parties 58–9; globalisation 274; health services 184; LGBTI individuals' rights 193–4, 196, 198, 204; margin of appreciation 42; obligation to assist 30, 72, 74–5, 85, 111–12, 181; organising, monitoring and supporting family 86, 181; United States: child/parents/state relations 78–81

stereotypes 96, 100–1, 102, 179, 185–6, 202, 204
sterilisation 196; forced 38
Stockholm Declaration 254, 255, 257, 260
suicide 57
surrogacy 41
survival and development, right to life 24, 25, 260–1; general principle of CRC 27–8, 52, 53–6, 57–8, 60, 61
sustainable development law 29

terminology: obligations 30; responsibilities 30
terra nullius 135
'third parties': rights, duties and responsibilities 5–6, 25, 29–31, 71–86, 102, 160–1, 162, 181; conciliation between children's rights and 72, 81–4, 85, 86; legal analysis of Arts 3(2) and (3), 5 and 18 CRC 72–5; other human rights law: third party inclusion 84–6, 86; parents *see separate entry*; religion: child's right to freedom of religion 75–8; state(s) *see separate entry*; US campaign to ratify CRC: children's rights/parental rights dichotomy 72, 78–81, 86
tokenism 141
Toonen v Australia 194
training 104, 124
transgender rights 95; *see also* LGBTI persons' rights and children's rights
transnational human rights obligations 275
transparency 23, 44
trusteeship 178

unborn child 132
UNICEF 25, 261, 279, 283, 285, 287–8, 289
United Nations 110, 141; Declaration on the Protection of Women and Children in Emergency and Armed Conflict (1974) 96; Declaration on the Rights of Indigenous Peoples (UNDRIP) 130, 139; Environment Programme (UNEP) 254; Framework and Guiding Principles on Business and Human Rights 275–7, 278, 279, 280, 281, 282, 283–5, 288–9, 292; General Guidelines on periodic reports (2009) 151–2; Global Compact 279, 283, 285, 288, 289, 290; Guidelines for the Alternative Care of Children 134; High Commissioner for Human Rights 115, 193, 285; High Commissioner for Refugees 37, 254; LGBTI individuals' rights 193, 194; media 232–4; older persons 147–9, 156, 160; Principles for Older Persons (1991) 148; Proclamation on Ageing (1992) 148; violence against children 84–5
Universal Declaration of Human Rights (UDHR) 77, 147, 156, 159, 174, 241

vaccination 79
values 42–3
Vienna International Plan of Action on Ageing (1982) 148
views of child, respect for *see* participation, right of/views of child
violence and abuse 151, 196; freedom from 118, 120, 160; *see also* corporal and physical punishment; domestic violence
vote, right to 113–14
vulnerable groups/individuals 93, 94, 96–7, 98, 114, 120, 134, 137, 149, 150, 162; best interests 26, 32, 38, 40, 43, 46–7; business and human rights 276; capabilities approach 153; dependent situations of care 160; environmental pollution 256, 265; nuanced vulnerability concept 211–13, 219–24; overlapping vulnerabilities 286; sexual orientation discrimination 194; tensions: women's rights and children's rights 187; undocumented migrants 213–19

wardship 178
welfare states 146
well-being 47, 72, 74, 81, 82, 83, 85; CRPD 85; women and children 186
women 133; CEDAW *see* Convention on the Elimination of All Forms of Discrimination against Women; and children in international human rights law 93–4; emancipation rights 94–5; (women's rights and children's rights as) 96–9; (crucial emancipation tool: Art 5 CEDAW) 99–102; lessons for

children's rights 102–4; night work 96; non-discrimination 23, 28; older 147, 149, 150, 153, 156; tensions: children's rights and rights of 187; workplace 102, 177
work 280; child labour 79, 96–7, 109, 132, 158, 277, 279, 286, 289, 290; dismissal 100, 177; minimum age 278, 279; right to 158; right to work in dignity 132; women 102, 177, 179, 184
World Assembly of Ageing 148
World Bank 253
World Health Assembly 184
World Health Organization (WHO) 25, 253, 260

Yogyakarta Principles (2006) 193–4, 195, 198, 203, 204
young adults 134

ZH Tanzania 46

For Product Safety Concerns and Information please contact our EU representative GPSR@taylorandfrancis.com
Taylor & Francis Verlag GmbH, Kaufingerstraße 24, 80331 München, Germany

www.ingramcontent.com/pod-product-compliance
Ingram Content Group UK Ltd.
Pitfield, Milton Keynes, MK11 3LW, UK
UKHW022011180926
475701UK00003B/301

* 9 7 8 0 3 6 7 1 9 6 5 8 5 *